STUDIES
IN
GALATIANS

JOHN G. REISINGER

Books By

John G. Reisinger

Abraham's Four Seeds
The Believer's Sabbath
But I Say Unto You
Chosen in Eternity
Christ, Lord and Lawgiver Over the Church
Grace
In Defense of Jesus, the New Lawgiver
John Bunyan on the Sabbath
Limited Atonement
The New Birth
Our Sovereign God
Perseverance of the Saints
Studies in Ecclesiastes
Tablets of Stone
The Sovereignty of God and Prayer
The Sovereignty of God in Providence
Total Depravity
What is the Christian Faith?
When Should a Christian Leave a Church?

STUDIES
IN
GALATIANS

JOHN G. REISINGER

5317 Wye Creek Drive, Frederick, MD 21703-6938
phone: 301-473-8781 or 800-376-4146 fax: 240-206-0373
email: info@newcovenantmedia.com
Website: www.newcovenantmedia.com

Studies in Galatians

Dedication

I use two computers, one is a Macintosh and the other a PC. Why I use two is a long story. In God's kind providence, he has given me two friends who are real computer buffs and willing to help me at any time. One, Moe Bergeron, is a Windows expert and the other, Joe Krygier, knows more about Apple computers than Apple. They have both helped me with technical stuff on more occasions than I can count. They have also read and critiqued material I have written. My sincere thanks to both of them.

John G. Reisinger

January 9, 2010

CONTENTS

CHAPTER ONE

INTRODUCTION

Most readers of Galatians recognize that Paul addresses a conflict that existed in the first century between his teaching and that of certain others still emotionally and theologically attached to the Mosaic law. It might seem as though that problem is far removed from issues that confront the twenty-first century church. Therefore, it would be quite logical to ask me, "John, why would you choose to do a study on the Book of Galatians? What would make you choose this particular book at this time?" I would answer, "Because we face the identical issues in our day that Paul faced in his day. When we look at the church, at secular society, or at our own personal lives, we find the same basic problems and questions today that Paul addressed in his day when he wrote this epistle to the Galatians."

Dr. Martyn Lloyd-Jones was my favorite preacher. He influenced my entire approach to preaching, especially to preaching from Paul's epistles. When Lloyd-Jones preached or wrote a sermon, his approach was always the same. He would first establish the context by explaining the problem that existed in the particular church addressed in the epistle. He would then carefully exegete the verses of Scripture that discuss the particular problem, thus showing how the author dealt with that issue. He would then detail how we face the same, or a similar, problem today. Lastly, he would apply the apostle's message to our circumstances.

In this book on Galatians, I intend to follow Lloyd-Jones's method. That means I will spend more time on certain sections than on others. I believe that many of our churches display notable examples of Galatian theology. While we may not experience identical manifestations of the theological issues present in the Galatian church, we do face three major problems that demonstrate the similarities between the twenty-first century and the Galatian church. Seeing how Paul dealt with these three problems in the first century gives us much-needed help as we face the same problems today.

Paul constructed his letter to the Galatians by organizing it into three distinct sections. We can divide these sections into groups containing two chapters each. Each section addresses one of the major problems confronting the Galatian church. The three problems are: *(1) the Question of AUTHORITY,* chapters 1 and 2, *(2) the Question of SALVATION,* chapters 3 and 4, and *(3) the Question of VICTORY OVER SIN,* chapters 5 and 6.

The Book of Galatians consists of a letter, written by Paul sometime between AD 48 and 58, to a Gentile church that he had previously established. This church was under attack from people Paul refers to simply as "they" and as "those who unsettle you" (Gal. 4:17; 5:12), and whom subsequent readers have labeled as Judaizers. These people are similar to those Paul had encountered when he had gone to Jerusalem, fourteen years after his conversion, but before he wrote the letter to the church at Galatia. Paul, in recollecting the Jerusalem incident, calls these people false brethren (2:4). He calls them "brothers" because they professed to be Christians. He calls them "false" because they were not true

Christians at all (2:4, 5). The same issue surfaces again in Antioch, where "certain men from James" (2:1–5, 11–14) had influenced Peter to withdraw from table fellowship with the Gentiles. These men implied that they had come from Jerusalem as representatives of the apostles there.

Paul is quite clear as to the Judaizers' intentions in Jerusalem. They "came in privately to spy out our liberty which we have in Christ Jesus that they might bring us into bondage" (2:4). The logical connection in Paul's mind between the false brothers in Jerusalem and the troublemakers in Galatia compels us to identify Paul's definition of both liberty and bondage. We cannot possibly understand the Book of Galatians without knowing what Paul meant by the phrases *spy out our liberty* and *bring us into bondage*. Exactly what liberty did Paul (and by implication, the Galatian Christians[1]) have that the Judaizers wanted to destroy, and what was the bondage that the Judaizers wanted to impose? Understanding these terms is crucial to understanding the Book of Galatians and lies at the heart of the theology of the new covenant.

---

[1] Paul, Barnabas, and Titus had gone to Jerusalem to meet privately with the leaders of the Jerusalem church. Their purpose was to explain the content of the gospel message they preached to the Gentiles. Paul and his companions resisted the efforts of the false brothers to alter the condition of the messengers (to require circumcision for Titus) or to alter the content of the message. Paul recognizes that to yield to either alteration is to compromise the truth of the gospel and to affect negatively anyone who might subsequently hear that altered message. Thus, he writes, "to them [the false brothers] we [Paul, Barnabas, and Titus] did not yield in submission even for a moment, so that the truth of the gospel might be preserved for you [the Galatians]" (Gal. 2:5 ESV).

One of the most common mistakes made in exegeting Galatians is to misunderstand the words _liberty_ and _bondage_. Many teachers correctly associate bondage with the Mosaic law but wrongly insist that the aspect of the Mosaic law to which Paul refers is the so-called ceremonial law. They teach that the bondage to which Paul refused to submit was the regulation of life with the dietary and cer-emonial laws of the Mosaic covenant. In this view, the liberty that Christ purchased is freedom from the Mosaic ceremonial system. Christ was born under the law (Gal. 4:4), meaning the ceremonial system, to redeem believers from the ceremonial law. In essence, this view means that Christ died so that a person could eat bacon with his eggs. It certainly is true that Christ delivers us from the so-called ceremonial law, but that is not Paul's point in Galatians. John Stott has some excellent comments on Galatians 5:1, where the Apostle Paul exhorts us to _"Stand fast therefore in the liberty with which Christ has made us free..."_

As the New English Bible puts it, 'Christ set us free, to be free men'. Our former state is portrayed as a slavery, Jesus Christ as a liberator, conversion as an act of emancipation, and the Christian life as a life of freedom. This freedom, as the whole Epistle and this context make plain, is not primarily a freedom **from sin,** but rather **from the law.** What Christ has done in liberating us, according to Paul's emphasis here, is not so much to set our _will_ free from the **bondage** of sin as to set our _conscience_ free from the **guilt** of sin. The Christian freedom he describes is **freedom of conscience**, freedom from the **tyranny of the law,** the dreadful struggle to keep the law, with a view to winning the favour of God. It is the freedom of acceptance with God and of access to God through Christ.[2]

Who can endure the pressure of applying God's holy law to the conscience without also knowing that the atoning sacrifice of Christ has silenced the threat of that law forever? This is the kind of bondage that a legalist is always trying to impose. It is a constant drumbeat of "law, law, law" and "do, do, do" without preaching full justification and the imputation of Christ's righteousness. The child of God must always remember, as Newton wrote so beautifully, "He has *hushed the Law's loud thunder.*" The greatest spiritual power that one will ever receive to live a holy life comes from the assurance in one's conscience that he is fully justified in God's sight, and, therefore, he is perfectly acceptable to Him *just as he is* because of the merits of Christ.

This assurance is the essence of the freedom that Paul's gospel puts into the heart of those that sincerely believe its message. This is freedom of conscience with respect to the "blessed assurance" of my personal relationship to God. I *know* he loves me and has accepted me, not because of what I did or ever will do by way of law-keeping, but only because Jesus died for me! This is the freedom that a legalist, with all of his earnest striving to keep the law, can never enjoy. This is what John Bunyan meant when he said:

> Wherefore whenever thou who believest in Jesus, dost hear the law in its thundering and lightening fits, as if it would burn up heaven and earth; then say thou, **I am freed from this law,** these thunderings have nothing to do with my soul; nay even

---

[2] John R. Stott, BST: *The Message of Galatians*, with Study Guide, (Leicester, England: Inter-Varsity Press, 1988), 132. Italics in the original; emphasis in bold face type added.

this law, while it thus thunders and roareth, it doth both allow and approve of my righteousness. I know that Hagar would sometimes be domineering and high, even in Sarah's house and against her; but this she is not to be suffered to do, nay though Sarah herself be barren; wherefore serve IT [the law] also as Sarah served her, and **expel her out from thy house.** My meaning is, when this law with its thundering threatenings doth attempt to lay hold on thy **conscience,** shut it out with a promise of **grace;** cry, the inn is took up already, the Lord Jesus is here entertained, and here is **no room** for the **law.** Indeed if it will be content with being my informer, and so lovingly leave off to **judge** me; I will be content, it shall be in my sight, I will also delight in therein; but otherwise, I being now made upright without it, and that too with that righteousness, which this law speaks well of and approveth; **I may not, will not, cannot, dare not** make it my Saviour and Judge, nor suffer it to set up its **government** in my **conscience;** for so doing I **fall from grace,** and Christ Jesus doth profit me **nothing.**[3]

We most certainly believe that people must become conscious of sin. Men and women should tremble before a holy God, but guilty sinners also must hear the gospel and find real joy and assurance in the presence of that holy God. Any right understanding of the gospel of justification by faith must lead us to quit trembling and to start rejoicing with joy unspeakable. John Newton, in his great hymn, "Amazing Grace," had it right:

'Twas *grace* that taught my heart to *fear,*
and *grace* my fears relieved.

We must never downplay the need of lost people to see and feel their sinfulness in the sight of a holy God. Oh, that

---

[3] From: *Of the Law and a Christian, The Works of John Bunyan,* (Edinburgh: The Banner of Truth Trust, 1999), 2:388. Bolding added.

we might see more unbelievers trembling under a sense of the judgment of God! It is *grace* that arouses the conscience and makes people fearful because of their guilt. Newton saw that fearful experience occurring only because of the grace of God. It was God's grace that taught him to fear. However, if the Spirit of God has truly wrought conviction, and if the preacher has faithfully declared the whole truth of God's saving gospel, the grace that leads to fear will also *relieve* that fear. Newton saw the second aspect of the Spirit's work just as clearly as he saw the first. Wherever a ministry leaves people in a state of fear, or encourages fear and doubt as healthy signs, that ministry represents Moses better than it represents Christ. You are worshipping in Galatia if you go to a church like that. Such preachers are strangers to the grace that John Newton loved and preached.

How do grace and freedom, law and bondage, and circumcision relate to each other? When Paul mentions circumcision as one of the alterations to which he would not allow Titus to submit, he uses the term metonymically. We will see this more clearly when we explore 5:3. The theological significance of circumcision extends beyond the physical act; it stands for the entire covenantal system symbolized by the imposition of circumcision. Paul refuses to yield, not to an insignificant ceremony (5:6), but to a religion of law and works symbolized by that ceremony.

By insisting on circumcision, the Judaizers were *not* denying the necessity of faith in Jesus Christ as the true Messiah. Both Paul and the Judaizers acknowledged that salvation was possible only by faith in Christ. The difference was that the Judaizers believed that salvation came through faith in Christ *plus* keeping the law. In effect, they were saying, "We know you have believed in Jesus Christ; that is right and necessary since he is the true Messiah. To be a true child of God, however, in addition to trusting Christ, you must also be circumcised and keep the law of Moses."

The Judaizers emphasized that circumcision was essential to salvation because in their scheme of theology, the law was still in full force. Salvation was by faith in Christ *plus* circumcision. Since circumcision clearly symbolized being bound over to keep the whole law, the Judaizers' message was that salvation is half by grace and half by law, or half by faith and half by works. Paul saw this mixing of law and grace as a denial of the total *sufficiency* of Christ to save a sinner's soul. Judaizing theology does not openly deny that sinners need the grace of God, but it does deny that grace and faith alone are *sufficient to meet the sinner's true need*. In reality and practice, it teaches grace *plus law,* which is a logical and theological contradiction.

The importance of this point will become evident when we look at the various ways that different current theologies attempt to understand Paul's words about Christian freedom from the law. The original Judaizers may have died, but some of their descendants are alive and well today.

As I mentioned earlier, understanding what Paul meant by the phrase "spy out our *liberty* which we have in Christ Jesus, that they might bring us into *bondage"* (2:4, 5) lies at the heart of the epistle to the Galatians as well as at the heart of the Christian faith. It is the center of the new covenant gospel of grace as well as the foundation of biblical Christian freedom and victory over sin. Both legalism and antinomianism experientially ignore this gospel liberty.

Once you see how deadly it is to mix law and grace, as the Galatians were doing, you will see why Paul was so incensed at the Judaizers for teaching such heresy and at the Galatians for listening to them. Paul was not merely concerned that there was a difference of opinion on the matter of circumcision as a physical ceremony. No, the real problem was that circumcision was a symbol of an entire theological system. Paul could say, "For I testify again to every man that is circumcised, that he is a debtor to do the whole law" (5:3). Circumcision, in the context of Galatians, symbolized giving up the gospel itself and yielding to a works religion of legalism. Paul said that *the truth of the gospel* was at stake.

As one writer stated, "To *supplement* Christ in any way is to *supplant* Christ altogether."[4] It is either all Christ or all law. It is all grace or all works. Paul's attitude comes through loud and clear.

> *I fear for you, that somehow I have wasted my efforts on you.... Mark my words! I, Paul, tell you that if you let yourselves be circumcised, Christ will be of no value to you at all.* (Gal 4:11 and 5:2 NIV).

In other words, Paul is saying, "The moment you let them put that knife in your flesh, you are agreeing with their whole theology and are denying Christ. You are saying, by agreeing to be circumcised, that their basic premise that Jesus Christ alone is not sufficient to save your soul is correct, and therefore you are adding circumcision and law-keeping to the finished work of Christ." The Galatians were sacrificing their consciences to the Judaizers, and in effect

---

4 Source unknown.

were denying the sufficiency of Christ. My dear Christian friend, that is exactly what you do when you allow any person or group to seduce your conscience by making their acceptance of you more important than your personal walk with Christ.

Let me state an important point by way of introduction.

In his letter to the Galatians, Paul couches becoming a true child of God, or being justified, in terms of being a true child of Abraham. The point over which Paul and the Judaizers disagree is not whether sinners need to trust Christ as the only Savior. Since Paul does not address this point anywhere in the letter, we may safely infer that the Judaizers were not denying the necessity of believing in Christ as the true Messiah. The message of the Judaizers was quite clear. The question was whether, in addition to trusting Christ, circumcision and law keeping also were essential in order to be truly saved or to become a true child of Abraham. When the Judaizers appeared in Antioch, Paul and Barnabas refuted their teaching: this disagreement resulted in the Jerusalem council in AD 49, recorded in Acts 15.

1 And certain men which came down from Judaea taught the brethren, and said, Except ye be circumcised after the manner of Moses, ye cannot be saved. (This action prompted the church in Antioch to send Paul, Barnabas, and others to Jerusalem).

5 But there rose up certain of the sect of the Pharisees which believed, saying, That it was needful to circumcise them, and to command them to keep the law of Moses. (This happened at the council meeting in Jerusalem.)

6 And the apostles and elders came together for to consider of this matter. (KJV)

The Judaizers, like the professing believers in Hebrews, were not interested in denying the gospel, but merely in adding circumcision and law-keeping to the gospel. They wanted to Judaize Christianity and Christianize Judaism. If we let go of this fact, we will miss the message of the Book of Galatians. Additionally, we must ask two essential questions as we consider this epistle: (1) exactly who is a real child of Abraham, and (2) how does one become a true child of Abraham?

How does Paul organize his letter and build his argument? Most people accept a three-fold outline of the book.

Chapters 1 and 2 form one section and are a defense of the Apostle Paul's authenticity and authority as a true apostle of Christ. He proves that he meets all the qualifications of apostleship. He was called and taught personally by the risen Christ. It would seem that one of the claims of the Judaizers was that Paul had not been called and commissioned by Christ, as the other twelve apostles were, since he had neither known Christ in the flesh nor been a witness of his resurrection. They insisted that Paul was not a true apostle; therefore, the Galatians need not listen to him.

Chapters 3 and 4, the second section, lay out the doctrine of justification by faith alone in Christ alone, totally apart from works and circumcision. To add anything at all to faith in Christ was to come under the curse of God. Any form of saying, "You haven't gone far enough" to someone who has trusted Christ is adding to the gospel.

Chapters 5 and 6 form the final section and apply this doctrine to the situation in which the Galatian church found itself. This section is one of the major places in Scripture that deals directly with the question of the new covenant believer's relationship to the old covenant or law of Moses.

Let us consider two important background factors as we begin to explore this letter.

First, the Galatian church was a Gentile church. No one would have needed to urge believing Jews to be circumcised. Second, certain people were telling these Gentiles that their faith in Christ was not enough for them to become true children of Abraham or to be truly saved: they must also submit to circumcision and keep the law to be justified. Passages such as 3:3, *"Are ye so foolish? having begun in the Spirit, are ye now made perfect by the flesh?"* (KJV) make it clear that the people addressed had started their Christian life by faith and were now being urged to add circumcision and law-keeping to be "really" saved.

Paul frames his argument by asking a series of questions in chapters 3 and 4. Each question functions to either (1) directly refute something the Judaizers were teaching, (2) clarify something the apostle had just said, (3) state Paul's theology, or (4) deliberately force the Galatians to see the implications of the Judaizers' position.

One of Paul's vital questions occurs at 3:2, *"This only would I learn of you, Received ye the Spirit by the works of the law, or by the hearing of faith?"* (KJV). The question, as some would wrongly insist, does not ask **IF** they had received the Spirit, but **HOW** they received the Spirit. Paul assumes that all those he is addressing had already received the Holy Spirit at conversion. This question concerns **the means** by which they had received the Spirit: did they **do** something, or did they **believe a message**? Paul, in this text, assumes that receiving the Spirit and getting saved are the same thing. He has just written two paragraphs that specifically address justification (being right with God) (2:15–21). Justification is by faith and not by works of the law; receiving the Spirit is by faith and not by works of the law. The two concepts are not merely parallel; they are identical. All Christians receive the Holy Spir-it at the time of conversion, and they receive him only by "the hearing of faith."

Paul follows up his first question with a second in 3:3 *"Are ye so foolish? having begun in the Spirit, are ye now made perfect by the flesh?"* (KJV). The first question involves **how** Paul's reading audience received the Spirit: his second question involves **when** they received the Spirit. They (and we) received the Spirit at conversion. Nothing that you learn (including the Reformed faith), no ceremony or ritual that you have administered to you (including baptism), nor any experience you have subsequent to conversion (including a supposed baptism of the Holy Spirit and speaking in tongues) can add one single thing to your justification. Paul is saying that you start your Christian life by faith in God's promise of grace, you grow in your Christian life by faith in that same promise, and you finish your Christian life the same way. You are once-for-all justified at conversion, and you are just as justified at the moment of conversion as you will be in heaven. I repeat, Christ is all in all. If you have Christ, you have all there is to get. If you miss him by simple faith, you have nothing at all, no matter how much you think you have.

Paul goes on to explain the promise to Abraham and its relationship to the law given at Sinai. This explanation prompts another question in 3:19, *"Wherefore then serveth the law?"* If the law cannot, in any way, help sinners gain the inheritance of justification by faith, then why did God give the law? Was he offering two ways of salvation and does this not mean that Moses contradicts Abraham? The answer is, "God presented humanity with two ways to earn righteousness." The first was the message preached to Abraham—justification by grace through faith. The other was the law covenant at Sinai that said, "Obey this law and live." God did not set these two ways before humanity in the hope that if some sinners rejected the first option they could earn life by obeying the Mosaic law. In essence, God was saying, "Take your choice between grace and law, between faith and works. However, I have news for you. Not a single soul will ever make it by law and works. The very law that you think you can obey to earn life is the very law that will condemn you to death the moment you fail to keep it perfectly." God held up these two ways for the distinct purpose of pushing sinners to see their inability to earn life by law-keeping. The person who contracts with God to earn righteousness by keeping the law will be dead before the ink is dry on the covenant.

In this epistle, Paul will show that the Mosaic law had two distinct functions before Christ came. First, it functioned as a handmaid of the gospel. The law covenant at Sinai forced a sinner to look to the way of faith for salvation. The law served an essential function in the scheme of grace. It was a preparatory ministry. It was a ministry of death in that it killed all hope of salvation by works and merit. It pushed sinners toward faith as their only hope.

Second, the law of Moses functioned as a pedagogue in the conscience of an old covenant believer. Old covenant believers were just as saved as we are today, and they were saved the same way—they were saved by grace through faith in the one gospel of sovereign grace. The old covenant believer was no longer "under the wrath of God" but was justified and secure before God. However, that justification did not provide all of the privileges that the new covenant does. Old covenant believers were no longer under the curse of the law, but they were still under the law as a pedagogue. The law as a pedagogue ruled every aspect of an Israelite's life whether he was saved or was lost. Justification did not free the conscience nor did it provide an Israelite with liberty to enter into the Most Holy Place. John MacArthur has stated this point well.

> One of the key theological themes in Hebrews is that all believers now have direct access to God under the new covenant and, therefore, may approach the throne of God boldly (4:16; 10:22). One's hope is in the very presence of God, into which he follows the Savior (6:19, 20; 10:19, 20). The primary teaching symbolized by the tabernacle service was that believers under the covenant of law did not have direct access to the presence of God (9:8), but were shut out of the Holy of Holies. The book of Hebrews may be summarized in this way: Believers in Jesus Christ, as God's perfect sacrifice for sin, have the perfect High-Priest through whose ministry everything is new and better than under the covenant of law.[5]

We dare not treat an old covenant believer as if he sat in his tent studying the footnotes in a Scofield Reference Bible, nor dare we think he had memorized the Westminster

---

[5] The MacArthur Study Bible, (Word Publishing, 1997), 1895.

Shorter Catechism. An old covenant believer's knowledge and experience could not exceed the revelation that he had.

CHAPTER TWO

GALATIANS 1:1–4

Several years ago, at a Bible conference, I spoke twice a day on the Book of Galatians. I began the first day with the following introduction:

> Do realize that your being here this week is a great testimony to the inspiration of the Word of God? All of you people have gone to quite a bit of expense to be here. Most of you took vacation time and traveled a great distance to get here. And to do what? To listen to two lectures every day about a letter written by an obscure Jew to a small congregation of insignificant Christians nearly two-thousand years ago. And why did you go to all that trouble and expense? You believe that the two-thousand-year-old letter has information that will help you understand yourself and your life and provide answers to some of your most pressing problems. Your presence here is a confession that you believe that an obscure Jewish man named Paul understands you better than any modern psychologist or philosopher and that his letter to the Galatians will help you strengthen your marriage, raise your children, maintain your walk with God, and live your life in general.

Do you know of any other meetings in this entire state or country where people are gathering to seriously study a two-thousand-year-old letter written by an obscure nobody to a congregation that ceased to exist well over a thousand years ago in the hopes their lives will be changed for the better? Why would you hope that? Why would you go to the trouble and expense that you did to come here? Because you believe that this letter to the Galatians is part of a book that is nothing less than the Word of God! You believe that the Holy Spirit of God inspired the words of this letter to the Galatians, and those words have a timeless message.

A man named Phillips produced a modern English paraphrase of the New Testament that is well worth having. He did not believe in verbal inspiration, but he made an amazing confession for an unbeliever. He said something to the effect that when he was deeply involved in his work with the New Testament, he would, at times, feel like a man working with electric wires which were supposed to have no electricity, but who was still getting shocked. God's Word has the power to accomplish whatever his will decrees it will accomplish. One of the purposes of Scripture is to reveal the character of God to his image-bearers so that they will know how to love and obey him. Jesus Christ is the ultimate revelation of God; he speaks with the authority of God and delegates that authority to his apostles.

The first two chapters of Galatians address the question of authority. False teachers were implying that Paul was not a true apostle of Christ; therefore, the Galatians did not have to accept his message. They claimed that Christ had not called and taught Paul as he had the other apostles, and that Paul had received his authority and message from the apostles at Jerusalem. In these opening two chapters, Paul defends his apostleship. His concern is not for himself but for his message. If his enemies destroyed his credibility, they would destroy the gospel message that he preached. Paul defended himself as an apostle in order to protect the authority of his message. The issue of authority extends beyond first-century Galatia and the believers there: it also affects both believers and unbelievers in our twenty-first century American culture.

The Question of AUTHORITY

How do we know what to believe? Who, if anyone, has the right to tell me what is right or wrong, and how I am to live? Is this not the heart of the problem between parents and their children today? Who has not heard someone say, "It may be wrong for you, but it is not wrong for me. You have no right to impose your moral convictions on other people"?

Is this not the real difference between liberalism and conservatism in politics, education, and religion? Is one of the real differences between the United States and totalitarian countries our conflicting concepts of what it means to be free? Castro believes that he liberated Cuba, and others believe that he destroyed the people's freedom. These different opinions grow out of our convictions concerning the extent of authority a government has over the conscience and life of its people.

The issue of authority underlies the refusal of some people to condemn a peer, regardless of how that peer lives. Who can criticize someone for taking drugs or being sexually active? Doesn't each person have the right to choose his own lifestyle, even if it is destructive? Where do personal rights to do as one pleases and personal responsibilities to keep another person from self-destruction begin and end? Someone has rightly said, "Your personal freedom ends a half inch from the end of my nose."

A society that rejects the authority of the Bible as the inspired Word of God is like a ship with neither a compass nor a rudder. No longer are there any moral absolutes, but every person does that which is right in his own eyes. The new morality (which is neither new nor moral, but simply the old immorality dressed in new clothes) controls our society from top to bottom, including churches, the legal profession, the medical profession, foreign policy, education, art, and science.

Fifty years ago, it was rare for an electorate to elect a politician who believed there were no absolutes. Today, it is the opposite. If a political candidate believes there are moral absolutes to which everyone is subject, he may bear the label "moral bigot" and will likely face defeat. If Paul were raised from the dead, he would be considered a dangerous moral absolutist. He is claiming authority to tell you and me how to act. He is saying, "I have the authority to speak for God! My words are inspired by God." Let me list some issues that our society faces today. These things affect our lives and the future of our society whether we like it or not. How do we decide the answers to these vital questions?

1. Is abortion ever right? If so, when? On what basis do we make the decision? Who decides: the doctor, the mother, the parents, a priest or preacher? A judge? Is the argument, "It is my body to do with as I choose" a legitimate argument? How would you advise a pregnant friend who had been raped by an escaped mental patient with AIDs?

2. Is capital punishment ever justified? If so, for what specific crimes?

3. Is war ever justifiable? When is it justified? Should we respect a conscientious objector's view?

4. Are mercy killings (euthanasia) acts of murder or of kindness? Who decides when to stop life support

when there is no medical hope the patient will ever regain consciousness? On what basis does that person decide to pull the plug?

5. Do I have the right to die with dignity and to refuse medication and hospitalization, or does the state have the right to force me to take medicine or to put me on a life-support system?

6. If two people sincerely love each other, would they be sinning if they lived together for a time before getting married? Dare we condemn them, and if so, on what basis?

7. Is extra-marital sex ever justified, or is it always a sin? Who makes the rules?

8. How should we respond if a woman says, "God has called me to preach and I want to be ordained"?

9. Should homosexuals be allowed to marry and get divorced? Should they be allowed to adopt children?

10. How many of the following people should not be allowed to teach in public school? Homosexuals? A person living with someone to whom he is not married? A person who openly ridicules the Bible and Christians? A person who mocks Judaism? A person who denounces Islam?

11. Are terrorists justified in bombing public buildings in order to call attention to what they perceive as injustice? Why would some church leaders and college professors support such actions while others see them as wrong?

In each of the above cases, we face the same problem. How do we know for sure what is right and what is wrong?

Is there such a thing as right and wrong, or is everything up to the individual to decide? Is there an authoritative pattern for a wife, a husband, a child to follow? Is there such a thing as a right choice where the opposite decision is always wrong? Is there a real source of authority? Can anyone speak for God and demand obedience to what he says, purely on the ground of God's absolute authority? Who, if anyone, can say, "Thus saith the Lord!"? Who can speak with the full authority of God himself behind every word? Paul says, "I can. My words as an apostle of Jesus Christ end all arguments about truth."

I remember a man coming into my office and saying, "Pastor, will you talk with my son Mike? He is adopting some really weird ideas." The father did not know that several days before his visit, Mike had come to see me and said, "Pastor, would you talk to my dad? He does not live in the real world." What had happened? Mike had come home from college during spring break and his father had asked him, "How is Jimmy doing in school?" Mike had answered, "He is doing fine. He moved in with a girl named Linda and they seem to be getting along great." The father had asked, "What do you mean by 'moved in'? Do we mean they are living together as if they were married?" Mike had replied, "Yes." The dad then said, "It's wrong for people who aren't married to live together." Mike had replied, "Dad, just because it is wrong for you does not mean it's wrong for everyone." At this point, Dad had exploded, "Wrong is wrong and right is right!" Mike had responded, "That is your hang-up, Dad! You want to impose your moral absolutes on everyone and deny people freedom to make their own moral choices. To you, everything is black or white, but in reality, there are no such things as pure black or white. Everything is a shade of grey."

I had tried to show Mike that both he and Jimmy had rejected Scripture as the Word of God and were acting as if they were God. He was defending what his friend Jimmy was doing as if Jimmy had a God-given right to do whatever he wanted to do. If he felt it was right, then it was right for him. Mike could not see that no one has a right to disobey God's Word.

In the Book of Galatians, Paul not only claims that he has a God-ordained message; he also says that to reject that message is to perish for eternity. He calls down the curse of God on those who reject his authoritative words. His claim is that as an apostle of Jesus Christ, he, Paul, speaks with the full authority of God himself. To disobey what Paul says is to disobey God. The concepts of authority and punishment hardly seem linked to the idea of liberty, yet Paul has no problem connecting all three. The theme of Galatians is *freedom:* true and lasting spiritual freedom. Paul focuses the readers' attention on the *liberty* Christians have in Jesus Christ by faith in the gospel promises. Galatians has been called the *Magna Charta* of the Christian faith, and Paul has been called the Apostle of Liberty.

Galatians falls into three sections: each section deals specifically with one of the three questions: *(1) the Question of AUTHORITY,* chapters 1 and 2, *(2) the Question of SALVATION,* chapters 3 and 4, and *(3) the Question of VICTORY OVER SIN,* chapters 5 and 6. We shall outline each section around the words *liberty* or *freedom.*

In this first section, Paul deals with the first problem—*the question of authority.* We could call this section "The Apostle of Liberty—or Liberty Declared."

Paul claims to have *authority* to speak for God because he is an *apostle* of Jesus Christ. When he speaks, it is the same as Jesus Christ himself speaking. To reject Paul is to reject God because God has directly sent Paul. That is what the word *apostle* means—"a sent one." Paul claims that God (in Christ) sent him as his personal representative with full authority to speak in his name. Notice Paul's opening remark:

> *Paul, an apostle—sent not FROM men nor BY man, but by Jesus Christ and God the Father...* (Gal. 1:1 NIV, emphasis added)

Did you catch Paul's point in his word choice—the words *from* and *by* in this verse? Paul wants both the source and the means of his authority clearly understood: his authority is neither *from* the church (the source), nor did it come to him *through* the church (the channel). The church did not call Paul, nor did his authority come through a church or any of its agencies. His authority originated outside himself, outside a school or society, and outside a church denomination. His authority came directly from Jesus Christ with no intermediary agents or agencies. This is a vital point in Paul's argument.

Not only did Paul receive his *authority* directly from Christ, he also received his *message* the same way: directly from Christ. Paul's gospel is neither an *insight* he gained through meditation, nor is it the result of *instruction* he received from human teachers. His understanding of the gospel was a direct and personal *revelation* from Christ. Paul later repeats this point for emphasis:

I want you to know, brothers, that the gospel I preached is not something that man made up. I did not receive it from man, nor was I taught it [by any man or group of men]; *rather I received it by* [direct] *revelation from Jesus Christ* [himself]. (Gal 1:11, 12 NIV)

Why was Paul so adamant about his authority? Was he an egomaniac who could not stand to be challenged? Not at all: as we shall see later, Paul defended himself as an apostle with apostolic authority only in order to defend the message of the gospel that he preached. Paul's concern is for the freedom of the gospel and not for his personal authority; however, in Paul's case, these two things are inseparable. Destroy Paul's unique authority as an apostle of Christ, and you destroy the authority of his message. If Paul was under any church authority, in any sense at all, then that church was also responsible to approve the doctrines that he presented in his letters. I will say more about this later.

Having established his authority in verse 1, Paul immediately moves to his greeting. One cannot help but notice that Paul incorporates the doctrine of justification by faith in his opening, right at the beginning of his letter. The idea of liberty, or freedom, lies at the heart of every argument throughout the Book of Galatians, and that liberty begins with freedom from the curse of the law. Later in the letter, Paul will defend the glorious redemption that comes through the atoning work of Christ against the works salvation of the Judaizers; he lays the groundwork for that defense early:

... who gave himself for our sins to rescue us [set us free] *from the present evil age ...* (Gal 1:4 NIV)

Paul was merely echoing the words of our Lord himself:

... If the Son shall make you FREE, ye shall be FREE indeed.... (John 8:36 KJV, emphasis added)

Paul's controversy with the congregation at Galatia concerned the freedom of which Jesus spoke. Paul viewed the conflict in terms of bondage to the law versus the freedom of grace. The bondage against which he argued was not only bondage to the world, but also bondage of the conscience to the Mosaic law as a means of gaining assurance with God. The same controversy continues to this day wherever the gospel of free grace is preached in simplicity and power. People with either a legalistic mentality or a pharisaical nature will always use the law incorrectly in an attempt to fetter the simple gospel. How many people do you know who would demand that Titus be circumcised (or whatever our contemporary analogy might be), regardless of how godly and blessed of God the individual might be? Before he is acceptable in our circles, he must first pass our personal inspection and have our distinctive mark of approval upon him. He must come through our schools and submit his conscience to our creed. It is true that Christ may have accepted him as one of his sheep, but before he can come into our sheepfold, he needs some additional preparation under our authority. Our understanding of doctrine, our interpretation of Scripture, or our particular practice becomes the new orthodoxy by which we measure heresy. My brother Donald used to remark, "It is dangerous to say, 'We know the Great Shepherd has put his mark upon you, but we must also put our peculiar mark on you before you are acceptable to us.'" How do Paul and the other apostles view these kinds of demands?

Not one of them intimated that Titus, because he was a Greek, ought to be circumcised. In fact, the suggestion would never have arisen but for the presence of some pseudo-Christians, who wormed their way into our meeting to spy on the liberty we enjoy in Christ Jesus, and then attempted to tie us up with rules and regulations. We did not give those men an inch, for the TRUTH OF THE GOSPEL for you and for the Gentiles was at stake (Gal. 2:3–6, Phillip's, emphasis added).

Later, we will study how the pseudo Christians managed to worm their way into the early church in the first place and gain such power. It will help us understand the cultic mentality in many churches today. Now, however, we will continue with the first five verses of chapter one.

Notice again in verse 1 Paul's method of defending himself. Some Baptists, called Landmark Baptists, insist that the only church in the New Testament is what is called the local/visible church. They reject as unscriptural the concept of a universal/invisible church. Other Baptists, called Reformed Baptists, have insisted that only a local church has the authority to send missionaries, start other local churches, or engage in the Lord's work. Some of these Baptists insist that even Paul was under the direction and authority of the church at Antioch.[6] If Paul, in *any* sense whatever, was ever under the authority of *anyone* other than Christ himself, then he is not being honest in Galatians 1:1. His defense is foundationless if the church at Antioch commissioned him, gave him authority, or sent him. It is essential to understand exactly what Paul is saying. He is claiming that he got both the message he preached and the authority, or commission,

---

[6] The primary proof text for this view is Acts 13:1-4.

to preach that message personally and directly from Christ himself.

The Landmark and the Reformed Baptist views of authority negate Paul's argument and defense against the Judaizers. The Judaizers' charge that Paul was not a *real* apostle would be true if Paul had received authority in any way or in any sense from either the church at Antioch or the other apostles. The Roman Catholic Church has been trying for centuries to convince Protestants of the very thing that Landmark and Reformed Baptists claim. Rome insists that Christ founded the Church before he appointed the Apostles. This makes the apostles "Churchmen," and makes the Church the source of the authorization and authentication of their writings. The Church gave birth to the Bible, and not the other way around. Therefore, the Church has the authority to add Church tradition to Scripture. We greatly appreciate the efforts of the Reformed Baptists to restore the biblical doctrine of the local/visible church that has sometimes been undermined by para-church organizations. Many organizations that claim to be arms of the church end up competing with the local church. However, if the cure for run-away individualism is tyranny over the individual's conscience, then the cure may be worse than the disease. Just as we must not minimize the local church, we must also not deny the absolute and the unique authority of the apostles. They were subject to Christ alone. We also insist there is no one today who has the same apostolic authority.

As I mentioned, the Landmark view of authority is identical to the Roman Catholic view. It, too, makes the apostles to be churchmen responsible to the church. The only difference lies in the identification of who constitutes that church. It is a contradiction to say that Paul's apostleship was indeed from Christ and directly under Christ's control, but that his commission and authority to start churches came from the local church at Antioch. There is no textual evidence of such a division in either the recommending episode in Acts 13 or the life and labor of Paul as recorded in the rest of the Scriptures. I repeat; this view is Romish as it respects the authority of Paul as an apostle and his relationship to the local church at Antioch.

The authoritative sender (Christ) has given his authorized messenger (Paul) an authoritative message (the gospel). The heart of the gospel message that Paul preached is "Jesus Christ crucified for sinners." The risen Christ, who sits at the Father's right hand, sent Paul to declare the promise of forgiveness and justification to all who believe his message about the death, burial, and resurrection of the Lord Jesus Christ. Paul's greeting contains a short   but sufficient declaration of the gospel in verse four:

… *who gave himself for our sins…*

That's it! That is the gospel. That is the entire gospel in six words. Jesus Christ was crucified for sinners like us. Do not add to it, and do not argue with it; simply believe it with all of your heart. Receive it with thanksgiving that it is true. Give thanks to God for giving his Son to die on the cross for our sins.

I want to close this section by earnestly urging you to apply Paul's words to your heart "… *Christ gave himself for our sin…*" My friend, let me say several things to you from these few words from God.

First, there is a message to you from God! You do not
have to cross the ocean, go down to the depths of the sea, or
climb up into heaven in order to know the truth. God has
clearly spoken (cf. Romans 10:6–10). I have repeated his
message to you. Read it again. Listen to God speaking!
"Christ gave himself for our sins ..."

Second, God has sent that message to you today. He sent
it through the Apostle Paul, and he sent it through me,
telling you what Paul said. Today, right now, is the hour of
salvation for you!

Third, the message is clear and simple. God does not tell
you just to believe vaguely in some undefined whatever.
No, he tells you exactly *what* you are to believe. You are to
believe that the death of Jesus Christ was for a sinner like
you. You are to believe that Christ, once and for all, has paid
your debt to God and *delivered* you from condemnation.

Fourth, that message has the authority of God himself
behind it. It is not the church speaking, and it is not a
preacher talking. It is the word of an inspired apostle of
Christ with all of the authority of Christ behind him.

Do you believe the gospel message that God has given
concerning his Son? Will you this moment believe it, and
will you right now, in an act of personal faith, receive Jesus
Christ the Son of God into your heart as your Lord and
Savior?

If you perish, it will not be because of ignorance on your
part. You can never say, "But I never heard the message."
My friend, you have heard it. If you die without God's free
forgiveness, it will be only because you deliberately chose to
reject his gospel message about his Son Jesus Christ. If you
are without God's free and gracious forgiveness, it is only

because you cling to your own righteousness and trust your own works instead of fleeing to Christ in repentance and trusting alone in his blood and righteousness.

We are not talking about joining a church nor are we talking about receiving baptism. We are not talking about whether you are moral and kind. God is not asking you to turn over a new leaf (the old one would still be dirty); he is urging you to trust the work of his Son. We are talking about God's wonderful message of grace. Have you acknowledged your need of his grace and have you thanked him for such a gift as Jesus Christ to save your soul? Have you believed the gospel in your heart, or are you insulting God by trying to save yourself by your own works?

Will you right now say in your heart, "Oh, God and Father of the Lord Jesus Christ, I thank you that you gave your only begotten Son to die on the cross for a sinner like me. I do repent and I do trust your promise to forgive me for Christ's sake. I pray in his name and I trust alone in his name. Amen!" The moment that you pray and mean that by the power of the Holy Spirit, you will be saved!

CHAPTER THREE

GALATIANS 1:1–10

I remember hearing a story about Donald Barnhouse's approach to problem solving. He and one of his elders were having difficulties and decided to have lunch and discuss the problem. Barnhouse began the discussion by saying, "Let's first list the things that we agree upon." He proceeded to list many areas where they were of the same mind. Before long, lunch was over and the two men had only talked about how much they agreed. The unresolved problem worsened. The elder asked Barnhouse to go to lunch again. Barnhouse again said, "Now remember all the things upon which we agree," and he started to list them. The elder stopped him and said, "No, no, we did that the last time. Let's start with where we disagree!"

Paul opens his letter to the Galatians with an implicit reference to a key point of his disagreement with them: the question of his authority. In our last chapter, we noticed that Paul protects the gospel message on two fronts. First, he establishes his authority as an apostle sent from Christ. Then, he validates the content of his message by pointing out that he received it directly from Christ. We noted that the implications of Paul's defense extend into contemporary issues of authority raised by both the Roman Catholic and the Landmark Baptist understanding of who may commission and start local churches.

We saw that Paul continues his greeting by mentioning the concept of justification, a second area of disagreement.

He introduces the topic here; later he explains that to demand any additional criteria to Christ's work on our behalf is to compromise the truth of the gospel. In this chapter, we will complete our examination of Paul's greeting (verses 1–4) and begin to explore his main point (verses 6–10).

> *Paul, an apostle—sent not from men nor by man, but by Jesus Christ and God the Father, who raised him from the dead—and all the brothers with me, To the churches in Galatia: Grace and peace to you from God our Father and the Lord Jesus Christ, who gave himself for our sins to rescue us from the present evil age, according to the will of our God and Father, to whom be glory for ever and ever. Amen.* (Gal 1:1–5 NIV)

As I mentioned in our last chapter, the very first sentence is loaded with a cannon ball. Paul often introduces himself as "Paul, an apostle, by the will of God" but here he adds an expansion that is unique to this epistle. He uses two different prepositions, "neither FROM men nor BY men," to demonstrate that neither the source of his apostleship nor the message that he preached came to him from or by any authority other than the risen Lord himself. Notice the entire short but powerful introduction.

The false teachers were claiming that Paul did not have the essential qualifications laid down in Acts 1:15–26 to be a true apostle. There are some who believe the apostles were wrong in choosing a successor to Judas. They feel Paul was God's choice and the action in Acts 1 was premature and without sanction from God. Whether that is right or wrong, the criteria for apostleship was that the person had been personally called and taught by the Lord himself and had been an eyewitness of the resurrection. Paul defends his apostleship to prove that he is a true apostle and not an imposter as the Judaizers claimed. He proves he was personally called, taught, and commissioned by Christ himself, "I am a true apostle, not an imposter as these false teachers claim. I was called personally by the risen Lord while on the road to Damascus. I spent three years in seclusion being taught by the Holy Spirit sent from the enthroned Lord."

Paul's claim of being a "sent one," or apostle, means that he is more than just a representative sent out by the mother church at Jerusalem. He is one of that small group known specifically as the "Apostles of Christ." In 1 Corinthians 9:1, he asks, *"Am I not an apostle? Have I not seen Jesus our Lord?"* Likewise, in 1 Corinthians 15:7–9, Paul insists that Christ had appeared to him just as he had to the other apostles. *"Then he appeared to James, then to all the apostles, and last of all he appeared to me also, as to one abnormally born. For I am the least of the apostles and do not even deserve to be called an apostle, because I persecuted the church of God."* Paul indeed had the credentials to claim apostleship.

The importance of these claims by Paul is vital in an ongoing argument about the authority of the church and its leadership. The Landmark Baptists reject the belief that there is such a thing as a universal/invisible church. They not only teach that the only church in the New Testament is the local/visible church; they also insist that only a local church has the authority to establish another local church. That means that a church must be able to trace its history from one church to another back to John the Baptist. This is "link succession."

Contemporary Reformed Baptists adopted part of the Landmark view. They rejected link succession but insisted that only a local church could start another local church. Some Reformed Baptists have backed off this view, but to my knowledge, none have openly repudiated this view. What we must see is that the Landmark view of authority (and its variations) is Baptist Roman Catholicism. Since the Reformation, Rome has been insisting that the church existed before apostolic authority existed. The apostles were churchmen and therefore under the authority of the church. The church produced and gave us the Scriptures, and it was the church's authority that authenticated which books should be in the Canon. It follows that the same church that gave us the Bible has the authority to add to Scripture. What the church adds is just as authoritative as that which was written by the first apostles in the Scripture. A present day papal bull has the same authority, as does the Epistle to the Romans. The Landmark Baptists do not claim to have authority to add to Scripture, but, like Rome, they claim to be the official and only God-ordained organization to interpret and apply the Scriptures.

As I noted previously, if Paul was given any kind of authority from a human source, or was under any kind of human authority in his apostolic ministry, then his whole claim for legitimate apostleship in Galatians 1:1 is illegitimate. If a local church, or a denomination, or a mission agency, or a seminary, or any other human organization, including the "college of apostles" either called Paul or taught Paul, then the Judaizers were correct and the Galatians did not need to accept Paul as an apostle of Christ. Nothing less than the priesthood of all believers and the single authority of the Scriptures over the individual's conscience are at stake. Paul sees the message of the Judaizers as robbing the Christian of his freedom and bringing believers into the very bondage from which Christ, in his vicarious death, delivered us (Gal. 2:4, 5 and 5:1).

We have already observed that Paul defends his authority by appealing to the source of that authority. We should also point out that in verses 1 and 2 Paul identifies both the Father and the Son as that source. He was *sent* (the word *apostle* means *a sent one*) *not from men nor by man, but by Jesus Christ and God the Father, who raised him from the dead.* This is one of the clearest New Testament texts that teaches the deity of Christ. Here, Paul declares (1) that he was not called or commissioned by *men*, but (2), instead was called by Jesus Christ and God the Father. What is the conclusion? If Christ is a mere man, then Paul's statement is nonsense. If Jesus is not God, then he is a man, and Paul has destroyed the basis of his apostolic authority.

In verse 3, Paul uses both the Greek greeting, *grace*, and the Hebrew greeting, *peace*. When used together, they constitute the new covenant Christian greeting. Grace is the source of every blessing a Christian enjoys; peace is the crown jewel of all those blessings. To have peace with God through the grace of our Lord Jesus Christ is to become a king with Christ and an heir of all that Christ secured as our substitute.

The moment Paul mentions the name of Christ, he (1) offers a short doxology of praise for such a Savior as our Lord, and (2) gives a short summary of the gospel of sovereign grace as it concerns Christ. However, his words of praise are not merely an emotional outburst. In verse 4, just as in verse 1, Paul carefully chooses his words and aims them at the Judaizers; *He gave himself for our sins to rescue us from the present evil age, according to the will of our God and Father.*

The first thing to notice is that Paul's declaration of the gospel contains nothing about circumcision or the law of Moses. The essence of the gospel is the cross work of Christ. "He gave himself" means he gave himself up to death on the cross. We must recognize the direction of this giving: he gave himself up *to* God the Father. When he died, Christ offered himself as a sacrifice to the Father. Our Lord's sacrifice is first of all God-ward before it is us-ward. Christ first satisfies the character of God (Eph. 5:2) before God sets him forth as a Savior for sinners. "For our sins" means that the death of Christ is vicarious. He died "for OUR sins," because he had no sin. Death comes as the wages of sin; since Christ had no sin of his own, and yet he died anyway, he must have been bearing someone else's sin. Otherwise, he could not have died. He died the death that we deserve:

He paid a debt he did not owe
I owed a debt I could not pay.[7]

In verse 4, Paul also points out that one of the goals of Christ's redemptive work was to *deliver us from this present evil world.* This is far different from much current preaching that has a theological emphasis almost entirely on deliverance from a future hell. Paul's gospel delivers us not just from a future hell, but also from this present evil world. Note again the emphasis on deliverance and freedom. From what does the gospel free Christians? What does Paul mean by *this present evil age*? Usually, when Paul writes about our

---

[7] Anonymous, "He Paid a Debt."

being set free, he has the curse of the Mosaic law in mind, but that referent is not broad enough to fit this context.

John Piper, in a sermon on this passage, comments on the meaning of "this present evil world."

What does it mean to be delivered from the present evil age? Jesus prayed for us in John 17:15, "Father don't take them out of the world, but keep them from evil." The present age is an evil age because sin has such a grip on our lives and on the institutions of our society, and because Satan is allowed so much power. In fact, in 2 Corinthians 4:4 Paul says, "The god of this age has blinded the minds of unbelievers to keep them from seeing the light of the gospel of the glory of Christ" (cf. Luke 4:6).

But for those who trust Christ, liberation has begun to take place. Colossians 1:13 says, "God has delivered us from the dominion of darkness and transferred us to the kingdom of his beloved Son."

The reason we are no longer enslaved to the fear and guilt and anger and pessimism and selfishness and greed and pride of the present evil age is that "we have tasted the powers of the *age to come*" (Hebrews 6:5), or as Jesus said, "the kingdom of God has come upon you" (Luke 11:20). "If anyone is in Christ, he is a new creation; the old has passed away, behold, the new has come" (2 Corinthians 5:17). The new age, with new powers and new ways, has broken into this evil age to deliver us from the present evil age.[8]

Paul probably intends for his readers to think of the entire system of this world as opposed to the will and purpose of

---

[8] John Piper, "Sermon on Galatians 1:1-5," January 23, 1983. Accessed on December 26, 2006 through http://www. desiringgod.org/ResourceLibrary/Sermons. Email: mail@desiringGod.org. Toll Free: 1.888.346.4700.

God. The child of God needs constant deliverance from the world's false goals: its futile status symbols, its animal lusts, its philosophy of life, its fantasies, and above all, its smile of approval and acceptance. This last problem is one of the most difficult for Christians to overcome. I have known great Christians who, by grace, conquered criticism and all temptations of the flesh but succumbed to the smile of the world. Sometimes, we fail badly and suffer defeat in our Christian walk. We must remember that it is God's revealed will that we ultimately prevail. Paul writes in Romans 8:37 that God's ordained purpose is that we will be more than conquerors. Our security and ultimate glorification is _according to the will of our God and Father_. It was not an accident that you became a Christian. God's sovereign election purposed your salvation. It was not your free will that brought you this far in your Christian life. God's sanctifying will keeps you by his grace. That same sovereign will has purposed to conform you to the image of Christ in spite of all the powers and purposes of the world, the flesh, and the Devil. That is why Paul does not compliment Christians for either their salvation or their sanctification.

In verse 5, he praises the one and only being responsible for every blessing—_to whom be glory for ever and ever. Amen._ Paul's words here remind us of another facet of the freedom the gospel brings: we are free from the pride that would ensnare us if any part of our salvation were accomplished through our own efforts, and we are free from the despair that would engulf us if we were responsible for our progress in holiness. Every child of God, along with Paul, will say amen to this doxology.

In verses 6–10, the apostle first expresses his amazement at how fickle the Galatians are, and then he shows how deeply he detests the heresy of the Judaizers. We need to avoid several dangers as we look at these verses. We must not minimize Paul's condemning to hell the false teachers who were upsetting the church at Galatia. Heresy is spiritual poison masquerading as medicine: this particular heresy (salvation by law-keeping) was a snare and a delusion that prevented those who accepted it from realizing their lost condition before God. Additionally, it implied that the messianic age, with its displacement of the Mosaic law, had not yet dawned. If the messianic age was still future, then Jesus's messianic claims were false, and he deserved to die under the curse of the Mosaic law. Any teacher who implies that Jesus was cursed deserves the same judgment on himself or herself.[9] Heresy is dangerous to spiritual health, and we must recognize and label it as such. However, we must not describe every sincere difference of opinion as heresy worthy of the curse of God. On the other hand, we must not misuse charity by putting heresy into the liberty-of-conscience category. We cannot allow Judaizers and their heresy in the church. I will say more about this later. Look with me at the verses under discussion.

6. I am astonished that you are so quickly deserting the one who called you by the grace of Christ and are turning to a different gospel–

7. which is really no gospel at all. Evidently some people are throwing you into confusion and are trying to pervert the gospel of Christ.

---

[9] F.F. Bruce, *NIGTC: Commentary on Galatians*, (Grand Rapids: Eerdmans, 1982), 83-84.

8. But even if we or an angel from heaven should preach a gospel other than the one we preached to you, let him be eternally condemned!

9. As we have already said, so now I say again: If anybody is preaching to you a gospel other than what you accepted, let him be eternally condemned!

10. Am I now trying to win the approval of men, or of God? Or am I trying to please men? If I were still trying to please men, I would not be a servant of Christ. (Gal 1:6–10 NIV)

Note that Paul expresses amazement not merely that the Galatians were forsaking the gospel but that they were doing it so quickly. Paul had established and taught this church. It must have seemed to him that he had barely shut the door when the Galatians began to listen to the Judaizers' criticism of both Paul and the gospel he had taught them. An old Methodist commentator commenting on this verse said, "Beware of those who push you for a quick decision about truth. Be especially wary if they will not allow you to ask questions but insist you immediately believe without question what they teach. Heresy is like fish. You must eat it quickly or it starts to smell. The truth is like gold, and the more it is examined, the more it proves itself to be gold."[10] Someone once told Spurgeon that he needed to be more careful in guarding free grace in his preaching. Spurgeon replied that the gospel is like a lion. Turn it loose, and it can take care of itself.[11]

Paul does not consider the teaching of the Judaizers as merely another acceptable interpretation, but as another *gospel.* He immediately clarifies, "I do not mean it actually is

---

10 Exact source unknown.

11 Exact source unknown.

another gospel, because there is only one true gospel. The Judaizers, with their view of circumcision and the law of Moses, do not really have a gospel at all. Their news brings bondage, not freedom." It is not good news but bad news. Their message is a perversion of the only gospel, and Christ's followers must not tolerate it as a sincere difference or a legitimate opinion. *Perversion* is the word Paul uses to describe the message that the Galatians were beginning to believe.

Paul's condemnation in verse 8 could not be more severe, "Let the person who preaches this bad news be condemned." The KJV reads, "Let him be accursed;" this means literally, "Let him be given up to destruction under God's wrath."[12] Notice several things in Paul's fearful condemnation. *But even if we or an angel from heaven should preach a gospel other than the one we preached to you, let him be eternally condemned!* First, Paul says, "I don't care if an angel appears to you. If he tells you anything contrary to the gospel I preached, then reject him as one who comes from Satan." Next, Paul includes even himself. "I don't care if it is an angel or if it is me. Do not let anyone contradict the truth of sovereign grace." In verse 9, Paul repeats himself. *As we have already said, so now I say again: If anybody is preaching to you a gospel other than what you accepted, let him be eternally condemned!* It is almost as if Paul is saying, "I'm sure you think I am so upset that I am not aware of the import of my words. Let me repeat myself so you are sure I said what I meant and meant what I said. I pray the wrath of God to fall on the heads of the Judaizers and on your heads also if you

---

12 Spiros Zodhiates, The Complete Word Study Dictionary: New Testament, s.v. "anáthema."

desert the gospel." Notice also that Paul views those who followed the Judaizers as not merely changing their theological view; they had forsaken ("deserted," v. 6) God himself!

I would love to have been in the Galatian congregation the morning they received this letter. A messenger would have delivered the epistle to one of the elders. The elder may well have been greatly influenced by the Judaizers. When he read the letter, he would have immediately called the other elders. The big question would have been, "Who is going to read this letter to the congregation?" I am sure no one wanted the job! Can you imagine the atmosphere when someone finally did read the letter? Can you imagine sitting next to a Judaizer who had visited you the night before and spent all evening trying to convince you that Paul was all right, but he was not a true apostle and he had not given you all the truth concerning circumcision and the Mosaic law? I think there would have been a lot of squirming and very little hanging around after the meeting.

It is imperative that we limit Paul's words of condemnation to what he calls _preaching another gospel_. Paul is not talking about those who differ with us in church polity, baptism, prophecy, or a host of other particulars. He is talking specifically about anyone who adds anything to "believe on the Lord Jesus" as essential for salvation. Let us be very clear. I believe that the Bible teaches believers-only baptism by immersion as clearly as it teaches the doctrine of justification by faith. However, if anyone says, "You must be immersed to be saved," he is a Judaizer and comes under Paul's anathema. The Bible may or may not teach a baptism of the Holy Spirit evidenced by speaking in tongues. If anyone says that the experience is necessary in order to go to heaven, he is a Judaizer and comes under Paul's curse. I believe the five points of Calvinism, but if anyone says that you must believe those five points to be a Christian, they are adding to the one true gospel. In other words, Paul's curse rests on anyone who adds anything to the cross work of Christ as essential to salvation. Someone has said, "To supplement Christ in any way is to supplant Christ all together."[13] Paul says that it is all Christ or no Christ at all.

I used to have a neighbor who was a Charismatic. I think he sincerely loved the Lord. He was always giving me literature about speaking in tongues and inviting me to special seeking-meetings. One day I asked him if he thought I was saved. He replied, "Brother John, you are okay as far as you have gone, you just have not gone far enough." I asked, "Do you think I will make it to heaven?" He replied, "Yes." I said, "That's all the farther I want to go." I challenged him on his use of the words *full-gospel*. I asked him if my gospel of believe-on-the-Lord-Jesus-Christ-and-thou-shalt-be-saved was a one-half or a three-quarter gospel. He finally conceded that he could not say that speaking in tongues was any part of the gospel.

Beware of Judaizers! A modern Judaizer is anyone who adds anything to faith in Christ as something that is essential to salvation and part of the gospel. In many cases, the particular thing added is something biblical in itself; it becomes heresy, however, when someone elevates it to an essential part of the gospel. My friend, the late D.J. Ward, said, "The main thing in preaching is keeping the main

---

[13] Exact source unknown.

thing the main thing—and the main thing is that Christ died for our sins."

A Judaizer is a legalist at heart. He is not free to have a life full of the joy of the Lord because the Holy Spirit does not endorse the feeble efforts of works as sufficient grounds for assurance. The legalist's insistence that you must be circumcised (or perform whatever particular work currently advocated) does not bring liberty and peace but instead brings your conscience into bondage and fear. As we will see, Paul uses the strongest possible language to condemn both the Judaizers for teaching heresy and the Galatians for stupidly and quickly accepting the heresy. He thought that they had been bewitched.

I love verse 10. It would seem that one of the charges made by the Judaizers was that Paul did not preach the entire gospel because he was a man-pleaser. He held back hard truth in order not to offend people. After consigning the Judaizers to divine condemnation, he asks, tongue in cheek, "*Am I now trying to win the approval of men, or of God? Or am I trying to please men? If I were still trying to please men, I would not be a servant of Christ.*"

The Judaizers' insistence on the necessity of certain old covenant practices implicitly denies Jesus as Messiah. If Messiah's advent was going to usher in a new age in God's economy (an era in which all who are in the covenant community rest from their own works [Heb. 4:6–11]), and yet the old economy with its insistence on work is still in force, then the messianic age has not come. Adherence to the Mosaic law diminishes Jesus to just another rabbi. In effect, the Judaizers are saying, "Follow this teacher from Galilee if you want, but the really important thing is to keep the

Mosaic law." Paul is pointing out that following Jesus is incompatible with following the Mosaic law. The two are mutually exclusive if we are seeking salvation. This same principle of mutual exclusivity applies to the Roman Catholic addition of works to grace. Our difference with Rome hinges on one word—the word *and*. Rome agrees with us that salvation is by grace through faith, but they then add "and also by works." Works, however, effectively negate grace. The addition contradicts the main proposition. Moreover, works cancel the freedom that grace brings by placing people under bondage. How can we rejoice in a salvation of which we are unsure? How can we confidently enter God's presence when we are unsure of our welcome? The practical problem with adding works to grace is that we never know when we have compiled enough good works to make God willing to deal with us. The Judaizers in Paul's day compromised the freedom of the gospel; every Judaizer since that time continues to do the same. They would say, "Paul was a good man, and he taught you a lot of truth. However, he left out some of the 'hard sayings' for fear of offending you. He failed to remind you that circumcision and obedience to the law of Moses is also necessary to be saved." When anyone talks like this, even if he is a bright shining angel, run as fast as you can.

It is necessary that we keep reminding ourselves that Paul's primary target is the Judaizers with their false teaching who unsettled the Galatian Christians. When we teach truth that is new to some people, they often become upset. They argue that what we are teaching must be wrong because it is upsetting the church. Both truth and error will upset a congregation. Truth will upset the goats, and error will upset the sheep. Paul was not condemning the Judaizers simply because the church was in turmoil, but because the confusion in the church stemmed from the Judaizers' contradiction of the Word of God. Someone has said, "If you feed the congregation sheep food, you will not have to worry about church discipline. The goats will not hang around."[14]

I am certain of one thing. Nothing you will ever believe or experience will add one single thing to the justification that you received the moment you trusted Jesus Christ. If you have Christ, you have everything you need for time and eternity. If you have everything in the world except Christ, you are hopeless in the sight of God.

---

[14] Exact source unknown.

CHAPTER FOUR

GALATIANS 1:11–23

We have emphasized that Paul's main thrust in Galatians is to defend the legitimacy of both his apostleship and the gospel message of grace that he preached. In 1:1, he stresses the truth that he is an authentic apostle. In Galatians 1:11 and 12, Paul stresses that his message, like his apostleship, came directly from God and not from man. He repeats his claim that the gospel he preached does not have its source or authority in man, but it is a direct and personal revelation by Christ himself to Paul. In Romans 1:16–17, Paul also speaks of the gospel as a "revelation from God," but in Galatians, his point is that Christ revealed it to him individually. It is true that the gospel is a revelation from God to all men, but it is also true that God effectually reveals it to individuals. In Paul's case, it even goes past that. Jesus was Paul's personal teacher, and he revealed the doctrines of the gospel to Paul. The divine origin of the gospel becomes clear upon a moment's reflection: what human (including Paul) would ever dream up a scheme of grace where a judge puts his son to death in order to set free and adopt into his family one of the worst of criminals? It is little wonder that some people think we are mad when we proclaim sovereign grace. Only a mad man would try to make us believe such a gospel!

I want you to know, brothers, that the gospel I preached is not something that man made up. I did not receive it from any man, nor

was I taught it; rather, I received it by revelation from Jesus Christ.
(Gal. 1:11, 12 NIV)

John Stott has stated the essence of the text very well.

Paul's claim, then, is this. His gospel, which was being called in question by the Judaizers and deserted by the Galatians, was neither an invention (as if his own brain had fabricated it), nor a tradition (as if the church had handed it down to him), but a revelation (for God had made it known to him). As John Brown puts it: 'Jesus Christ took him under his own immediate tuition.' This is why Paul dared to call the gospel '*my* gospel' (*cf.* Rom. 16:25). It was not 'his' because he made it up but because it had been uniquely revealed to him. The magnitude of his claim is remarkable. He is affirming that his message is not his message but God's message, that his gospel is not his gospel but God's gospel, that his words are not his words but God's words.[15]

From 1:13 through the end of chapter 2, Paul answers the false accusation of the Judaizers in three stages. First, in 1:13–24, he argues that he had learned and preached the gospel of sovereign grace long before he had ever met any of the Jerusalem apostles. His immediate action after his conversion was to proclaim Jesus as Messiah in the synagogues in Damascus (Acts 9:19b–22). From Damascus, he went into Arabia for an unspecified amount of time, and then he returned to Damascus. Three years passed between his return to Damascus and his first meeting with any of the apostles in Jerusalem, and then he met only Peter and James. After that meeting, Paul spent fourteen years traveling and preaching the gospel before returning to Jerusalem to meet

---

[15] John Stott, *Only One Way: The Message of Galatians*, (Downers Grove, IL: IVP, 1968), 30.

the other apostles. Second, when he finally did meet the other apostles, they sat down in a conference and fellowshipped as equal apostles. The Jerusalem apostles fully accepted Paul and the gospel he was preaching (2:1–10). Third, he, Paul, had publicly rebuked Peter, one of the most famous of the Jerusalem apostles, for actions that denied the very doctrine of grace that Paul preached (Gal. 2:11–14).

The first stage of his argument offers three proofs that his gospel and apostleship came neither from men nor through any agency of man: both his authority and message came directly from the risen Christ and not from the other apostles. Paul uses his own personal experience to prove his point. In 1:13 and 14, he reminds the Galatians of how deeply he hated Christ and Christians and how he was wholeheartedly committed to destroying Christ's church. In verses 15 and 16, Paul reminds them of the circumstances of his conversion on the road to Damascus, and then in verses 17–24, the apostle describes his behavior immediately after his conversion. Let us notice how each element helps establish Paul's primary point in this section. How does, (1) what he was like before he was converted, (2) how he got converted, and (3) what he did immediately after his conversion prove he was called and taught personally by the risen Lord?

First, Paul's pre-conversion life:

For you have heard of my previous way of life in Judaism, how intensely I persecuted the church of God and tried to destroy it. I was advancing in Judaism beyond many Jews of my own age and was extremely zealous for the traditions of my fathers. (Gal 1:13, 14 NIV)

Paul described his life before his conversion as that of a zealot filled with hatred and bent on nothing less than destroying Christ's church. His zeal caused him to advance in Judaism. However, the Judaism that rejects Christ as Messiah turns into a religion that hates Christ, his people, and the gospel they preach. Paul intensely persecuted God's people and tried to destroy them. Luke, in Acts 9:1–16, 22:1–16, and 26:9–18 records Paul's conversion and his attitude and actions before he became a Christian. He was a zealot. He was similar to other religious crusaders and terrorists throughout history. John Stott refers to Paul's zeal as fanatical on two fronts:

> Here the apostle describes his pre-conversion state 'in Judaism', that is, when I was still a practising Jew' (NEB). What he had been like in those days was well known. 'You have heard of my former life,' he says, for he had told them. He mentions two aspects of his unregenerate days, his persecution of the church, which he now knew to be 'the church of God' (verse 13), and his enthusiasm for the traditions of his fathers (verse 14). In both, he says, he was fanatical.[16]

These two things, love of tradition for its own sake and hatred of any who seek to change it, no matter how justified, often go together. We believe in some traditions, but we dare not revere them for their own sake. Nor do we want to rationalize wrong behavior on the grounds of defending or protecting tradition. Luke records Paul's conversion in Acts 9:1, 2 and shows how Paul's attitude worked itself out in his actual behavior.

> _Meanwhile, Saul was still breathing out murderous threats against the Lord's disciples. He went to the high priest, and asked_

---

[16] Ibid., 31.

him for letters to the synagogues in Damascus, so that if he found any there who belonged to the Way, whether men or women, he might take them as prisoners to Jerusalem. (Acts 9:1–2 NIV)

Later, in Acts 26, Luke records Paul's own testimony and description of what kind of person he was before being converted.

"I too was convinced that I ought to do all that was possible to oppose the name of Jesus of Nazareth. And that is just what I did in Jerusalem. On the authority of the chief priests I put any of the saints in prison, and when they were put to death, I cast my vote against them. Many a time I went from one synagogue to another to have them punished, and I tried to force them to blaspheme. In my obsession against them, I even went to foreign cities to persecute them." (Acts 26:9–11 NIV)

What is Paul's point? Why does he detail how committed he was in his wicked treatment of Christians? A zealot may seem irrational to others, but he is convinced that his attitude is reasonable and just. You cannot reason with a zealot, because he does not view your position as reasonable. The facts and logic you present mean nothing to a true zealot. A confrontation between you and a zealot is a clash of two opposing worldviews. Only a miracle can change a zealot. Paul is saying that his worldview produced such bigotry and hatred of Christ that nothing but a personal encounter with the risen Lord could have convinced him to become a Christian. No amount of arguments and proofs could have overcome this zealot's mind and heart.

The Greek word translated as *Judaism* occurs only twice in all of the Scriptures: in Galatians 1:13 and 14. The KJV translates the word as *the Jew's religion*. Up until our Lord came, Judaism was God's only ordained true religion. When

Christ came as the Messiah promised all the way through the Old Testament Scriptures, he fulfilled the promises made to the Jewish fathers, and Judaism ceased to be God's religion. It became "the Jew's religion." It was now only an empty shell, devoid of any spiritual reality. It was a spiritual corpse—a religion of death.

In verses 15 and 16, Paul briefly describes his conversion. Nothing less than a miraculous revelation that Christ indeed was raised from the dead could have convinced him. The risen, living Savior literally appeared to him and talked to him. As I said earlier, zealots do not respond to even the most convincing evidence or ironclad arguments. All you can do with a zealot is to knock them on the head. That is exactly what God did. He knocked Saul on the head—hard.

But when God, who set me apart from birth and called me by his grace, was pleased to reveal his Son in me so that I might preach him among the Gentiles, I did not consult any man ...(Gal. 1:15, 16 NIV)

Paul's testimony presents a striking contrast to some testimonies we hear today. First, Paul attributes everything that happened that day on the Damascus road to God's grace and power. Paul was determined to do all he could to destroy the church. He eagerly sought authority to beat, bind, and drag off to prison every Christian he found in the synagogues. However, even though Paul was filled with hate, God's heart was filled with purposes of sovereign grace toward Paul. God had already ordained that the world's greatest Christ-hater would become the world's greatest Christ-lover. The persecutor would become an apostle.

Today, people sometimes testify, "I am glad when I was given the gospel that I took advantage of God's wonderful offer and gave God a chance. I have never been sorry for that decision I made." No, there is not a word in Paul's testimony about what he did. It was "when God" did in time that which he had decided in eternity to do—bring Saul of Tarsus, the blaspheming zealot, to a saving knowledge of sovereign grace—to bring a rebel to bow to Christ as Lord.[17]

For Paul, there was no "when I got ready," but "when it pleased God!" It was not "that day I decided," but "that time in eternity that God set me apart by sovereign electing grace." It was not "I made a decision," but "God revealed his Son in me." Salvation does not lie at the end of a "you do your part and God does his part" proposition. Biblical conversion is a sovereign, personal, powerful revelation of Jesus Christ as Lord to an individual's mind, heart, and will. Notice the following: (1) Paul's conversion did not take place "when I decided to accept," but *when it pleased God.*" (2) It was not when Paul decided to "open my heart and let Jesus come in," but when (a) God *"called me* [effectually, or regenerated me] *by his grace,"* and (b) *"revealed his Son in me."* A new heart does not result from a dead sinner's willingness to be made alive, but it is the direct result of a divine revelation of the Holy Spirit's power. (3) Paul did not need a personal worker or counselor to convince him that he had been converted. He did not have to "confer with flesh and blood" to be assured that "Jesus had indeed come into his heart." When the Lord of glory takes up his abode in a poor sinner's heart, that sinner knows something amazing

---

[17] I urge everyone to read my booklet on the doctrine of election, *Chosen In Eternity,* available from New Covenant Media.

has happened. If a sinner must be badgered and argued into believing that Christ has indeed come into his heart, would we not be justified in asking if it was worthwhile to have such an experience?

There was nothing ambiguous about the value of Paul's experience that day! When God struck him down and said, "Saul, Saul, why are you persecuting me?" Saul replied, "Who are you, Lord?" He knew it was some Lord, but not which one. Can you imagine Paul's amazement when the voice said, "I am Jesus, whom you are persecuting"? These words must have shocked Paul deeply. Paul never forgot those words. There was never a time in Paul's life that he forgot that sovereign grace alone had saved him. He learned at conversion that Jesus is Lord. One of the reasons that Christianity is often shallow today is that there is little realization of the absolute lordship of Christ. As you listen to people who believe in free will give their testimony, you get the distinct impression that *these people did God a favor by allowing him to save them.* Not so the conversions in the Bible. Some years ago, one seminary professor claimed that preaching the lordship of Christ in evangelism was another gospel. He insisted that you receive Christ as Savior in conversion and then later receive him as Lord. To insist that Christ must be received as Lord at conversion was, to him, another gospel!

We should mention two more points before moving on. Concerning the doctrine of sovereign election, some people say we should (1) teach it to mature Christians only, and (2) never mention it at all when speaking to lost people. Paul's conversion, and his testimony about it, proves that statement is biblically unfounded. The very first truth that

Paul learned as a newborn babe in Christ was *election*. Ananias's words to Paul, and Paul's experience, contradict both these objections.

Then he said: 'The God of our fathers has chosen you to know his will and to see the Righteous One and to hear words from his mouth. (Acts 22:14 NIV)

Notice that Paul was chosen to know God's will and to hear God's words. It was not that he heard, understood, and decided to believe, but rather that he was *chosen to believe*. This is Paul's consistent testimony about God's grace. Not only does he always attribute his conversion to God's sovereign election, he also attributes every other conversion to the same source. Notice in the following text from Acts that he refers back to that Damascus road experience and then boldly states that all who were appointed (or chosen) to be saved believed the gospel.

For this is what the Lord has commanded us: "I have made you a light for the Gentiles, that you may bring salvation to the ends of the earth." When the Gentiles heard this, they were glad and honored the word of the Lord; and all who were appointed for eternal life believed. (Acts 13:47–48 NIV)

The second thing to note is that when Paul recounts his conversion experience, he is neither lecturing at a seminary nor talking to mature Christians. *He is giving his testimony to lost sinners who were contradicting the gospel of grace he preached in Antioch.* Paul is neither ashamed nor afraid to preach sovereign electing grace to lost people. I am not suggesting that we stress election every time we preach. I am saying that there are some people who have to be hit on the head with sovereignty! When I was in university years ago, an arrogant classmate mocked my faith and said, "Give me one good reason why you believe the Bible is the Word of God." I replied, "Because God in his sovereign mercy and power opened my heart and gave me faith to believe it. Apparently, he has not done the same thing for you. I pity you and will pray that God will show His mercy to you and give you the same ability to believe." I smiled and walked away. Notice that Romans 9, a great chapter on absolute sovereignty, is followed by Paul's deep concern to see his fellow Jews saved (Rom. 10:1). He pleaded with God for their souls and pleaded with them to believe the gospel.

Paul closes this account of his conversion with this statement, *"I did not consult any man"* (verse 16). Someone has said, "There were no personal workers there to give Paul assurance that he was converted." Something is terribly wrong when evangelistic meetings need highly emotional appeals to get people saved (meaning to come up to the altar), and then need trained workers to give those people assurance that they now are Christians.

In Galatians 1:17–24, Paul introduces his post-conversion experiences as the third proof that he was called and taught by Christ personally and not by the other apostles. His pre-conversion days and the circumstances of his conversion prove that he had seen and spoken to the risen Lord. He now shows that it was years after his conversion before he met any of the other apostles. God had already established and accredited Paul's ministry long before Paul met the other apostles. It was not possible that they either taught him or gave him authority.

[N]or did I go up to Jerusalem to see those who were apostles before I was, but I went immediately into Arabia and later returned to Damascus. Then after three years, I went up to Jerusalem to get

acquainted with Peter and stayed with him fifteen days. I saw none of the other apostles—only James, the Lord's brother. I assure you before God that what I am writing you is no lie. Later I went to Syria and Cilicia. I was personally unknown to the churches of Judea that are in Christ. They only heard the report: "The man who formerly persecuted us is now preaching the faith he once tried to destroy." And they praised God because of me. (Gal. 1:17–24 NIV)

Almost immediately upon conversion, Paul went into Arabia. Someone has said, "Paul went into Arabia with a warped view of the Old Testament Scriptures in his mind and the Holy Spirit as a personal teacher. He came back with Romans, Ephesians and Galatians in his heart." Part of this was a new understanding of the Hebrew Scriptures that was radically different prior to his sojourns in Arabia, and part was by direct revelation of the Holy Spirit. Three years after his return to Damascus from Arabia, Paul went up to Jerusalem to become acquainted with Peter. He stayed with him for fifteen days, preaching among the disciples and refuting the Greek-speaking Jews. Fifteen days with Peter did not provide enough time to learn all the theology that Paul had obviously already grasped. He must have learned it in Damascus and Arabia. The only other apostle that Paul met on that visit to Jerusalem was James, and that seems to have been a one-time meeting. Paul then went to Syria and Cilicia, and he said he was personally unknown to the churches in Judea except by reputation. John Piper explains how this statement proves that Paul did not receive some kind of commissioning from the Jerusalem church.

> Even more, in verse 22 Paul says that the churches in Judea do not know him personally. The point here is: If Paul had been an understudy of the apostles in Jerusalem, these are precisely the churches where he would have worked. But they

don't even know him. Therefore, the whole attempt of the Judaizers to discredit Paul's independent apostleship is a failure. On the basis of evidence which the Galatians could check out, Paul makes a compelling case that his amazing 180° turn from persecutor to apostle can only be explained by a revelation and commission from Jesus Christ. Therefore, his *apostleship* is "not from men or through man" (as verse 1 says), and his *gospel* (as verse 12 says) "he did not receive from man, nor was he taught it, but it came through a revelation of Jesus Christ." Therefore, the point of verse 11 is well established: "This is not man's gospel." It is God's gospel: good news that comes from God and accords with his great heart of holiness and love.[18]

One the vital lessons we learn in this section is that we need to be valiant for truth, but motivated by true love of the truth alone. When we treat tradition as truth that no longer needs to be checked and confirmed with Scripture itself, we are in danger. We risk becoming zealots who can act viciously in the name of Christ while sincerely believing that we are glorifying God. Every pastor's study should contain a framed print of the words of John 16:1–3:

> I have said all these things to you to keep you from falling away. They will put you out of the synagogues. Indeed, the hour is coming when whoever kills you will think he is offering service to God. And they will do these things because they have not known the Father, nor me. (ESV)

We conclude this section with a summary statement by John Stott.

---

[18] John Piper, "This Is Not Man's Gospel: Sermon on Galatians 1:11-24," February 13, 1983. Accessed on February 2, 2007 through http://www.desiringgod.org/ResourceLibrary/ Sermons. Email: mail@desiringGod.org. Toll Free: 1.888.345.4700.

What Paul has been saying in verses 13 to 24 may be summarized thus: The fanaticism of his pre-conversion career, the divine initiative in his conversion, and his almost total isolation from the Jerusalem church leaders afterwards together combined to demonstrate that his message was not from man but from God. Further, this historical, circumstantial evidence could not be gainsaid. The apostle is able to confirm and guarantee it by a solemn affirmation: 'In what I am writing to you, before God, I do not lie!' (verse 20).

This, then, is our dilemma. Are we to accept Paul's account of the origin of his message, supported as it is by solid historical evidence? Or shall we prefer our own theory, although supported by no historical evidence? If Paul was right in asserting that his gospel was not man's but God's (*cf.* Rom. 1:1), then to reject Paul is to reject God.[19]

Paul has defended the legitimacy of his apostleship and his message. He has proved the divine origin of both. In chapter 2, he will explain that justification is by faith, not by works of the law, and he will warn the Galatians of the consequences of accepting the message of the false gospel of the Judaizers.

---

[19] Stott, *One Way*, 36, 37.

CHAPTER FIVE

GALATIANS 2:1–10

We have noted thus far in our study that Paul, in chapter 1 of Galatians, begins to defend the integrity of both his apostleship and the gospel of grace that he preached to the Gentiles. He pronounces a curse from God on anyone who denies or changes the gospel he preached. His gospel was from *God* and not from man, either in its source or in its transmission to Paul. Christ himself called, taught, and commissioned Paul personally.

Paul uses his personal testimony as evidence that nothing short of a personal encounter with the risen Christ could have convinced him to become a Christian. Paul's arguments indicate the nature of the Galatians' error. They were starting to believe the message of the Judaizers—Paul had received both his commission and message secondhand from the Jerusalem apostles. He points out that it was years after his conversion that he first met with the leaders of the Jerusalem church. That meeting is described by Paul in 2:1–10 of Galatians and by Luke in Acts 15. Read carefully Paul's account of that historic meeting.

Fourteen years later I went up again to Jerusalem, this time with Barnabas. I took Titus along also. I went in response to a rev-elation and set before them the gospel that I preach among the Gentiles. But I did this privately to those who seemed to be leaders, for fear that I was running or had run my race in vain. Yet not even Titus, who was with me, was compelled to be circumcised, even though he was a Greek. [This matter arose] because some false brothers had infiltrated

*our ranks to spy on the freedom we have in Christ Jesus and to make
us slaves. We did not give in to them for a moment, so that the truth
of the gospel might remain with you. As for those who seemed to be
important—whatever they were makes no difference to me; God does
not judge by external appearance—those men added nothing to my
message. On the contrary, they saw that I had been entrusted with
the task of preaching the gospel to the Gentiles, just as Peter had been
to the Jews. For God, who was at work in the ministry of Peter as an
apostle to the Jews, was also at work in my ministry as an apostle to
the Gentiles. James, Peter and John, those reputed to be pillars, gave
me and Barnabas the right hand of fellowship when they recognized
the grace given to me. They agreed that we should go to the Gentiles,
and they to the Jews. All they asked was that we should continue to
remember the poor, the very thing I was eager to do.* (Gal 2:1–10
NIV)

Notice that Paul's actions set up a confrontation.
Confrontation can force dialogue and action in a given
situation when some people involved have no desire for
either. The issue that is the subject of the confrontation is
usually controversial. In the early 1950s, a young pastor was
scheduled to preach in a large church in the south. On the
way to the church, he picked up two young African-
American men and tried to witness to them. He invited
them to go along with him to church and hear him preach.
They laughed and said, "Sir, that church does not allow
blacks to attend." The young pastor insisted they go with
him. He appeared at the church door with his two new
friends. An elder of the church said, "I'm sorry, this is a
segregated church." The young pastor said, "If they cannot
come in to listen to the gospel, then I cannot come in to
preach. Which will it be?" That is setting up a confrontation
that forces others to take sides.

What was Paul's confrontation? Paul went to the center of Judaism–Jerusalem–and took with him a Gentile named Titus, a baptized member of the Antiochean church, but one who had not been circumcised. By taking Titus with him, Paul initiated a test case concerning circumcision and the Gentiles. Titus served as a classic example of the results of Paul's ministry among the Gentiles. The Jerusalem apostles, and the church there (which was made up of nearly all Jewish Christians), were forced to examine the issue of Gentile circumcision and the law of Moses. They had two choices: (1) Extend the right hand of fellowship and accept Titus as a true fellow believer in Christ even though he was not circumcised, and thus endorse Paul's ministry as an apostle, or (2) say, "Titus, you must be circumcised before we will accept you as a true Christian," and thus endorse the message of the Judaizers. What was happening was simple but momentous. John Stott has caught the seriousness of Paul's action:

> Such were the two vital features of his visit. He took with him to Jerusalem a Gentile companion and a Gentile gospel. It was a tense and crucial situation, an occasion fraught with great peril and equally great possibility for the subsequent history of the Christian church. What would be the reaction of the apostles in Jerusalem to Paul's Gentile companion and Gentile mission? Would they receive Titus as a brother or repudiate him because he was uncircumcised? Would they endorse Paul's gospel or attempt to modify it in some way? These were the questions in everybody's mind. Behind them was the fundamental question: would the liberty with which Christ has made us free be maintained, or would the church be condemned to bondage and sterility? Had the Judaizers any

ground for their rumour that there was a rift in the ranks of the apostles?

Paul tells his readers what happened at that epoch-making consultation. His Gentile companion Titus was not compelled to be circumcised (verses 3–5), and his Gentile gospel was not contradicted or even modified in any way (verses 6–10).

Of course, it was a daring step of Paul's to take Titus with him at all. Thus to introduce a Gentile into the headquarters of the Jerusalem church could have been interpreted as a deliberate act of provocation. In a sense, it probably was, although Paul's motive was not provocative. It was not in order to stir up strife that he brought Titus with him to Jerusalem, but in order to establish the truth of the gospel.[20]

It is difficult for us to imagine the tremendous implications of that one act on Paul's part. He was risking his ministry. If the Jerusalem apostles had not accepted uncircumcised Titus, but forced circumcision on him, then the church at large would have had grounds to view Paul as a false apostle and his gospel as incomplete. If the Jerusalem church had not received Titus as a true brother in Christ, then today we would have two different churches of Christ—a Jewish church and a Gentile church. There would also be two gospels. One would say, _"Believe on the Lord Jesus Christ and thou shalt be saved,"_ and the other one would say, _"Believe on the Lord Jesus Christ,_ **be circumcised, keep the Law,** _and thou shalt be saved."_ That one act of confrontation and the action it forced settled the issues concerning Jew/Gentile and law/grace. It established that the gospel of sovereign grace did not need a single thing in addition to faith in Christ.

---

[20] Stott, _One Way_, 41, 42.

We need to mention one other point before looking at the individual verses. The Judaizers would later accuse Paul of inconsistency when he had Timothy circumcised. Luke records that incident in Acts 16.

He [Paul] *came to Derbe and then to Lystra, where a disciple named Timothy lived, whose mother was a Jewess and a believer, but whose father was a Greek. The brothers at Lystra and Iconium spoke well of him. Paul wanted to take him along on the journey, so he circumcised him because of the Jews who lived in that area* [southern Galatia], *for they all knew that his father was a Greek.* (Acts 16:1–3)

At first reading, it would be easy to say, "Paul, you are inconsistent. In Jerusalem, you were so bull-headed that you would not even discuss the possibility of circumcising Titus, and here you have Timothy, a half-Jew, circumcised and that 'because of the Jews.' Make up your mind and quit waffling." The key to harmonizing the two passages is the phrase, *"Paul wanted to take him along on the journey, so he circumcised him because of the Jews."* The phrase "take him along" meant taking Timothy on an evangelistic trip through areas whose populations consisted of both Gentiles and Jews. In Jerusalem, with Titus, the issue centered on circumcision and adherence to the Mosaic law as means for Gentile salvation, and the setting was among believers. The circumcision of Timothy had nothing to do with his acceptance as a Christian by other professing Christians. The setting of Acts 16 did not involve Jews who professed to believe and who were members of the church. In Timothy's case, circumcision had nothing to do with salvation, but with stopping the mouths of unbelieving Jews. Timothy's uncircumcised condition could have been an impediment to his speaking in the synagogues. In the case of Timothy, circumcision was a matter of Christian liberty:

"circumcision, un-circumcision, who cares? If it helps in our evangelistic efforts among Jews, then let us be circumcised." In the other setting (Acts 15), with Titus in Jerusalem, the issue was the Judaizers' claim that circumcision was an essential component of the gospel. In that case, to submit to circumcision was to deny the sufficiency of Christ. Paul was acting in two entirely different situations and circumstances.

Sometimes, momentous and decisive events in history shape vital issues for years to come. Such was Paul's confrontation with the Judaizers in Jerusalem. This meeting addressed the content of the gospel message. Will the gospel be "believe on the Lord Jesus Christ and you will be saved," or will it be, "believe on the Lord Jesus Christ, be circumcised and keep the law of Moses, and you will be saved"? The church at Jerusalem settled the issue conclusively when they decided that the Mosaic law was a yoke that no one could or should be told to bear. Jews and Gentiles alike are saved solely through the grace of the Lord Jesus (Acts 15:10–11).

Let us now look at the individual verses. Paul specifically notes that he returned and met most of the Jerusalem apostles *fourteen years after* his initial trip to Jerusalem to visit Peter. In verse 1, Paul tells the Galatians that he took Titus and Barnabas with him. Barnabas was a logical choice to accompany Paul. He had interceded for Paul on his initial trip to Jerusalem. Later, the Jerusalem church dispatched Barnabas to Antioch; on his way, he fetched Paul from Tarsus to help him. Then, the church at Antioch sent Paul and Barnabas to the elders in Judea with famine relief. Upon their return, the Holy Spirit commanded the church at Antioch to set Barnabas and Paul apart for special work

(Acts 9:26–30; 11:25–30; 13:1–12). The two men had traveled and worked together for most of the fourteen years Paul mentions in verse 1. Barnabas was one of those "loved by all" people who had the gift of "pouring oil on troubled waters." His presence would have forestalled accusations that Paul's choice of Titus as a traveling companion was designed simply to make trouble. Scripture indicates that Barnabas was a godly man who loved peace and earnestly sought harmony, but who also contended whole-heartedly for the truth of the gospel of grace. Luke portrays both Paul and Barnabas as responding to the Judaizing teaching in Antioch with "sharp dispute and debate" (Acts 15:2).

Verse 2 is an important part of Paul's defense of his apostleship and message.

I went in response to a revelation and set before them the gospel that I preach among the Gentiles. But I did this privately to those who seemed to be leaders, for fear that I was running or had run my race in vain. (Gal.2:2 NIV)

Paul makes it clear that he did not go to Jerusalem to answer a summons and appear before the other apostles as if he were somehow under their authority or in some way needed their approval or authentication. He was not unsure of his calling or in need of confirmation from the other apostles. He went up because our Lord revealed to him that he was to do so. Paul's going to Jerusalem was in response to a revelation from Christ and not in response to a summons from the other apostles. Both Paul and Barnabas reported to the entire church at Jerusalem concerning the fact of the conversion of many Gentiles, but Paul met privately with the leaders (the apostles and the elders) to present the content of his gospel message. This was a matter of correct protocol and common sense, not a matter of uncertainty about either his message or his authority. Paul did not intend to circumvent the other apostles. With the Judaizers making false claims and their false teaching corrupting the church at Antioch, Paul wanted everyone to know that he and the church at Jerusalem were in agreement. The place to start was with the top men. Paul's primary concern was for everyone to agree that the Gentiles were not under the Mosaic law, nor did they need circumcision to be saved. The meeting to address that concern, first with the apostles, then with the whole church, cleared the air and forever settled the circumcision/law and the Jew/Gentile questions.

> Yet not even Titus, who was with me, was compelled to be circumcised, even though he was a Greek. (Gal. 2:3 NIV)

The key word here is _compelled_. The Judaizers wanted to compel Gentile believers to be circumcised in order to be saved. They would not have accepted Titus as a true child of God. Paul is not arguing here that believers must not be circumcised (remember Timothy in Acts 16), but refuting any notion that they must be circumcised _to be saved_. The first is a matter of Christian liberty, and the second is adding to the gospel. By refusing to press circumcision on Titus, an uncircumcised member of the delegation from Antioch and a member of the church there, the Jerusalem church and the other apostles supported Paul's ministry and message. Furthermore, by sending members of the Jerusalem church back to Antioch with Paul, Barnabas, and Titus, the Jerusalem church implicitly embraced Titus, and by extension, all Gentile believers, as equals in the church (Acts 15:22–30). Circumcised Jewish believers and uncircumcised

Gentile believers traveled together, which would have included eating together, an activity forbidden by the Mosaic law but demanded by Christ's gospel.

Verses 4 and 5 are the heart of the Book of Galatians as well as the heart of the gospel of sovereign grace. A misstep at this point will confuse everything that follows. We will return later to do a lengthy study on what Paul means by the words *liberty* and *bondage*, and especially by the phrase, *the truth of the gospel* in these texts. Now, however, we will examine five points that will enable us to avoid the misstep that leads to confusion.

[This matter arose] *because some false brothers had infiltrated our ranks to spy on the freedom we have in Christ Jesus and to make us slaves. We did not give in to them for a moment, so that the truth of the gospel might remain with you.* (Gal. 2:4, 5 NIV)

First, note the source of the problem that led to the Jerusalem council. Some people had come to the church at Antioch with a false message. They claimed that the apostles at Jerusalem had sent them. Some in the church at Antioch were beginning to listen to them. Then, some men from the Pharisees promoted the same false message at the Jerusalem council. Luke refers to them as "believers who belonged to the party of the Pharisees" (Acts 15:5), but Paul calls them "*false* brothers." These false brothers professed to be saved, but in their hearts, they were still wedded to Judaism and the law of Moses. Paul calls these troublemakers "brothers" because they professed faith in Christ and were members of the church. He calls them **false** brothers because they were not convinced that salvation was by grace alone. This same teaching and these same kinds of people had resurfaced in

Galatia. Unfortunately, they continue to resurface throughout history to this present day.

Second, these people (false brothers) may have been sincere when they made their confession of faith. There were many Jews, including Pharisees, who believed that Christ had risen from the dead. The evidence for the resurrection of Christ was overwhelming. Some Jews had believed Christ was the Messiah, but they did not bow their hearts to his Lordship. They could not let go of the old covenant and move into the new covenant. Some of these pseudo-Christians would fit the description of the people in Hebrews who wanted to go back to Judaism. Neither Paul nor Luke indicates the motive behind the Judaizing teaching in Antioch and Jerusalem. However, the particular Judaizers in Galatia appeared to be staying in the church for the deliberate purpose of opposing Paul and his gospel. They were determined to Judaize Christianity. They never denied the necessity of trusting Christ, but insisted that faith alone was not enough. Gentile believers had to undergo circumcision and keep the law of Moses. The Judaizers would have said something like this: "Paul was a great preacher and taught you a lot of truth. However, he neglected to tell you that you must be circumcised and keep the law of Moses in order to be a true child of Abraham and go to heaven. We agree with Paul that you must trust Christ as the Messiah. All we are insisting on is that Paul failed to teach you a vital part of the true gospel, namely, that you must also be circumcised and keep the law of Moses."

Third, Paul insisted that the message of the Judaizers would do two things. One, it would rob the Galatian Christians of the "freedom they have in Christ" that came to them when they believed the gospel that Paul preached, and two, it would bring them into spiritual bondage or slavery to the law. That was why he opposed the Judaizers at Antioch and Jerusalem, and why he is opposing them now at Galatia.

Fourth, Paul sees the freedom believers have in Christ as nothing less than the truth of the gospel. This was not an argument that could be settled by agreeing to disagree. This argument centered on an essential part of the gospel. Paul will show in chapters 3 and 4 that this freedom is freedom of conscience or assurance of salvation. In chapter 5, he will exhort the Galatian believers to "stand fast in the liberty wherewith Christ has made us free and be not entangled again with the yoke of bondage" (Gal. 5:1). As we shall see, the yoke of bondage is not the so-called cer-emonial law. If that were the case, then all that Paul was teaching was that Jesus shed his blood so I could eat bacon with my eggs. Our Lord's blood shedding allowed the worst of sinners to come boldly to the throne of grace with full assurance of acceptance. That privilege is a freedom that no old covenant believer had as long as the veil in the temple was in place. Unrestricted access into the Most Holy Place was not possible until our Lord shed his blood on the cross.

The message of old covenant religion was "stay away because God is holy and you are a sinner." God specifically designed the old system to teach that lesson. Hebrews is explicit:

> *The Holy Spirit was showing by this* [The old covenant system of worship just described] *that the way into the Most Holy Place had not yet been disclosed as long as the first tabernacle was still standing. This is an illustration of the present time, indicating that*

the gifts and sacrifices being offered were not able to clear the
conscience of the worshiper. They are only a matter of food and drink
and various ceremonial washings – external regulations applying
until the time of the new order (Heb. 9:8–10 NIV).

The ministry of Aaron was unable to open the veil and
bring sinners into the presence of God. That was the
message the Holy Spirit was teaching. As long as the veil in
the temple was in place, there was no entrance into the Most
Holy Place where the presence of God dwelt. The message
was "stay away—don't even touch." How different is the
message now that Christ has made the once-and-for-all
great and sufficient sacrifice. The message now is "come and
welcome." We will look carefully at this later.

Fifth, Paul sees the need to maintain this gospel liberty of
access into the presence of God as paramount. It is not
negotiable or even discussable. To either deny or in any way
corrupt this gospel liberty is to deny the very gospel itself
and to come under the curse of God. People corrupt this
gospel whenever they put anything between a sinner's
conscience and God except the person and work of Jesus
Christ.

The Old Testament Scriptures conclude with God and the
sinner separated by a veil that could have posted a sign
saying, "No Admittance upon Pain of Death." The veil
between the Holy Place and the Most Holy Place closed God
in and shut the sinner out. The cross opened up two things:
(1) It allowed God to come out from behind the veil and, in
perfect righteousness, freely invite sinners to himself
because the blood atonement of Christ forever satisfied his
holy character. (2) It allowed the guilty sinner to come
boldly to the throne of grace with a conscience void of

offense. In other words, the cross brought true and everlasting reconciliation between a holy God and a guilty sinner.

We can easily misunderstand verses 6 and 7. At first reading, it almost sounds as though Paul is being disrespectful. However, when we look at the broader context, it is obvious that he is not. Paul acknowledged in 1:17 that these men were apostles before he was. He viewed them as men of repute (verse 2) and as those "reputed to be pillars" (verse 9). Is he then being sarcastic in saying, *"As for those who seemed to be important—whatever they were makes no difference to me; God does not judge by external appearance"*? I think he was aiming his remarks at the Judaizers among the Galatian church, and perhaps at those whom the Judaizers had swayed. They were ascribing great authority to the Jerusalem apostles and Paul is saying, "Even these whom you hold in such high regard agree with me." He is rubbing their noses in their own words and showing that they were unaware of the apostles' decision and their subsequent letter to the church at Antioch. The authority to which they appeal actually supports Paul. It is always gratifying when someone drops the name of an important person to support his argument and you are able to claim, and prove, that the person is an ally in agreement with you.

John Stott points out that Paul's laying out his gospel to the other apostles had two effects—one negative and the other positive.

> The negative outcome is seen at the end of verse 6: they *added nothing to me*. In other words, they did not find Paul's gospel defective. They made no attempt to add circumcision to it, or to embellish it any other way. They did not say to Paul,

'Your gospel is all right as far as it goes, but it does not go far enough; you must add to it." In fact, they changed nothing. Significantly, Paul describes the gospel that he laid before the apostles as 'the gospel which I preach' (present tense). It is as if he wrote: 'the gospel which I submitted to the other apostles is the gospel I am still preaching. The gospel which I am preaching today was not altered by them. It is the same as I preached before I saw them. It is the gospel which I preached unto you and which you received. I have added nothing, subtracted nothing, changed nothing. It is you Galatians who are deserting the gospel; it is not I.' This then was the negative result. They 'added nothing to me.'

The positive outcome of the consultation was that they *gave to me ... the right hand of fellowship* (verse 9). They recognized that they and Paul had been entrusted with the same gospel. The only difference between them was that they had been allocated different spheres in which to preach it. The Authorized Version rendering of verse 7 is a little misleading. It refers to 'the gospel of the uncircumcision' and 'the gospel of the circumcision', as if they were two different gospels, one for the Gentiles and one for the Jews. That is not so. What the apostles realized was that God was at work in His grace through both Peter and Paul (verses 8, 9). So they gave Paul the right hand of fellowship, which means that they 'accepted Barnabas and myself as partners, and shook hands upon it' (NEB). They simply recognized *that we should go to the Gentiles and they to the circumcised'* (verse 9).[21]

The next few verses record one of the most tense and dramatic events in the New Testament Scriptures. Two of the leading apostles, Peter and Paul, are in open conflict with each other over applying the implications of the

---

[21] Ibid., 45, 46.

doctrine of justification by faith alone. It is truly an amazing passage. We will look at it in the next chapter.

CHAPTER SIX

GALATIANS 2:11–16

The last chapter ended with Galatians 2:10. In the previous verses, Paul had been making two crucial points: (1) his full acceptance by the Jerusalem apostles, and (2) their validation of his claim that the gospel message he preached was in agreement with that which they preached. The next few verses record an open confrontation between Paul and his fellow apostle, Peter. Read carefully the report of this astounding episode.

> [11]*But when Peter was come to Antioch, I withstood him to the face, because he was to be blamed.* [12]*For before that certain came from James, he did eat with the Gentiles: but when they were come, he withdrew and separated himself, fearing them which were of the circumcision.* [13]*And the other Jews dissembled likewise with him; insomuch that Barnabas also was carried away with their dissimulation.* [14]*But when I saw that they walked not uprightly according to the truth of the gospel, I said unto Peter before them all, If thou, being a Jew, livest after the manner of Gentiles, and not as do the Jews, why compellest thou the Gentiles to live as do the Jews?* [15]*We who are Jews by nature, and not sinners of the Gentiles,* [16]*knowing that a man is not justified by the works of the law, but by the faith of Jesus Christ, even we have believed in Jesus Christ, that we might be justified by the faith of Christ, and not by the works of the law: for by the works of the law shall no flesh be justified.* (Gal. 2:11–16 KJV)

John Stott has captured the heart of this situation well.

This is without a doubt one of the most tense and dramatic episodes in the New Testament. Here are two leading apostles of Jesus Christ face to face in complete and open conflict.

The scene has changed from Jerusalem, the capital of Jewry, to Antioch, the chief city of Syria, even of Asia, where the Gentile mission began, and where the disciples were first called Christians. When Paul visited Jerusalem, Peter (together with James and John) gave him the right hand of fellowship (verses 1–10). When Peter visited Antioch, Paul opposed him to the face (verses 11–16).[22]

In the early part of chapter 2, we saw Paul vehemently defend the gospel of free and sovereign grace against people known as Judaizers. They were professing Christians, but in reality were "false brothers." Paul and Barnabas had encountered these people in Antioch, debated their claim of the necessity of circumcision, and then traveled to Jerusalem to discuss the question with the elders and apostles there (Acts 15:1–2). While in Jerusalem, the Judaizers reappeared, raised the issue again, and forced the council to resolve the controversy. These false teachers likely were insisting that Titus, a Christian Gentile (and by implication, all other Gentiles who professed faith in Christ), had to be circumcised before he could become a true child of Abraham. Paul used the situation to prove several things.

First, he publicly defeated the Judaizers in Jerusalem by insisting on, and receiving, public acceptance by the church of the uncircumcised Titus as a brother in Christ. His action openly demonstrated that he, Paul, was fully accepted as a true apostle by the apostles at Jerusalem.

---

[22] Stott, _One Way_, 49.

Second, he proved that the truth of the gospel applies to sanctification as well as to justification. In verses 11–16, the scene changes from Jewish Jerusalem to Gentile Antioch, and the particulars of the argument change from circumcision to dietary laws. In Jerusalem, the question was theological and dealt with justification or, more specifically, "Must you be circumcised in order to be saved?" In Antioch, the question was practical and dealt with sanctification or, more specifically, "How does a new covenant child of God relate to the law of Moses in his personal life?" John Piper explains that the two questions are different sides of the same coin.

Now in 2:11–14 the "truth of the gospel" is again at stake but in a different manner. Again Gentiles are about to be compelled to live like Jews. In Jerusalem the issue was circumcision. In Antioch the issue is Jewish dietary laws. Two terms make the connection between the Titus affair and the Antioch affair explicit. First, the term "compel." In verse 3 Paul says, "But even Titus ... was not *compelled* to be circumcised." And in the last part of verse 14 he says to Cephas, in Antioch, "If you, though a Jew, live like a Gentile and not like a Jew, how can you *compel* the Gentiles to live like Jews?" The other term is "the truth of the gospel." In verse 5 Paul says, "We did not yield submission even for a moment, that *the truth of the gospel* might be preserved for you." And in verse 14 he says, "When I saw they were not straightforward *about the truth of the gospel* ... " So in verses 11–14 Paul teaches us that we can contradict the gospel in our life not only by requiring circumcision, but also by other kinds of ritual demands as well.[23]

---

[23] John Piper, "In Sync with the Gospel: Galatians 2:11-14," February 27, 1983. Accessed on March 31, 2007 through

We need to understand both what happened at Antioch and why it happened. At some point after the Jerusalem Council, Peter had come to Antioch. He had eaten freely with Christian Gentiles there (vv. 11, 12), which was consistent with his Jerusalem speech defending Jewish and Gentile equality and salvation by grace alone (Acts 15:6–11). Next, some men claiming to be sent from Jerusalem by James (they were lying) had come to Antioch. This group had intimidated Peter, whose fear then caused him to withdraw from eating and fellowshipping with the Gentile Christians (v. 12). The rest of the Jewish believers in Antioch, even openhearted Barnabas, Paul's partner, had withdrawn and joined the hypocrisy (v. 13).

The fear that controlled Peter was fear of criticism. It caused him openly to contradict what inwardly he knew was true and what he had publicly defended in Jerusalem. Paul rightly rebukes Peter to his face in front of the other believers, simply because Peter was so wrong (v. 11). Verses 14–16 record Paul's assessment of the situation and the content of his rebuke. Peter, in his actions, was contradicting the gospel that he had preached, defended, and, until the Judaizers from Jerusalem came, had openly practiced. Peter's behavior was clearly contrary to the gospel of free grace.

We need to note two points: (1) This confrontation involved two of the chief apostles. These two men are so significant for the development of Christianity that nearly the entire Book of Acts is devoted to the history of their ministries. (2) Peter was denying the gospel, not in his teaching, but in his behavior. For the rest of this chapter, I will follow John Stott's outline for this section. He builds it around Peter and Paul, showing what each apostle did, why he did it, and with what result. He begins with Peter.

What did Peter do that upset Paul so deeply? Paul writes in verse 12, "Before certain men came from James, Cephas *ate with the Gentiles.*" The imperfect past tense of the verb indicates that it was his regular, on-going practice. Phillip's paraphrase renders it, "He ... was in the habit of eating his meals with the Gentiles." Or, as Paul puts it in verse 14, though Cephas was a Jew, he was *living like a Gentile.* I once heard Donald Barnhouse imaginatively describe the occasion this way: Peter loved ham. He was visiting a home where the hostess was a master at fixing ham. She gave Peter a doggy bag with a few ham sandwiches to take home. As he was walking home, he met several Judaizers who asked him what was in the bag. Peter stuttered for a moment, and one of the Judaizers said, "Peter, that smells like ham," and poor Peter threw the bag of ham sandwiches away.

Peter was a Jew. The law of Moses would have forbidden his eating with Gentiles. To remain with Barnhouse's scenario, not only the company was taboo, but also the food was wrong. Ham was specifically on the "do not eat" list. Why would Peter openly disobey the law of Moses and not only eat with Gentiles, but eat **ham** with them? The answer is simple. Peter had learned by a personal revelation from God that he was no longer to live under the law of Moses. He had learned that he was to live under the freedom of the gospel. Luke records that lesson in Acts 10:9–16. This revelation stemmed from God's intention and subsequent preparation of Peter to evangelize a Gentile named Cornelius at Caesarea. John Piper has caught the truth of Peter's experience and its implications.

To prepare Peter, a Jew, to visit the home of Cornelius, a Gentile, which was forbidden by the law of Moses, God gave Peter a vision ... A sheet was lowered from heaven with all kinds of animals that the Old Testament pronounced unclean (Leviticus 11). A voice from heaven said, "Rise, Peter, kill and eat" (v. 13). But Peter responded, "No, Lord, I have never eaten anything that is common or unclean." And the voice came back, "What God has cleansed you must not call common."

This is a tremendously important turning point for Peter, and indeed, for the mission of the church, and for world history. God was saying, "Peter, a new era of redemptive history has dawned; the Messiah has come. The sacrificial and ceremonial laws of the Old Testament have done their preparatory work; let them go (cf. Mark 7:19). I will show you something great at the house of Cornelius." So when Peter is called for, he goes—to the house of a Gentile! Verse 28 shows how he understood the vision in relation to Cornelius. He says to the Gentiles there, "You yourselves know how unlawful it is for a Jew to associate with or to visit anyone of another nation; but God has shown me that I should not call any man common or unclean." *That doesn't mean that men aren't sinners. It means that nothing in a Gentile should keep a Jew from being with him to seek his salvation. So Peter preached the gospel to them, and as he was preaching, the Holy Spirit fell upon them. And it utterly astonished the Jews that uncircumcised Gentiles who kept none of their ceremonial laws could receive the Holy Spirit simply by hearing the gospel with faith.*[24]

---

[24] Ibid, emphasis in the original.

Peter was so rattled by the Judaizers in Antioch that he seems to have forgotten that incident. It is not as though this was the first time he encountered opposition to his eating with Gentiles. Luke records early criticism from the circumcision party, "So when Peter went up to Jerusalem, the circumcision party [cf. Galatians 2:12!] criticized him, saying, 'Why did you go to uncircumcised men and eat with them?'" (Acts 11:2, 3). Peter gave a thoroughly new covenant answer. This defense comes to a climax in Acts 11:17. After recounting the vision and the evidence of the Holy Spirit in the believing Gentiles, he says (v. 17), "If then God gave the same gift to them *as he gave to us when we believed* in the Lord Jesus Christ, who was I that I could withstand God?" This was a life-changing experience for Peter. He evidently inferred from it that not only did Gentiles not have to keep the Old Testament law of circumcision or the Old Testament ceremonial laws in order to have the same spiritual blessings as Christian Jews, but also (rightly) that he as a Jew was free from those same laws. Slowly but surely, Peter and Paul had been moving independently by revelation to the same understanding of the truth of the gospel. The condition for receiving the Holy Spirit and enjoying all his benefits is a living faith in Jesus Christ (cf. Galatians 3:2). That is all. That is the truth of the gospel, and therefore, when Peter ate with Gentile brothers and sisters in Antioch, he was in harmony with the gospel. He was standing fast in *freedom*, honoring the all-sufficiency of Christ by *faith*, and walking in *love*.

Paul's logic in refuting Peter is itself irrefutable. Peter had stopped living like a Jew when he understood that he was no longer under the law of Moses. He visited and ate with

Gentile believers. With thanksgiving and a conscience void of offense, he ate foods on the unclean list under the old covenant. How could anyone who acted like a Gentile, as Peter did, *and especially when he was conscious of why he was doing it,* turn around and demand that a Gentile start acting like a Jew? It was indeed hypocritical of Peter to demand that a Gentile act like a Jew when Peter himself had quit acting like a Jew and was acting like a Gentile.

The next question is, **"Why did Peter do what he did"?** The answer is simple. Peter is a person with feet of clay, just as you and I are. He acted out of fear of criticism, which stems from fear of other people. His behavior is understandable, but inexcusable. That is why Paul is so upset. We can understand his denying Christ before the maid by the fire. The circumstances there were different from those surrounding this incident. Then, Peter feared for his life. In addition, the former denial occurred before the revelation with the sheet from heaven. The Peter who had refused to "withstand God" ate with Cornelius at Caesarea; he now "withstands God" by refusing to eat with the Gentile Christians in Antioch.

Paul's charge is serious. He charges Peter and the others with acting in insincerity (the word means *hypocrisy*) and not from personal conviction. Their withdrawal from table-fellowship with the Gentile believers was not prompted by any theological principle, but by craven fear of a small pressure group. In fact, Peter did in Antioch precisely what Paul refused to do in Jerusalem, namely, yield to pressure. The same Peter who denied his Lord for fear of a maidservant now denied him again for fear of the circumcision party. He still believed the gospel, but he failed to practice it. His conduct did not "square with it" (NEB). He contradicted it by his action, because he lacked the courage of his convictions.

What would have happened as a result of Peter's action if Paul had not openly rebuked him? Everything that was settled at the Jerusalem council would have been undone. There would have been two churches, one Jewish and one Gentile, and there would have been two gospels. One would declare the all-sufficiency of Christ's free and sovereign grace plus nothing in order to be saved. The other gospel, which is not a gospel at all, would be, "Believe on the Lord Jesus Christ **and keep the law of Moses,** and you will be saved." At best, there would be one church but two Lord's tables.

Now look at what Paul did. We cannot describe his action any better than John Stott has done.

> Verse 11: Paul 'withstood' (AV) or 'opposed' (RSV) Peter 'to his face'. The reason for Paul's drastic action was that Peter 'stood condemned'. That is to say, 'he was clearly in the wrong' (NEB). Not only so, but Paul rebuked Peter 'before them all' (verse 14), openly and publicly.
>
> Paul did not hesitate out of deference for who Peter was. He recognized Peter as an apostle of Jesus Christ, who had indeed had been appointed as an apostle before him (1:17). He knew that Peter was one of the 'pillars' of the church (verse 9) to whom God had entrusted the gospel to the circumcision (verse 7). Paul neither denied nor forgot these things. Nevertheless, this did not stop him from contradicting and opposing Peter. Nor did he shrink from doing it publicly. He did not listen to those who may well have counselled him to be cautious and to avoid washing dirty theological linen in public. He made no attempt to hush the dispute up or arrange (as we might) for a

private discussion from which the public or the press were excluded. The consultation in Jerusalem had been private (verse 2), but the showdown in Antioch must be public. Peter's withdrawal from the Gentile believers had caused a public scandal; he had to be opposed in public too. So Paul's opposition to Peter was both 'to his face' (verse 11) and 'before them all' (verse 14). It was just the kind of open head-on collision which the church would seek at any price to avoid today.[25]

The next question is, **"Why did Paul do what he did?"** What made Paul publicly contradict and rebuke a fellow-apostle? Was Paul just a nitpicker looking for an excuse to make himself look important? Was Paul jealous of Peter and desirous of taking down a famous apostle? Did he have an uncontrollable temper and just could not keep his mouth shut? Was Paul really just a negative personality spoiling for a fight? I am sure none of these things describe Paul's actions or motives. I believe Paul not only loved the gospel; he also loved Peter. Paul acted in true love. This is the kind of love of which our society knows little. In a postmodern culture, everyone is right and no one is wrong. The only sin worthy of condemnation is to criticize another person for being wrong. When anyone says, "Our church shows real love," I always ask, "Do you discipline your members when they sin? If you don't, then you do not know what love is." Likewise, a parent who says, "I love my child too much to spank him" really means, "I love myself too much to endure the pain involved in biblical discipline." Paul was a gentle and gracious man who knew how to fulfill his duty in defending the truth. Again, John Stott has stated it clearly.

---

[25] Stott, *One Way*, 53.

Why then did he do it? The answer is simple. Paul acted as he did out of a deep concern for the very principle which Peter lacked. He knew that the theological principle at stake was no trivial matter. Martin Luther grasps this admirably: 'he hath here no trifling matter in hand, but the chiefest article of all Christian doctrine ... For what is Peter? What is Paul? What is an angel from heaven? What are all other creatures to the article of justification? Which if we know, then we are in the clear light; but if we be ignorant thereof, then are we in most miserable darkness.'[26]

Exactly what was the theological principle at stake? Paul twice calls it the "truth of the gospel." Those familiar with Paul's other writing will recognize that he is talking about justification—exactly how poor sinners are forgiven and put right in the sight of God. Sinners are justified by faith alone in Jesus Christ alone and his atoning sacrifice upon the cross alone. The truth of the gospel was, is, and always will be, "Believe on the Lord Jesus Christ [period] and thou shalt be saved." Stott explains,

> Any deviation from this gospel Paul simply will not tolerate. At the beginning of the Epistle he pronounced a fearful *anathema* on those who distort it (1:8, 9). In Jerusalem he refused to submit to the Judaizers even for a moment, 'that the truth of the gospel might be preserved' (2:5). And now in Antioch, out of the same vehement loyalty to the gospel, he withstands Peter to the face because his behaviour has contradicted it. Paul is determined to defend and uphold the gospel at all costs, even at the expense of publicly humiliating a brother apostle.[27]

---

[26] Ibid, 54.

[27] Ibid, 54.

What are some of the lessons we should learn from this confrontation? First, we may have many different physical sheepfolds of varying stripes and colors dividing Christendom, but there is only one true spiritual sheepfold and one true Shepherd. A church leader is an under-shepherd and never a law unto himself. Likewise, a local church, as a sheepfold of Christ, cannot add essential membership qualifications that Christ the Chief Shepherd has not made. My brother Donald used to ask, "If Christ has accepted an individual into his sheepfold, dare we refuse to accept him into our sheepfold?" If Christ's mark is on an individual, dare we say, "Sorry, but you must also have our peculiar mark on you before we will accept you into our sheepfold?" If we are unwilling to accept God's sheep on the same terms on which he accepts them, then we have earned Paul's censure as much as Peter did.

There is another lesson to be drawn from this situation. We must have the courage to oppose men and women who oppose the gospel, whether in teaching or in practice. Their stature and popularity should not influence us to be quiet when the gospel itself is at stake. Most of us will never be in Paul's situation, but we will face similar situations. Let us ask God for courage. We should pray that God would raise up more men like Athanasius, who stood against the whole world when most of Christendom was succumbing to the Arian heresy, and like Luther, who as he faced enemies of the truth, with his life at stake, refused to deny the truth, and cried out, "I will not and cannot recant. Here I stand, so help me God."

There are all kinds of pressure groups inside and outside the church today. Where are the men and women of the caliber of Luther and Athanasius who are standing up and being counted? We must do everything we can to promote harmony and unity among the brethren, but never at the expense of the gospel. Every person's right to their own opinion does not mean an individual has a right to teach or practice error in the church and go unchallenged. We must all walk in step with the truth of the gospel, or our Christianity becomes something less than the life of Christ manifest in us, which is no Christianity at all.

We must mention one last point. The Roman Catholic Church teaches that Peter was the first pope. He is supposed to be the "rock" upon which the church is built. Peter certainly did not act like a solid rock before the taunting of the slave girl during the trial of Jesus and the criticism of the Judaizers at Antioch. While we appreciate all that Peter accomplished for the good of the church, we refuse to acknowledge any Vicar of Christ on earth other than the Holy Spirit.

CHAPTER SEVEN

GALATIANS 2:16–21

In the last chapter, we saw Paul publicly rebuking Peter for his inconsistent behavior. Paul viewed Peter's actions as incompatible with the "truth of the gospel" (2:14). This is the second time in chapter two that Paul uses the term "truth of the gospel" (see 2:5). Paul was a patient and gracious man. His love of peace and harmony comes through in all his writings. However, the one thing that Paul would not tolerate for a second is anything that threatens or in any way denies the gospel of God's sovereign grace. The gospel was a sacred trust that Paul guarded at any cost, including that of publicly rebuking Peter, a fellow apostle.

Those familiar with Paul's writings will know what he means by "the truth of the gospel." He is talking about justification by faith. Paul himself summarizes this concept in Galatians 2:16.

[A] *man is justified not by performing what the Law commands but by faith in Jesus Christ. We ourselves are justified by our faith and not by our obedience to the Law, for we have recognized that no one can achieve justification by doing the "works of the Law."* [28]

The heart of the Christian faith is that faith in Christ's atoning death can and will put guilty sinners right before a holy God. The truth of the gospel answers the greatest of all questions: How then can a sinner be made just in the sight of

---

[28] Phillips, New Testament

a holy God? Paul is clear and emphatic in his letter to the Romans.

Now how does all this affect the position of our ancestor Abraham? Well, if justification were by achievement he could quite fairly be proud of what he achieved—but not, I am sure, proud before God. For what does scripture say about him? 'Abraham believed God, and it was accounted to him for righteousness.'

Now if a man works, his wages are not counted as a gift but as a fair reward. But if a man, irrespective of his work, has faith as righteousness, then that man's faith is counted as righteousness, and that is the gift of God. This is the happy state of the man whom God accounts righteous, apart from his achievements, as David expresses it: 'Blessed are those whose lawless deeds are forgiven, and whose sins are covered; blessed is the man to whom the Lord shall not impute sin.'

Now the question, an important one, arises: is this happiness for the circumcised only, or for the uncircumcised as well? (Rom. 4:1–9a Phillips)

In this passage from Romans, Paul deals with the same subject that he does in his letter to the Galatians. How are sinners justified and made Abraham's true children? The answer is simple. Sinners are justified today the same way that Abraham himself was justified—by faith alone with no help from the law. How was David justified? By faith alone with no help from the law. How were you and I justified? By faith alone with no help from the law. Notice that Paul uses Abraham (who lived before the law was given), David (who lived under the law), and himself and us (who live after the law was fulfilled and abrogated). Paul covers every possible era, and shows that justification has always been by faith and never by law and works.

We should mention that the Jews would have considered these words of Paul as grounds for stoning. Imagine their reaction to hearing that the holy God of Israel actually *loved and justified guilty sinners.* And worse, God justified sinners not only without their not earning it, but actually deserving the worst of wrath! The pious Jew would have been horrified to hear Paul say that the lawless deeds of ungodly sinners would be covered and that free righteousness would be imputed to those same ungodly sinners. Not only would guilty hell-deserving sinners not get what they deserved, they would get the exact opposite.

In his letter to the Galatians, Paul answers his question from his letter to the Romans (4:9a):

Now the question, an important one, arises: is this happiness for the circumcised only, or for the uncircumcised as well?

The answer is twofold. (1) The very same justification that came to the Jews comes to the Gentiles, and (2) it comes to both Jew and Gentile the same way—by faith in Jesus Christ without the works of the law.

Let us review Paul's description of Peter's sin of denying the "truth of the gospel." Here is Phillips' paraphrase of the section.

Later, however, when Peter came to Antioch I had to oppose him publicly, for he was then plainly in the wrong. It happened like this. Until the arrival of some of James' companions, he, Peter, was in the habit of eating his meals with the Gentiles. After they came, he withdrew and ate separately from the Gentiles—out of sheer fear of what the Jews might think. The other Jewish Christians carried out a similar piece of deception, and the force of their bad example was so great that even Barnabas was affected by it. But when I saw that this behaviour was a contradiction of the truth of the Gospel, I said to Peter so that everyone could hear, "If you, who are a Jew, do not live like a Jew but like a Gentile, why on earth do you try to make Gentiles live like Jews?" (2:11–14, Phillips)

Some of Paul's argument describing Peter's sin is hard to follow. The central thrust, however, is clear: Peter, in his new Christian attitude to the Law of Moses, had ceased to act like a Jew. However, for fear of the Judaizers, he went back to practicing Judaism. He quit eating with the Gentile believers. Peter was demanding, by his behavior, that Gentile Christians become Jews. That demand was nothing less than open hypocrisy. In verse 14, Paul refers to "walking not uprightly according to the truth of the gospel." This un-upright walking demanded that Peter not eat with Gentile believers. Peter had been doing this but stopped for fear of being criticized by the Judaizers. This was denying, by behavior, the doctrine of justification by faith alone. This was adding law-keeping to the gospel of grace. This was saying, by example, that the gospel is, "Believe in Christ and keep the law in order to be saved."

Paul's first argument is clear: *"Peter, If thou, being a Jew, livest after the manner of Gentiles* [by not following the Law of Moses], *and not as do the Jews, why compellest thou the Gentiles to live as do the Jews* [by forcing them to live under the Law of Moses instead of living under the freedom of the gospel]? (Gal. 2:14 KVJ)

Paul next reminds Peter of the truth that Peter knew, believed, and taught, but was currently denying by his behavior. The problem was not whether circumcision or the food laws were good or bad in themselves, but whether the Mosaic law was essential to salvation. Peter, by eating with Gentile believers, in effect was saying, "What you eat or whether you are circumcised has nothing to do with salvation. Salvation is dependent on faith alone. Gentiles who trust Christ are just as saved as us Jews." By discontinuing eating with Gentile believers, he was changing his message. He was now saying, "In addition to faith in Christ, you must also follow the Law of Moses to be saved."

Paul's logic in refuting Peter is impeccable: "Peter, why did you trust Christ in the first place? Was it not because you understand that we Jews are as guilty as the Gentiles are, in spite of our circumcision and law-keeping?"

> And then I went on to explain that we, who are Jews by birth and not Gentile sinners, know that a man is justified not by performing what the Law commands but by faith in Jesus Christ. We ourselves are justified by our faith and not by our obedience to the Law, for we have recognized that no one can achieve justification by doing the "works of the Law." (2:15, 16 Phillips)

When Peter ate with Gentile believers, he was living out the truth that the "all" in *"All have sinned"* included Jews. He was acknowledging that the Jews, of whom he was one, knew that they were just as guilty before God as were the Gentiles. In effect, he was saying, "We need to be saved just as badly as the Gentiles need to be saved." *There is no difference* really means that there is no difference. Both Jews and Gentiles are guilty sinners before God in need of salvation, and they can only receive salvation the same way—by faith alone. Peter knew this! He knew, as did his fellow believing Jews, that law-keeping had nothing to do with their acceptance before God. However, he stopped eating with the Gentiles; he was denying all this and saying by his actions the exact opposite. He was saying that living like a Jew by keeping the Law of Moses was indeed essential to salvation.

Paul next addresses what would be a problem in the mind of some Jews. Before Christ came, the Jew was indeed part of a nation that had a special relationship with God. All the following words applied to them: *"holy, loved, chosen, redeemed, and called."* However, one word was conspicuously absent from any description of Israel: it was the word *justified.* Failure to see that Israel was "holy, loved, chosen, redeemed and called" but *not* justified, and therefore not really God's saved people, confuses the issue.

Israel, despite being *"holy, loved, chosen, redeemed, and called,"* never was the true people of God. Remember, Moses spoke the following words (from Deuteronomy) of the same people whom he called holy, loved, chosen, redeemed, and called. God could never say the following about his church. No justified person could ever be described the way God described Israel in Deuteronomy 29:2–4.

> *And Moses called unto all Israel, and said unto them, Ye have seen all that the LORD did before your eyes in the land of Egypt unto Pharaoh, and unto all his servants, and unto all his land; The great temptations which thine eyes have seen, the signs, and those great miracles:* **Yet the LORD hath not given you an heart to perceive, and eyes to see, and ears to hear, unto this day.** (Deut. 29:2–4 KJV, emphasis mine)

The word *holy* sometimes means separate and sometimes means morally pure. When used of Israel, it never means morally pure, but always means separate. Altars, spoons, days, robes, and many other things were holy (separate) in exactly the same sense that Israel was holy. Israel was indeed a nation holy (separate from all other nations), loved (as a special nation, even though most were unbelievers), chosen (as a physical nation, but not chosen in Christ unto salvation), redeemed (physically with animal blood, but not redeemed spiritually with the blood of Christ), and called (out of bondage in Egypt, but not out of bondage to sin). These great redemptive words do not mean the same thing when used of the church as they do when applied to the nation of Israel.

The Jew of Paul's day made two great mistakes. First, he believed that God loved the Israelites just because they were Israelites, regardless of how they lived. Second, he believed that God hated the Gentiles just because they were Gentiles, regardless of how they lived. It is sad, but true, that many religious people, including Calvinists, fall into this same trap today. They believe that God loves Calvinists, just because they are Calvinists, irrespective of how they live, and he hates Arminians just because they believe in free will, regardless of how they live. The Jew would have hated the words, *there is no difference.* Before the coming of Christ, there had indeed been a great difference between Jew and Gentile, as far as privilege was concerned, but not according to their ultimate spiritual state before God. Some would say that the Jew was better off before Christ came. There is one sense in which that is true. Paul delineates that truth in Romans 2 and 3.

The Jews had the Scriptures, the covenants and covenant signs, and the gospel. The Gentiles were without any of these great blessings. However, having privileges is not the same as obeying and taking advantage of the promised blessings and privileges. If the Jew was better off in one sense before Christ, he was far worse off after Christ came. In fact, the Jew was guiltier than was the Gentile, because the Jew had more light and truth (Romans 2). By rejecting the very Messiah that their Scriptures clearly promised, the Jews were guilty of crucifying the Lord of Glory.

Among the many things that happened on the day of Pentecost, two were especially significant. (1) The believing Jew was raised from childhood to adult sonship, and (2) the pedagogue (the law) was dismissed. For the purposes of our study, there were two other things of great significance as well. (1) The believing Gentile was given equal status with the believing Jew in the Body of Christ, or the 'new man' spoken of in Ephesians, and (2) the unbelieving Jew was stripped of all his special status and made equal with the unbelieving Gentile dog.

Paul's next argument in Galatians closes his case. "If I, a Jew, earnestly seeking to know the truth about how to be justified before God, discover in the process that I am just as guilty before God as is a Gentile, did Christ and the gospel make me guilty?"

> *Now if, as we seek the real truth about justification, we find we are as much sinners as the Gentiles, does that mean that Christ makes us sinners?* [Is it the gospel's fault that I am guilty?] *Of course not! But if I attempt to build again the whole structure of justification by the Law* [Believing that you must, in addition to trusting Christ, keep the Law, is nothing less than denying the gospel and going back to the very law that you renounced at conversion.] *then I do, in earnest, make myself a sinner.* [The very Law to which you return will show you how doubly guilty you are in your apostasy.]
>
> *For under the Law I "died"* [The law killed any hopes I had of attaining righteousness by keeping its demands.] *and now I am*

dead to the Law's demands so that I may live for God. [Compare this with Rom. 7:1–5.] (Gal. 2:17–19)[29]

The purpose of our freedom from the law is that we might be married to a new husband, even Christ himself, and bear fruit by him. Our old husband, the law, was sterile. He could not impregnate us with a seed that could produce life. Our new husband's words are alive and can produce acceptable fruit unto God.

As far as the Law is concerned, I may consider that I died on the cross with Christ. [The law can no more condemn me than it can again condemn Christ. I can no more be judged and condemned than Christ can die again. (cf: Rom. 8:1)] (Gal. 2:20a)[30]

And my present life is not that of the old "I," [There is a record book of the life of John Reisinger, born March 21, 1924, that was nailed to the cross. It is completely blotted out and will never be seen again. As far God as is concerned, that old record book never existed!] *but the living Christ within me. The bodily life I now live, I live believing in the Son of God, who loved me and sacrificed himself for me.* [There is another John Reisinger, who was born of God in September 1948. The entire motivation of this new John Reisinger's life is gratitude to the Christ who loved him and died for him.] (Gal. 2:20b)[31]

Consequently, I refuse to stultify the grace of God by reverting to the Law. For if righteousness were possible under the Law, then Christ died for nothing! [One thing is clear. You cannot mix law and grace without destroying the "liberty of the gospel." You frustrate the very purpose and concept of grace by adding the law to the gospel.] (Gal.2:21)[32]

---

[29] Ibid.
[30] Ibid.
[31] Ibid.
[32] Ibid.

We usually are concerned with using the word *me* too much. Here is one time that using the word *me* is vital. We must read Galatians 2:20 and emphasize that little word *me*. Christ loved **ME** and gave himself for **ME**.

CHAPTER EIGHT

GALATIANS 3:1–5

In most of Galatians chapter 1 and 2, Paul defends the divine origin and authority of both his apostleship and the gospel message of sovereign grace that he preached. He had been accused of being a false apostle and of preaching a false gospel. To counter that, he presented evidence that he had been personally called and taught by Christ himself, and both his apostleship and his message were neither "of men" (as to their source) or "through men" (as to the means by which they were conveyed). Paul's reason for defending himself as a true apostle was not his personal feelings, but the integrity of the gospel that he preached. His enemies were using an *ad hominem* argument: the old tactic of "discredit the messenger to destroy the message."

In chapter 3, Paul again addresses the fickleness and unfaithfulness of the Galatians that had resulted from the corrupting influence of false teachers. In verses 1 and 3, Paul uses strong words of ridicule to emphasize the Galatians' degree of stupidity. He twice calls them "dear idiots." Paul is sincere in saying they are indeed dear to him, but they still are spiritual idiots by their actions! The title "dear idiots" fits them well.

In 1:6, Paul accused them of being turncoats. By deserting the gospel, they were guilty of spiritual treason. In 3:1–5, his charge changes to stupidity. The Galatians' action was so stupid that Paul suggests that they were "bewitched." These people had openly confessed Christ. They had been justified by faith and had received the Holy Spirit as the assurance of their faith. What could possibly add to what they had received in Christ at conversion? Paul states that there is no rational way to explain their behavior.

One lesson we must learn from these verses is that nothing (and nothing really means not one single thing) can add to the salvation we received when we believed the gospel. Nothing subsequent to our conversion can make us "more saved." We were just as justified in God's sight the moment we trusted Christ as we will be in heaven. Nothing we have learned or experienced after we were born of God can make us any more a child of God, a true seed of Abraham. What can either law or circumcision add to the finished work of Christ on the cross? Granted, we will grow in our appreciation of what God has done for us, and we may have mountaintop experiences, but nothing will add anything to our justification. The least experienced saint has Christ, and having Christ is having everything there is to have!

We must be suspicious of anything that in any way adds to the atoning work of Christ. Every form of a "second work of grace" is automatically suspect. A second work of grace logically necessitates a deficient first work of grace. If anything extra is taught as an essential to the salvation that we already possess, we can be certain it is wrong.

Our basic disagreement with Roman Catholicism is over one word—the word *and*. We say that the Bible is the Word of God. Rome will say, "We too believe that the Bible is the Word of God. We believe the Bible **and** we also believe our church tradition." When we say we believe in justification by faith, Rome will say, "We believe in justification by faith

and by works." When the word *and* is added to a clear biblical doctrine, the result is a half-truth that has become an anti-truth.

It was reported that someone asked Spurgeon's grandfather if he felt he could ever preach the gospel as well as his grandson could. He replied, "Young Charles can preach a far better sermon than I ever could, but he cannot preach a better gospel than I can preach." In Galatians, the Judaizers may have been very eloquent in their arguments. However, even the least educated of all the saints would have had a better grasp of the true gospel than all the Judaizers put together. John Piper has caught the main point.

In 3:1–5 Paul does the same thing to the Galatians that he did to Peter in 2:11, 14ff.—he confronts them head-on with their folly and the inconsistency of their behavior. They have begun to be taken in by the Judaizers, and Paul shows them that their action contradicts the work of Christ on the cross and contradicts the work of the Spirit in their lives. Let's see how he does it. If you want to know the main point in advance, it is stated in 5:5. Galatians 3:1–5 is a series of rhetorical questions that do not come right out and state Paul's point. However, 5:5 does: "Through the Spirit, by faith, we wait for the hope of righteousness." The hope and confidence of every Christian is that at the end of the world, when he stands before the Judge of the universe, the verdict he will hear is "righteous." And the point of this verse is that the only way to hear that verdict is to wait for it through the Spirit, not the flesh, and by faith, not by works. That's the main point of 3:1–5, indeed, of the whole book. So let's listen carefully to 3:1–5 and let the Lord teach us how to live through the Spirit by faith rather than through the flesh by works. For as Paul says in Romans 8:13, "Those who live according to the flesh will die."[33]

Paul frames his argument around several simple questions. We will look at them carefully. Paul's astonishment stems from wondering how anyone could see and understand the meaning of the finished work of Christ as the Galatians had, and then turn from that and look to Moses for salvation. Let us look at the verses as paraphrased by Phillips.

> *O you dear idiots of Galatia, who saw Jesus Christ the crucified so plainly, who has been casting a spell over you? I will ask you one simple question: did you receive the Spirit of God by trying to keep the Law or by believing the message of the Gospel? Surely you can't be so idiotic as to think that a man begins his spiritual life in the Spirit and then completes it by reverting to outward observances? Has all your painful experience brought you nowhere? I simply cannot believe it of you! Does God, who gives you his Spirit and works miracles among you, do these things because you have obeyed the Law or because you have believed the Gospel? Ask yourselves that.* (Gal. 3:1–5)

In 1:6, Paul expressed his amazement at how quickly the Galatians had forsaken the truth. In these verses, he cannot understand the depth of their foolishness and stupidity. They had heard and professed to understand the gospel that he had so clearly preached. The KJV says, *"before whose eyes Jesus Christ hath been evidently set forth, crucified among you."*

---

[33] John Piper, sermon, "Can You Begin by the Spirit and Be Completed by the Flesh" Gal. 3:1-5, March 13, 1983, http://www.desiringgod.org/ResourceLibrary/Sermons/ByDate/1983/ 381 _Can_You_Begin_by_the_Spirit_and_Be_Completed_by_the _Flesh/, accessed June 01, 2007.

This does not mean that Christ was crucified in Galatia, nor does it mean the Galatians were eyewitnesses of his actual crucifixion. "Evidently set forth" means "publicly displayed" or "clearly preached." Paul had preached the message about Christ openly and clearly. There was no excuse for the present actions of the foolish Galatians. They were turning their backs on the gospel of grace in Jesus Christ. They were rejecting both Paul as an apostle and the gospel he preached.

It is vital that we see how Paul emphasizes that he had preached Christ as *crucified*. Paul preached Christ, not merely as a great teacher and prophet (which he was), not merely as a great miracle worker (which he was), but as crucified. Paul's emphasis is "Christ as *crucified*." It is not Christ as a babe in a manger, but Christ on a cross—dying under the judgment of God. It is not Christ the miracle worker, but Christ shedding his redeeming blood. The heart of the gospel is the person and work of Christ on the cross. Paul's immortal words in Galatians 6:14, 15 should be carved into every pulpit and tattooed on every preacher's heart and conscience.

> But God forbid that I should glory, save in the cross of our Lord Jesus Christ, by whom the world is crucified unto me, and I unto the world. For in Christ Jesus neither circumcision availeth any thing, nor uncircumcision, but a new creature. (Gal. 6:14, 15 KJV)

The gospel is not good advice; it is good news about forgiveness of sins. Its message is not that it is my duty to obey the law and thus to merit favor with God; it is the news that Christ has kept the law as my surety and died under its curse in my place. It is not an exhortation to examine myself to see if I am holy enough; it is an invitation to examine

Christ and to trust him as Lord and Savior. The gospel does not tell me to try harder and to be a better person; it tells me to come, just as I am, to a throne of grace, sprinkled with the blood of Christ. If only poor sinners could understand that it is not what they do, but what Christ has done for them that they cannot do for themselves. It is not what they feel; it is what he felt as he stood in their place and bore their guilt.

The Galatians had known, understood, and professed to believe these great truths about Christ. They had experienced the joy and assurance of salvation. But now they were acting like spiritual idiots, and I must say as gently as I can, that every one of us is just as much a stupid spiritual idiot if we have allowed a legalist preacher to bring our conscience into bondage to the law, to the church, or to himself. We all, like the Galatians, need to be warned of our danger. Paul's admonition to all who look to the law, hoping to find help or grace, is clear: *"Christ is become of no effect unto you, whosoever of you are justified by the law; ye are fallen from grace"* (Gal. 5:4 KJV).

Paul proves the stupidity of the Galatians two ways. First, he argues from their personal experience, and then he argues from the Scripture. In 3:1–2, Paul reminds them they had started well, and in verses 3–6 he wants to know who bewitched them and turned them aside. Reformed people have the tendency to reject any use of experience as an argument. Other evangelicals in general do the exact opposite; they use mostly experience in arguments. Paul uses both experience and Scripture to prove his point in Galatians 3:1–9.

To *"not obey the truth"* in verse 1 means to not believe and put into practice what the truth states. Obeying the truth certainly starts with understanding what the truth of the gospel is saying, but it is more than just mental assent. One of the tragic mistakes of our generation of believers is to equate "faith in Christ" or "believing the gospel" with nothing but mental assent. Too often, we present faith as something done with our brains alone. In Galatians, obeying the gospel had practical aspects: in daily living, it involved Jews eating with Gentiles; it involved abandoning circumcision as essential to salvation; it involved replacing living by the law with living by grace.

John Stott has some excellent comments on verse 2 and verse 4.

> *This only would I learn of you, Received ye the Spirit by the works of the law, or by the hearing of faith … Have ye suffered so many things in vain? if it be yet in vain.* (Gal. 3:2, 4 KJV)

Paul assumes that they have all received the Holy Spirit. His question is not whether they have received Him, but whether they received Him by works or by faith (verse 2). He assumes also that this is how their Christian life began (verse 3: *having begun with the Spirit*). What he is asking concerns *how* they received the Spirit and so began the Christian life. What part did they play in the process?

It is important to be clear about the possible alternatives, which the apostle terms 'by works of the law' *(i.e.* by obeying the law's demands) and 'by hearing with faith' *(i.e.* 'believing the gospel message', NEB). The contrast, already adumbrated in 2:16, is between the law and the gospel. As Luther writes: "Whoso … can rightly judge between the law and the Gospel, let him thank God, and know that he is a right divine.' This is the difference between them: the law says 'Do this'; the gospel says 'Christ has done it all'. The law requires works of human achievement; the gospel requires faith in Christ's achievement.

The law makes demands and bids us obey; the gospel brings promises and bids us believe. So the law and the gospel are contrary to one another. They are not two aspects of the same thing, or interpretations of the same Christianity. At least in the sphere of justification, as Luther says, 'the establishing of the law is the abolishing of the Gospel'.[34]

Probably no single passage so clearly refutes the Charismatic teaching concerning the baptism of the Holy Spirit as does Galatians 3:1–5. Paul insists not only that every Christian has the Holy Spirit, but also that he received the Holy Spirit at conversion. Put that together with Romans 8:9, where Paul states that if a person does not have the Holy Spirit then they are not really a Christian, and you have destroyed any possibility of a second blessing being essential to salvation.

Paul's primary concern in these verses is *how* believers receive the Holy Spirit. The questions he presses are simple but crucial. Paul insists that at conversion, the Holy Spirit witnesses to a person's heart that his sins are forgiven. The vital question is this: did this happen to you because you *did something*, had something *done to you*, you *joined something*, or was it because you *believed something* that you were told? Did you *do* something, or did you simply *believe* some news from the Bible? Paul could tell the Galatians, "Your personal experience of assurance of salvation proves beyond question that you started your Christian life completely by faith in the promises of God. What in the world makes you so stupid as to think you can go back to the very empty works from which you turned when you turned to Christ? If the works of law could not begin your salvation, how can they

---

[34] Stott, *One Way*, 71.

possibly finish it? What insane thinking allows you to believe that you could begin the Christian life by grace and faith only, but you could finish it with law and works?"

In verse 5, Paul uses the same argument as he does in verse 2, but from a different point of view. He has already argued concerning *how* the Galatians received the Spirit. Now he argues concerning how God *gave* the Spirit. The question (how did something happen) and the answer (not by law) are the same in both verses. When Paul preached the gospel in Galatia, God's Spirit empowered Paul to perform miracles. "How did God do these miracles among you?" is answered with "it had nothing to do with keeping the law" but was solely "through the hearing of faith."

> *He therefore that ministereth to you the Spirit, and worketh miracles among you, doeth he it by the works of the law, or by the hearing of faith?* (Gal. 3:5 KJV)

John Stott summarizes this section very well.

This, then, was a fact of their experience. Paul had come to Galatia and preached the gospel to them. He had publicly portrayed before their eyes Jesus Christ as crucified. They had heard the gospel and with the eye of faith had seen Christ displayed upon His cross. They had believed the gospel. They had trusted in the Christ exhibited in the gospel. So they had received the Spirit. They had neither submitted to circumcision, nor obeyed the law, nor even tried to. All they had done was to hear the gospel and believe, and the Spirit had been given to them. These being the facts of their experience, Paul argues, it is ludicrous that, 'having begun with the Spirit', they should now expect to be complete 'with the flesh'. This is another way of saying that, having begun with the gospel, they must not go back to the law, imagining that the law was needed to supplement the gospel. To do so would be not 'improvement' but 'degeneracy'. [35]

We should note that Paul changes his terminology somewhat throughout this section. In verse 2, he contrasts the *works of the law* with the *hearing of faith*. In verse 3, he contrasts *beginning in the Spirit* and trying to *finish by the flesh*. Paul uses the word *flesh*, not in the sense of our physical body, but in the sense of our old sinful nature. Piper believes that Romans 8:7 says, "Flesh is the autonomous self, so in love with its personal power of self-determination that it does not and cannot submit to God's absolute authority."[36] The world and its many manifestations of sin and immorality can easily bewitch the flesh. But in Galatians, the bewitched flesh to which Paul refers is not carnal and irreligious flesh. Paul's reference is to *religious flesh*, with its power to rationalize and destroy truth. The world has the bewitching power to make sight more important than faith, even to Christians. In its most insidious form, religious flesh is the skilful use, or misuse, of the holy, just, and good law of God to make self-righteous legalists out of simple and sincere Christians. Religious flesh rears its ugly head whenever we try to mix law and grace.

In the next chapter, we will look at Paul's second argument: the example of Abraham. Paul not only argues from Scripture; he uses the very Scriptures that the Judaizers are using and distorting.

---

[35] Ibid,. 72.

[36] Piper, sermon, "Can You Begin by the Spirit."

CHAPTER NINE

GALATIANS 3:6–9

In the last chapter we covered Galatians 3:1–5. Paul expressed his amazement that the Galatians were accepting the false gospel of the Judaizers and rejecting the true gospel that he had taught them. In Galatians 3:1–5, Paul demonstrates the Galatians' utter folly by using their personal experience. They had started their Christian life by faith and not by works. They were now forsaking the truth of sovereign grace for the tyranny of the law. In verses 6–9, Paul argues from the Scriptures. Their personal experience proved them wrong, and their own Scriptures also condemned them. The Judaizers kept using God's dealing with Abraham to prove their claim that circumcision and keeping the law was essential to being a "true" child of Abraham. Paul takes the argument of the Judaizers and shows how they were twisting the Scriptures that spoke of Abraham's justification.

You can go right back to Abraham to see the principle of faith in God. He, we are told, 'believed God, and it was accounted to him for righteousness.' Can you not see, then, that all those who "believe God" are the real "sons of Abraham"? The scripture foreseeing that God would justify the Gentiles "by faith" really proclaimed the Gospel centuries ago in the words spoken to Abraham, 'In you all the nations shall be blessed.' All men of faith share the blessing of Abraham who "believed God." (Gal. 3:6–9)[37]

---

[37] Phillips, New Testament

This is really a masterstroke by Paul. In essence Paul is saying, "You want to talk about Abraham and circumcision to prove your point. You picked the wrong man. God's dealing with Abraham proves my point, not yours." Paul then begins to carefully unpack what the Old Testament Scripture actually says about Abraham being justified.

First of all, the religion of Abraham is a religion based entirely on grace and faith. It has nothing to do with works and law. Paul first quotes Genesis 15:6, Abraham _"believed God, and it was accounted to him for righteousness."_ Why is this verse so important? It totally destroys the Judaizer's argument. They were insisting that it was essential to be circumcised in order to be justified and be one of Abraham's children. However, Abraham was justified by faith _many years before he was circumcised._ Abraham's experience of salvation by grace through faith alone, before he was circumcised, proves it is impossible for circumcision to have anything at all to do with becoming God's child in justification.

Secondly, Abraham was justified by faith many years before the law was given at Mount Sinai. Actually, Abraham was in the grave when the law was given. The Biblical facts prove the gospel message that Paul preached and refutes the false gospel the Judaizers preached. Paul applies these facts in verse 7. "Can't you not see then ("Understand then ..." NIV) that all those who "believe God" are the "real of sons Abraham"? It is Abraham "the believer" who was justified, not Abraham "the circumcised law-keeper." Abraham did not _do_ something to be justified but rather Abraham _believed_ something.

Paul's point is proved. When we look at the biblical facts, they are quite clear. Abraham was indeed a justified man. He was "counted righteous in God's sight." Scripture is just as clear that Abraham was justified entirely by faith in God's promise *before* he was circumcised and *before* the Law was given to Moses. Conclusion: First, neither circumcision nor law-keeping played any part in Abraham's justification, and second, this proves that the Judaizers' claim that circumcision and law-keeping were essential to salvation was absolutely wrong and totally contrary to the Biblical facts.

In Romans 4, Paul argues at length that Abraham's justification by faith without works is the prototype of all justification. His amazing statement in 4:5 would have been utter blasphemy to the Judaizers. They would have screamed, "Can you imagine Paul claiming that the Holy One of Israel actually justifies *ungodly sinners?*"

Now to him that worketh is the reward not reckoned of grace, but of debt. But to him that worketh not, but believeth on him that justifieth the ungodly, his faith is counted for righteousness. (Rom. 4:4, 5 KJV)

Paul proceeds to show that (1) Abraham was justified by faith before the law was given, (2) David was justified by faith while living under the law, and (3) Gentiles today are justified by faith after the law has been fulfilled and done away with. Justification has always been, and will always be, by grace through faith alone.

In Romans 4, Paul gives the best definition in all of Scripture of gospel faith that issues in true salvation. He recounts the Scripture account of God making a promise to Abraham that seemed impossible to be fulfilled. In spite of all the evidence to the contrary, Abraham still believed God's promise.

He staggered not at the promise of God through unbelief; but was strong in faith, giving glory to God; And being fully persuaded that, what he had promised, he was able also to perform. And therefore it was imputed to him for righteousness. (Rom. 4:20–22 KJV).

Look carefully at verse 21. (1) Faith needs a foundation. There is no true faith without a clear promise for faith to lay hold of. Abraham did not "have faith in God" in a vacuum. His faith was "in what God had specifically promised." I cannot emphasize this too strongly. Faith does not begin with us; it begins with God's Word. Faith does not begin with our needs and wants; it begins with God's promise. No promise—no faith! (2) Abraham's faith was in God's character. He believed God was faithful to His promise, and he also believed God's sovereign power could bring to pass what He had promised. (3) Abraham was "fully persuaded" that God meant what he said and not only fully intended to do exactly what had been promised but He had the power to do it. True faith always has expectancy as long as it has a promise. (4) "Therefore it was imputed to him for righteousness."

Paul's application of his main point is beautiful. The history of Abraham was not recorded just for his sake or for the sake of the nation of Israel. The account of Abraham's justification was written for you and me to learn and experience the same truth that Abraham experienced. It was the very truth the Judaizers in Galatians were denying. You and I will receive the same justification and friendship with God that Abraham enjoyed if we believe the same God and the same promise. Notice that the object of our faith is God the Father's action of raising "Jesus our Lord from the dead." The resurrection of our Lord is the Father's testimony of approval of the atoning work of our Lord. We literally "believe the Father's testimony concerning His Son."

> *Now it was not written for his sake alone, that it was imputed to him; But for us also, to whom it shall be imputed, if we believe on him that raised up Jesus our Lord from the dead; Who was delivered for our offenses, and was raised again for our justification.* (Rom. 4:23–25 KJV).

In Galatians 3:6, Paul quotes Genesis 15. In verses 7–9, Paul goes back to an earlier reference to Abraham in Genesis 12:1–3. Galatians 3:7–9 are key verses. Let's look again at the verses and then try to follow Paul's argument.

> *Know ye therefore that they which are of faith, the same are the children of Abraham. And the scripture, foreseeing that God would justify the heathen through faith, preached before the gospel unto Abraham, saying, In thee shall all nations be blessed. So then they which be of faith are blessed with faithful Abraham.* (KJV)

Verse 7 is the theological point which is the heart of Paul's whole theology. All who have saving faith, regardless of which dispensation they lived in or under what covenant they were born, are truly justified and are the children of Abraham. Verse 8 states that the Old Testament Scriptures clearly foretold, in a promise to Abraham, that God was going to extend the Gospel message past Israel to include the Gentiles. These verses contain three important points.

One: Exactly what is the "blessing" promised?

Two: How will this blessing be received?

Three: To whom is the blessing promised?

First, exactly what is the blessing "promised"? It is clear that the phrase *to justify* and *to bless* in verse 8 are the same thing.

The blessing is justification. Galatians 3:14 says the same thing.

Second, how will the blessing be received? It has nothing to do with birth, whether it be into the nation of Israel or into a Christian home. It has nothing to do with wearing a covenant sign whether it be circumcision or baptism. It has nothing to do with obeying the law. The Scriptures are clear: they foresaw *"that God would justify the heathen through faith."* Both verses 7 and 9 speak of "they which be of faith" being Abraham's children and also being "blessed (with justification) with faithful Abraham." Note again it is Abraham the believer and not Abraham a circumcised law-keeper who is blessed.

Third, to whom is the blessing promised? (1) In verse 6, the promise is made to Abraham. (2) In verse 7, the promise is made to Abraham's children. Since the blessing is justification, this must be referring to Abraham's spiritual children and not the nation of physical Israel. (3) The blessing was to all the elect among the entire heathen world.

Verse 9 is a beautiful summation of Paul's argument. All of Abraham's true seed will receive the blessing of justification, and they will receive it the same way that Abraham did *by faith.* Go back again and read Romans 4:23–25! The Galatians would have realized and rejoiced in this glorious truth if they had just kept their eyes on Christ crucified. The primary source of all spiritual problems has its source in not keeping our eyes on Christ alone. John Piper keeps insisting that we must constantly "preach the gospel to ourselves." The gospel is Christ crucified in the room and stead of sinners. We must hear, understand and believe that message to be saved, and we must keep on hearing it over and over again to grow in grace. The hymn writer had it right.

> Tell me the old, old story
> Of unseen things above,
> Of Jesus and His glory,
> Of Jesus and His love.
> Tell me the story simply,
> As to a little child;
> For I am weak and weary,
> and helpless and defiled.

> Tell me the story slowly,
> That I may take it in
> That wonderful redemption,
> God's remedy for sin.
> Tell me the story often,
> For I forget so soon;
> The early dew of morning,
> Has passed away at noon.

> Tell me the same old story
> When you have cause to fear
> That this world's empty glory
> Is costing me too dear.
> Yes, and when that world's glory
> Is dawning on my soul,
> Tell me the old, old, story:
> "Christ Jesus makes thee whole."[38]

I pity people that sit under a ministry where they must listen to the same sermon every week with no real change except the text. Such ministries usually end with a prolonged altar call. However, having said that, I must add that when I hear some people complaining about "hearing

---

[38] Words by A. Katherine Hankey, 1866

nothing but the gospel," I wonder if the problem may be a wrong appetite as much as sermon content. One of the greatest compliments I ever received for a sermon came from a lovely older lady. I preached a gospel sermon (I refuse to say "simple" gospel sermon), and this lady came up to me with tears in her eyes and said, "Pastor, as I listened to the gospel tonight, my heart was overwhelmed. I was almost wishing I was lost just so I could believe and experience salvation all over." My dear Christian, beware when a good old gospel sermon does not make you want to cry.

You will grow in ignorance, fear and superstition until you hear and believe the message of the cross. If you sit under a Galatian message of legalism, you can only feel despair. You can only grow in grace and joy under a ministry that exalts Christ crucified.

Do you want to "get the blessing"? I mean the real blessing. I mean the blessing that made Abraham God's friend. Actually, you can get a double blessing. First, you can be justified (v. 8) and have the status of "child of Abraham." Second, you can have the very Holy Spirit of God put in you (verses 2–5) and know the joy of son-ship. Being justified and having the Spirit is a package deal. If you are justified, you have received the Spirit. If you received the Spirit, then you are justified.

It was reminding himself of God's promise that kept Abraham persevering in faith and hope. Abraham had the promise of a coming Christ. Paul says that, "God preached the gospel to Abraham" (verse 8). The gospel is, "Believe on the Lord Jesus Christ and you will be saved." Where are those words found in Genesis? Look carefully at exactly what Paul says in verse 8.

And the scripture, foreseeing that God would justify the heathen through faith, preached before the gospel unto Abraham, saying, In thee shall all nations be blessed. (Gal. 3:8 KJV)

According to this verse, the gospel preached to Abraham was *"In thee shall nations be blessed."* The promise to Abraham was a seed through whom the blessing would come to all nations. That seed is Christ, and the blessing is justification. "In thy seed" is the same as saying, "Believe in the coming Messiah." That is exactly the way Abraham and the old covenant believers understood the promise of a seed. The Seed of woman in Gen. 3:15 is Christ. The Seed of Abraham in Genesis 12 is the same Christ. The Seed of David in 2 Samuel 7, now raised to sit on the throne, is the same Christ. Saying, "Believe in a coming Seed" is the same as saying, "Believe on the Lord Jesus Christ."

Everyone believes God gave Israel the hope of a coming Messiah all the way through the Old Testament. They also agree that Genesis 3:15 is the first intimation of that promised Messiah. Where is the second, third, etc. promise held out? How do we trace the gospel promise down through the Old Testament? Tracing the promise of "a seed" is one way. Peter, on the day of Pentecost, changes the word *seed* in the promise God made to David to *Christ.* There is no question the seed line is the line of a coming Savior.

Genesis 12:1–3 is an important passage just as Abraham is an extremely important man. Theologians differ on the implications of Abraham's role in the history of redemption. Dispensationalism sees Genesis 12 as God beginning a new program. The importance of Abraham in that system is that he is the father of the Jewish nation, and as such, he receives some very specific and special promises. One of those promises is inheriting and living in peace in the "promised land" of Palestine. God has two peoples, an earthly and a heavenly people. They are both under different covenants and have different destinies. Non-dispensational theologians say that God is not starting a new program with a new people, but rather he is taking the first step in fulfilling the prophecy in Genesis 3:15. In this second system the importance of Abraham is not that he is the father of a new spiritual people but that he is the father of the nation that will bring forth the promised Seed. Both Abraham and Israel's purpose is tied up with the coming of the Seed to fulfill the hope of old covenant believers. The latter group of theologians feel that dispensationalism destroys the unity of the Bible. Dispensationalists insist that non-dispensationalists will not take the Old Testament Scriptures "literally."

I have godly friends on both sides of this issue. I have more questions than answers. One thing I know for sure, looking at our present world and where it is moving, especially in the Middle East, it is a lot easier to look at the nation of Israel as still being, *in some sense,* a special people before God than it was twenty years ago.

Regardless of your prophetic view, hold on to the truth that God has one elect people for whom his Son died. God will bring those elect people to faith through the preaching of the gospel of sovereign grace. The next time you look up into a starry sky, remember that Abraham looked at those same stars and believed the promise of the gospel. He was instantly justified and made God's child. If you would be

God's friend, then imitate father Abraham and believe the gospel.

CHAPTER TEN

GALATIANS 3:10–14

For as many as are of the works of the law are under the curse: for it is written, Cursed is every one that continueth not in all things which are written in the book of the law to do them. But that no man is justified by the law in the sight of God, it is evident: for, The just shall live by faith. And the law is not of faith: but, The man that doeth them shall live in them. Christ hath redeemed us from the curse of the law, being made a curse for us: for it is written, Cursed is every one that hangeth on a tree: That the blessing of Abraham might come on the Gentiles through Jesus Christ; that we might receive the promise of the Spirit through faith. (Gal. 3:10–14 KJV)

Galatians 3:10 begins a new paragraph containing a new argument. Earlier, Paul had argued that both the personal experience of the Galatians and the testimony of Scripture contradicted the message of the Judaizers (3:1–5). Then he argued from the promise to Abraham (3:6–9). Now he will argue against the Judaizers by using their own appeal: the Mosaic law. In order to understand Paul's point, we must understand the phrase he uses to introduce his argument: "as many as are of the works of the law." This refers to anyone who is expecting that he will earn favor or justification before God by obeying the law. Paul declares that anyone who has such a hope is self-deluded. Those who seek to be justified by keeping the law must realize that they already have broken the law and therefore already are under its curse. It is spiritual insanity for me to look to the law for help in earning the favor of God when that law already has cursed me. The same law cannot bless and curse the same people at the same time. Paul not only shows how the very nature of the case shows its absurdity; he shows the same thing from Scripture itself. Thus, he shows again that salvation by obedience to the law is both unreasonable and unscriptural. Paul quotes Deuteronomy 27:26 to prove that his point is the biblical position.

> *Cursed be he that confirmeth not all the words of this law to do them. And all the people shall say, Amen.*(KJV)

When Israel went into Canaan, Moses and the elders told the people to inscribe the law with its curses and promised blessings on large plastered stones. Representatives from half the tribes were to stand on Mount Gerizim and read the blessings in store for those who obeyed the law. Members of the remaining six tribes were to stand on Mount Ebal and read the curses waiting to befall those who disobeyed the law. Then the Levites were to declare to all the people of Israel a list of eleven individual, specific curses, to which all the people were to give vocal assent. Verse 26 follows this list and contains the sum and substance of the entire list. The verse literally means, *"cursed is he who maketh not to stand the words of this law."* In other words, those who obey the precepts make them stand; those who disobey do what lies in their power to overthrow them.

Paul then quotes Habakkuk 2:4b to demonstrate the outcome of this principle: *"The just shall live by faith."* The *New Scofield Reference Bible* says this about Habakkuk 2:4:

> Here is the central theme of the Bible. The cause of life and death is presented. Trust in God brings life (Gen. 15:6; Jn. 3:16;

Rom. 6:23); pride leads to death, because it will not accept by faith the grace of God (Rom. 1:17; Gal. 3:11; Heb. 10:38).[39]

Habakkuk had received a revelation from God, who then told the prophet to publish the message. God assured Habakkuk that the promise would surely come to pass, even if its actualization seemed slow or uncertain. Those who believed the message, in spite of its delayed fulfillment, would live, or be saved by grace through faith, and those who rejected God's promise would be damned. Here is the watershed for all humanity. One group (implicitly represented by Habakkuk and the oppressed Israelites) is described as bowing down in the humility of faith in God's revealed truth. Regardless of the current evidence to the contrary, God will right the wrongs in Israel. This group (the just) will conduct their lives in the light of their belief in God's faithfulness. The other group (implicitly represented either by the wicked and greedy among Israel, or by the Chaldeans, who were even more wicked and greedy than their Hebrew counterparts) is pictured as standing up in rigid unbending unbelief and rejection of God's revealed truth. This group will conduct their lives in the light of their unbelief in God's future action. The one group will be justified by their faith, and the other will be condemned for their unbelief.

The New Testament writers quote Habakkuk 2:4b three times. Each time, the author stresses a different word from the phrase. In Romans 1:17, "the just shall live by faith," Paul lays stress on the word *just*. The just one is the person

---

[39] *New Scofield Reference Bible* (NY: Oxford University Press, 1967), 954, ftnt. 3.

who believes God's word. In Hebrews 10:38, the idea is perseverance. The stress there is on the word *live*. The truly just person will believe, keep on believing, (living by faith), and will not give up. In our text, Galatians 3:11, the idea is the means by which a person becomes justified or gains life. No one will ever be made just or be converted by any means other than faith. The stress is on "faith." Paul uses the phrase to set forth three truths. (1) "Justified" people are those to whom God has given life through "grace alone and through *faith* alone." (2) Those who have faith are the truly *just*, or justified. (3) The truly just ones not only receive life through faith; they *continue to live by that faith* until the day their faith gives way to sight.

So what connection does Paul draw between the passage in Deuteronomy and the passage in Habakkuk? It is this: Habakkuk had been complaining that the law was paralyzed—it was ineffective. Wicked people within the covenant community flagrantly violated the law with impunity. They prospered, in spite of the threatened curses listed in Deuteronomy. Those who obeyed the law were not receiving its promised blessings. It looked, from the evidence at hand, as though God's word was not to be believed. God assured Habakkuk that the law would indeed work—it would bring its threatened curses and its corrective justice, but the law itself was of no help in encouraging the Israelites to believe that God was faithful. In fact, it was a hindrance. For belief that pleased God, they needed faith. Paul's point is that the righteous—the just—do not need the law to believe God. He has demonstrated that principle earlier by appealing to Abraham (verse 6); now he strengthens his argument by appealing to Habakkuk. The law promotes action based on immediate results—it operates on the principle of sight and works. Faith is concerned with belief in the face of no results.

We must grasp one major point here: Paul is clear and emphatic in verses 11 and 12 about his doctrine of law and grace: *The just shall live by faith. And the law is not of faith.* The law cannot help a sinner become justified, nor can the law help a justified sinner become sanctified. Both law and grace, and works and faith, operate on opposite principles. We need to cement in our minds: "The law is not of faith." If you grasp that fact, then you will not look to the law to help save you or to keep you saved. Not only will you not hope for life by the law; you will not try to sustain that life through the law.

We should also mention Paul's use of the word *continues* in Galatians 3:10. Although justification is a once-for-all declaration by God that can never change, it does not mean that a child of God must not persevere in faith until the end. The idea that a Christian is eternally secure regardless of how he lives is not the biblical doctrine of the perseverance of the saints. Perseverance until the end is vital to true salvation. The glory of the doctrine of perseverance is that God pledges his grace to every believer enabling that believer to persevere until the end. We must persevere, and God's grace will enable us to do so.

Verse 13 is an example of Paul answering an obvious objection without actually stating the problem. If the Jews were under the law, and therefore under its curse, as Paul has so clearly proven, then how can a Jew in such a condition ever be justified? How can one who is justly condemned by the law ever escape that condemnation? That surely is a legitimate question, and it would naturally enter the mind of anyone carefully following Paul's logic.

> *Christ hath redeemed us from the curse of the law, being made a curse for us: for it is written, Cursed is every one that hangeth on a tree.*

The answer to this question is that Christ has redeemed "us" from under the curse of the law. Christ's atoning work completely satisfied every demand of the "just, holy, and good" law. That redemption by the blood of Christ brought those who had believed out from under the curse of the law.

The first item to establish concerns to whom Paul refers when he says "us." The apostle uses the pronoun "we" many ways. Sometimes, he means we *people;* sometimes, we *sinners;* sometimes, we *Jews;* sometimes, we *believers,* whether Jew or Gentile; sometimes, we *believing Jews;* sometimes, we *apostles.* Context must establish the correct uses. John Brown states that nearly all commentators say that the referent of "us" in verse 13 is either "us elect *sinners,*" or "us *believers.*" He disagrees and proceeds to give what he feels is the correct meaning.

> But to a person who is familiar with the modes of thinking and speaking of the primitive age, and who carefully attends to the context, it will appear plain that this is not the apostle's meaning. It is obvious, that they who are "redeemed from the curse of the law," are distinguished from "the Gentiles," to whom the blessing of Abraham comes through means of their redemption. The direct subject of the discussion is the impossibility of being justified by obedience to the Mosaic law; and it is the curse of the Mosaic law which is spoken of in the 10th verse. The Gentile believers were, previously to their conversion, under sin and condemnation, as well as the Jewish believers; but not being subject to the Mosaic law, they could

not be considered as exposed to *its* curse, and, of course, they could not be represented as redeemed from a curse to which they were never subject.

Every principle of rational interpretation, therefore, requires us to consider the statement made in this verse as referring to those Jews who had become Christians. They had been under that law which the Judaizing teachers were so anxoius to impose on the Gentile believers; but so far from being justified by that law, they had incurred its curse, in consequence of their "not continuing in all things written in its book to do them," and must have taken the tremendous consequences had not "Christ redeemed them from the curse of the law, by becoming a curse for them." [40]

Every Jew was exposed to the curse of the law of Moses, or the old covenant. His circumcision committed him to obey that law as covenant terms. The death of Christ redeemed the believing Jew from the curse of the broken law. Our Lord was born under that law for the express purpose of earning its righteousness and enduring its curse. He bore the curse of the law and delivered those described from its just condemnation. Notice the text does not say, "Christ *delivered* us," even though that is true. Redemption is more than deliverance. To substitute "deliverance" for "redemption," as the *Good News for Modern Men* paraphrase does, misses a key ingredient in redemption. Redemption requires the necessity of a redemption price which is acceptable to the one to whom it is paid. If I drug a jailor, steal his keys, and then turn all his prisoners free, I have "delivered" them but I certainly have not "redeemed" them.

---

[40] John Brown, *An Exposition of the Epistle of Paul the Apostle to the Galatians,* (Edinburgh: William Oliphant and Sons, 1853), 129-30.

We must remember that redemption from the curse of the law was not accomplished by an act of God's power. Nor was that redemption accomplished by the love of God. Not all the love in the universe, including all the love in God's heart, could forgive one single sin. Strict justice demands payment for sin, and nothing can pay for sin except the atoning blood of Christ. God will be satisfied with only one sacrificial offering—the once-for-all, blood-shedding sacrifice of his Son on the cross. The hymn writer was correct when he wrote, "What can wash away my sin? Nothing but the blood of Jesus."[41]

Paul then quotes another Scripture reference (Deut. 21:23) to prove his point:

> *Cursed is every one that hangeth on a tree:* (Gal 3:13 quoting Deut. 21:23)

In ancient Israel, after a person was put to death for committing a capital crime, his body was "hung on a tree" in a public place. The Israelites also hung the dead bodies of vanquished non-Israelite kings on trees (see Joshua 8:29; 10:16–29). This treatment was to show all who passed by that the person who had died was under the curse of God. Our Lord was not cursed because he died on a cross; he died on a cross to show *he was being cursed by God!* Dying the death of the cross was the proof that he was dying the death of an enemy of God. This was the great stumbling block for the Jews. They would ask, "How can Jesus be the Messiah when he dies under the curse of God? How can the anointed one be God's enemy?" They were correct that he died under God's curse, as though he was God's enemy, but they did

---

[41] Robert Lowry, "Nothing but the Blood," (1826-1899).

not understand that he was bearing that curse vicariously. It is true that Christ died a true sinner's death under the wrath of God, but he was no sinner. He had neither deserved nor earned that death. He was treated as if he were a guilty sinner only because he took our sins upon himself. He was treated as a sinner so that we might be treated as if we were without sin.

Verse 14 was never clear to me until I started to understand new covenant theology. I could not see the connection of the truth set forth in verse 14 to the truth in verse 13. I missed the connecting word "that." Verse 14 is stating that the Jewish believer's redemption from under the curse of the law was essential in order to make several things possible.

The first result of Christ redeeming the Jewish believer from the curse of the law was that it enabled the "blessing of Abraham," which is justification, "to come on the Gentiles." Why was the justification of the Gentiles not possible until the Jewish believer was redeemed from the curse of the law? What is the connection between those two things?

The second thing made possible by the Jewish believer's redemption from the curse of the law was that *"we might receive the Spirit by faith."*

> *That the blessing of Abraham might come on the Gentiles through Jesus Christ; that we might receive the promise of the Spirit through faith.* (Gal. 3:14)

Again we ask, what is the connection between the Jewish believer's need for redemption from the curse of the law and his *receiving the Holy Spirit by faith?* (I highly recommend a careful reading of John Brown, pages 131–140 on these verses). As we look at these verses, we need to "gird up the loins of our minds." John Brown lays out the problem.

> But it may be asked, What connection is there here? What has Christ's enduring the curse of the Mosaic law in the room of his people who were subject to it [the Jews] to do with another class of persons altogether [the Gentiles] obtaining justification from the offences they had committed against God in doing what they knew to be wrong and neglecting to do what they knew to be right?[42]

Understanding these verses and answering Brown's questions requires a clear understanding and application of the following biblical facts.

Fact one: The nation of Israel "had the law" in *some clear sense* that the Gentiles did not.

Fact two: The nation of Israel, and every Jew in it, by virtue of his being "under the law," was therefore also under the "curse of the law."

Fact three: The Gentiles were not under the law, meaning the law of Moses or the old covenant, and therefore were not under the "curse of the law." The "curse of the law" must, of necessity, follow the breaking of those of God's revealed laws under which a person lives.

Fact four: This does not mean that Gentiles were not guilty sinners. It does mean their guilt was not measured by specific transgressions of a law that was never given to them. Romans 4:15 is greatly misunderstood. This text says, *"Because the law worketh wrath: for where no law is, there is no transgression."* (Rom. 4:15). This text usually is misquoted, especially by Covenant Theologians, as saying, *"for where no*

---

[42] Brown, *Galatians*, 134.

*law is, there is no **sin**."* They then proceed to misuse the verse to prove the necessity of all human beings, including Gentiles, as being under the law. The logic of this position is as follows: since there must be law before there can be sin, and we know all people are sinners, we know that all people must be under the law. Paul, however, is not saying that there must be law in order for there to be sin, that is—"no law, no sin." He says that sin cannot be credited as **transgression of law** unless that law is known. The whole world, apart from Noah and his family, was judged as guilty sinners deserving death and died in the flood long before the law was ever given to Moses at Sinai. Nobody first became a sinner at Sinai, but the Jews became the first "transgressors of revealed and codified law" at Sinai.

Fact five: The primary purpose of the law of Moses, which was the old covenant, was to reveal sin and make those under it feel their guilt. The law did not cause sin, but it did bring to the surface the sin that was already in people's hearts.

Fact six: The law covenant at Sinai not only separated sinners from God; it also separated Israel from all other nations. The law created, by God's design, a wall of partition that not only segregated all who were under it from God, but also segregated Israel, as God's chosen nation, from the Gentiles. The Jews were not allowed even to eat with Gentiles.

Fact seven: As long as that wall of partition was in force, there was no possibility of Gentiles being reconciled with either God or with Jews unless they converted to Judaism. There could never be any kind of fellowship between Jews and Gentiles as long as the middle wall of partition was in place.

Fact eight: Gentiles were not under the curse of the law of Moses because they had never been given the law of Moses. The Gentiles, however, were still sinners under the wrath of God because there was, and is, a revelation of God in the heart of all people, as well as in creation, that leaves all people, whether they have been given the law of Moses or not, guilty and condemned before God (Romans 1).

Fact nine: Since it was the law as covenant that segregated the Jews and Gentiles, that segregated situation had to remain in place as long as the law of Moses, or the old covenant, was in force. The middle wall of partition had to be removed before the gospel of free justification could come to the Gentiles and they could be "fellow heirs" with the Jews. The distinction of "Jew and Gentile" mandated by God in the old covenant must stand in force as long as the old covenant stood in force.

Fact ten: Nothing less than the atonement of Christ, establishing the new covenant and the gift of the Holy Spirit to create the Body of Christ, could fulfill and do away with the old covenant.

When you put all of these things together, they explain Paul's statement concerning the need for the Jew's redemption from under the law and the gift of the Holy Spirit so that Gentiles could be saved. Nothing less than the cross could satisfy God and bring reconciliation between him and sinners. Likewise, nothing but the cross could destroy the enmity between Jews and Gentiles and reconcile them to each other (See Ephesians 2:10–22). You can reconcile enemies but you cannot reconcile enmity. In order to reconcile enemies, you must remove the enmity that is the cause of their being enemies. This Christ did when he nailed the old covenant to the cross.

John Brown's summary of this section is excellent. He shows how the "promise of the Spirit" was to be "one of the grand characteristics of the Messiah's reign (See Isa. 44:3; Ezek. 36:27; Joel; John 14:16, 17; 15:26; 16:7)."

The sum, then, of what the apostle says in these two most important verses is this: 'We believing Jews owe our salvation not to the law, but entirely to Christ, and obtain it entirely through believing. We, by violating the law, to which we were subject, had incurred its curse; but Christ has delivered us from this curse by enduring it in our room. As his sufferings and death are sufficient and intended to avail, not only as the propitiation for our sins, but also for those of the whole world; and as, by completely satisfying all the demands of the Mosaic law, they have put an honourable termination to that order of things, which, during its continuance, necessarily excluded the great body of the Gentiles from the blessing of Abraham—an order of things which, now that the Messiah is come, has completely served its purpose,—the consequence is, that justification by believing is extended to men of every nation; and we Jews obtain the promised Spirit through believing the gospel, and not by obedience to the law.'[43]

Brown then adds a footnote saying: "It scarcely requires to be noticed, that it is through the channel of the atonement that the Spirit comes to Gentiles as well as Jews."[44]

In the next chapter, we begin to get into the heart of new covenant theology. The section we will examine, which

---

[43] Ibid., 138, 39.
[44] Ibid., 139

tends often to be misunderstood, explains the real purpose and function of the law of Moses.

Chapter Eleven

GALATIANS 3:15–19

In Galatians 3:15, Paul begins to compare God's covenant with Abraham with his covenant with Moses. Paul has already pointed out the contrasting natures of law and of faith; now he will develop the contrast in more detail. As he does so, he will ask and answer an obvious and vital question; namely, "If the law can neither justify nor even help justify a sinner, then why did God give the law in the first place?" Paul has been fighting the Judaizers in Galatia by hammering home the truth that justification is by grace through faith without the works of the law. He has demonstrated the error of the Judaizers' position by arguing from their own starting place—the Old Testament Scriptures that refer to the law of Moses. Paul has used a correct understanding of those Old Testament Scriptures to prove his point. His argument, however, would raise a logical question in the minds of his readers—the question of "why the law?" Let us read the passage.

Brethren, I speak after the manner of men; Though it be but a man's covenant, yet if it be confirmed, no man disannulleth, or addeth thereto. Now to Abraham and his seed were the promises made. He saith not, And to seeds, as of many; but as of one, And to thy seed, which is Christ. And this I say, that the covenant, that was confirmed before of God in Christ, the law, which was four hundred and thirty years after, cannot disannul, that it should make the promise of none effect. For if the inheritance be of the law, it is no more of promise: but God gave it to Abraham by promise. Wherefore then serveth the law? It was added because of transgressions, till the seed should come to whom the promise was made; and it was ordained by angels in the hand of a mediator. (Gal. 3:15–19 KJV)

John Stott gives an excellent summary of this section.

a. The history

Paul takes us back to about 2,000 BC, to Abraham, and then on to Moses who lived some centuries later. Moses is not named here, but he is without doubt the 'intermediary' (verse 19), through whom the law was given.

Let me remind you of this part of the Old Testament story. God called Abraham from Ur of the Chaldees. He promised that He would give him an innumerable 'seed' (or posterity), that He would bestow on him and on his seed a land, and that in his seed all the families of the earth would be blessed. These great promises of God to Abraham were confirmed to Abraham's son Isaac, and then to Isaac's son Jacob. But Jacob died outside the promised land, in Egyptian exile, to which a famine in Canaan had driven him. Jacob's twelve sons died in exile too. Centuries passed. A period of 430 years is mentioned (verse 17), which refers not to the time between Abraham and Moses, but to the duration of the bondage in Egypt (Ex. 12:40; *cf.* Gn. 15:13; Acts 7:6). Finally, centuries after Abraham, God raised up Moses, and through him both delivered the Israelites from their slavery and gave them the law at Mount Sinai. This, briefly, is the history which links Moses to Abraham.

b. The theology

God's dealings with Abraham and Moses were based on two different principles. To Abraham He gave a promise ('I will show you a land ...I will bless you...', Gen. 12:1, 2). But to Moses He gave the law, summarized in the Ten Commandments. 'These two things (as I do often repeat), 'comments Luther, 'to wit, the law and the promise, must be diligently distinguished. For in time, in place, and in person, and generally in all other circumstances, they are separate as far asunder as heaven and earth ....' Again, 'unless the Gospel be plainly discerned from the law, the true Christian doctrine cannot be kept sound and uncorrupt.' What is the difference between them? In the promise to Abraham God said, 'I will ... I will ... I will ...'. But in the law of Moses God said, 'Thou shalt ... thou shalt not ...'. The promise sets forth a religion of God—God's plan, God's grace, God's initiative. But the law sets forth a religion of man—man's duty, man's works, man's responsibility. The promise (standing for the grace of God) had only to be believed. But the law (standing for the works of men) had to be obeyed. God's dealings with Abraham were in the category of 'promise', 'grace' and 'faith'. But God's dealings with Moses were in the category of 'law', 'commandments' and 'works'.[45]

The point that Paul is seeking to establish is that the Christian religion is the religion of Abraham and not the religion of Moses. The gospel is the story of the fulfillment of the promise made to Abraham and fulfilled in Christ. The church is not merely the religion of Moses with the Gentiles added to it. It is not, as some have said, "God adding another room to his house." The gospel establishes a new house (Heb. 3:1–6). The gospel is not a continuation of the religion of Moses. Christians today, both believing Jews and Gentiles, are presently living in the blessings promised to Abraham. The Christian faith and church, viewed as the "body of Christ," is the "new man" described in Ephesians 2:15. However, after clearly contrasting the religion of promise given to Abraham with the religion of law given to

---

[45] Stott, *One Way*, 86, 87. The passages from Luther to which Stott refers are from Luther's *Commentary on the Epistle to the Galatians,* based on lectures delivered by Luther in 1531. Published in 1953 by James Clarke; pages 291, 302.

Moses, Paul then shows the integral relationship between the two. We must always remember that the same God who gave the promise, or the gospel, to Abraham also gave the law to Moses. We have understood neither the religion of Abraham nor the religion of Moses until we have seen that even though they are radically different, they both are essential and serve the same ultimate purpose of the same God. They have different functions, but nonetheless, they both are essential parts of the single history of redemption. We will see that the same law functioned differently in the life and worship of the Israelite than it does in the church and the Christian life. The vital question, then, *"What is the real purpose of the law?"* (Gal. 3:19) includes why, from whom, and to whom: what is the purpose of God in giving the law to the nation of Israel?

Paul answers in two parts. In verses 15–18, he gives the negative side of the answer, and in verses 19–22, the positive. First, he shows that regardless of what God's purpose was in giving the law to Israel, it cannot in any way deny, change, or do away with the gospel promise he made to Abraham. The promise of the gospel given to Abraham, salvation by grace through faith, is as unchangeable as is God himself. At Sinai, God did not change horses in the middle of the stream of redemption. Moses furthered the promise of God and contributed in fulfilling God's one, sovereign, unchanging purpose of electing grace. Paul tells his readers what the purpose of the law was not. Next, he explains what its purpose was: the law had an essential ministry that necessarily preceded a personal experience by the "heirs according to the promise" made to Abraham. However, as just mentioned, the law does not serve that same function today in the heart of a Christian or in the life and worship of the church. It is amazing to watch Paul work out the theology of grace in Scripture! Let us look at the verses carefully.

In verse 15, Paul uses an everyday illustration that his readers will understand and accept.

> *Brethren, I speak after the manner of men; Though it be but a man's covenant, yet if it be confirmed, no man disannulleth, or addeth thereto.* (Gal 3:15 KJV)

Some insist that the word *covenant* should be translated *testament* and that it means *a will*. It does not matter which is correct, since the point proved in the text is the same in either case: once a covenant between two parties is established or once the terms of a will are written, especially if the person making the will has died, nothing can be changed in the covenant or in the will. Once the covenant is cut, or confirmed, nothing except the unanimous agreement of all concerned can disannul it or change it in any way. In the case of a will, only the one making the will can change it. If this is true of the covenants that humans make, how much more does it hold when we speak of a covenant that God has made?

Paul is emphatic in verse 16. God made a specific promise to Abraham and confirmed it with an oath. That promise involved the good news of a coming Messiah and the doctrine of justification by faith in that Messiah for all in every nation who believe. God's *promise* and God's *covenant* refer to the same thing—the gospel of salvation by grace through faith. The point is clear. *Now to Abraham and his seed were the promises made,* and they were made on the ground of grace, not on the ground of law.

The second clause in verse 16 is striking. Paul insists that the recipients of God's promise are Abraham and his seed. This seed is *singular*, not *plural*—"*He saith not, And to seeds, as of many; but as of one, And to thy seed, which is Christ.*" The Abrahamic promise made in Genesis 12:1–3 must be fulfilled in one single seed. Paul further establishes that the specific singular seed is Christ, the Messiah—"*And to thy seed, which is Christ.*" Why is this so important? Some theologians insist that God's unconditional promise to Abraham and his seed is a promise to Abraham's physical seed, the nation of Israel, and it concerns the land of Canaan. It is obvious in this text that this is not the promise to which Paul refers, since that promise's fulfillment would involve a plural seed. Other theologians insist the promise to Abraham and his seed is a promise to believing parents that their children are included in the covenant. This also cannot be correct for the same reason—its fulfillment would involve a plural seed. Whether infant baptism is valid or not, one thing is certain—you cannot use the promise to "Abraham and his seed" as a proof text for it. The same is true of Israel's inheriting the land of promise in the future. That may or may not be true, but you cannot use "the promise to Abraham and his seed" to prove it. The object indicated by the promised seed (1) has to be singular, (2) has to be Christ and (3) has to someway provide a justification by faith that includes Gentiles. Isn't it interesting that both dispensationalism and covenant theology use the same Old Testament text to prove mutually exclusive points in their theologies? Additionally, both of them ignore Paul's clear statement in Galatians 3:16.

I think we can lay down a biblical fact, which when consistently applied, will greatly help us in understanding

Paul's theology of grace. "Listen up," as they say today. *No one, including a circumcised Jew or a baptized baby, ever received an eternal, spiritual blessing from God apart from personal repentance and faith.* Every eternal, spiritual blessing that anyone ever received from God was by virtue of his being joined in living faith to Christ, the true Seed promised to Abraham. There is not a single eternal, spiritual blessing promised to any individual, regardless of his family tree, or the ceremonies performed on that person, that will come unless that individual is united to Christ in true repentance and faith.

In verse 17, Paul reaffirms the obvious.

And this I say, that the covenant, that was confirmed before of God in Christ, the law, which was four hundred and thirty years after, cannot disannul, that it should make the promise of none effect." (KJV)

God made a promise to Abraham. He then confirmed that promise with an oath. To confirm means to sanction, ratify, make or declare valid. The signature of the president of the United States on a piece of legislation passed by Congress "confirms" it as binding law. Only another enactment by Congress and another signature of the president can change it. Any future legislation that appears to, or in fact actually does, contradict the original legislature must be reconciled by a decision of the Supreme Court. Neither the former nor the latter legislation can contradict either each other or the Constitution. This same principle applies to all legal contracts. Paul is insisting that once you admit that God made a promise to Abraham and then confirmed it with an oath into a covenant, you also must admit that the confirmation precludes changes. It cannot, in any way, be added to, taken away from, or changed. Justification by faith alone is the gospel promise to Abraham, and it included the justification of the Gentiles. _That covenant promise cannot be changed._ Our understanding of Moses dare not, in any way, change God's promise to Abraham. If it does, then we clearly do not understand one or the other. Justification by grace through faith without the works of the law stands as the one and only gospel of sovereign grace for all persons in all ages.

In verse 18, Paul states two undeniable facts. _First,_ it is a fact beyond dispute that justification cannot be both by law and by promise. It is clearly one or the other and cannot be a mixture of the two—_"For if the inheritance_ [remember, the inheritance is justification] _be of the law, it is no more of promise."_ This is the same principle that Paul sets forth in Romans 4:4, 5. _Second,_ it is also a clear fact that God gave justification to Abraham purely on the basis of faith, without either circumcision or the works of the law—_"but God gave it to Abraham by promise."_ So cut it any way you like, in the end you must admit that the Scripture clearly teaches that Abraham was justified by faith alone without the works of the law, and that justification took place before he had been circumcised and before God had given the law at Sinai. Since God did this (justified Abraham by faith) in fulfillment of a covenant promise, and (1) that promise included the Gentiles, and further, (2) nothing can change or disannul that covenant, it follows (3) that if the Galatian Gentiles had believed the gospel of faith preached to Abraham, then they were already Abraham's seed and had already inherited the true promise of justification. Neither circumcision nor keeping the law could make them any more justified than either of those things would have made Abraham more justified. End of discussion!

Paul now asks the crucial question and gives an amazing and unexpected answer—"Wherefore then serveth the law? It was added because of transgressions, till the seed should come to whom the promise was made" (Gal. 3:19). Phillips paraphrases it this way:

> *Where then lies the point of the Law? It was an addition made to underline the existence and extent of sin until the arrival of the "seed" to whom the promise referred.*

By *law*, Paul means the law of Moses, or the covenant of law given to Israel at Sinai. There is no question that this law played a central role in Israel's history. It controlled every aspect of an Israelite's life. Its meaning and purpose have been the subject of many intense arguments. The answer to Paul's question is one of the most discussed points in Reformed Theology today. Paul raises that specific question and gives us his clear answer. His answer, however, provokes another question. In verse 19, Paul has asked the first question concerning the purpose of the law that logically grows out of what he had just stated (that the law cannot affect the promise made to Abraham). After giving his answer, "it was added because of transgressions," he then, in verse 21, asks another question that grows out of that answer. If it was true that (1) the law provoked sin and increased transgressions, and (2) if the law not only does not give the sinner any help at all in gaining justification but actually hinders his quest, then (3) does it not logically follow that "the law is actually against the promises of God"? Paul immediately states that such a thing is impossible—"God forbid." That would mean that God was acting in self-contradiction. But does it not surely appear that there is indeed a very real contradiction in God's dealing with Abraham and with Moses?

I think it is vital that we realize an important fact. If there were not an apparent, deep contradiction between promise—the religion of Abraham—and the law—the religion of Moses—Paul would never have raised either of these questions. We do not protect God from the charge of being inconsistent by reading the text in a way that denies an apparent tension between law and promise. The failure to recognize and acknowledge this apparent contradiction prevents many theologians from clearly understanding the problem, let alone arriving at the answer. We simply must see that Paul asks about the purpose of law only because it certainly appears on the surface that God is contradicting himself, and we know that is impossible. Paul asks the second question, in verse 21, "Is the law against the promise?" only because that seems to be, on the surface, exactly what Paul's answer to the question in verse 19 implies. It appears that the real fault lies with the giving of the law, but as Paul keeps insisting, "That can never be."

As we work through Paul's answer to the first question (why then the law?), we must ask to *what* the law was added. It could not have been added to the Abrahamic covenant, since that would clearly violate verse 15 (no one adds to a ratified covenant). I am not positive that I have the answer; however, it would seem to be one of two things, or maybe both. Paul could mean that the law was added to the revelation of God. He could also be teaching that it was added to conscience. At Mount Sinai, God put Israel under the law as a covenant of life and death. That covenant controlled the entire life and worship of Israel. It demanded perfect obedience, which no one could give, and when a person inevitably sinned against that covenant, it demanded an acceptable offering, which no one could bring. Israel's conscience was sandwiched between the law's constant reminders of failed duty and earned guilt. Their diet, their clothing, their rituals, the veil in the tabernacle, and multiple other such things constantly reminded the Israelites of their duty and of their failure to obey that duty. There was no help available to keep the law, and there was no permanent way to silence its just accusations. The sacrificial system, especially the Day of Atonement, gave temporary and partial relief, but nothing could deliver an Israelite from the hands of the pedagogue, which was the function the law served in the Israelite's conscience. We will discuss the meaning of the pedagogue when we get to 3:24.

The next thing to note is that the law's specific function as a pedagogue had both a historical beginning and a historical ending. The phrase *it was added* must mean added to, and different from, something already in existence. It denotes a beginning of law, or perhaps a new function of law, at a specific point in time. Some theologians simply will not accept this fact. Paul is quite emphatic that the law "entered" (Rom. 5:20) at Sinai. Something cannot **enter** if it is already there. He says, **"Before the law,** sin was in the world" (Rom. 5:13). If the law, **in some sense,** does not have a historical beginning at Sinai, then Paul is speaking incoherently. The law of God did not come into being at Sinai, but the law, codified, made the terms of a covenant, and functioning as a pedagogue in the conscience, did begin at Sinai.

The law's function as a pedagogue not only had a historical beginning at Sinai, Paul says it also had a historical ending at the coming of Christ. It is clear that verses 19, 23, 24, and 25 all refer to the coming of Christ and the subsequent ending of the law's ministry as a pedagogue. The law, in some sense, must be dismissed with the coming of the true seed to whom the promises were made. *"Till the seed* (Christ) *should come"* (verse 19); *"We were kept under the law, shut up* **unto the faith which should afterwards be revealed** (verse 23); *"The law was our schoolmaster* **to bring us unto Christ,** *that we might be justified by faith. But* **after that faith is come, we are no longer under a schoolmaster"** (vs. 24, 25). Each verse teaches that the coming of Christ ended a relationship that Israel alone had with the law that began at Sinai.

The phrase in verse 19, that the law was added "because of transgressions," would have seemed incomprehensible to many Jews. Unfortunately, some theologians today also struggle with Paul's statement. Phillips' paraphrase has caught the idea Paul is expressing.

> It was an addition made to underline the existence and extent of sin until the arrival of the "seed" to whom the promise referred.

The law was not given to destroy sin, since that is beyond the power of law. Nor was the law given to diminish or control sin. God gave the law to make transgressions increase. Galatians 3:19 is not an isolated text that teaches that this is the purpose of the law. This is the consistent theology of the law throughout the entire New Testament. Paul's classic statement about the law appears in Romans 5:20.

Moreover the law entered, that the offence might abound. But where sin abounded, grace did much more abound. (KJV)

I can easily imagine the Jewish leaders picking up stones as they shout at Paul, "Antinomian, antinomian!" We, too, want to shout, "Paul, do you realize what you are saying? You are claiming that God gave the law so that the offenses, or sins against God's law, might increase instead of decrease. You are laying yourself wide open to the charge of antinomianism when you say that the "more we sin, the more God's grace is glorified." I think that the Jewish leaders misunderstood Paul, but I can sympathize with their struggle in trying to understand his view of the law.

In order to understand the biblical relationship of law and grace, it is essential to understand the true purpose for which God gave the law at Sinai. In 2002, I published four articles on the New Perspective on Justification. One of those articles dealt with the purpose and function of the law (see *Sound of Grace,* Issue 142, page 3). There is some small overlap between that article and this. I urge you, however, to read that article in its entirety. You can access all four articles online at www.soundofgrace.com. Follow the John G. Reisinger Library link under Main Features and look for the articles on "The New Perspective."

Paul is quite clear on the purpose of the law. (1) The law was given to make the offenses increase. (2) It was not given for the purpose of curbing sin. (3) The law was not given "to believing people" as a means of aiding their sanctification, since the law can no more sanctify than it can justify. (4) It was not given primarily as a "fence" to protect the gospel given to the nation of Israel. I repeat; Paul is clear! The law was given to "make the offense abound" (Rom. 5:20).

We must make a distinction between making the "offenses increase" and making a *person* more sinful. A sinner is no more sinful at eighty years old than at five years old. The only difference is that the older person has had seventy-five more years to demonstrate his sin. The law does not make a person more sinful. It does, however, provoke demonstrations of the already-present sin in that person's heart. Prior to Sinai, the law could not and did not provoke acts of *transgression* simply because no codified law or covenant of law existed then. On several occasions, we have mentioned how some theologians misuse Romans 4:15, but it bears repeating here. That text does not say, "Where there is no law, there is no *sin.*" It says there was "no transgression." Sin takes on a different character whenever known law exists.

CHAPTER TWELVE

GALATIANS 3:21-25

In the last chapter, we considered both Paul's vital question about the law and the answer he provided: What was God's purpose in giving the law? To add transgression! We looked at Paul's teaching that prompted the question concerning law and justification and at Paul's development of his answer—the law, instead of curbing sin, actually caused sin to be magnified. This explanation provoked another obvious question that brings us to the first verse in the passage now under consideration. *Is the law, therefore, opposed to the promises of God?* (Gal. 3:21 NIV). John Stott explains verse 21 in the light of the Judaizers' likely reaction to Paul's teaching about the law:

> One can almost hear the indignant expostulations of one of the Judaizers, saying something like this: 'Really, Paul, you are the limit! If it is through faith only that a man is in Christ and becomes a beneficiary of God's promise to Abraham, what is the point of the law? Your theology so fuses Abraham and Christ, that you squeeze out Moses and the law altogether. There's no room for the law in your gospel. You wicked, turbulent fellow, your message is akin to blasphemy. You are "teaching men everywhere against…the law"' (Acts 21:28).[46]

Paul's immediate response is, *Absolutely not!* What reasoning led Paul to both ask and answer his second question?

---

[46] Stott, *One Way*, 89.

> *Is the law, therefore, opposed to the promises of God? Absolutely not! For if a law had been given that could impart life, then righteousness would certainly have come by the law. But the Scripture declares that the whole world is a prisoner of sin, so that what was promised, being given through faith in Jesus Christ, might be given to those who believe.* (Gal. 3:21–22 NIV)

Many commentators will not admit that Paul's view of the law implies, on the surface, a radical difference between the religion of Moses and that of Abraham. They insist that the law that was given to a "redeemed" people was, and is, the chief instrument in their sanctification. They stop short of admitting that Paul's view of law, on the surface, appears to imply that the law is "opposed to the promises" of the gospel of grace. If such an appearance were not the case, Paul would never have raised the question in verse 21. The question, *"Is the law, therefore, opposed to the promises of God?"* logically follows the implications of the answer to his first question. Paul anticipates the question because he knows that what he has said appears to pit the law given to Moses against the promise made to Abraham. The apostle's adamant rejection of such an idea shows how wrong the Judaizers were in understanding what Paul meant.

The primary reason that so many people misunderstand the law is their failure to see that it was "added because of transgressions" (verse 19) and *not* as a means of sanctification. The law's primary function had nothing to do with sanctification. God gave the law to prepare people to understand experientially that justification is by faith alone. John Stott develops this idea:

> The apostle's own statement of the purpose of the law is given in verse 19: *Why then the law? It was added because of transgressions.* He elaborates this in his Epistle to the Romans:

'through the law comes knowledge of sin' (3:20); 'where there is no law there is no transgression' (4:15); and 'if it had not been for the law, I should not have known sin' (7:7). So the law's main work was to expose sin. It is the law which turns 'sin' into 'transgression', showing it up for what it is, a breach of the holy law of God. 'It was added to make wrongdoing a legal offence' (verse 19, NEB). It was intended to make plain the sinfulness of sin as a revolt against the will and authority of God. And it was added *till the offspring should come to whom the promise had been made* (verse 19). Thus, the law looked on to Christ, Abraham's seed, as the Person through whom transgression would be forgiven.[47]

One of the key statements in the above quotation is this: *"It is the law which turns 'sin' into 'transgression'..."* One could illustrate what happened at Sinai (the giving of the law) by making an analogy to volleyball. Imagine a group of people deciding to play volleyball. They put up the net, but they have no way of establishing boundary lines to define the playing field. They decide to put a stone at each corner and trust each other's integrity. You can predict what would happen. In a few moments, there would be an argument as to whether the last shot was in or out of bounds. Without a clear boundary line defining the playing field, there would be no way of settling the argument. Suppose one player remembered that they had a large ball of string in the trunk of their car. The players fasten the string to the ground, and now the playing field is clearly marked. The established boundaries make it possible to judge each shot. Add a referee with a whistle, and you have a picture of what happened at Sinai. God (1) clearly defined the boundaries of

---

[47] Ibid. 90.

sin, and (2) gave the law the authority of a pedagogue—a referee with a whistle. The group playing volleyball may have been close friends, but the argument over the validity of the disputed shot reveals a heart attitude that wants to win at all costs. That is exactly how the law functioned as a pedagogue in the conscience of an Israelite. The lines on the volleyball court were not responsible for either the attitude in the heart of the players or the arguments over whether the ball was in or out of bounds. All that the lines did was to bring heart attitudes to the surface and make it inexcusable if people tried to cheat.

Stott has summarized the function of the law well:

> ...the Judaizers held falsely that the law annuls the promise and supercedes it; Paul teaches the true function of the law, which is to confirm the promise and make it indispensable.[48]

Paul anticipates the question, based on his doctrine of law, but then he turns the question against his opponent's doctrine of law. Paul asserts that it was not his view of law but that of the Judaizers that actually made the law contradict the gospel promise. They were teaching that a person could gain life by obeying the law. Whether that is true or false was irrelevant, because every child of Adam had already sinned and was already under condemnation. The law came to people who were *sinners*.

The text does not say, as is usually assumed, that the law cannot give life. The law can indeed give life, but unfortunately, there is no law that *sinners* can keep to earn the promised life. Likewise, the text does not ask if the law promised life, since it clearly promised life for obedience just

---

48 Ibid. 91.

as clearly as it promised death for disobedience. "What was promised" in verse 22 is nothing less than righteousness and justification. If the law does not promise life or if it cannot reward perfect obedience with righteousness, then we have no righteousness, since it was law-keeping that earned the righteousness in our justification. True, it was not our law-keeping, but that of our substitute, but nonetheless, our righteousness was an earned righteousness—a reward for keeping the law. We base the doctrine of the active and passive obedience of Christ on this truth.

Look carefully at the text. Paul does not say that the law does not have the authority to reward perfect obedience with righteousness. Paul's argument includes both verse 21 and verse 22, and we must not separate them. The clear implication of his argument is that all persons without exception are sinners and are unable to keep the law and thereby earn the righteousness it promised. There has never been a law given that *sinners could keep and earn righteousness.* However, the problem is not with the inability of the law to give righteousness; the problem lies with the sinner and his inability to keep the law and earn its promised righteousness. Our Lord alone could solve the problem by obeying the law in his sinless humanity and then dying under its curse. Christ literally earned the righteousness the law promised. He laid his sinless humanity, with our sin imputed to him, on the altar of his perfect deity and secured a perfect redemption.

Having said all this, we must insist, however, that the law does not take the place of the promise. Moses does not replace Abraham and start a new ball game. The purpose of the law was to show how badly sinners needed the promise in order for the goal of redemption to be reached. It was the law that made Israel aware of its guilt and need of a savior to earn righteousness and pay for sin. The law, instead of replacing the promise, showed the Israelites how badly both the law and the promise were needed. The law drove people under it to see the promise as their only hope. The law was an essential ingredient in God's plan of salvation. In order for God's plan of grace to succeed, he had to make things worse before they could get better. There must be a realization and admission of sin before there can be an appreciation of grace. Hard-hearted sinners need a wilderness experience before they can appreciate the land of Canaan.

Again, John Stott has stated it well:

> After God gave the promise to Abraham, He gave the law to Moses. Why? Simply because He had to make things worse before He could make them better. The law exposed sin, provoked sin, condemned sin. The purpose of the law was, as it were, to lift the lid off man's respectability and disclose what he is really like underneath—sinful, rebellious, guilty, under the judgment of God, and helpless to save himself.[49]

As we will see shortly, that is not the main function of the law today. The law is no longer the pedagogue in the conscience of believers.

Verse 22 requires a careful exegesis of the actual words Paul uses. Look carefully at what the text says and does not say.

> _But the Scripture declares that the whole world is a prisoner of sin, so that what was promised, being given through faith in Jesus Christ, might be given to those who believe._ (Gal. 3:22 NIV)

---

[49] Ibid. 92

First, the Scripture, meaning the Old Testament, "declares that the whole world is a *prisoner of sin.*" It is not law that imprisons the world; it is sin. The Gentiles were "without the law" (Eph 2:11–13), meaning the law of Moses, but they were still prisoners of sin. As we will see later, the law, acting as a pedagogue, functioned in the conscience of an Israelite to convict of sin. The Gentiles had only conscience, with no pedagogue, and were basically allowed to run wild (Acts 17:30). They were, however, prisoners of sin, which brings us to the second important point in this verse.

Second, *the whole world* is held as a prisoner in sin's grip. The book of Genesis, recording a time before the law, shows that all the inhabitants of the world were nonetheless guilty—that is why God destroyed them with a flood. The book of Psalms and the books of the Prophets also show that everyone in the whole world was a "prisoner of sin" and knowingly guilty. The Jews were doubly imprisoned. Sin had locked them up, and the law guarded the prison door. The Gentiles had neither the law nor the gospel, but they had some knowledge of God and were thereby justly condemned. Romans 1, Ephesians 2 and Psalm 14:1–6 clearly establish the truth that "all," without exception, are guilty before God.

Third, the Scriptures show the whole world is *guilty of sin*. The Gentiles are not guilty of rejecting a gospel they never heard, nor are they guilty of breaking a covenant that they never were under. They are guilty on the grounds of creation and conscience (Romans 1 and 2). All people have some revelation from God, but no one obeys the revelation that he is given. The Jews were given much more revelation than the Gentiles were (Rom. 2) and therefore were guiltier than the Gentiles were.

Fourth, the reason that "all people" (or the whole world) must be proven guilty before God is "so that" (vital words): (1) the gospel might be preached to the whole world, and (2) all who believe, in spite of their guilt, might receive "what was promised," which can only mean justification.

Paul emphasizes one more time that justification has always been by faith in Jesus Christ, and not by the works of the law, ceremonies, or any sort of effort. All those who believe the gospel are in present possession of the very righteousness that God promised to Abraham. We inherit the same blessing that God gave Abraham, and we inherit it on the same basis—faith alone.

We now come to an important section. As with most sections, this one is the subject of more than one doctrinal argument. As I approach this section, I am reminded of the old adage, "fools rush in where angels fear to tread." Believe me when I say that I still have unanswered questions raised by this passage.

> But before faith came, we were kept under the law, shut up unto the faith which should afterwards be revealed. Wherefore the law was our schoolmaster to bring us unto Christ, that we might be justified by faith. But after that faith is come, we are no longer under a schoolmaster. For ye are all the children of God by faith in Christ Jesus. For as many of you as have been baptized into Christ have put on Christ. There is neither Jew nor Greek, there is neither bond nor free, there is neither male nor female: for ye are all one in Christ Jesus. And if ye be Christ's, then are ye Abraham's seed, and heirs according to the promise. (Gal. 3:23–29 KJV)

Verses 23 and 24 describe the status of an old covenant believer while "under the law," verse 25 describes the status of those believers after "the law is over," and verses 26–29 describe the status of all new covenant believers, Jew and Gentile—"in Christ." It is essential that we notice the change of pronouns from *we* to *you*. I will come back to this point in the next chapter. It is also necessary that we note the time references. There is a "before" and an "after" the coming of faith; some believers (Paul's *we*) were, past tense, under the law as a pedagogue, but after the "coming of faith," they are no longer under the law in that sense. We must see what changed the conditions or status of old covenant believers in relation to the law and what changed a Gentile believer's relationship to Jewish believers and to the Abrahamic covenant.

First, we will look at the Jewish believers. Though truly converted, they were still under the law. Paul uses two pictures to describe old covenant believers and their relationship to the law. The first simile is that of a prison: *we were kept under the law, shut up* (v. 23). The word translated *kept under* means *to protect by a military guard*. The idea is that of guarding a city. The soldiers not only kept the enemy out; they also kept the inhabitants of the city inside—as a protective measure. The believers were imprisoned, but the intent was for their own good. They were not being punished; they were in "protective custody." To be "shut up" means to be "hemmed in" or "cooped up." Again, the idea is "protective custody." Old covenant believers were "cooped up" the same way farmers treat chickens to keep them from wandering away. It was a confining situation, but it was essential for the believing Israelite's own good.

The second descriptive simile Paul uses is "schoolmaster" or "pedagogue" in verse 24. The KJV translation is unfortunate. The Greek word transliterates as *paedagogus* and does not refer to the child's teacher, but to a disciplinarian. Wealthy families entrusted their young, school-aged sons to the care of a trusted slave. The slave was not the boy's teacher. He was responsible to take the boy to school and to pick him up after school. He made sure the boy did his homework and any other duties he had. If the boy got in any kind of trouble, the pedagogue would discipline him harshly. We could say that pedagogue's job was to "make a man" out of the boy. The pedagogue began his job when the boy was between six and eight years old and usually ended his task when the boy was eleven (when many boys would have finished their schooling). Some boys from wealthy families went on to higher education and finished their schooling at age fifteen. Others finished their training in advanced literature and public speaking at eighteen or twenty-one.[50] Regardless of the duration of the education, the pedagogue was responsible for the boy's behavior and safety. John Stott writes,

> He [the pedagogue] was often harsh to the point of cruelty, and is usually depicted in ancient drawings with a rod or cane in his hand. J. B. Philips thinks that the modern equivalent is 'a strict governess'. Paul uses the word again in 1 Corinthians 4:15, saying 'You may have ten thousand *tutors* in Christ, but you have only one father' (NEB). In other words, 'there are plenty of people to discipline you, but I am the only one to love you.' Later in the same chapter he asks: 'Am I to come to you

---

[50] *Cambridge Latin Course*, North American 4th ed., Unit 1 (NY: Press Syndicate University of Cambridge, 2001. Reprint, 2004), 175.

with a rod in my hand (*i.e.* like a *paidagogos*), or in love and a gentle spirit (*i.e.* like a father)?' (1 Cor. 4:21, NEB).[51]

We need to ask what truth Paul meant to imply by using the two similes to depict the law of God as a prison warden and as a child's disciplinarian. The prison warden illustrates the law imprisoning the conscience. The law demands perfection and when its demands are not met, it justly condemns all those who are under its authority. The law spells out the duty to God and to fellow human beings. It imprisons the conscience because all who are under the law constantly fall short of both of those duties. The law functioning as a pedagogue keeps screaming, "out of bounds, out of bounds." No one can bring an offering that can free or quiet the conscience. No one can bring to the law the perfect obedience it demands, nor can anyone bring an acceptable sacrifice that will cover sin once the law has been broken.

The metaphor of a child first under the authority of a pedagogue and then out from under that authority (the pedagogue dismissed) pictures the state of the Jewish believer before and after Christ came. Before the Holy Spirit came on the day of Pentecost, the Jewish believer was treated as a child under the constant supervision of a pedagogue. With the coming of Christ and the Holy Spirit, and the dismissing of the pedagogue, the Jewish believer was given the status of sonship in the family of God. This sonship has nothing to do with either gender or membership in the family. It has everything to do with

---

[51] Stott, *One Way*, 97.

status and privilege. The sonship Paul is talking about in Galatians 3 and 4 is strictly a new covenant doctrine.

Christians disagree over the interpretation of verses 24 and 25. We will do well to look carefully at them.

Wherefore the law was our schoolmaster to bring us unto Christ, that we might be justified by faith. But after that faith is come, we are no longer under a schoolmaster. (Gal. 3:24–25 KJV)

The verses clearly state that the coming of Christ had a definite effect on a believer's relationship to the law. The pedagogical function of the law ended with the advent of the Holy Spirit. Up until recently, many Christians understood verse 24 this way: "The law, meaning the Ten Commandments, convicted us of sin and led us to trust Christ in order to be justified." One of my late brother Ernest's clichés was, "If you lock the schoolmaster out of the school, the pupils will never learn their needed lessons." His point was that only the law, acting as a schoolmaster, could effectively prepare sinners for faith. The covenant theology mantra, following the Puritans, said, "The law will bring you to Christ to be justified, and Christ will take you by the hand and lead you back to Moses to be sanctified." This interpretation usually omitted an explanation of verse 25, because it did not fit. It was difficult to insist that the law, which was essential for conviction unto salvation as well as the chief instrument of sanctification, could be dismissed in any sense. If the law was dismissed, how could it function as either the instrument of sanctification or the means of preparing sinners for salvation?

Today, most people in the Reformed tradition, especially Reformed Baptists, understand the verse this way: The law is dismissed, but law here cannot refer to the moral law, or the Ten Commandments, because the moral law cannot in any sense be dismissed. This verse therefore addresses the ceremonial law or the Mosaic administration apart from the moral law. This ceremonial law guarded both Israel and the gospel, as a fence, until the coming of Christ. Now that Christ has come, we are no longer under the ceremonial law. Walter Chantry has articulated this view very clearly.

"It [the law] was added because of transgressions" is the stated reason for God's affixing a Mosaic rider to the original pact. In the Israelites, there was a tendency to wander away from Jehovah—especially into idolatry. This presented two dangers: The revelation of God's grace deposited with the Jews would perish unless they were prevented from straying utterly. Secondly, the chosen people would abandon God's grace, being drowned in iniquity and transgression. The Mosaic system was a fence erected to impede the decline of Israel from the Lord. But it was not intended to be permanent: "till the seed should come."[52]

This interpretation has several problems. (1) To attach a rider to the covenant made with Abraham ("the original pact") seems to violate verse 15 of chapter three (no one can set aside or add to a covenant once that covenant has been established). (2) It seems to me that if the above two reasons for adding the law are correct, then God's purpose failed miserably. Even with the law, Israel constantly fell into idolatry. The generation alive when Jesus came had him crucified.

---

[52] Walter J. Chantry, *God's Righteous Kingdom* (Carlisle, PA: Banner of Truth Trust, 1980), 104.

In Galatians 3 and 4, Chantry will allow the words *the law* to mean anything as long as it does not include the Ten Commandments.

> Here we see plainly why "schoolmaster" cannot be an illustration of the moral law. For after the full revelation of the truth in which we believe, the schoolmaster has been dismissed. We are not under him anymore. Surely this does not contradict the rest of Scripture. It means the Mosaic economy (meaning the ceremonial law) is no longer appropriate to us. Its usefulness passed away at the coming of Christ.[53]

By "see plainly," Chantry means, "That will not fit into my covenant theology." Because Chantry cannot admit that the tables of the covenant, meaning the Ten Commandments given as covenant law, are a vital part of the law that is dismissed, he is forced to twist the meaning of Galatians 4:4, 5. Here are his comments:

> 'When the fullness of time was come—the time appointed by the father for this tutorial system to end and our lordship to begin—'God sent forth his son under this rigid, tutorial system of Moses. But why? What need had the Son of God for this 'bondage'? He was not a child in character (verse 3), neither had he any tendency to transgression (3:19). His submission to the Mosaic administration was to 'redeem them that were under the law' (the Mosaic covenantal arrangement). He released all saints from the Mosaic system. Part of the liberty or our adoption in Christ is freedom from the confining statute! Now all saints enter upon full and mature sonship.[54]

---

[53] Ibid. 106.
[54] Ibid. 108.

In other words, Christ was born under the so-called *ceremonial* law and not the so-called moral law. He shed his blood to redeem us from the bondage of that confining ceremonial law. Cut that any way you want to, and it will always mean that our Lord shed his blood so I could eat bacon with my eggs! As we shall see when we get to 5:1, the bondage from which we are freed is the bondage of a conscience threatened by the holy law of God. It is true that the inauguration of the new covenant brought with it, as a by-product, dismissal of the food laws, among other things. However, the real freedom we enjoy in Christ is not freedom to eat bacon, but the freedom of the conscience to come into the presence of God wearing the perfect robe of the righteousness of Christ. Our Lord purchased that righteousness and deliverance for us on the cross. The "curse of the law" from which our Lord delivered poor sinners is the curse spoken of in Galatians 3:13. Even if the category of "the ceremonial law" were biblical, we could not state that Christ was born under that law alone. The curse he bore was not for violations of part of the law, but for the entire law, including the Ten Commandments.

CHAPTER THIRTEEN

GALATIANS 3:25–4:7

Certain passages of Scripture require us to "gird up the loins of our minds" and do some heavy thinking. When we engage in this kind of serious thought, we are in good company. Even the apostles struggled at times with theology. Peter said, "Our brother Paul has written some things hard to be understood." As we approach the passage before us, we must prepare to think hard, for this text contains the heart of both the letter to the Galatians and new covenant theology.

The proper understanding of the relationship of the Christian to the law is a theological problem of long standing. Sincere believers have disagreed on this subject as far back as the time of the writing of the New Testament. The primary purpose of Paul's letter to the Galatians is to address what it means to be "free from," or, "not under" the law. All Christians agree, because the text is so clear, that **in some sense,** Christians are not under the law **in some way** that Israelites were under the law. Likewise, today, a Jewish believer is "free from the law" in some sense that they could never have been before Calvary and Pentecost. The debate centers, however, on the identity of *law* in any given text, and the meaning of being *under* that law.

Galatians 3:23–29 contains both theological and practical teaching.

But before faith came, we were kept under the law, shut up unto the faith which should afterwards be revealed. Wherefore the law was our schoolmaster to bring us unto Christ, that we might be justified by faith. But after that faith is come, we are no longer under a schoolmaster. For ye are all the children of God by faith in Christ Jesus. For as many of you as have been baptized into Christ have put on Christ. There is neither Jew nor Greek, there is neither bond nor free, there is neither male nor female: for ye are all one in Christ Jesus. And if ye be Christ's, then are ye Abraham's seed, and heirs according to the promise. (Gal. 3:23–29 KJV)

Verses 23 through 26 present a theological truth; verses 27 through 29 unpack the implications of that statement. If we disagree about the theology presented in the first part of the passage, we will also disagree about how that theological teaching affects our lives— the second part of the passage. The first disagreement centers on the word *faith* in verses 23–25. One view sees this text as referring to the convicting work of the law that prepares sinners for faith and salvation. Faith in this view is subjective. Until the recent flare-up of the law/grace issue, most commentators took this view. A second view insists that Paul cannot be talking about personal faith that leads to salvation. This view of the word *faith* explains that Paul uses the word here the same way we do when we say "the Presbyterian faith," or the "Christian faith," or the "faith once for all delivered to the saints." It means a body of objective truth. In effect, Paul is saying, "Before the objective truth of the full revelation of God in Jesus Christ, or the New Testament Scriptures, was made known." Paul does not mean personal faith, but the "age of faith," or the era of the gospel. He cannot mean, "Before anyone was saved by faith." All readers agree that there is no question that faith, in the sense of personal salvation, did not begin with the coming of Christ. We need only look at Hebrews 11 to be assured that saving faith operated in the lives of many people long before Christ came. The saints described there were just as saved as we are today.

A further point of controversy hinges on the word *wherefore* in verse 24. All readers agree that the word signals that what follows is the reason why the "custody of the law" was necessary. Some people who hold the second view mentioned above (faith is the era of the gospel) see Paul teaching that the so-called "ceremonial" law protected the nation of Israel by keeping her separate (set apart or holy) from all other nations until Christ came. This is sometimes called the *fence view of the law*. The three major problems with this view are: (1) It is an anachronistic reading of the text. This view requires that both Paul and we accept the later (seventeenth century) theological division of the law into three codes: moral, civil, and ceremonial. There is no hint in all of Scripture that Paul or any other writer viewed the law that way or expected readers to do so. (2) The law failed to keep Israel from idolatry or any other sins. They not only forsook God; they crucified the Messiah when he came. (3) This view does not account for verse 24. This verse specifically says that the schoolmaster's work in bringing those under his supervision to Christ was for the express purpose of their being "justified by faith." No one believes that real justification of sinners did not begin until the incarnation.

One solution to the disagreement of the function of the law is to see that both views are half true, but do not have all the truth. The law actually functioned differently in two different periods of time. During the first period, from Sinai to the coming of Christ, the primary function of the law was conviction of sin unto salvation or justification. That truth is clearly taught in many texts. During this period, the same law functioned as a guardian to the individual who was truly converted. At the coming of Christ, the law ceased to be the primary God-ordained means of conviction that brought people to faith. Our Lord made that very clear.

> *Nevertheless I tell you the truth; It is expedient for you that I go away: for if I go not away, the Comforter will not come unto you; but if I depart, I will send him unto you. And when he is come, he will reprove the world of sin, and of righteousness, and of judgment: Of sin, because they believe not on me; Of righteousness, because I go to my Father, and ye see me no more; Of judgment, because the prince of this world is judged.* (John 16:7–11 KJV)

Notice Jesus does not say, "The Comforter will convict the world of sin because they broke the law." That was the ministry of the pedagogue under the old covenant. Under the new covenant, there has been a change. This is not to say that the law cannot still convict people of sin and thereby lead them to Christ. It only means that the law is no longer the ordained and essential means of convicting sinners unto salvation. Under the old covenant, the issue was the obeying or disobeying of the law. Under the new covenant, the issue is the person and work of Christ. Under the law, the issue was obeying the authority of God expressed in that law. Under the gospel, the issue is refusing to bow to the Lord's anointed King. Regardless of how we understand the text, one thing is clear; the ministry of the schoolmaster, or the law (however we define it), is finished. The Holy Spirit is now the believer's teacher, comforter and disciplinarian. We live in the age of grace and the Holy Spirit.

In verse 26, Paul returns to the idea he was developing in verse 22, "What was promised (to Abraham) is given to those who believe in Jesus Christ." What was promised was sonship in Abraham's family, with all its attendant privileges, and the sending of the Holy Spirit. The reason why new covenant believers are not under the schoolmaster is the fact of their personal union with Christ (accomplished through the incarnation) and the subsequent sending of the Holy Spirit. The law now functions as a teacher and helper of our faith, but it has no authority to either "accuse" or "excuse." The law can neither bless us nor can it curse us, because Christ has earned every blessing the law promised and endured every curse it threatened. We are free from the law as a pedagogue. It is no longer a tutor or a governor.

The book of Galatians is the only New Testament book that specifically asks and answers the question, "What is the purpose and function of the law for believers today?" The book of Hebrews does not ask the question, but it does clearly set forth the purpose and end of the law's ministry. If we fail to see the authors' purposes, we will grossly misunderstand both Hebrews and Galatians. The author of Hebrews is not comparing the condition of a weak and immature Christian with a strong and mature Christian; he is comparing the status of God's people under the old covenant with their status under the new covenant. John MacArthur explains this well.

> The central theme and message of the Book of Hebrews is the superiority of the New Covenant to the Old, that is, of Christianity to Judaism. Within this theme are the subthemes of the superiority of the new priesthood to the old, the new sacrifices to the old ones, the new Mediator to the old ones, and so on. This is the key that unlocks every section of Hebrews, and to use any other key is, I believe, to make forced entry.

In the Book of Hebrews the Holy Spirit is not contrasting two kinds of Christianity. He is not contrasting immature Christians and mature ones. He is contrasting Judaism and the redeemed Jew in Christianity. He is contrasting the substance and the shadow, the pattern and the reality, the visible and the invisible, the facsimile and the real thing, the type and the anti-type, the picture and the actual.

The Old Testament essentially is God's revelation of pictures and types, which are fulfilled in Christ in the New Testament. The Book of Hebrews, therefore, compares and contrasts the two parts of God's revelation that our division of the Bible reflects.[55]

The section of Galatians we are discussing deals with the same subject from a slightly different angle. Like Hebrews, Galatians 3 and 4 presents a series of contrasts, including the following:

1. Two time periods: The first is the time period when the old covenant was in force, or the time before Christ came and established the new covenant. The second time period is the age after Christ came.

2. Two relationships: The first is a believer's relationship, during the time of the law, or old covenant, as being "under the law." The second is the believer being set free from the law under the new covenant.

3. Two statuses: The first is the status of a believer as an immature child while under the law, or pedagogue. The immature child, or old covenant believer, was an heir in waiting under the tutelage of the law as a pedagogue. The second is the status of full sonship of believers, free from the

---

[55] John MacArthur, Jr., *Hebrews*, The MacArthur Commentary (Chicago: Moody Bible Institute, 1983), 128.

law, under the new covenant. The new covenant believer has come into the inheritance and is free from the "tutors and governors," or the law. The Holy Spirit indwells every new covenant believer.

4. Two degrees of revelation: The first is the limited revelation of the gospel in shadows and types during the age of learning the ABCs. The second is the full revelation of the grace and freedom the new covenant believer has in Christ.

It is essential to see that in this section of Galatians, the apostle is not contrasting believers and unbelievers, or writing about how one becomes a Christian. He is contrasting the state of "childhood" and "being grown up." He is not talking about getting into the family of God, since every old covenant believer was just as much a member of the family of God as we are today. Paul is showing that the privileges of an adult son, living under the new covenant and indwelt by the Holy Spirit, far surpass those of a minor child under the old covenant. It is impossible to understand the meaning of Paul's statement in verse 25, *"But after that faith is come, we are no longer under a schoolmaster,"* without seeing this truth. John Brown has said it well.

"We are no longer under a schoolmaster." These words seem a statement not only of the fact, but of the reason of it. It is as if the apostle had said, 'We are no longer, and we no longer need to be, under such a restrictive system as that of the law.... Till faith came, it was necessary that we should be under the tutelage of the law; but now that faith is come, we need our tutor no longer. When the child, in consequence of the development of his faculties, and the completion of his education, becomes a man, and capable of regulating his conduct by internal principles, the tutor is dismissed, and his pupil is freed from external restraints now understood to be superseded by the expanded, instructed, disciplined, rational and moral powers of his nature.

It is plainly on this principle that the apostle reasons; for he immediately adds, "For ye are all the children of God by faith in Christ Jesus." 'Faith being come, you no longer need a tutor; for by faith in Christ Jesus ye are all the children of God.' The change of the person from the first to the second, from *we* to *ye,* is easily accounted for. The language in the 25th verse is strictly applicable to believing Jews only, who once were under the tutelage of the law; the statement made in the 26th verse is equally applicable to believers, whether Jews or Gentiles, to all the Galatians converts, and is plainly intended to lay a foundation for this conclusion—'if the coming of the faith emancipates those believers who were under the tutelage of the law [meaning the Jews], it surely must prevent those believers who were never subject to it [meaning the Gentiles] from being brought under its bondage.'

… in the passage before us, it obviously describes the state and character of saints under the Christian dispensation, in contrast with the state and character of saints under the Jewish dispensation. The persons spoken of as having been under the law, previously to the coming of faith [the old covenant believer], are not represented as aliens from the family of God. They belonged to it; but being under age, they were "under tutors and governors till the time appointed of the father," when they were to receive, what our translators call, "the adoption of sons"—the privileges of grown-up children. There can be no reasonable doubt then that the phrase "children of God" is here equivalent to *grown-up children.*[56]

---

[56] Brown, *Galatians,* 176, 77.

With this essential point in mind, let us give a short overview and paraphrase of this section, starting at Galatians 3:23. We will then unpack each verse.

23 But before [the age of] faith came, **we** [Jewish believers] *were kept under the law* [the covenant given to Moses], *shut up unto the faith* [the gospel age of faith] *which should afterwards be revealed* [The promise, as prophesied, was fully revealed and fulfilled in the gospel age in the work of our Lord and the gift of the Holy Spirit.]

24 Wherefore the law [covenant] *was our schoolmaster* [who prepared Jewish believers for Christ] *to bring us unto Christ* [by showing them their guilt], *that we might be justified by faith.* [Thus, the law functioned as a handmaid of the gospel and brought Jewish believers to trust the promise of justification by faith made to Abraham—believing this promise was accredited to them as saving faith or righteousness.]

25 But after that faith [the age of faith as opposed to the age of promise] *is come, we* [Jewish believers] *are no longer under a schoolmaster.* [Jewish believers are full-fledged adult sons, indwelt by the Spirit of truth as their teacher. The pedagogue has been dismissed. His essential job is finished.]

26 For ye [Gentile believers] *are all the children* [This should be "sons." The Greek word is not (1) *nepois*—an infant or minor—used in Galatians 4:3, or (2) *teknon*—child—used in Galatians 4:25, but (3) *huios*—sons] *of God by faith in Christ Jesus.*

27 For as many of **you** [Gentile believers] *as have been baptized into Christ* [and become part of his body that was created on the day of Pentecost] *have put on Christ* [have put on the *toga virilis* indicating their coming of age and possessing the full rights and privileges of adult sons.][57]

---

[57] In the Roman Empire, male sons who had reached the age of adulthood (somewhere between 14 and 17, usually an age appointed by their fathers) donned the garment that marked their new legal

28 There is neither Jew nor Greek, there is neither bond nor free, there is neither male nor female: for ye are all one in Christ Jesus. [All of these categories were mandated and enforced by the law. The Jew was not allowed even to eat with a Gentile. Women were almost second-class citizens. There were slaves and a whole theology of slavery. All of these categories, as mandated under the old covenant, disappeared under the new covenant. The baptism of the Holy Spirit of all believers of all ages into one body forever makes these categories impossible. You cannot be under the law and NOT have these categories in force, and likewise you cannot be in Christ and have these categories in force. Believers in the gospel age relate to each other as equals; all have the privileged status and rights of adult heirs. No one is more of an adult than anyone else. No one is granted or denied privilege based on ethnicity, gender, or class. Just as the old covenant created and enforced these three categories, the new covenant eliminated them. One example would be the impossibility of the Jew and the Gentile ever being "one in Christ" before Christ broke down the "middle wall of partition." The Jewish and Gentile believers, by being united to Christ in his death, burial, resurrection, and ascension, are now reconciled to each other and to God. That would have been contrary to the law before the death of Christ and the coming of the Holy Spirit on the day of Pentecost.]

---

status as full adult citizens of the Empire. Although a boy was registered as a citizen within thirty days of his birth, he was not enrolled as a citizen nor accorded full rights as a citizen until he put on the *toga virilis* — the toga of a man. After this event, the father often placed the son in the care of a prominent man from either the military or civilian life to spend a year in training. From Sumair Mirza and Jason Tsang, *Rome Exposed — Roman Life* 1999-2007. http://www.classicsunveiled.com/romel/html/romechildren.html./Accessed January 27, 2008.

29 And if ye [Gentiles] *be Christ's, then are ye* [Gentiles equally] *Abraham's seed* [along with us Jewish believers], *and* [equal] *heirs* [along with us believing Jews] *according to the promise.* (Gal. 3:23–29 KJV)

The Jewish believer under the old covenant was a true heir, but could not come into or spend his/her inheritance. That inheritance was the experience of the full redemption and kingdom promises made to the fathers. They are the "things hoped for" and only seen afar off by the believing Israelite. Believing Israelites came into the experience of their promised inheritance when Christ, in his atoning work, earned the right to send the Holy Spirit to indwell every believer.

Let us continue our paraphrase with Galatians 4:1–7. These are important verses in our discussion. Paul is going to summarize and carefully explain what he has just said in chapter 3. One of the key ideas he develops is who qualifies as a true heir, what is the inheritance, and when and how the heir comes into his heirship.

1 Now I say [Let me be sure you understand what I just said], *That the heir* [In this case, the Jewish believer], *as long as he is a child* [under the pedagogue], *differeth nothing from a servant, though he be lord of all;*

2 But is under tutors and governors until the time appointed of the father.

3 Even so we [That was exactly our status, as old covenant believers, before Christ came], *when we were children* [in our minority, we were in the same situation, (we, meaning Jewish believers)], *were in bondage under the elements of the world:* [the ABCs, another term for the law]

4 But when the fulness of the time was come [the age determined by the father for the pedagogue to be dismissed],

God sent forth his Son, made of a woman [a true human being], *made under the law* [a true Israelite and son of Abraham],

5 *To redeem them that were under the law* [the old covenant believer], *that we* [old covenant believers] *might receive the adoption of sons* [not become children of God, but receive the status of full adult sonship and be on equal footing with the believing Gentile].

6 *And because ye* [Gentile believers] *are sons* [not children born into the family of God, but full-fledged grown-up sons in Christ. The Gentile believers were never under the pedagogue. They became full-fledged sons the moment they were born into the family.] *God hath sent forth the Spirit* [as the Spirit of adoption and the seal of redemption] *of his Son into your hearts, crying, Abba, Father.*

7 *Wherefore thou art no more a servant, but a son; and if a son, then an heir of God through Christ.*

The old covenant believer was a true heir-in-waiting who became a grown-up son in Christ. The Gentile was not an heir of Christ. He was an heir of nothing but wrath. He had no covenants or promises. He had neither the law nor the gospel. Notice how Paul reverses the order. The Jewish believer was first an heir-in-waiting who came into possession of his inheritance when he became a mature son at the coming of Christ and the dismissal of the pedagogue and gift of the Holy Spirit. Prior to the coming of Christ, the Gentile was neither an heir nor a son. With the extending of the gospel to the Gentiles, a believing Gentile became a full-fledged son (with equal privileges as the Jewish believer) the moment they were born of God. And because such Gentiles were full-fledged adult sons, they also became heirs. In the first scenario, an heir-in-waiting—the Jewish believer—becomes a full-fledged grown-up son and comes into the enjoyment of his inheritance. In the second scenario, a full-fledged grown-up son (by adoption)—the Gentile believer—becomes an equal heir (because he is a son). The order is reversed—an heir becomes a full-fledged son/a full-fledged son becomes an heir. This is another example and proof that the apostle is writing about the different status of believers under the old and new covenants. This status has to do with privilege within the community of God's people, and not with the status of actual justification. Justification was the same for believers under both covenants. Paul's point here is not how *God* views ethnicity, gender, and class under two different ages, but with how *those within the community of God's people* view each other in the two ages. The law mandated separation. The gospel mandates unity. Peter had violated that unity by refusing to eat with the Gentiles, for fear of the Judaizers (Gal. 2:12). The Galatians, by considering circumcision, and by implication, full implementation of the Mosaic law, were flirting with the same thing—destroying the unity of the body of Christ.

CHAPTER FOURTEEN

GALATIANS 3:24–29

In our study of Galatians 3, we have looked at two major questions that Paul asks and answers. The first question is in Galatians 3:19, "What, then, was the purpose of the law?" Paul's answer to that question provoked the second question, found in 3:21, "Is the law, therefore, opposed to the promises of God?" Understanding the answer to these two questions, and why the first answer necessitated the second question, helps us understand Paul's theology of law. Paul illustrates his view of the purpose and function of the law by comparing it to the work of a *pedagogue* (Gal. 3:24) in Roman and Greek society. The ministry of the pedagogue is the key idea around which his argument in Galatians 3 and 4 centers.

In order to follow Paul's argument, we must understand the role of a pedagogue in Paul's day. We touched on this in an earlier chapter, but it bears repeating here. A wealthy man would put his son into the custody of a trusted slave called a *paidagogos*, from which we get our English word *pedagogue*. It is unfortunate that the KJV renders the word *paidagogos* as *schoolmaster* in 3:25. The connotations of the Greek word would have been familiar to Paul's audience, but unless we are familiar with the culture of Paul's day, we will miss those nuances and therefore miss the point of Paul's argument in verse 25. The English word *schoolmaster* brings to mind a far different picture than does the word *slave-who-is-a-child-trainer*. The NIV translates *paidagogos* as *supervisor* and makes the connection for us: "Now that faith is come we are no longer under the **supervision of the law.**" The *paidagogos* controlled the boy's life from the time the child woke up until he went to bed. He took the boy to school, brought him home, checked his homework and his clothing, supervised his recreation, made sure the boy ate his spinach, and other such things, *ad infinitum.* The boy was under the direct supervision of the pedagogue in the totality of his life. The pedagogue was an overseer, but he was **not** a teacher. The life of an Israelite under the law was the same as the life of a boy under a pedagogue. The law dictated acceptable and forbidden food and clothing; the law told the Israelite how to cut his beard; it controlled socialization. In short, the law supervised every aspect of the life of an Israelite. The law, in Paul's argument in this section, is analogous to the pedagogue.

A second point that we must understand about the pedagogue is the duration of his task. The supervisory function of the pedagogue began at a specific point of time and ended at a specific point of time. This point is vital. Paul applies it to the ministry of the law as a pedagogue. The law, in the function of a pedagogue, had a historical beginning at Sinai and a historical end with the coming of Christ. The words *added, until, no longer,* and the like establish specific points of time. They all qualify Israel's experience and relationship to the law by indicating given periods of time. A. T. Robertson provides a good description of both of these salient points of the pedagogue.

> **Our tutor unto Christ** *paidagoogos humoon eis Christon.* See 1 Cor 4:15 for the only other New Testament example of this old and common word for the slave employed in Greek and

Roman families of the better class in charge of the boy from about six to sixteen. The paedagogue watched his behaviour at home and attended him when he went away from home as to school. Christ is our Schoolmaster and the law as paedagogue kept watch over us until we came to Christ.

That we might be justified by faith _hina ek pisteoos dikaioothoomen_. This is the ultimate purpose of the law as paedagogue.

Now that faith is come _elthousees tees pisteoos_. Genitive absolute, "the faith (the time of the faith spoken of in Gal 3:23) having come."

Under a tutor _hupo paidagoogon_. The pedagogue is dismissed. We are in the school of the Master. [58]

Robertson notes that the pedagogue began to supervise the boy when the child was about six years of age and was usually dismissed when the boy reached the age of sixteen. In the case of the law functioning as a pedagogue over Israel, the supervision began with the covenant made with Israel at Mount Sinai and ended with the enthroned Christ sending the Holy Spirit to replace the law in its function as a pedagogue. It should be noted that Israel alone was put under the supervision of the law as a pedagogue. Israel "had the law" in a sense that no other nation ever did. Many theologians ignore both the clear time references in Galatians 3 and the fact that Israel alone "had the law." By doing this, they miss the point in Paul's argument. The following verses all refer to a specific point in time.

---

[58] _Robertson's Word Pictures in the New Testament,_ Electronic Database. Copyright © 1997, 2003, 2005, 2006 by Biblesoft, Inc. Robertson's Word Pictures in the New Testament. Copyright © 1985 by Broadman Press.

3:17 - "the law introduced"

3:19 - "it [the law] was added"

3:19 - "until"

3:19 - "the law was put into effect"

3:23 - "before this faith came"

3: 23 - "until faith should be revealed"

3:25 - "no longer under the supervision of the law"

4:3 - "even so, when we were"

4:4 - "But when the fullness of time had come"

This emphasis on a specific point of time for the beginning and ending of the law is not peculiar to Paul's writing in Galatians 3 and 4. In Romans 5, Paul outlines the history of redemption around the law having a specific beginning and ending point.

Romans 5:13—*"Before the law was given."* If the law was already present in Exodus 20 and was not being given for the first time at Sinai, Paul's words here are nonsense. There must be a clear sense in which the law has a historical beginning at Sinai and a historical end at the coming of Christ. Granted, we may differ on what that sense is, but to deny the fact of a historical beginning and a historical end of the law *in some sense* is to deny clear statements of Scripture. We ought not to ask **if** the law had a historical beginning at Sinai and a historical end at Calvary. That is a clear Biblical fact. The appropriate question is, **"In what sense** does the law begin at Sinai and end at Calvary?" Likewise, the question, "Is a Christian not under the law?" is not a valid one. Romans 6:14 clearly states that a Christian is *"not under the law."* The better question is, **"In what sense** is a Christian 'not under the law'?" What does Paul mean by, "not under the law, but under grace"? Most commentators will provide page after page of what Paul cannot mean, but they never clearly explain what he does mean.

Romans 5:14—"*death reigned from the time of Adam to the time of Moses, even over those who did not sin by breaking a commandment.*" The nature of sin **as transgression of known law,** or "breaking a commandment," began at Mount Sinai. Paul did not say or imply that sin and guilt began at Sinai, but sin as **transgression of known law,** or "breaking a commandment," began at that point in history. Sin and guilt existed from the time of Adam's sin in the garden. In order for sin to be defined as transgression of codified law, there must first be codified law that can be consciously broken. There must be a law given that can be consciously transgressed before there is "transgression of a law." The kind of sin described in Romans 4:15 awaited the "giving of the law" at Sinai.

Romans 5:20—"*the law entered.*" It could not "enter" if it was already present.

The passages from Paul, quoted above, do not suggest that the law of God did not exist in any way before Mount Sinai. All that Paul is saying is that God gave the law to Israel, in codified form as the terms of the covenant, for the first time at Sinai. He put Israel "under law" in a unique and distinct sense. The law of God, as an expression of God's holy character, took on a new character and function at Sinai. The law was put into Israel's conscience as covenant terms and now began to function as a pedagogue. It was the conscience that was "shut up," and "held prisoner of the law." The "law was put in charge;" that is, the law began to function as a pedagogue. It began to supervise every aspect of life in a minute way. The law continued that function in the conscience until the Redeemer came and freed those who were under the law, or the pedagogue. At that point, the immature child was declared grown up and hence would function as an adult, and not as a child under age. The adult would be governed by principles and sincere love. The pedagogue would be dismissed because he had served his purpose.

Several passages in Hebrews and one in Romans will further elucidate the purpose of the law's function as a pedagogue in the conscience. We will look at the passage in Romans first. Since this is such an important text, we must be sure we understand its meaning in its immediate context.

Paul's point in the first three chapters of Romans is to show that all people, without a single exception, are guilty before God and are deserving of death and hell. "For all have sinned" really means every offspring of Adam and Eve without exception and without distinction. Jews and Gentiles alike are guilty of not believing God, and their actions prove it. Everyone knows something about God, but no one acts upon that revelation. In fact, people reject what light God has sent them. This is why all people, without exception, are guilty sinners. The Jews are not exempt from this charge; in fact, since they have more revelation, they are more responsible and hence guiltier than the Gentiles are.

In Romans 1, Paul explains about three characteristics of God and the means by which God reveals each characteristic. First, the gospel reveals God's righteousness. Second, human wickedness reveals God's wrath. Third, creation reveals God's invisible attributes. By establishing these three facets of God's self-revelation, Paul shows that no one may plead ignorance as an excuse for unbelief. All people who have no faith, including pagans who have never read or listened to the Scripture, are nonetheless guilty before God. Paul shows that there are no such people as those who have never received revelation. All people have some revelation from God.

Paul, in Romans 2, addresses those who pass judgment on other people. Paul may be talking about the Jew, or he may be talking about the educated and cultured Gentile. His point is that when you point your finger at someone else, you have three fingers pointing back at yourself. The fact that you pass judgment on others is proof that you not only know what is right and wrong; you also are ready to hold people responsible for not doing the right thing. Your very judgment of others puts a noose around your own neck if you practice that which you condemn in others. All people are guilty of judging others, which proves that all people have a conscience. When a person is put under the law as a pedagogue, as Israel was, his conscience gets sharper. The NIV brackets verses 14 and 15, thereby marking them as an explanation of verse 13—what it means to obey the law and be declared righteous. The KJV also brackets verses 13 through 15, thereby marking all three verses as an explanation of verse 12—what it means to sin with and without the law. These are important verses and we will look closely at them.

(... For when the Gentiles, which have not the law, do by nature the things contained in the law, these, having not the law, are a law unto themselves: Which shew the work of the law written in their hearts, their conscience also bearing witness, and their thoughts the mean while accusing or else excusing one another;) In the day when

God shall judge the secrets of men by Jesus Christ according to my gospel. (Rom 2:14–16 KJV)

We need to clarify several points before we show the bearing these verses have on our subject under discussion (the purpose and the nature of the Mosaic law). First, many writers and preachers misquote verse 15 unless they are actually reading it directly from the Bible. They will say, "Romans 2:15 says, 'the Gentiles have the law written in their hearts.'" The text actually says, "the *work* of the law written in their hearts." This misquoted text is then used as a proof text for the idea that God has tattooed the Ten Commandments on the hearts of all people. However, that is not what the text says. What does Paul mean by "the work of the law"? Paul may be saying, "The Gentile's feelings of guilt when they do things specifically forbidden in the written law given to the Jews, but not given to the Gentiles in that same form, proves that the same laws are written in all people, regardless of whether that person ever heard Torah or not."

However, "the work of the law" can mean something else. Later, in the same letter, Paul wrote, "Because the law worketh wrath: for where no law is, there is no transgression" (Rom. 4:15 KJV). Here, Paul specifically describes "the work of the law" as "the working of wrath," or conviction of sin. Again, we have to point out that this verse, like Romans 2:15, also is frequently misquoted. A speaker or writer will usually say, "Paul says in Romans 4:15 that where there is no law, there is no *sin*." The text does not say that at all. It says that there is no *transgression*.

Because the law worketh wrath: for where no law is, there is no transgression. (Rom. 4:15 KJV)

Those who misquote this verse think it proves the necessity of pushing the law back into the Garden of Eden and denying its historical beginning at Sinai. Paul never said or implied that there was no sin before the law was given at Sinai. He said there was no *transgression*, or *breaking of a known commandment*, of law before Sinai, simply because the law had not yet been given as codified law. The law, as codified covenant law, was first given at Sinai and was given only to the nation of Israel. Human beings did not become sinners for the first time at Sinai, but those who received the law did become far more responsible and guiltier sinners at Sinai. Sin took on a different aspect at Sinai, but that new aspect was God's deliberate intention. There was not an ounce of grace in the law, but it was most gracious of God to give the law to Israel. It was the law that made the gospel able to work. The law clearly defined, measured, and classified sin. The law made the Israelite feel his guilt and prepared him for faith. The law "worked wrath" by giving the Israelite an awareness of guilt before God. According to Paul, human wickedness reveals the presence of God's wrath. Wickedness is the punishment for unbelief. The law brings (worketh) more wrath (more punishment), thereby revealing more clearly the plight of the person without faith. The *means* has no grace, but the *end* is a gracious one.

Romans 2:15 is important to our study of the law.

(... Which shew the work of the law written in their hearts, their conscience also bearing witness, and their thoughts the mean while accusing or else excusing one another;) (KJV)

The *work of the law* is conviction of sin or working wrath in the conscience. The law uses conscience in this work.

Conscience is not a lawgiver. It does not make laws or even reveal laws. Conscience acts as a judge, either "accusing" or "excusing" every action, and meting out either internal punishment (a guilty conscience) or feelings of having "done good." Conscience uses the standard provided for it. Different people will have different views of sin because their consciences have been trained by different standards. If a given action is inconsistent with the standard a person has acknowledged as right, then conscience cries, "Guilty! You are a hypocrite." If an action is consistent with what a person believes is right, then conscience applauds, "Good boy! You did good." When the holy law of God is given to conscience as the standard in a person's relationship to God, then the verdict will always be "guilty" and will never be "good boy, God is pleased with you." The reason for this is that the law can only approve of perfection, and no sinner can render a perfect life according to the law standard. No sinner can live a sinless life. The conscience can never be quieted as to our relationship with God until it has been silenced in its condemning ministry. Its condemning ministry can only be silenced when two things happen. First, the law that informs the conscience must be presented with a perfect, sinless life that has earned righteousness. Second, a sacrifice that sufficiently pays for sin and satisfies God's holy character must be offered. We can present either of these only when we come before God in the name and merits of our Lord Jesus Christ and plead his bloody sacrifice and righteous life.

It is vital to see the above in the light of an individual's relationship to God, and to God alone. Our individual actions toward ourselves and toward our fellow human beings may be "right" and conscience may approve. This is what David claimed in his relationship to Saul. He praised God for "rewarding him for his righteousness" (2 Sam. 22:21). He was not asserting that God had saved and justified him in an eternal sense because of his actions toward Saul. He was saying that God had vindicated him in the here and now, because he had done the right thing in relationship to King Saul. Our conscience may be justifiably clear as far as our actions toward another person in a given relationship, but our conscience before God in respect to our actions in his sight can never be totally clear, except as we understand and plead the free and full justifying action of God in our behalf. We cannot *feel* free to come into Christ's presence until we *see* ourselves robed in the perfect righteousness of Christ.

When Scripture speaks of the "liberty of conscience" that results from the dismissal of the pedagogue, it is speaking of freedom from the law's tyranny over the conscience in a person's relationship to God. Later, in Galatians 5:1, Paul will plead with the Galatians (and us, too, by implication) to stand fast in the liberty with which Christ has made them free, and to not be entangled again with the yoke of bondage. This is another misunderstood passage. It is almost universally taught that Paul is referring to freedom from the so-called "ceremonial law" and does not refer to the "moral law." We will cover this more thoroughly when we come to chapter five. For now, notice John Stott's excellent comments on Galatians 5:1.

> As the New English Bible puts it, 'Christ set us free, to be free men'. Our former state is portrayed as a slavery, Jesus Christ as a liberator, conversion as an act of emancipation and

the Christian life as a life of freedom. This freedom, as the whole Epistle and this context make plain, is not primarily a freedom from sin, but rather from the law. What Christ has done in liberating us, according to Paul's emphasis here, is not so much to set our *will* free from the bondage of sin as to set our *conscience* free from the guilt of sin. The Christian freedom he describes is freedom of conscience, freedom from the tyranny of the law, the dreadful struggle to keep the law, with a view to winning the favour of God. It is the freedom of acceptance with God and of access to God through Christ.[59]

Paul is not the only New Testament writer to address the issue of conscience. The writer of Hebrews uses the word *conscience* in three passages. All three passages are helpful in our discussion of law.

> *Which was a figure for the time then present, in which were offered both gifts and sacrifices that could not make him that did the service perfect, as pertaining to the **conscience;*** (Heb. 9:9 KJV)

The author's point in this extended passage (Heb. 9:9–15) is that under the old covenant, animal sacrifices "covered" sin and made the worshipper *ceremonially* clean, but could not *cleanse the conscience*. The author is emphatic on that point. The reason for this is that not one of the old covenant sacrifices and offerings, or even all of them combined, could pay for one single sin. There was no true atonement or propitiation until the cross. If we took all the animal blood shed on Jewish altars and put it together, it could not pay for one single sin. The sinner who lived under the old covenant could never hear the message "paid in full" on the basis of animal blood. The conscience of an Israelite, wedded to the law as the accuser and excuser, could never be quieted until

---

[59] Stott, *One Way*, 132. Italics in the original.

the terms of the law covenant, housed in the ark of the covenant, were thoroughly met. The terms of the law written on the tablets of the covenant, or the Ten Commandments, demanded a perfect, sinless life or an acceptable sacrifice to pay for breaches of the covenant. Neither the worshipper nor the high priest could provide either the sinless life of obedience or the adequate and acceptable sacrifice for disobedience. Both of these conditions waited for the coming of a substitute in the person and work of Christ.

Our Lord, in his atoning work, accomplished what the law never could. His holy life and his blood sacrifice perfectly satisfied the law in all of its demands. His work forever set the sinner's conscience free. All believers, Jewish and Gentile, now have free access into the Most Holy Place that formerly was closed off to everyone except the Jewish high priest, and even he was allowed in only once a year.

In the second passage containing the word *conscience*, the author of Hebrews points out the superiority of Christ's sacrifice in its essence, its administrative means, and its effectiveness.

> *How much more shall the blood of Christ, who through the eternal Spirit offered himself without spot to God, purge your* **conscience** *from dead works to serve the living God?* (Heb 9:14 KJV)

The "dead works" are the old covenant rituals and ceremonies that could only affect the outside and could not touch the conscience. In verse 15, the author links the superiority of Christ to the glory of the new covenant.

> *And for this cause he is the mediator of the new testament, that by means of death, for the redemption of the transgressions that were*

under the first testament, they which are called might receive the
promise of eternal inheritance. (Heb. 9:15 KJV)

The phrase, *for this cause*, means that in order to effect this necessary cleansing of the conscience, our Lord established and mediated a new covenant. His death pays for the sins that were "covered," but not paid for, under the old covenant. On the ground of that all-sufficient sacrifice, those who live under the new covenant receive not a mere one-year redemption, but an eternal redemption and inheritance. The author, in the tenth chapter of Hebrews, gives the glorious conclusion and application of this truth.

> *For the law having a shadow of good things to come, and not the*
> *very image of the things, can never with those sacrifices which they*
> *offered year by year continually make the comers thereunto perfect.*
> *For then would they not have ceased to be offered? because that the*
> *worshippers once purged should have had no more **conscience** of*
> *sins. But in those sacrifices there is a remembrance again made of*
> *sins every year. For it is not possible that the blood of bulls and of*
> *goats should take away sins. Wherefore, when he cometh into the*
> *world, he saith, Sacrifice and offering thou wouldest not, but a body*
> *hast thou prepared me* (Heb 10:1–5 KJV).

Aaron and his descendents who filled the office of high priest could do nothing to bring the sinner into the Most Holy Place. The necessity of yearly Days of Atonement demonstrates the inability of the old covenant to effectually deal with sin. If Passover lambs could have satisfied God's holiness, there would not have been another Day of Atonement the next year. However, what the blood of bulls and goats could not accomplish, the blood of Christ could and did accomplish. His offering satisfied both God's holy character and the sinner's guilty conscience. The law was a shadow and a blurry outline of the good things that were coming. In the fullness of time, God sent the good things: his son, a true human being and son of David, born of Mary (Gal. 4:4), whose coming established the new covenant, and redeemed, fully and eternally, not for merely one year, those who were under the law. This new covenant redemption made possible the giving of the spirit of adoption and the freeing of the old covenant believer from the pedagogue — the law (Gal. 4:5).

But when the fulness of the time was come, God sent forth his Son, made of a woman, made under the law,

To redeem them that were under the law, that we might receive the adoption of sons.

And because ye are sons, God hath sent forth the Spirit of his Son into your hearts, crying, Abba, Father. (Gal 4:4–6 KJV)

We will unpack these verses in a later chapter. For now, notice two things in verse 5. (1) Paul does not say "to redeem them," but "to redeem them that were *under the law.*" Paul is referring to Jewish believers under the old covenant. (2) Paul does not say, "that we might be saved," but "that we might receive the *adoption of sons.*" Paul is not talking about becoming a member of the family of God or being converted. He is talking about the changed status of old covenant believers. Their status has been raised from that of immature children to that of adult sonship. Paul is talking about the dismissal of the pedagogue, or the freedom from the law's functioning as a pedagogue. Think back to the analogy. The boy who had been under the supervision of the pedagogue had always been a member of the family. It was that familial standing that provided for the pedagogue. The neighbor's son was not under the supervision of the same pedagogue. The son did not *become* a member of the family when the pedagogue was dismissed.

In the same way, a Jewish believer did not become a child of God when the law was dismissed. He was already a member of God's household. That is why he was under the supervision of the law. The neighboring Gentiles were not under that same supervision. When the time was right, the immature son (the Jewish believer) received the status of full sonship with all of the adult privileges that go with that status. The "adoption of sons" in Paul's theology is not the sonship of salvation; it is the status of new covenant believers. We will say more about this later.

In the next chapter, we will look at the phrase *baptized into Christ* (Gal. 3:27) and consider its implications. One of the most important things to remember from our study of law in Galatians is that Paul bases everything he teaches about freedom on the truth of justification by faith alone. We must understand and protect this great doctrine at all costs. When we fight all attempts to add anything to the gospel of free justification, we fight for the glory of Christ realized in the new covenant, and for our own eternal well-being, also realized in the new covenant.

CHAPTER FIFTEEN

GALATIANS 3:24–29, CONTINUED

In this chapter, we will continue to follow Paul's answer to the vital question he asked in Galatians 3:19, "For what purpose was the law given?" Historically, theologians have agreed about the question, but disagreed over how to interpret Paul's answer. The 1917 edition of the Scofield Reference Bible has the following notes at Galatians 3:19, summarizing one interpretation of Paul's answer to that question.

The answer is sixfold:

(1) The law was added because of transgressions, i.e., to give to sin the character of transgression.

(a) Men had been sinning before Moses, but in the absence of law, their sins were not put to their account. Romans 5:13. The law gave to sin the character of "transgression," i.e., of personal guilt.

(b) Also, since men not only continued to transgress after the law was given, but were provoked to transgress by the very law that forbade it, Romans 7:8, the law conclusively proved the inveterate sinfulness of man's nature, Romans 7:11–13.

(2) The law, therefore, "concluded all under sin." Romans 3:19, 20, 23.

(3) The law was an *ad interim* dealing, "till the seed should come." Galatians 3:19.

(4) The law shut sinful man up to faith as the only avenue of escape. Galatians 3:23.

(5) The law was to the Jews what the pedagogue was in a Greek household, a ruler of children in their minority, and it had this character "unto," i.e., until Christ. Galatians 3:24.

(6) Christ having come, the believer is no longer under the pedagogue. Galatians 3:25.

Paul, in Galatians 3:25, draws the conclusion to his answers concerning the purpose of the law. It functioned as a pedagogue to infant Israel, or to the believers in Israel, until Christ came. When they grew up, or came under the new covenant, the pedagogue, or the law, was dismissed. Verse 26 begins with the explanatory word *for,* which connects what follows with what has just gone before. All of the changes Paul will now mention (v. 26 ff.) result from the abrogation of the law covenant. The law, as a pedagogue, has been dismissed because the child has come of age. What does Paul present as practical consequences of this coming of age? One major point involves the implied analogy between the state of adulthood and the work of the Holy Spirit. There is some sense in which the Holy Spirit now directly (internally) performs the work in a believer's conscience that the law performed (externally) under the old covenant.

> *For you are all sons of God through faith in Christ Jesus. For as many of you as were baptized into Christ have put on Christ. There is neither Jew nor Greek, there is neither slave nor free, there is neither male nor female; for you are all one in Christ Jesus. And if you are Christ's, then you are Abraham's seed, and heirs according to the promise.* (Gal. 3:26–29 NKJV)

Several points call for comment. The first is **vocabulary**. Notice that both the NKJV and the NIV correctly change the KJV translation of the Greek word *huio* from *children* to *sons.* As we demonstrated in our last chapter, Paul is not explaining here how one enters the family of God, i.e., how one becomes a child of God. We become "children of God" by birth: the new birth enables us to repent and to believe the gospel. In some places, biblical authors do indeed use the two terms synonymously: thus, the phrase *sons of God* can, and sometimes does, mean *Christians,* i.e., *a son (child) of God.* However, that is not how Paul uses it here. In the book of Galatians, Paul uses the word *son* to refer to a new status of someone who is *already* a believer. This new status results from the inauguration of the new covenant, which dismisses the pedagogue.

Someone has said, "God has no grandchildren." I agree with that. We can also say, "All of God's children, whether male or female, living under the new covenant, are *sons* of God." There is only one text of Scripture in the New Testament that uses the phrase, *daughters of God,* and that is 2 Corinthians 6:18.

> *Therefore, "Come out from among them, And be separate, says the Lord. Do not touch what is unclean, And I will receive you. I will be a Father to you, And you shall be My sons and daughters, Says the LORD Almighty." (2 Cor. 6:17–18 NKJV)*

The phrase, *I will be a Father to you, And you shall be My sons and daughters, Says the LORD Almighty,* seems to be a quotation from the Old Testament, but the entire phrase, as quoted by Paul, does not occur in the Old Testament.[60]

---

[60] Portions of the phrase occur in various places in the Old Testament Scriptures. "I will be a father to you," appears, with a slight variation in wording, in 2 Samuel 7:14 with reference to David's son (cf. 1 Chron. 17:13). The idea of God's sons and daughters appears in Isaiah 43:6, where they are called the offspring of Israel. The concept of becoming the people/sons of God occurs in Hosea 1:10 with

In Galatians 4:5, Paul uses the phrase *adoption as sons*. The Greek text has a compound word (*son-placing*) that we translate with the phrase *adoption as sons*. In order to understand the meaning of the Greek word, we must define the two root words within the compound.[61] When Paul uses the word *adoption*, he is not always referring to God's adopting a pagan into his family. When Paul uses the word *sons*, he is not always referring to gender. Sometimes, Paul refers to the change of status from Israel's spiritual childhood under the law as a pedagogue to their status as adult sons (the state of son-ship) lived under the new covenant. This status change implies a corresponding actual change in attitude and behavior: one of the main differences is between a minor whose status/behavior necessitates the external control of the law, and an adult whose status/behavior results from the inward control of principles, applied by the indwelling Holy Spirit.

The KJV is inconsistent in translating two different Greek words that bear on this text. Both the NIV and NKJV correctly translate the two words in nearly all instances. The one word is *teknon*, which means "child" and the other word is *huios*, which means "son." The latter word can mean son in the sense of gender—a male offspring; it can mean a child (of either gender) of a father; or it can mean, in Scripture and in some cultures, an adult as opposed to a child. We have

---

respect to those who formerly were told, "You are not my people." Paul amalgamates all these phrases/concepts into a loose quotation.

61 In the New Testament, only Paul uses the word *huiothesia*. He does so five times. It is not just adoption, but adoption as *sons*. The word is a combination of the word "son" (*huios*) and the word "placing" (*tithemi*). It literally means, "placing as a son."

already seen in Galatians 3:26 that *huio,* translated "children" in the KJV, should be translated "sons." We find the opposite case in John 1:12. The KJV translates that text, "But as many as received him, to them gave he power to become the **sons** of God..." There the Greek word is not *huio,* but *tekna.*[62] The NKJV and NIV correctly translate it as, "... to them gave he the right to become the **children** of God..."

We become **children** of God, or come into the family of God, by being born of God and receiving Christ as our Lord and Savior. God, as our father, literally has begotten us. This "begetting" experience was also true under the old covenant. However, being placed into the position of sonship, or spiritual adulthood, by the baptism of the Holy Spirit into Christ, and being given the gift of the indwelling Holy Spirit, is true only of believers under the new covenant. Both the baptism of the Holy Spirit and the indwelling of the Holy Spirit are new covenant blessings possible only because of the advent of the Holy Spirit at Pentecost.

My wife is just as much a child of God as I am. Both of us are born of God. She also is just as much a *son of God,* as Paul uses that word in Galatians, as I am. Both of us have the same spiritual status as adults. If we were Jewish and had been born under the old covenant, we both would have become children of God when we believed the promise of the gospel, but neither one of us would have been sons of God as Paul uses that word in Galatians 3 and 4. When I pray, I do not pray on the basis of being a white male or a

---

[62] The plural of *huios* is *huio,* and the plural of *teknon* is *tekna.*

clergyman. I pray on the same basis and grounds upon which my wife prays. We both are equally *children of God* as opposed to lost people. We both are also equally *sons of God* as opposed to old covenant infant believers. We both are equally the true children of Abraham, even though neither of us has a drop of Jewish blood in us.

The second important point is **grammar**. Paul changes pronouns from "we," meaning old covenant believers, in 3:25, to "ye," meaning Gentile believers under the new covenant, in verse 26, and he does this deliberately. We must remember that Gentiles were never "under the law" as a pedagogue in the sense that Israel was. Verses 26 and 27 are bold and dogmatic statements. Every believer under the new covenant is a full-fledged grown-up son of God because he has been baptized into Christ. The experience of a new covenant believer looks like this: they are born of God; they believe God about Christ; they are baptized into Christ; they receive the status of full adults. Under the new covenant, new converts become children (members in the family) and grown-up sons at the same time, but the two things are not the same. You and I, as new covenant believers, were baptized into the **body of Christ** (Eph. 1:22, 23) the moment we believed the gospel. The same was not true of the old covenant believer. That experience could not, and did not, take place until the ascension of Christ and the coming of the Holy Spirit. The body of Christ was not created until the day of Pentecost.

There were true believers under the old covenant. They were like parts of a building, gathered in preparation for construction. When we construct a building, we gather the lumber, the bricks, the wire, the plumbing, and the like.

Then we begin to put them all together into one building that will be inhabited as a dwelling place. The old covenant believers were analogous to the bricks, the lumber, and other such framework components. The new covenant believers were like the wire and plumbing that had been ordered, but had not yet been delivered. The day of Pentecost was the day that the wire and plumbing started to arrive and the builder began "putting it all together into one building." In the mind and purpose of God, the house is all finished; but in time, all the pieces must actually be put in place. The work of building Christ's church has been going on for nearly two thousand years. When it is complete, which will be when every single brick is laid and every nail is driven in, our Lord will permanently occupy his "house."

The third important point to notice as we read Galatians 3:25–29 is **Christology**. These verses are full of Jesus Christ. We are sons of God because we are **"in Christ"** (v. 26). We have been **"baptized into Christ"** and have **"put on Christ"** (v. 27). We are all **"one in Christ"** (v. 28). We are **"Christ's"** (v. 29). The emphasis is twofold. Christians are one in Christ before God. We belong to God as a child belongs to a father. This is a vertical aspect of the "in Christ" experience. We also belong to each other in a unique and special way as brothers and sisters. This is a horizontal aspect of the "in Christ" experience. The Christian king and the Christian servant both eat the same bread and drink from the same cup at the Lord's Table, even as both remain king and servant. Paul emphasizes this "in-Christ" experience and then lists ensuing changes in three horizontal distinctions.

First, *there is the distinction of race.* There is neither Jew nor Greek (verse 28). God called Abraham and gave him a promise that would include "all families of the earth." He fulfilled that promise in Christ. That promise could not be fulfilled under the law, because the law enforced separation between Jews and Gentiles. Christ unites believing Jews and believing Gentiles by giving them both a new identity—his own. Ethnic identity no longer dictates behavior; it is no longer prescriptive.

Second, *there is no distinction of rank.* There is neither slave nor free (verse 28). Every society has some form of caste system built around skin color, wealth, education, or membership in a group that divides people from one another. This was true of the theocratic society of Israel, and that division affected all members of that society, believers and unbelievers alike. It is not true, however, of the spiritual nation of Christ-believers. There is no such thing as Christian snobbery or class distinction in the body of Christ.

Third, *there is no distinction of sex.* There is neither male nor female (verse 28). Paul made this amazing statement centuries before the modern move toward emancipation of women and social equality of the sexes. Nearly every culture in Paul's day, including Judaism, mistreated and exploited women and promoted male privilege. Paul finds no place in the new covenant community for either practice. It is amazing that some readers of the New Testament regard Paul as being anti-female when it is the theology in his epistles that provides the rationale for liberating women. Feminists with a correct understanding of Paul's theology should make Paul their patron saint.

The old covenant governed how sinners approached God, but it also governed interpersonal relationships. Under the old covenant, the Jew was forbidden to even eat a meal with a Gentile. Remember how scandalized the Pharisees were and how vehemently they denounced the behavior of our Lord. One of his acts that especially irked them was that Jesus went so far as to "even eat with sinners." Under the new covenant, not only may a Jewish believer eat with a Gentile, they may marry a Gentile believer. In no sense does Galatians 3:28 mean that a person who was born a Jew who then becomes a Christian is no longer an ethnic Jew. Likewise, a Gentile, upon conversion, is still an ethnic Gentile. Paul, in Galatians 3:28, means that the "in-Christ" status puts an end to that special old covenant status (along with its ensuing behavior) of the Jew. The Gentile is now on equal terms with a Jew before God. The new covenant, in some way, renders the identity categories of the old covenant irrelevant. The result of "putting on Christ," in some way, ends those old covenant categories. Two things happened at Pentecost. The believing Gentile was raised to a position of equality with the believing Jew, and the unbelieving Jew was lowered to a place of equality with the unbelieving Gentile "dog." Under the old covenant, Jews had many privileges and spiritual benefits from which Gentiles were excluded. Under the new covenant, those privileges are open to Gentile brothers and sisters in Christ.

In Galatians 3:28, Paul is talking about the spiritual relationship of all believers "in Christ" to God and to each other. Paul is not saying that the actual categories of Jews/Gentiles, slaves/freepersons, and men/women are obliterated under the new covenant. He is not saying that gender no longer exists or that gender has nothing to do with roles within the covenant community created by the new covenant. The law (old covenant) both defined and enforced the categories that Paul lists in verse 28. Now, the new covenant defines and enforces those categories. There are still males and females, and they still have different roles. However, we know this, not from the old covenant law, but from the new covenant. Paul's point about putting on Christ is that all people in the new covenant—Jews, Gentiles, males, females, slaves, free-persons—wear the same garment (Christ) that marks them all as adult citizens with all the ensuing privileges of full citizenship in the kingdom of grace.

While all believers are citizens of one kingdom, they still have to live and function in a different kingdom. Peter's first letter helps us understand that believers are "in Christ" at the same time that they are "among the Gentiles." When an earthly king became a Christian, he was still the king and he still exercised the duties and enjoyed the privileges of being the king, *among the Gentiles*. When a servant became a Christian, he was still a servant, *among the Gentiles*. It was still his duty, as a servant, to obey his master. The master was still a master, but he must now consider his Christian servant as a brother *in Christ* as well as a servant *among the Gentiles*. To say that the in-Christ experience makes the king and the subject, or the servant and the master, equal in all things without exception is to ignore the distinctions Peter explains. Paul sets up a similar tension in Colossians, when he writes that here [*in Christ*] "there is not Greek and Jew ... slave or free, etc." He then goes on to acknowledge the fact that there are servants and masters and to explain how these masters and slaves ought to treat each other (Col. 3:1–4:1 cf. Eph. 4:17–6:9—what it means to walk *among the Gentiles* by walking *in Christ*). The same principle applies to relationships between men and women. *In Christ*, men and women relate to each other as siblings; *among the Gentiles*, we not only observe the conventional proprieties, we transform them by infusing our actions with love. We must see that Paul, throughout the New Testament documents, makes two different contrasts: one is *in Christ* (under grace) versus *under the law*; the other is *in Christ* (part of the new creation) versus *among the Gentiles*. We cannot treat the two contrasts as identical.

Henry Ironside has some good comments on Galatians 3:28.

> "For as many of you have been baptized into Christ have put on Christ." He probably has two thoughts in mind here. Outwardly we put on Christ at our baptism. That ordinance indicates that we have professedly received the Lord Jesus Christ, but I think he also has in mind the baptism of the Holy Spirit, and by that we are actually made members of Christ and, in the fullest, deepest sense, we put on Christ. And now as members of that new creation, "there is neither Jew nor Greek;" national distinctions no longer come in. In this connection there is "neither Jew nor Greek, there is neither bond nor free, there is neither male nor female: for you are all one in Christ Jesus." He does not ignore natural distinctions. Of course we still retain our natural place in society, we remain servants or masters, we remain male and female, but as our place in the new creation, God takes none of these distinctions into account. All who believe in the Lord Jesus Christ are made one in Him, "members of His body, of his flesh, and of his bones" (Eph. 5:30). How we need to remember this![63]

John Stott also has some excellent comments.

---

[63] H. A. Ironside, *Galatians* (Neptune, NJ: Loizeaux Brothers, 1940), 129.

A word of caution must be added. This great statement of verse 28 does not mean that racial, social and sexual distinctions are actually obliterated. Christians are not literally 'colour-blind', so that they do not notice whether a person's skin is black, brown, yellow or white. Nor are they unaware of the cultural and educational background from which people come. Nor do they ignore a person's sex, treating a woman as if she were a man or a man as if he were a woman. Of course every person belongs to a certain race and nation, has been nurtured in a particular culture, and is either male or female. When we say that Christ has abolished these distinctions, we mean not that they do not exist, but that they do not matter. They are still there, but they no longer create any barriers to fellowship. We recognize each other as equals, brothers and sisters in Christ. By the grace of God we would resist the temptation to despise one another or patronize one another, for we know ourselves to be 'all one person in Christ Jesus' (NEB).[64]

Several people had told me that they could not wait until we arrived at Galatians 3:28 and explained Paul's statement, "there is neither male nor female." Those on both sides of the issue of the role of women in the church, especially the question of women preachers, will probably be disappointed. I tried to read a fair sampling of recent articles, both from the pro side and the con side of the issue. The result, for me, was a basic confirmation of what I have believed for a long time. Paul, in Galatians 3:28, is not teaching an egalitarian view of either the church or society, nor do I believe that we can extrapolate justification for the ordination of women to be pastors of churches from the words *neither male nor female*.

---

[64] Stott, *One Way*, 100, 101.

To be equal does not mean that we all have the same gifts, functions, or roles. Equality does not mean there are not some people who may deserve more honor than others, nor that some, by virtue of position, have more authority than others do. Paul insists that servants are to honor their masters *just because they are masters* (1 Tim. 6:1.) It is true that the servant's obedience is so that *God and the gospel message will be honored,* but that does not change Paul's argument. Does a husband have specific duties to his wife *just because she is his wife,* and likewise does a wife have specific responsibilities toward her husband *just because he is her husband* (Eph. 5:22–25)? It is clear that both of these relational categories (servant/master; husband/wife) continue under the new covenant. We may discuss forever what constitutes the duties and responsibilities of each category and how those categories relate to our contemporary culture, but we cannot deny that such God-ordained categories exist. Each category, by definition, implies specific duties; those duties, however, are governed by the new covenant. New covenant equality of men and women does not abolish the categories/responsibilities of husband and wife. Neither does it mean that any woman or any man automatically has a "right" to become a pastor. We must look outside of Galatians 3:28 to determine the qualifications for the uniquely new covenant role of pastor.

Paul concludes his argument (begun in 3:19) in verse 29.

And if you are Christ's, then you are Abraham's seed, and heirs according to the promise.

Remember, in Galatians, Paul couches "being a Christian" in terms of "being Abraham's seed." The Judaizers were trying to force circumcision and law-keeping on the Gentiles as essential for salvation. They said, "You cannot be a true child of Abraham until you are circumcised and commit yourselves to keeping the law." The implication is that uncircumcised Gentile believers were nobodies with neither hope nor heritage. Paul argues that if you belong to Christ, you are a child of Abraham, and every true child of Abraham is in possession of the promise made to Abraham and his seed. Therefore, believing Gentiles have both a well-grounded hope and a royal heritage. Every single believer, regardless of race, social status, or sex, is a living part of the most important family the world has known or will know. We are the true "blue-bloods." We all take our place in our family tree, listed in Hebrews 11. Abraham is our father and John Calvin is our uncle. King David is our grandpa and Sarah is our grandma. We all have the same spiritual genes. Paul wants us to live with each other in the light of this shared family heritage.

Again, I think Stott has caught the truth.

These, then, are the results of being 'in Christ', and they speak with powerful relevance to us today. For our generation is busy developing a philosophy of meaninglessness. It is fashionable nowadays to believe (or to say you believe) that life has no meaning, no purpose. There are many who admit that they have nothing to live for. They do not feel that they belong anywhere, or, if they belong, it is to the group known as 'the unattached'. They class themselves as 'outsiders,' 'misfits.' They are without anchor, security or home. In biblical language, they are 'lost'.

To such people comes the promise that in Christ we find ourselves. The unattached become attached. They find their place in eternity (related first and foremost to God as His sons and daughters), in society (related to each other as brothers and sisters in the same family), and in history (related also to the succession of God's people down the ages). This is a three-dimensional attachment which we gain when we are in Christ—in height, breadth, and length. It is an attachment in 'height' through reconciliation to God who, although radical theologians repudiate the concept and we must be careful how we interpret it, is a God 'above' us, transcendent over the universe He has made. Next, it is an attachment in 'breadth,' since in Christ we are united to all other believers throughout the world. Thirdly, it is an attachment in 'length,' as we join the long, long line of believers throughout the whole course of time.

So conversion, although supernatural in its origin, is natural in its effects. It does not disrupt nature, but fulfills it, for it puts me where I belong. It relates me to God, to man and to history. It enables me to answer the most basic of all human questions, 'Who am I?' and to say, 'In Christ I am a son of God. In Christ I am united to all the redeemed people of God, past, present and future. In Christ I discover my identity. In Christ I find my feet. In Christ I come home.'

The apostle has painted a vivid contrast between those who are 'under the law' and those who are 'in Christ,' and everyone belongs to one or the other category. If we are 'under the law', our religion is a bondage. Having no knowledge of forgiveness, we are still, as it were, in custody, like prisoners in gaol or children under tutors. It is sad to be in prison and in the nursery when we could be grown up and free. But if we are 'in Christ', we have been set free. Our religion is characterized by 'promise' rather than by 'law'. We know ourselves related to God, and to all God's other children in space, time and eternity.[65]

We will begin to explore chapter 4 next.

---

[65] Ibid., 101, 102.

CHAPTER SIXTEEN

GALATIANS 4:1–7

In the last chapter, we mentioned that in Galatians 4:1–7, Paul advances his argument about the function of the law by explaining the concept of adoption as sons. This is an extremely important subject, and, as usual with vital sections, commentators disagree over how to understand it. Our analysis will begin with questions raised by the text.

> *Now I say that the heir, as long as he is a child, does not differ at all from a slave, though he is master of all, but is under guardians and stewards until the time appointed by the father. Even so we, when we were children, were in bondage under the elements of the world. But when the fullness of the time had come, God sent forth His Son, born of a woman, born under the law, to redeem those who were under the law, that we might receive the adoption as sons. And because you are sons, God has sent forth the Spirit of His Son into your hearts, crying out, "Abba, Father!" Therefore you are no longer a slave but a son, and if a son, then an heir of God through Christ* (Gal. 4:1–7 NKJV).

In order to explain the passage, we must learn the answers to the following questions:

1. What does the "elements of the world" mean?
2. To what law does Paul refer?
3. Who are the people that are under the law?
4. What does Paul mean by redeem?
5. What does the phrase *adoption as sons* mean?
6. What slavery was Israel under before Christ came?

7. Were the Gentiles under the same slavery?

8. What is the main argument in the passage?

In verses 1 and 2, Paul uses an illustration from the secular world. The point of his analogy is that an heir to wealth, while an immature child, lives under some form of guardianship until he reaches a specified adult age. It does not matter if the parent who gave the inheritance is dead or alive, or at what age the child will be considered an adult. The phrase *the heir, as long as he is a child* governs the context. The heir, while a child, is a true member of the family but functionally is little better off than a slave. He is not free to make his own decisions or to spend any of his inheritance. This condition remains until the time appointed by the child's father. This was usually at either eighteen or twenty-one, depending on the culture.

In verse 3, Paul explains the main point in this analogy. *Even so we, when we were children...* The words *even so* mean that this situation of being under guardians is identical to the state of Jewish believers prior to the coming of Christ. How do we know that Paul's analogy applies exclusively to Jewish believers? Paul has been using this pronoun to refer to old covenant Jewish believers ever since 2:15. Nothing in the text allows us to understand *we* as referring to all believers. John Calvin is quite emphatic about this point.

> Let this point be first of all settled, that Paul here compares the Israelitish church, which existed under the Old Testament, with the Christian church.[66]

I would modify that quotation to read, "Paul here compares the state of true believers in the nation of Israel

---

[66] Brown, *Galatians*, 391. Quoting Calvin's exposition of Galatians 4:1-7.

under the old covenant with the state of true believers under the new covenant." Regardless, both Calvin and John Brown understand Paul's point to be that the analogy of childhood applies to old covenant believers prior to the coming of Christ.

Before Christ came, *we*, Jewish believers, were like the children described in verses 2 and 3—*we* (Jewish believers) were truly saved and were part of the family of God. *We* (Jewish believers) were true heirs of Christ, but *were in bondage under the elements of the world*. To what does the phrase, *elements of the world*, refer? Paul uses it in a twofold sense here so that it functions to describe the Mosaic law. John Stott has defined it well.

'So with us,' Paul continues (verse 3). Even in the Old Testament days, before Christ came and when we were under the law, we were heirs—heirs of the promise which God made to Abraham. But we had not yet inherited the promise. We were like children during the years of their minority; our childhood was a form of bondage.

What was this bondage? We know, of course, it was a bondage to the law, for the law was 'our custodian' (3:24) and from it we needed to be 'redeemed' (4:5). But here the law appears to be equated with 'the elemental spirits of the universe' (verse 3). And in verse 9 these 'elemental spirits' are called 'weak and beggarly'—'weak' because the law has no strength to redeem us, and 'beggarly' because it has no wealth with which to bless us.

What are these 'elemental spirits'? The Greek word is *stoicheia*, 'elements'. Broadly speaking, in Greek as in English, the word 'elements' has two meanings. First, it can be used in the sense of 'elementary' things, the letters of the alphabet, the ABC which we learn at school. It occurs in this sense in

Hebrews 5:12. If this is Paul's meaning here, then he is likening the Old Testament period to the rudimentary education of the people of God, which was completed by further education when Christ came. The margin of the New English Bible takes it thus as 'elementary ideas belonging to this world' and J. B. Philips as 'basic moral principles'. Such a translation is certainly appropriate to the childhood metaphor which Paul is developing, but on the other hand an elementary stage of education is not exactly a 'bondage.'

The second way in which the word 'elements' can be interpreted is, as in the Revised Standard Version and New English Bible, 'the elemental spirits of the universe'. These were often associated in the ancient world with either the physical elements (earth, fire, air and water) or with the heavenly bodies (the sun, the moon and the stars), which control the seasonal festivals observed on earth. This fits in with verse 8, where we are said to have been 'in bondage to beings that by nature are no gods', namely demons or evil spirits.

But how can a bondage to the law be called a bondage to evil spirits? Is Paul suggesting that the law was an evil design of Satan? Of course not. He has told us that the law was given to Moses by God not Satan, and mediated through angels (3:19), good spirits, not bad. What Paul means is that the Devil took this good thing (the law) and twisted it to his own evil purpose, in order to enslave men and women. Just as during a child's minority his guardian may ill-treat and even tyrannize him in ways which his father never intended, so the Devil has exploited God's good law, in order to tyrannize men in ways God never intended. God intended the law to reveal sin and to drive men to Christ; Satan uses it to reveal sin and to drive men to despair. God meant the law as an interim step to man's justification; Satan uses it as the final step to his condemnation. God meant the law to be a stepping-stone to liberty; Satan uses it as a cul-de-sac, deceiving his dupes into supposing that from its fearful bondage there is no escape.[67]

Paul uses the phrase *elementary things* in the same way as the writer of the letter to the Hebrews uses the phrase *first principles of the oracles of God* (Heb. 5:12). There, the writer refers to the earlier self-revelation of God (recorded in what we call the Old Testament), comparing it to the revelation of God embodied in Jesus Christ (explained in what we call the New Testament). MacArthur's comments on Hebrews 5:12 in his commentary on Hebrews are excellent.

> **Oracles of God** does not refer to the gospel. Those being addressed were Jews, and to them the oracles of God meant the Old Testament. The oracles of God were the laws of God, the mind of God revealed in the Old Testament. Having been entrusted with God's oracles was a great advantage for the Jews (Rom.3:1–2). It was the rudiments of the Old Testament revelation, the law, that they needed to be taught again. They had considerable exposure to the New Covenant, but they did not even comprehend the Old, as evidenced by their lack of ability to handle deeper truth about Melchizedek.
>
> These Jews did not even understand the meaning of their own law. They needed someone to go back and show them the pictures again. They were not ready to read a book; they had to go back to the ABCs—the elementary pictures-truths of ordinances, ceremonies, sacrifices, holy days, washings. These foreshadowed Christ, and they could not recognize Him unless they understood the pictures.
>
> The **elementary teaching about the Christ** (Messiah) that the unbelieving Jews were to leave was the Old Testament teaching about Him—another indication that it is not immature Christians ("babes") that are being addressed. We

---

[67] Stott, *One Way*, 104, 105.

are never to leave the basics, the elementary teachings, of the gospel, no matter how mature we grow in the faith. Remember, the issue here is not that of growing in spiritual maturity as a Christian, but of coming into the first stage of spiritual maturity by *becoming* a Christian. It is a matter of dropping, leaving, putting away that which we have been holding onto and taking up something entirely new. Therefore it can only be a reference to unbelievers, because at no time does the Word of God suggest that a Christian drop the basics of Christianity and go on to something else.

It is the provisions and principles of the Old Covenant, of Judaism, that are to be dropped. It is not a question of adding to what one has. It is a question of abandoning what you have for something else. This is precisely what the Holy Spirit asked the Hebrews to do—to abandon the shadows, the types, the pictures, and the sacrifices of the old economy and come to the reality of the New Covenant in Jesus Christ. A paraphrase could be, "Leave the picture of the Messiah and go on to the Messiah Himself," or "Drop the Old Covenant and accept the New." [68]

Both Paul and the writer of Hebrews address the same problem. In Galatians, Paul warns his readers about the danger of missing the revelatory change from the old covenant to the new covenant and all that ensues from that change—the danger of living as though one is a child when one is, in fact, grown up. There is a time to act like children and a time to put away childish things (1 Cor. 13:11; 14:20). The law was a shadow, but people now live in the light of the full revelation brought by Christ. The ABC age of immaturity is past, and the child has become an adult.

---

[68] John MacArthur, Jr., *Hebrews*, The MacArthur Commentary (Chicago: Moody Institute, 1983), 132, 133, 137.

Paul continues his argument by referring to *the fullness of time* (Gal. 4:4). Sadly, many preachers and teachers misunderstand and misuse this text, especially at Christmas time.

> But when the fullness of the time had come, God sent forth His Son...

Some preachers describe the *fullness of time* as an age that was well suited for Christ to come, thus God took advantage of it and sent his Son. That misses Paul's point completely. I agree that Christ came at the time that was perfect for him to come, but that was not because the time *happened* to be right. The time was perfect because a sovereign God prepared every detail that was essential for Christ to come. This preparation and timing included a pagan king who issued a decree that, quite unknown to him, would facilitate the fulfillment a prophet uttered years before. That decree brought a pregnant woman named Mary to Jerusalem to have her baby, "as it was written." Read again those amazing words, preserved for us by Luke.

> And it came to pass in those days, that there went out a decree from Caesar Augustus, that all the world should be taxed. (And this taxing was first made when Cyrenius was governor of Syria.) And all went to be taxed, every one into his own city. And Joseph also went up from Galilee, out of the city of Nazareth, into Judaea, unto the city of David, which is called Bethlehem; (because he was of the house and lineage of David:) To be taxed with Mary his espoused wife, being great with child. And so it was, that, while they were there, the days were accomplished that she should be delivered. And she brought forth her firstborn son... (Luke 2:1–7 KJV)

"And it came to pass" (v. 1). What was *it* that just happened to come to pass? Exactly what God had ordained as the means to fulfill his word. "And so it was" (v. 6). It was what? It was exactly what God decreed. An economist might explain that the taxing was necessary because the empress was spending too much on clothes and the emperor needed some money. A military man might connect the taxing to gathering funds to prepare for war. Psychologists, historians, and even an astrologist might explain why that particular tax was made at that particular time. In actual fact, the taxing took place because one pregnant Hebrew woman had to give birth to her baby in Jerusalem in order to fulfill the Hebrew Scriptures. Don't you just love the way the Holy Spirit records things? Paul, writing from within the framework of God's sovereignty, would not have thought of *the fullness of time* as something upon which God had to wait. He would not use it to refer to something that just *happened* to come to pass.

Paul's use of the phrase *fullness of time* has to fit the metaphor in which it occurs. *The fullness of time* does not mean the perfect time as far as having all the circumstances placed exactly right. It means the time that the father had appointed to end the heir's minority: the time set by the father for the son to become a legal adult and thus to move into his majority, with all of the privileges and responsibilities entailed by this move. As we saw before, this move from the status of a minor to the status of an adult occurred regardless of convenient circumstances.

Paul explains the details of this move. First, something had to occur to signify that the appointed time had indeed arrived. A Greco-Roman boy would know when he had reached the age set by his father. Birthdays are easy to count. What would serve that same function in Paul's analogy? How would the Jewish believers know that their minority had ended? They knew that God was going to make a new covenant with them, but they did not know when he would do it. Next, something had to occur that would legitimately end the old covenant. It is one thing to announce that the time had come for the old covenant to end. It is quite another to end it in fact. Its terms had to be fulfilled. Finally, the heir had to receive his inheritance. The transition from minor to adult would be incomplete unless the heir actually took possession of his inheritance. Paul sees one thing as satisfying all these conditions.

> ...God sent forth His Son, born of a woman, born under the law, to redeem those who were under the law, that we might receive the adoption as sons.

We need to note several points about this sentence. First, notice the voluntary nature of God's "sending" of his son. God "gave" his son for the specific purpose of accomplishing an ordained work. God purposed and carefully planned the birth, life, and death of Christ. We already mentioned that God set up the events that would lead to the circumstances of Christ's birth. In the same way, God brought about all the details that would lead to the circumstances of the death of Christ. The cross was not the result of God's plans going astray and God's being forced to adopt a plan B. No event in history was as carefully planned and orchestrated as the death of Christ.

Second, to accomplish God's purposes, his Son needed a human mother. God's Son must be "born of a woman" in order to be a kinsman for all believers, not just for those who were Jewish. He had to be part of the *human* family. Our Lord was just as much a true human being as you and I are. The humanity of the Son of God fulfills God's promise to

Abraham that in his seed, *all* the families of the earth would be blessed.

Third, God's Son was also "born under the law" in order to accomplish that blessing promised to Abraham. We have seen that to earn and to give us the "blessing of Abraham," or justification, the Son had to be a child of Abraham. In addition to that, he also had to be a son of David. God had promised to send a Messiah who would establish a new kingdom and who would rule over it is as king. In order to sit on David's throne (a metaphor for ruling), the Messiah had to come from David's family line. The Messiah had to be a true Israelite, born under the law, in order to redeem those who also were "under the law" (the believing Jew). This supports the interpretation that understands "we" in this section to refer, not to all believers, but to the Jewish believer.

The Gentiles never were "under the law" and therefore never would have needed redemption from it (Eph. 2:11, 12). They would indeed have needed redemption from the guilt of sin, but that is not Paul's point here. Paul uses redemption here as something that was necessary for "the adoption as sons." As we saw in our last chapter, this adoption was not adoption into the family of God in salvation, but it was an adoption that reflects status: old covenant believers acquiring the status of adulthood. This is further evidence that Paul is talking about Jewish believers who have been delivered from the law, which was *their* pedagogue.

The result of this redemption from the law into full sonship is the giving of the Holy Spirit. This giving is significant, so we must understand what it means. The Holy

Spirit was active in some sense during the old covenant era. He must have regenerated individuals, or else they would not have been able to believe the promise of the gospel. However, the indwelling of the Holy Spirit, as the "spirit of adoption" who cries out "Abba, Father," could not take place until our Lord had accomplished the atonement and had ascended to the Father's right hand. The Son "sent forth the Holy Spirit" in the same sense that the Father "sent forth the Son." The Son did this by becoming incarnate—embodied. It is the **man** Christ Jesus who has been "given all power" as an earned right, and this includes the power to send forth the Holy Spirit. Pentecost and the advent of the Holy Spirit ushered in a distinctly new and different era, just as the birth, life, death, and resurrection of the Son established a new and different kingdom—that of grace. covenant theology minimizes this new and unique coming of the Holy Spirit on the day of Pentecost, simply because they do not believe that the new covenant is different both in nature and in substance from the old covenant. In their view, the new covenant is merely a better administration of the so-called one unchanging "covenant of grace." We would do well to refer to the day of Pentecost as the "advent of the Holy Spirit" just as we refer to the coming of our Lord as "the advent of Christ." During the time prior to the first-century day of Pentecost, the Holy Spirit was no more present, *in the sense in which he "came" on the day of Pentecost,* than the Son was present physically on earth prior to his "coming" in the incarnation.

It would seem that biblical writers see the sending forth of the Holy Spirit as happening on two different levels. The first level is broad—it is the fulfillment of God's promise to inaugurate the last days (Acts 2). This directly affects all who believe, both at the time of the advent of the Holy Spirit and in the future ("they all shall prophesy ... and everyone who calls on the name of the Lord shall be saved"). The second level, however, is narrower and affects Jewish believers specifically. God sent the Holy Spirit into the hearts of Jewish believers to enable them to see and feel their new status as adult sons. The broad level involves empowerment and is somewhat objective. The narrow level is far more subjective and accomplishes a different purpose.

The "giving of the Spirit" was contingent on two events. First, the incarnate Son had to ascend to the Father as the glorious victor and thus receive the reward for his atoning work. Second, the Jewish believers had to receive the adoption of sons—that is, they had to come into full sonship, which of necessity entailed the dismissal of the pedagogue. The indwelling Spirit now performs the function that the law did as a pedagogue in the conscience of an old covenant believer. Being "under the law" meant having every aspect of life, down to the smallest detail, laid out in a book of rules. This would have helped the tender conscience with regard to knowing right from wrong. Yet, at the same time, it would have terrified that conscience with the constant threat of just punishment for failure to comply in every aspect. Additionally, while the Mosaic law was extensive, it was not comprehensive. It could not have anticipated _every_ possible circumstance that might arise. In the event of one of those unanticipated circumstances, how would the conscience know what was the right thing to do?

Let me digress for a moment and say a word about the pedagogue's dismissal. Some folks claiming to be new covenant theologians either state or imply an attitude toward the Mosaic law that I do not share. The "holy, just, and good" Mosaic law can be a believer's best friend or worst enemy. It depends on how the believer understands the true intent of the law. The dismissal of the pedagogue in no way implies a hatred of the pedagogue or his service any more than the dismissal of Aaron evinces a hatred of Aaron or his service. If a boy who had been under a pedagogue had truly become an adult in character as well as in years, he would have tears in his eyes when his family dismissed his pedagogue. He would be grateful that the pedagogue had made "a man out of him." He would not have spit in the pedagogue's face just because the pedagogue had lost his authority. He would continue to love the pedagogue for all that he had taught him. A contemporary illustration for us might be that of a strict Army sergeant who trains a recruit. At first, the young man would likely resent the rigid rules and discipline. He might hate being told what to do, what to wear, when to go to bed, and when to get up. He probably would complain about the rugged obstacle courses and the unending mind-numbing drills. However, once on the battlefield, with his life spared by his conditioned response to those lessons, the young man would thank God for that rugged boot camp experience, especially for the work of the rigid sergeant.

I trust that all new covenant people who have been influenced by me in any way will always see two things. First, the "holy, just, and good" Mosaic law, as a pedagogue, has been completely dismissed. The Holy Spirit now indwells us, functioning internally to inform us about what is right to do in every situation. He empowers us so that we desire to do the right thing, and then we actually do the right thing. In this way, the Holy Spirit functions both similarly and dissimilarly to the pedagogue. He is our teacher and trainer, but he is more than that. He harmonizes our knowing, wishing, and doing in agreement with God's will. This is something that the law, as an external agent, could not do, nor did God intend it to. So we are indeed "free from the law" and all its condemning power. Second, I pray we all will view the "holy, just, and good" Mosaic law as a gracious gift from God to help us to better understand God's will for our lives. The Mosaic law is an enemy only when you put a sword in its hand and use it to instill fear. As long as Moses wears a teacher's hat and is without a sword, he is a friend. As long as we see him through the eyes of the new covenant, he is a helper of our faith. I agree with what John Bunyan said of the law, "Indeed if it will be content with being my informer, and so lovingly leave off to judge me; I will be content, it shall be in my sight, I will also delight therein…"[69]

The sending of the Holy Spirit on the day of Pentecost proved several things. First, it validated the person and work of Jesus Christ. Not only did it prove and establish his claim of absolute deity; it also proved that the Father accepted the Son's atoning work as effective. The day of Pentecost not only justified God's people; it also justified both the Father's and the Son's work and purpose in redemption. Second, the gift of the Spirit at Pentecost was proof that the long-anticipated kingdom promises had been fulfilled. The last days—the days of the Messiah—had

---

[69] *Of the Law and a Christian, Works of Bunyan*, 2:388.

dawned and the liberty and promises given to the fathers were now a reality in the new creation or body of Christ.

I asked a fellow pastor for his comments on the last few paragraphs above. He responded as follows.

I believe this articulates Paul's chief argument in Galatians. The Mosaic law is good, IF it is used "lawfully" (1 Tim. 1:8) i.e., for what it was designed. It was never designed to save; therefore it cannot. It was never designed to sanctify; therefore, it cannot. It WAS designed to "instruct" *(The LORD said to Moses, "Come up to me on the mountain and wait there, that I may give you the tablets of stone, with the law and the commandment, which I have written for their **instruction"** [Exod. 24:12]). Like an X-ray machine, the law is designed to be diagnostic, to provide us with information, but it has NO power whatsoever to deal with what it reveals.

For instance, the Ten Commandments as instruction teach us to:

Know that God alone is God.

Know that He cannot be quantified.

Know that His very name is precious above all things.

Know that He made us to rest in Him.

Know that He places infinite value on the lives of human beings made in His image.

Know that He is utterly faithful.

Know that He is the supplier of all things.

Know that He is truth.

Know that He is sufficient.

God's commandments instruct us about His attitude toward sin, tell us what kinds of things He designates as sin, and promise us that He has a provision for sin, typified and then fulfilled in His Son. If we use the law that way—let it be so. If we use it as a scourge, let us be anathema. It is revelation, not salvation.

A believer under the old covenant was just as saved as is a believer under the new covenant. That old covenant believer was converted exactly the way that we are today—justified by grace through faith. However, an old covenant believer's justification did not give him the privileges described in Romans 5:1–3. A justified Israelite did not have access into the Most Holy Place. He was not yet "seated in heavenly places in Christ Jesus" (Eph. 2:6). Jesus had not yet opened up that experience by his atoning death. He himself had not yet ascended to heaven and taken his seat of authority at the Father's right hand. A believer could not experience the knowledge of being seated in heaven with Christ when Christ himself was not yet seated there.

The language of "Abba, Father" is strictly new covenant speech. J. I. Packer has an excellent statement stressing this point.

> Some years ago, I wrote:

> You sum up the whole of New Testament teaching in a single phrase, if you speak of it as a revelation of the Fatherhood of the holy Creator. In the same way, you sum up the whole of New Testament religion if you describe it as the knowledge of God as one's holy Father. If you want to judge how well a person understands Christianity, find out how much he makes of the thought of being God's child, and having God as his Father. If this is not the thought that prompts and controls his worship and prayers and his whole outlook on life, it means that he does not understand Christianity very well at all. For everything that Christ taught, everything that makes the New Testament new, and better than the Old, everything that is instinctively Christian as

opposed to merely Jewish, is summed up in the knowledge of the Fatherhood of God. 'Father' is the Christian name for God (*Evangelical Magazine* 7, p 19-20).

This still seems to me wholly true, and very important. Our understanding of Christianity cannot be better than our grasp of adoption. [70]

Packer uses the word *adoption* differently than we would in this passage (Gal. 4:5), but this in no way undermines his claim that "Abba, Father" is strictly new covenant terminology.

Paul concludes his section on sons and heirs by shifting his focus to the Gentile believers in his audience.

Therefore you are no longer a slave but a son, and if a son, then an heir of God through Christ. (Gal. 4:7 NKJV)

Paul reverts to *you*, meaning Gentiles, instead of continuing with *we*, meaning Jews. This is the context he established in 2:15. We pointed out earlier that in verse 7, Paul reverses the order of "son" and "heir." The Jewish believer living under the old covenant was a true child of God by virtue of the fact that they were born of God. The believer's experience of being "under the law" as a pedagogue until the time appointed by the father demonstrated the factuality of their status as an "heir-in-waiting." The heir-in-waiting could not possess the full inheritance until Christ came and redeemed him from the law. The experience of inheriting all the promised "wealth in Christ" was conditioned on deliverance from the law and adoption (placing) as a son. The old covenant believer was an heir who became an adult with full sonship privileges,

---

[70] *Knowing God*, by J. I. Packer, IVP, p. 201.

and who was now governed by principles applied by the indwelling Spirit.

On the other hand, the Gentiles were heirs of no promises. They were heirs of nothing but wrath. Paul describes their plight in Ephesians 2.

> *That at that time ye were without Christ, being aliens from the commonwealth of Israel, and strangers from the covenants of promise, having no hope, and without God in the world:* (Eph. 2:12 KJV).

The Gentiles were not under the slavery or bondage of the law ("the elemental principles" of verse 3). Rather, they were in bondage to false gods (Gal. 4:8) and their own lusts. The Gentiles lived and functioned with a willful ignorance of God's revelation of themselves in nature and conscience (Romans 1). When the Gentile came into Christ, through hearing and believing the same gospel, and by means of the same gift of the Holy Spirit as the believing Jew, he instantly became an adult son with the same sonship status of the Jewish believer now under the new covenant. The Gentile believer under the new covenant is equal in every sense to a Jewish believer. They both are "joints heir in Christ." They both are son-placed and given an equal inheritance. The only difference is in the order of heirship and sonship. The Jewish believer under the old covenant was a true heir of Christ, waiting for the time of his maturity. He was kept under the law as a pedagogue until Christ came. On the other hand, the Gentile new covenant believer was a full-fledged son the moment he trusted Christ. The Gentile believer received the Spirit of adoption the moment he was saved. Gentile believers did not have to wait to grow up to be considered adults. The new covenant Gentile believer never was under the pedagogue and that long period of preparation for sonship. They did not receive the inheritance because they were "heirs in waiting," but because they were a full-fledged son at birth. In a sense, Gentile believers were born (spiritually) as adults.

In summary, the believing Jew was an heir-in-waiting until he was son-placed by the gift of the Spirit, and the Gentile believer was son-placed at conversion and then, because he was a son, he was given an inheritance. In the first case, an heir becomes a son, and in the other case, a son becomes an heir. In both cases, the received inheritance is the same.

CHAPTER SEVENTEEN

GALATIANS 4:8–11

God endowed human beings with both intellect and affections. Both of these affect each other. You cannot secure a true commitment of the affections without persuading the intellect, and likewise you cannot truly persuade the intellect without having the affections sincerely desiring the same thing. That is the way God wired us. The same sentiments and arguments, when coming from a friend, will appear differently and affect us differently than they will when coming from an enemy. We are inclined to believe what a friend says, simply because we like and trust a friend. We look for every possible reason to accept what a friend says. Likewise, we are inclined to reject what an enemy says, just because they are an enemy. We look for reasons to reject what someone whom we dislike says. Political campaigns illustrate this human tendency. Each candidate uses every means to make voters mistrust the other candidate. The object is to destroy the message by destroying the messenger.

The Judaizers used this method in the Galatian church, and it appears they were being successful. They were attacking Paul's integrity as a means of destroying his message. In the verses we will examine in this chapter, we will see Paul defend himself. His concern is not for himself but for the spiritual peril of the Galatians. In chapters 1 and 2, we encounter Paul the apostle: chapters 3 and 4 show us Paul the theologian and defender of the faith; Chapters 4 through 6 show us Paul the man and pastor, concerned with the spiritual health of men's souls. The early chapters of Galatians show an apostle laying out theology line upon line. In 4:8–20, we find a pastor opening his heart and emotionally appealing to people he dearly loves in spite of their changed attitude toward him.

Let us first look at 4: 8–11 as paraphrased by Phillips, including his headings.

> *Consider your own progress: do you want to go backwards?*
>
> *At one time when you had no knowledge of God, you were under the authority of gods who had no real existence. But now that you have come to know God, or rather are known by him, how can you revert to dead and sterile principles and consent to be under their power all over again? Your religion is beginning to be a matter of observing certain days or months or seasons or years. Frankly, you stagger me, you make me wonder if all my efforts over you have been wasted!* [71]

In verses 8–11, Paul reminds the Galatians of their days of ignorance while living in paganism. At that time, they were in bondage to false pagan gods who were not real gods at all. They had been set free by the gospel and were now in danger of trading one kind of bondage for another kind of bondage. These verses are full of practical application. First, ignorance of the true nature of God breeds legalism, whether it be in a pagan religion or in an orthodox religion. Legalism may take many forms, but it will always be rule centered and will emphasize the external. Legalism flourishes where there is knowledge neither of God (Rom. 1:18–22) nor of the freedom of the gospel of grace. Paul asks the Galatians how they could be so spiritually stupid as to go back into the very same kind of bondage from which the

---

[71] Phillips, New Testament

gospel had rescued them. John Brown explains the nature of that bondage.

> It is as if the apostle had said, 'Ye are no more slaves; but there was a time when ye were slaves.' "When ye knew not God," — that is, 'when you were ignorant of the true God and Father of our Lord Jesus Christ, when you were in a state of heathenism,' — ye did service unto them which are no gods." The English phrase *do service,* which suggests no other notion than worship, does not by any means come up to the apostle's idea: "Ye were enslaved to them who are by nature no gods," — ideal beings, dead men, evil spirits, heavenly luminaries. 'You served your false divinities, and you served them like slaves: you had the feelings of slaves in reference to them, and your conduct was like that of slaves engaged in a toilsome, profitless round of external services.' In false religion in all its forms, nothing is more remarkable than its enslaving, degrading influence on the minds of its votaries. [72]

It is understandable that those who are ignorant of the true knowledge of God are slaves to rituals and pagan services, but it is pure spiritual stupidity for anyone who has been set free by the grace of God and has been given a clear knowledge of God and his grace to go back into the bondage of ignorance. The Galatians had experienced the joy and freedom of the gospel. They had received and loved Paul "as an angel from heaven," but were now ready to abandon both Paul and the gospel of grace that he preached.

Verse 9 is one those verses that suggests that both Paul and the Holy Spirit have a sense of humor. Paul says, *"Now that you know God – **or rather are known by God.**"* It is almost as if after saying, "Now that you know God," Paul is

---

[72] Brown, *Galatians*, 206, 07.

afraid someone might misunderstand him and think he has become an Arminian in his theology, so he adds, "or rather you are known by God." We know God only because he first knew us. *"We love him* [only] *because he first loved us"* (1 John 4:19). To know is to love. To know God is to love God. For God to know us is not for God to be aware of who we are. He knows the ungodly in that sense. God knows his own in a way of electing love. God's loving us is the same as God's choosing us unto salvation.

God knows us by deliberate sovereign choice. *To know* means the same as *to elect*. He also knows us by his sovereign power working in us. His Holy Spirit works in us in regeneration. His Son knows us as his own, and that is why he died for us (John 10:14–15). Our Lord was conscious of us individually when He died on the cross. When his soul made an offering for sin, "he saw his seed" (Isa. 53:10). Our Lord's death was not an indefinite atonement that made salvation a possibility for all, but secured it for none; it was a substitutionary atonement that made salvation certain for those he knew, or loved.

The Galatians were ready to exchange that kind of salvation for an obey-the-law theology. They were deserting a finished work that provided a perfect seamless robe of righteousness, and they were starting to weave a robe of righteousness out of their personal works in a vain attempt to find an acceptance with God. Little wonder that Paul calls them "you dear idiots" (3:1, Phillips).

In the early part of chapter 4 (verses 1–7), Paul has described the new covenant believer's position as adopted, or son-placed. He has compared the difference between immature children (old covenant believers) who were "no better off than a servant" (4:1–3) with grown son-placed believers. There is a great difference between being treated as a servant and being treated as a grown son. One of the greatest differences lies in having an inheritance to spend. The son is rich, while a servant is, for all practical purposes, poor. A Christian is a son with a great and glorious inheritance. The Galatians were turning their backs on the true and eternal riches of grace, and leaning toward a religion of law with neither power nor riches. The law was "weak and beggarly." It was weak in that it had no power to motivate us to obey God, and it was beggarly in that it could bestow no spiritual blessings. Hendriksen quotes Luther (with no reference) in an amusing but potent illustration.

> People who prefer the law to the gospel are like Aesop's dog who let go of the meat to snatch the shadow in the water… The law is weak and poor, the sinner is weak and poor: two feeble beggars trying to help each other. They cannot do it. They only wear each other out. But through Christ, a weak and poor sinner is revived and enriched unto eternal life.[73]

The Galatians, though Gentiles by birth, were both sons and heirs of God through Christ. Under the new covenant, they were son-placed and could immediately draw on their inheritance in Christ. God made available the riches of his grace (Eph. 1:7; 2:7), the riches of his glory (Phil. 4:19), the riches of his goodness (Rom. 2:4), and the riches of his wisdom (Rom. 11:33)—and all of the riches of God are found in Christ (Col. 1:19; 2:3). They were turning their back on those riches and looking instead to something "weak and beggarly"—their obedience to the law, which could only

---

[73] William Hendriksen, *Galatians,* New Testament Commentary (Grand Rapids, MI: Baker Book House, 1968), 169.

give them grief and shame. Believers today have the same riches, and Paul's exhortation to protect those riches is the same for us as it was for the Galatians.

Bondage to religion for its own sake is one of the more prevalent and dangerous kinds of bondage. There have been more people killed by sincere religion than by all wars put together. Someone has said that all of the world's problems are religious. In the European Dark Ages, the professing Christian church slaughtered countless true Christians. If all professing Christians believed what Paul preached to the Greeks about God being the creator of all men (Acts 17:26–27), Christians would be in the forefront of the fight to end racism. The Puritans were surely orthodox in their view of "salvation by grace," but that did not keep them from drowning and burning at the stake their religious enemies. When your religion deteriorates to obeying rules and church authorities, and becomes *"a matter of observing certain days or months or seasons or years,"* you have already deserted the gospel of sovereign grace. All that matters in such a case is that you bow in the right direction at the right time and on the right day. Little wonder that Paul says, *"You stagger me. You make me wonder if all my efforts over you have been wasted."*

When Paul asks, *"How can you revert to dead and sterile principles* (NIV, "weak and miserable principles;" KJV, "weak and beggarly elements") *and consent to be under their power?"* he is talking about the old covenant, the law of Moses, or Judaism. He is warning against the same grievous error that the author of the letter to the Hebrews warns against: namely, professing faith in Christ the Messiah, but then abandoning him by turning back to Judaism, or the old covenant. The entire Mosaic administration was God's ordained religion under the old covenant. It governed the life and worship of the nation of Israel. After Christ fulfilled the old covenant by living under the law, dying under its curse, and thus establishing the new covenant, what had once been God's ordained religion, Judaism, was now merely the "Jew's religion" (Gal 1:13). The entire Mosaic law was now obsolete — an empty shell. That is why Paul refers to it as "dead and sterile principles." There was no route more wrong to take than that which led to Moses and the law. Warren Wiersbe points out why it was so wrong.

> The phrase *weak and beggarly elements* tell us the extent of their regression. They were giving up the power of the gospel for the weakness of the law, and the wealth of the gospel for the poverty of the law. The law never made anyone rich or powerful; on the contrary, the law could only reveal man's weakness and spiritual bankruptcy. No wonder Paul weeps over these believers, as he sees them abandon liberty for bondage, power for weakness, and wealth for poverty.
>
> How were they doing this? By adopting the Old Testament system of religion with its special observations of "days, and months, and times and years" (v. 10).
>
> Does this mean it is wrong for Christians to set aside one day a year to remember the birth of Christ? Or that a special observance of the coming of the Spirit at Pentecost, or the blessing of the harvest in autumn is a sin?
>
> Not necessarily. If we observe days likes slaves, hoping to gain spiritual merit, then we are sinning. But if in the observance, we express our liberty in Christ and let the Holy Spirit enrich us with His grace, then the service can be a spiritual blessing.
>
> The New Testament makes it clear that Christians are not to legislate religious observances for each other (Rom. 14:3–13).

We are not to praise the man who celebrates the day, nor are we to condemn the man who does not celebrate. But if a man thinks he is saving his soul, or automatically growing in grace, because of a religious observation, then he is guilty of legalism.

Our evangelical churches have many different kinds of observances, and it is wrong for us to go beyond the Word of God in comparing, criticizing, or condemning. But all of us must be aware of that legalistic spirit that caters to the flesh, leads to pride, and makes the outward event a substitute for the inward reality.[74]

When Paul says, *"You observe days ...."* he is accusing them of allowing their religion to degenerate into an external formalism. They once knew God in the free and joyful communion of adult children with their father. Their religion had now degenerated into a dreary routine of rules and regulations. John Stott describes their attitude as completely backwards.

Oh, the folly of these Galatians! We can understand the language of the Prodigal Son, who came to his father and said 'I am no longer worthy to be called your son; treat me as one of your hired servants' or 'slaves.' But how can anyone be so foolish as to say: 'You have made me your son; but I would rather be a slave'? It is one thing to say 'I do not deserve it'; it is quite another to say 'I do not desire it; I prefer slavery to sonship.' Yet that was the folly of the Galatians, under the influence of their false teachers.[75]

This section raises two pressing questions: *(1) Exactly what is the true Christian faith?* Is it merely a list of rules and ceremonies that we obey and perform; is it primarily living a

---

[74] Warren Wiersbe, *Be Free* (Wheaton, IL: Victor Books, 1977), 94.

[75] Stott, *One Way*, 108.

correct lifestyle? Being a true Christian and manifesting that I am a Christian certainly involves rules, ceremonies, and a lifestyle. However, the essence of the Christian faith in my daily life involves much more. True Christianity begins with understanding the truth, or theological doctrines, that God has revealed in Scripture. It must include an attitude of love toward God and toward my fellow human beings. The lifestyle that I then adopt flows from and is in harmony with this new knowledge and these new desires. *(2) Exactly how is the Christian faith lived out in our day-to-day life?* John Stott raises and answers these very questions.

a. What the Christian life is

The Christian life is the life of sons and daughters; it is not the life of slaves. It is freedom, not bondage. Of course, we are slaves of God, of Christ, and of one another (See, *e.g.,* Rom. 6:22; 1 Cor. 7:22, 23; 2 Cor. 4:5.) We belong to God, to Christ, to one another, and we love to serve those to whom we belong. But this kind of service is freedom. What the Christian life is not, is a bondage to the law, as if our salvation hung in the balance and depended on our meticulous and slavish obedience to the letter of the law. As it is, our salvation rests upon the finished work of Christ, on His sin-bearing, curse-bearing death, embraced by faith.

Yet so many religious people are in bondage to their religion! They are like John Wesley in his post-graduate Oxford days in the Holy Club. He was the son of a clergyman and already a clergyman himself. He was orthodox in belief, religious in practice, upright in conduct and full of good works. He and his friends visited the inmates of the prisons and work-houses of Oxford. They took pity on the slum children of the city, providing them with food, clothing and education. They observed Saturday as the Sabbath as well as Sunday. They went to church and to Holy Communion. They gave alms, searched the Scriptures, fasted and prayed. But they were bound in the fetters of their own religion, for they were trusting in themselves that they were righteous, instead of putting their trust in Jesus Christ and Him crucified. A few years later, John Wesley (in his own words) came to 'trust in Christ, in Christ only for salvation' and was given an inward assurance that his sins had been taken away. After this, looking back to his pre-conversion experience, he wrote: 'I had even then the faith of a *servant,* though not that of a son.' Christianity is a religion of sons, not slaves.

b. How to live the Christian life

The way to live the Christian life is to remember who and what we are. The essence of Paul's message here is: 'Once you were slaves. Now you are sons. So how can you revert to the old slavery?' His question is an astonished, indignant expostulation. It is not impossible to turn back to the old life; the Galatians had in fact done it. But it was preposterous to do so. It is a fundamental denial of what we have become, of what God had made us if we are in Christ.

The way for us to avoid the Galatians' folly is to heed Paul's words. Let God's Word keep telling us who and what we are if we are Christians. We must keep reminding ourselves what we have and are in Christ. One of the great purposes of daily Bible reading, meditation and prayer is just this, to get ourselves correctly orientated, to remember who and what we are. We need to say to ourselves: 'Once I was a slave, but God has made me His son and put the Spirit of His Son into my heart. How can I turn back to the old slavery?' Again: 'Once I did not know God, but now I know Him and have come to be known by Him. How can I turn back to the old ignorance?'

By the grace of God we must determine to remember what once we were and never to return to it; to remember what God has made us and to conform our lives to it.

A good example of this is John Newton. He was an only child and lost his mother when he was seven years old. He went to sea at the tender age of eleven and later became involved, in the words of one of his biographers, 'in the unspeakable atrocities of the African slave trade'. He plumbed the depths of human sin and degradation. When he was twenty-three, on 10 March 1748, when his ship was in imminent peril of foundering in a terrific storm, he cried to God for mercy, and he found it. He was truly converted, and he never forgot how God had had mercy upon him, a former blasphemer. He sought diligently to remember what he had previously been, and what God had done for him. In order to imprint it on his memory, he had written in bold letters and fastened across the wall over the mantelpiece of his study the words of Deuteronomy 15:15: 'Thou shalt remember that thou wast a bondman (a slave) in the land of Egypt, and the Lord thy God redeemed thee.'

If only we remembered these things, what we once were and what we now are, we would have an increasing desire within us to live accordingly, to be what we are, namely sons of God set free by Christ.[76]

It never ceases to amaze me to see someone trade freedom for bondage. Any true shepherd's heart would break to see someone gloriously saved by grace, and openly rejoicing in the assurance that grace brings, become a legalist and lose it all. As we will see in the next chapter, the goal of a false shepherd is to bring a sheep under his personal control, but the goal of a true shepherd is to bring the sheep more and more under the personal control of the Scripture and the Holy Spirit. It is painful to watch the joyful expressions of praise to God for his grace give way to

---

[76] Stott, *One Way*, 108-110.

constant lamentations of hopeless despair; to see a happy countenance replaced by a long face that no longer knows how to smile; to see the same people who would joyfully say, "praise the Lord" now constantly beating up on themselves until they are spiritually black and blue; to see people who once used to share comforting truth from Scripture now speaking only of their struggles, failures, and despair. Their joy has been turned into sorrow; their religion has left grace and has adopted law. All hope and assurance have been replaced by doubts and fear.

What happened that produced such a glaring difference? A false shepherd, like the Judaizers in Galatia, persuaded them that the law could do for them what the gospel alone could not do. These dear sheep, like their Galatian counterparts, were seduced into taking their eyes off Jesus, and had started to look to Moses for help and strength. They once could sing the following:

> Turn your eyes upon Jesus,
> Look full in His wonderful face;
> And the things of earth
> Will grow strangely dim,
> In the light of His glory and grace.

Now their theme song is:

> Turn your eyes upon Moses,
> Look full on those tablets of stone;
> The strength that you need
> To conquer your sin
> Is found in those tablets alone.

Spurgeon has described these people far better than I could. In the following quotation, Spurgeon has given us a description that, sad to say, fits some present day churches.

He was preaching on the "Full Assurance of Faith" and answering common objections made by people who felt that full assurance can be dangerous. He sounds like he has just finished arguing with some "law-centered" elders that I know.

> I have one more class of objectors to answer and I am finished. There is a certain breed of Calvinist, whom I do not envy, who are always jeering and sneering as much as ever they can at the full assurance of faith. I have seen their long faces; I have heard their whining periods, and read their dismal sentences, in which they say something to the effect "Groan in the Lord always, and again I say, groan! He that mourneth and weepeth, he that doubteth and feareth, he that distrusteth and dishonoureth his God, shall be saved." That seems to be the sum and substance of their very ungospel-like gospel. But why is it they do this? I speak now honestly and fearlessly. It is because there is a pride within them—a conceit which is fed on rottenness, and sucks marrow and fatness out of putrid carcasses. And what, say you, is the object of their pride? Why, the pride of being able to boast of a deep experience—the pride of being a blacker, grosser, and more detestable sinner than other people. "Whose glory is in their shame," may well apply to them. A more dangerous, because a more deceitful pride than this is not to be found. It has all the elements of self-righteousness in it."[77]

Please note that in no way am I suggesting that Christians are not to examine themselves and see if they are in the faith. Scripture is clear that this a duty (2 Cor. 13:5). Examination, however, does not consist of checking oneself against a list of some sort, nor is the checking to be

---

[77] C. H. Spurgeon, "Full Assurance" (Metropolitan Tabernacle Pulpit, 1861), 292.

continual. The question, "Are you in the faith?" could be asked this way: "Are you placing all your trust in Christ alone? Do you think of yourself as a follower of Christ and does that inform your desires and your actions?" Checking up on yourself in this manner occasionally is one thing. Making a constant occupation out of legalistic self-examination is another thing. We could call people who do the latter "belly-button Christians," since all they do is look at themselves. Their course of action is likely to produce either spiritual pride or spiritual despair, neither of which honors Christ. He calls his followers to lead joyful lives, full of love.

Our generation of evangelicals desperately needs to be told, "examine yourselves." Anyone who is afraid to test honestly their faith should automatically be suspect. We need to heed Paul's admonition to examine ourselves. However, we also need to follow M'Cheyne's advice. He said, "Take one good look at yourself and feel the depth of your sin and shame and then take ten-thousand looks at Jesus Christ."

In the next chapter, we will look at what one writer has called one of the most gripping paragraphs in all of Paul's epistles.

CHAPTER EIGHTEEN

GALATIANS 4:12–20

In the last chapter, we covered Galatians 4:8–11. There, Paul rebuked the Galatians for allowing themselves to be seduced into returning to the bondage. Formerly, they had been slaves to paganism; now they were contemplating becoming slaves to the law. They were trading the bondage of heathenism for bondage to the sterile religion of Judaism. In the section we look at now, 4:12–20, we see Paul pleading with the Galatians as a mother pleads with a wayward child. Hendriksen notes the change in Paul's tone:

> It is characteristic of the tactful shepherd of souls, the warm-hearted master-psychologist, that his rather sharp reproof (vv. 8–11) is followed immediately by tender, urgent, intensely personal appeal. This paragraph is one of the most gripping in all of Paul's epistles.[78]

Many people picture Paul as a cold, logical theologian with a massive intellect, but without emotions or feelings. This passage contradicts that image. Here we see a man with deep feelings and immense tenderness. He addresses the Galatians as his siblings: "brethren," and then, in verse 19, uses another familial metaphor to describe his relationship to them. He likens them to "children." In verse 19, he compares himself to a mother in labor, striving with all that is in her to deliver a healthy child. Paul worries that his

---

[78] William Hendriksen, *Galatians*, New Testament Commentary (Grand Rapids, MI: Baker Book House, 1968), 169.

labor was in vain; the child he has birthed (the Galatians) seems stillborn. No passage of Scripture better describes the correct attitude that a pastor should have for Christ's flock or the biblical attitude the sheep should have for an under-shepherd.

Let us first look at the passage as paraphrased by Phillips.

4:12–16—*I do beg you to follow me here, my brothers. I am a man like yourselves, and I have nothing against you personally. You know how handicapped I was by illness when I first preached the Gospel to you. You didn't shrink from me or let yourselves be revolted at the disease which was such a trial to me. No, you welcomed me as though I were an angel of God, or even as though I were Jesus Christ himself! What has happened to that fine spirit of yours? I guarantee that in those days you would, if you could, have plucked out your eyes and given them to me. Have I now become your enemy because I continue to tell you the same truth?*

4:17–20—*Oh, I know how keen these men are to win you over, but can't you see that it is for their own ends? They would like to see you and me separated altogether, and have you all to themselves. Don't think I'm jealous—it is a grand thing that men should be keen to win you, whether I'm there or not, provided it is for the truth. Oh, my dear children, I feel the pangs of childbirth all over again till Christ be formed within you, and how I long to be with you now! Perhaps I could then alter my tone to suit your mood. As it is, I honestly don't know how to deal with you.*[79]

Paul urges the Galatians to be like him in their present attitude toward the law, reminding them that when he first brought the gospel to them, he had become like them with respect to the law. He urges the attitude of mutual accommodation. He then reminds them of their past attitude toward him: the feelings of deep love they expressed for

---

[79] Phillips, *New Testament*

him, and this in spite of some debilitating problem he had. He contrasts that past attitude of joy and affection with their present attitude of rejection. Finally, he contrasts his attitude toward them with the attitude of the Judaizers, or false teachers.

In verse 12, Paul writes, "Follow me." In one sense, this statement should preface every exhortation that a pastor makes. In another sense, such an exhortation can be the epitome of popery and spiritual conceit that leads to tyranny. Paul does not hesitate to urge believers to "Be ye followers of me ..." but he adds, **"... as I also am of Christ"** (cf. 1 Cor. 11:1 KJV). It is the height of spiritual pride and arrogance to point people to ourselves, but it is our duty as leaders to be able to tell people to follow us **as we follow Christ.** Leaders not only have a right to ask that we follow them as we see Christ in them; they have a duty to do so. However, they have a right and duty to make sure they can see the mark of spiritual oil on their foreheads.

I often quote 1 Chronicles 12:32 when talking about leaders. Notice the three things outlined (with the bold numbers inserted).

> And of the children of Issachar, men that **(1)** had understanding of the times, **(2)** to know what Israel ought to do; the heads of them were two hundred, and **(3)** all their brethren were at their commandment (ASV).

We could say that (1) the men of Issachar were relevant: they understood the times in which they lived. They knew where they were in history and how they had gotten there. However, they were also men with (2) spiritual discernment, who knew how to solve the problems Israel faced. They not only understood the times in which they lived; they also knew what "Israel ought to do." They were not merely experts in their field; they also understood how to apply God's promises to the present situation, and (3) the people saw the mark of grace in the leaders and gladly followed their leadership.

The sons of Issachar led by example: they brought their loyalty and their expertise to serve David. Paul is doing the same thing. He is using his gifts to serve great David's greater son. He serves Christ by preaching the good news about Christ to Gentiles. To accomplish this end, Paul has to be free from the Mosaic law. In his attitude toward the law, Paul sets an example for the Galatian believers to follow.

The second thing to note is Paul's attitude toward zeal. In Galatians 4:19, he writes, *I feel the pangs of childbirth all over again till Christ be formed within you.* The Galatians were impressed with the religious zeal of the Judaizers. Paul saw that zeal as a false zeal that dishonored Christ. Religious zeal that is not rooted in truth is dangerous. Attacks on civilians by Muslim fundamentalists illustrate this danger. The Galatians were becoming more zealous in their religion, but their new religion did not enthrone Christ in their life. It was Moses that was being formed within them and not Christ. They were becoming zealots for the law. Wherever rules and rituals become the primary substance of our religion, we will see Christ formed less in the conscience and expressed less in daily living. The fruit of the Spirit will be replaced with the work of the flesh. As we shall see in chapter five, when we measure godliness by obedience to rules and ceremonies, we have put legalism in charge.

Paul is beginning to view the Galatians as stillborn, that is, as those who are not true believers born of God. Paul pleads with them "to become like me." John Stott has said it well.

In the context, following his agonized complaint that the Galatians were turning back to the old bondage from which Christ had redeemed them, this appeal can mean only one thing. Paul longed for them to become like him in his Christian faith and life, to be delivered from the evil influence of the false teachers, and to share his convictions about the truth as it is in Jesus, about the liberty with which Christ has made us free. He wanted them to become like himself in his Christian freedom. He expressed a similar sentiment to King Agrippa when the latter said, 'In a short time you think to make me a Christian!' Paul replied, 'Whether short or long, I would to God that not only you but also all who hear me this day might become such as I am—except for these chains' (Acts 26:28, 29). In other words, Paul said to the king: 'I do not want you to become a prisoner like me; but I do want you to become a Christian like me.' All Christians should be able to say something like this, especially to unbelievers, namely that we are so satisfied with Jesus Christ, with His freedom, joy and salvation, that we want other people to become like us.[80]

When Paul writes that he has become like them, he probably means the same thing he does in 1 Corinthians 9:20–22, *To the Jews I became a Jew, in order to win Jews...To those outside the law I became as one outside the law...that I might win those outside the law. To the weak I became weak, that I might win the weak. I have become all things to all men, that I might by all means save some.* If we would win people to Christ, we must become like them in all ways except participating in their sin.

---

[80] Stott, *One Way*, 112.

The night before I was to preach my last sermon in a church from which I had just resigned, a woman from the congregation phoned me. She said, "You'd better have a good sermon tomorrow or I will shoot you!" I asked her why she was so uptight. She told me she had just come from a two-hour "hat-making" party. She hated hats and had been bored at the party. I told it was her own fault for going to such a party when she knew she would hate it. She replied, "I have been witnessing to a fellow teacher and she invited me to this stupid hat-making party. I agreed to go with her provided she would come to church with me tomorrow. She agreed to come. I endured two hours of wasted time because I wanted her to hear the gospel, and you had better be good tomorrow!" That sister had caught the spirit of Paul's theology of "Be like me for I have become like you."

In verses 12b–16, Paul reflects on the past and present attitudes of the Galatians toward him.

> *You know how handicapped I was by illness when I first preached the Gospel to you. You didn't shrink from me or let yourselves be revolted at the disease which was such a trial to me. No, you welcomed me as though I were an angel of God, or even as though I were Jesus Christ himself! What has happened to that fine spirit of yours? I guarantee that in those days you would, if you could, have plucked out your eyes and given them to me. Have I now become your enemy because I continue to tell you the same truth?*[81]

"… when I first preached the Gospel to you" likely refers to Paul's initial visit to Galatia. When Paul first visited them, their treatment of him had nothing wrong in it. On the contrary, they could not have treated him any better.

---

[81] Phillips, New Testament

Apparently, Paul had not planned to stop in Galatia, but an illness forced him to do so. We do not know what his sickness was, but it appears to have made him somewhat repulsive. He reminds the Galatians that they did not allow his illness or its effects to affect their reception of him. They received Paul as an angel from heaven or "even as though [he was] Jesus Christ himself." Paul asks what happened to their love for him. Why was there a dramatic change of attitude?

The phrase, *"you welcomed me as though I were an angel of God, or even as though I were Jesus Christ himself"* (v. 14) is an amazing and bold statement. How does Paul dare to make such a statement? Again, John Stott has clearly understood Paul's intention.

> This is an extraordinary expression. It is another plain indication of Paul's self-conscious apostolic authority. He sees nothing incongruous about the Galatians receiving him as if he were one of God's angels, or as if he were Christ Jesus, God's Son. He does not rebuke the Galatians for paying an exaggerated deference to him, as he did when the crowd attempted to worship him in Lystra, one of the Galatians cities (Acts 14:8–18). On that occasion, after Paul had healed a congenital cripple, the pagan multitude cried out, 'The gods have come down to us in the likeness of men!' Priests and people tried to sacrifice oxen to Paul and Barnabas, until they rebuked and stopped them. Here, however, Paul does not rebuke them for receiving him as if he were God's angel or God's Christ. Although personally he knew that he was only their fellow-sinner, indeed 'the foremost of sinners' (1 Tim. 1:15), yet officially he was an apostle of Jesus Christ, invested with the authority of Christ and sent on a mission by Christ. So they were quite right to receive him 'as an angel of God', since he was one of God's messengers, and 'as Christ Jesus', since he

came to them on the authority of Christ and with the message of Christ. The apostles of Christ were His personal delegates. Of such it was said in those days that 'the one sent by a person is as this person himself'. Christ Himself had anticipated this. Sending out His apostles, He said: 'He who receives you receives me' (Mt. 10:40). So, in receiving Paul, the Galatians quite rightly received him as Christ, for they recognized him an apostle or delegate of Christ.[82]

Paul's words in verses 15 and 16 show that a remarkable change had taken place in the Galatians' attitude. What had happened to their original openhearted reception?

What has happened to that fine spirit of yours? I guarantee that in those days you would, if you could, have plucked out your eyes and given them to me. Have I now become your enemy because I continue to tell you the same truth?

How could one who had been received "as an angel of God" suddenly become an enemy? The Galatians' altered attitude was a direct result of listening to and accepting the false message of the Judaizers. The false teachers were accusing Paul of holding back on the hard doctrine of obedience to the law. He was, in their eyes, teaching the first-century equivalent of easy believism by discarding both circumcision and the Mosaic law.

The implications of the Judaizers' message linger in our day. One of the present tragedies in Reformed circles is the inability of some to distinguish between *easy* believism and *only* believism. The former is heresy, and the latter is the gospel. By nature, the human heart opposes both. We want

---

[82] Ibid., 114, 115.

to work penance and law-keeping into salvation. It takes a sovereign work of God's Holy Spirit to teach a person the truth of absolute, unconditional sovereign grace. By nature, we all want to do our part. And if our part is difficult, we believe that it is more meritorious. We see this in Reformed circles when the difficult contribution from the sheep involves unquestioning obedience to tyrannical rulers. It seems the harsher the treatment from leaders, the more devoted the followers become. Nor is this anything new. We find it illustrated in the Old Testament Scriptures. Some of the following comments come from a paper I did several years ago, entitled "When Should a Christian Leave a Church?"

> *The prophets follow an evil course and use their power unjustly* (Jer. 23:10b NIV).
>
> ... *"This is what the Sovereign LORD says: Woe to the shepherds of Israel who only take care of themselves! Should not shepherds take care of the flock? You eat the curds, clothe yourself with the wool and slaughter the choice animals, but you do not take care of the flock."* (Ezek. 34:2b, 3 NIV)

I would to God that leaders who have split churches over the issue of "elder authority" would ponder Ezekiel 34. Usually, when the leadership runs people out of a church for refusing to obey the "duly authorized elders" (which, interpreted, means refusing to sell their consciences in "unquestioning obedience" to the eldership), the pastors/elders never visit those people. The contact usually is limited to a "duly authorized" letter that quotes a lot of verses (mostly out of context) and then informs the "rebel" that they have been "duly"[83] excommunicated from the church, or cult, as the case may be. Sometimes, not too often, the letter informs the rebel that the elders are willing to consider reinstatement, as soon as the rebel manifests genuine repentance, which, in this case means the Reformed equivalent of kissing the pope's ring in submission.

Because true sheep have tender consciences, leaders can pummel them to death with two big clubs. When the Mosaic law (club number one) is swung by the "duly authorized prophet of God" (club number two), the effect on a tender conscience is subjection and fear. Week after week, many preachers cut the sheep and then rub salt into the open wound. When one of these wounded and bleeding sheep finally gets enough courage to leave such a church, or in one writer's words, "...with a sigh of relief some sheep escape such ministries," the abusive leadership accuses them of rebellion against God's "duly authorized church." I guarantee you that God does not view it that way: he views it as a refusal by a sheep to follow a false shepherd. When a child of God flees from that kind of tyranny, they are obeying the voice of the one true Shepherd and rejecting the authority of a false prophet. Do not ever feel guilty for leaving a church that was either into, or moving toward, a cultic mentality.

Ironically, many sheep in evangelical churches submit to a form of Romanism. It seems not to occur to them to challenge the situation with Scripture. The word of Jeremiah is true in many churches today:

---

[83] Institutional legalists rely heavily on the phrase "duly authorized." I would like to meet this person "Dooley" who authorizes others to act in his name!

A horrible and shocking thing has happened in the land: The prophets prophesy lies, the priests rule by their own authority, and my people love to have it this way. (Jer. 5:30, 31a NIV)

The content of the gospel matters. It is essential. It mattered to Paul, and it matters to us in the twenty-first century. The issue is twofold:

ONE: What is the gospel message that we are to give to poor sinners? Must we start with Exodus 20 and stay there until some essential "preparatory law work" occurs in the heart? Then, and not until then, do we offer the gospel. Or, can we evangelize sinners with the Gospel of John and immediately present the Savior himself?

TWO: How do we produce holy living among the saints of God? Do we send them back to Moses and put their consciences under his threat? Or, do we keep them standing under the cross, beholding their Savior, and put their consciences under his lordship and his clear objective commandments?

We are talking about nothing less than the essence of the gospel message in evangelism and the biblical means used to make believers grow in grace and sanctification. We are talking about two distinctly different approaches to preaching justification and sanctification. We are examining the true role of the church, the goal of its ministry, and the essence of its message to both sinners and saints.

These are the issues and arguments Paul addresses in his letter to the Galatians concerning the relationship of law and grace. In verses 17–20, Paul draws a sharp contrast between his attitude to the Galatians and the attitude displayed by the Judaizers.

Oh, I know how keen these men are to win you over, but can't you see that it is for their own ends? They would like to see you and me separated altogether, and have you all to themselves. Don't think I'm jealous—it is a grand thing that men should be keen to win you, whether I'm there or not, provided it is for the truth. Oh, my dear children, I feel the pangs of childbirth all over again till Christ be formed within you, and how I long to be with you now! Perhaps I could then alter my tone to suit your mood. As it is, I honestly don't know how to deal with you.[84]

The Judaizers were paying all kinds of attention to the Galatians. They were not evangelizing pagans, but exerting all their proselytizing efforts to impose Judaism on the Galatian church. It is a strange but real phenomenon—those whose religion is made up of rules and ceremonies cannot allow others any kind of liberty. Legalistic leaders need their converts far more than their converts need them. The security and self-esteem of legalists grows by bringing others into bondage to their authority. Their egos thrive on others' obedience to their every whim. Legalists need a stage to demonstrate their superior spirituality (meaning their keeping of all their own rules). A legalist feels safe only when everyone agrees with him. This is why legalists destroy affection for or loyalty to other religious leaders. As Paul says, "they want you all to themselves," but not for your benefit, but so they "can have you all to themselves." False leaders feed on the attention their devotees give them. Paul says, "It is good to have people pay attention to you if it is for the right reason," but not for the reason evidenced by the Judaizers.

---

[84] Phillips, New Testament

I have never been able to figure out why some leaders cannot allow people to love more than one pastor. An under-shepherd may labor for many years in one church, and see people saved and growing in grace. Then he retires, or moves to another church, and the new pastor comes in. Sometimes, the new pastor feels compelled to destroy the influence of the former pastor. He not only feels that he deserves the same love, respect, and confidence the former pastor earned over many years of faithful service, but he also feels the congregation should recognize, as he thinks he does, the weaknesses and failures of the former pastor. An even greater mystery is that far too often, many people in the congregation will go along with the new pastor's efforts to destroy the past. Like the Galatians, they forget all that the former pastor did on their behalf.

I hate to say it, but many pastors are among the most severely insecure people I know. I spent ten years in evangelism and conference ministry. I preached in about forty churches a year. Some churches, where God seemed to honor my preaching the most, did not invite me back because of the pastor's objection. I remember one instance where the chairman of the board of deacons professed to become converted. He testified that he had been a member of the church for twenty years, but had not been born again during that time. The pastor, instead of rejoicing that the man was finally converted, was upset. He felt that the deacon's former condition was a bad reflection on him and his ministry.

Every human being wants to be liked and appreciated. Preachers are no different from other people in this case. The Apostle Paul was not someone who looked for people to hate him. He, too, enjoyed being loved and appreciated. It is not wrong for us to seek to win people to ourselves as long as we do so as a means of winning them to Christ. It is not wrong for us to pay attention to people to demonstrate our Christian love for them. Once we have won their affection and respect, however, we must avoid a temptation inherent in that relationship of trust. We must not think for them or allow them to set us up in the place of their consciences. True leaders not only teach others how to lead and thereby work themselves out of a specific job in many areas; they also teach converts to be more directly dependent on the guidance of the Holy Spirit. New converts require special attention, but that is temporary. The process of weaning a growing disciple is difficult for both leader and follower. Sometimes, the follower feels personally rejected. Regardless, the goal of teaching is not to establish personal friendships, but to bring a person to the place where they are growing in grace.

John Stott summarizes this section well.

Notice, finally, the references to Christ in verses 14 and 19. Verse 14: *You ... received me ... as Christ Jesus. Verse 19: I am again in travail until Christ be formed in you!* What should matter to the people is not the pastor's appearance, but whether *Christ* is speaking through him. And what should matter to the pastor is not the people's favour, but whether *Christ* is formed in them. The church needs people who, in listening to their pastor, listen for the message of Christ, and pastors who, in labouring among the people, look for the image of Christ. Only when pastor and people thus keep their eyes on Christ will their mutual relations keep healthy, profitable and pleasing to almighty God.[85]

It is a sad commentary on a pastor's ministry when the only measuring stick used to gauge the growth of the sheep is faithful attendance at all church meetings and unquestioned loyalty to all of the pastor's ideas. As long as this "growth" is evident, the pastor is satisfied. What happened to the "fruit of the Spirit" as evidence of growth in grace?

In every pastorate where I served, I emphasized the following: You do not owe me a single thing for my own sake. However, to the gospel of sovereign grace that I preach, you owe all that you are and all that you have.

In the next chapter, we will come to the heart of Paul's theology of law as he expresses it in Galatians. In 3:19, Paul had asked, *"What, then, was the purpose of the law?* In 4:21, he asks, *"Tell me, you who want to be under the law, are you not aware of what the law says?"* If we can answer those two questions as Paul himself answers them, we can say that we understand Paul's doctrine of law and grace.

---

[85] Stott, *One Way*, 119.

CHAPTER NINETEEN

GALATIANS 4:21–28

We have now reached the heart of Paul's letter to the Galatians as it concerns the Christian's relationship to the law. After laying out the doctrine of justification by faith without the deeds of the law in chapters 2 and 3, Paul raised and answered the question, "What then was the purpose of the law?" (3:19). His answer reveals the radical difference between his theology of the law and that of the Judaizers. Paul asserts that, contrary to the Judaizers' position, God's primary purpose in giving the law was neither to curb sin nor to motivate holy living. God gave the law to do just the opposite. The law magnifies and exposes sin, thus revealing humanity's hopeless condition. Pressing the law on the conscience will cause transgressions to increase (Rom. 4:15 and 5:20). Paul has shown the utter ineffectiveness of the law to deal with sin in both the sinner and the saint.

Paul realizes that his stance on the law raises a logical question. If the Mosaic law does not help us in any way to be either justified or sanctified, and, in the case of sanctification, the law actually can be a real hindrance, then why did God give the law in the first place? Paul answers by explaining two distinct functions of the law. The primary purpose of the Mosaic law for the unbelievers in Israel was to convict them of sin and their inability to earn righteousness by their own efforts. This pushed them to faith in God's promise given to Abraham of a coming Messiah. The law also functioned as a pedagogue in the conscience of the believing Israelite during the period of his minority prior to the coming of the promised seed.

Paul then poses a question of his own to the Galatians: "Do you people know what the law really says?" (4:21). The question implies that the Galatians did not understand what the law actually taught, because if they had understood, they would have been insane to want it.

Paul wants the Galatians to see exactly what a dangerous position they will put themselves in if they adopt the Mosaic law. If they follow the Judaizers and go "under the law," they will be "alienated from Christ" and will "fall from grace." Christ and his atoning work will "be of no value" to them at all (5:2–4). To add any ceremony as an essential component of salvation, whether that ceremony is circumcision, baptism, or any other, is to believe far more than just bad theology; it is to deny completely the gospel of God's sovereign grace. Such an addition is heresy of the deepest dye. The same principle applies if we add law-keeping *in any way* to the terms of salvation. In such a case, we effectively reject the doctrine of the cross and the blood atonement our Savior made. To knowingly put oneself "under the law" in the sense the Judaizers were advocating was to deny Christ and to reject his all-sufficient grace by trusting in personal works to gain justification. Such a course consigns one to hell.

This situation in the Galatian church sounds a warning to believers in any century and in any setting. Even the most dedicated Christians are not immune from the kind of legalism that the first-century Judaizers were promoting. The church constantly faces two problems related to the law. On the one hand, we must guard against the threat of the "black devil" of antinomianism—being against all law—and on the other hand, we must avoid the danger of the "white devil" of legalism—adding law to the gospel. As Spurgeon said, these two enemies are both devils, and either one is capable of destroying a church or a Christian's profession of faith. If you do not acknowledge the real danger of these two enemies of the gospel, you know very little about either your own heart or the truth of Scripture. We must remember that the Galatians were the product of the mighty apostle's ministry. They had been converted and indoctrinated under his personal teaching. If such people could be beguiled into forsaking a gospel of grace for a mess of pottage that mixed law and grace, then we surely are capable of doing the same thing today. In the book of Galatians, Paul deals with both perversions of law: the black devil, antinomianism and the white devil, legalism.

Before we dig any deeper into Paul's questions and answers about the law, we need to say a word about methodology. Question-asking as a method of teaching and argumentation dates back at least to Socrates. Asking and answering penetrating questions is one of Paul's favorite methods of teaching. In order to interpret the questions a person has used to teach, we need to ask some questions of our own. (1) *What* is being asked in the question we want to interpret? (2) *Why* was that particular question asked *when* it was (at that particular point in the argument)? In other words, what prompted or necessitated that specific question? (3) Do we understand the answer the biblical author provided to the question? (4) Lastly, how do we apply the question and the answer to our situation?

Lloyd-Jones exemplifies this interpretive methodology. He first describes the problem that the biblical writer faced in his day; he then shows how the writer answers and solves that problem. He next shows how we today face the same basic problem which that particular writer faced; and lastly, he shows how to apply the answers to our problem today.

So, before we interpret Paul's questions and answers, we must ask our questions. What do the words that Paul uses mean? What provoked Paul to ask these specific questions? Why did he find it necessary to ask those specific questions at that particular time in his argument? It is obvious that Paul has said, or clearly implied, something that he felt needed additional explanation. He must have said something about the law that was contrary to what his hearers were thinking about it. Paul seems to have assumed that his first question about the law (3:19) would still be in the minds of his hearers when he asked the second question (4:21). Paul has said something about the law that made them want to say, "If the law was not given for the purpose which we have believed it was, then what was God's purpose in giving it?"

The first thing we must do is define some terms. (1) What does Paul mean by his words *the law*? How would the Galatians, and especially the Judaizers among them, have understood Paul's vocabulary? (2) What does it mean to be *under the law* in a wrong way? (3) What does it mean to *hear the law*?

What does Paul mean when he uses the word *law*? Exactly what law is Paul talking about? Whatever law it is, new covenant believers have never been under it and must never allow themselves to be beguiled into going under it (4:24–28).

Commentators on the book of Galatians generally offer three answers to the question of to what law Paul refers in verse 21. One view sees *the law* as referring to the Old Testament Scriptures, since Paul immediately quotes, in verses 22–31, from Genesis. This section of the Old Testament Scriptures covers a period of time before the old covenant was made with Israel. This would mean that Paul thinks the Galatians are wrong to put themselves under the Old Testament Scriptures. This seems highly unlikely on two counts. At this point in the early church's development, the concept of the Old Testament did not exist. Such a view is anachronistic, reading later developments back into the text. Then, just a few paragraphs later, he tells the Galatians that Scripture says to cast out the law/bondwoman (4:30). This interpretation makes Paul refer to the Scripture as the basis for casting out the Scripture. It is a logically incoherent statement. Furthermore, Paul tells the Galatians that the historical women (Sarah and Hagar) represent the Mosaic and the new covenants.

Another view states that by the word *law* Paul is referring to the *ceremonial law* since Paul would never think of casting out the *moral law*. This view also is anachronistic. The division of the Mosaic law into three distinct segments is a much later development.[86] Furthermore, as we will see in a later chapter, even if the category were valid, the so-called ceremonial law would not have been a yoke of bondage.

---

[86] Generally, historians credit Thomas Aquinas (14th century) with the division.

This view seems more concerned with protecting a particular theological view of the Ten Commandments than in carefully exegeting the biblical texts.

Still others say that Paul means the old covenant, since he immediately mentions "the two covenants" (v. 24). This is my view. Paul advances his argument by comparing the two major covenants to which the Scripture of his day referred, namely, the old covenant made with Israel at Sinai and the new covenant promised and then fulfilled in and through Christ. It seems to me that Paul, by the words _the law_, means _the law covenant made with Israel at Sinai._ Certainly, Paul's point is not merely to establish the historical fact that Sarah expelled Ishmael and his mother from Abraham's household. The expulsion of Hagar and her son are important in Paul's theology because they illustrate the necessity for a child of God to cast out the law covenant and its fruits. A note of warning is in order here. Paul takes a historical account from Genesis involving troubles in Abraham's household and uses it as a spiritual allegory. Writers of Scripture have liberty, when moved by the Holy Spirit, that we do not have. Just because Paul assigned an allegorical meaning to a passage in the Old Testament Scriptures, we do not have license to do the same thing with other passages.

On this third view, to be _under the law_ is to have the conscience under the burden of keeping the law to earn standing with God. We will see this more clearly when we come to Galatians 5:1 where the law is called a "yoke of bondage." To be _under the law_ in the sense Paul means here is to be under the obligation, upon threat of death, to perfectly obey the law in its entirety or suffer the consequences of eternal death.

One of the difficulties in defining the word *law* is that the writers of Scripture do not assign one and only one meaning to it. R. L. Dabney lists eight different uses of the words *the law*.

> The word "Law" [*torah* and *nomos*] is employed in the Scripture with a certain latitude of meaning, but always carrying the force of meaning contained in the general idea of a regulative principle. First, it sometimes expresses the whole of Revelation, as in Psalm 1:2. Second, the whole Old Testament, as in [John] 10:34. Third, frequently the Pentateuch, as in Luke 24:44. Fourth, the perceptive moral law (Proverbs 28:4; Rom. 2:14). Fifth, the ceremonial code, as in Heb. 10:1. **[Notice the word *code*.]** Sixth, the decalogue, Matt. 22:36–40. Seventh, a ruling power in our nature, as in Rom. 7:23. Eighth, the covenant of works, Romans 6:14.[87]

In this discussion, we will be using two definitions. The first is the first one in Dabney's list, the "whole of Revelation" or the Scriptures as special revelation as opposed to natural revelation (as in Psalm 19:7). The second will be the eighth in Dabney's list, the "covenant of works." Dabney would not define the covenant of works the same way that we would, but we will discuss that later. John Owen saw these two definitions as covering the major uses of *the law* in Scripture. In a sermon on Romans 6:14, *Ye are not under the law, but under grace*, published by his wife five years after his death, Owen elucidates the point under discussion. We agree with and accept Owen's definition of

---

[87] R. L. Dabney, *Lectures in Systematic Theology* (Grand Rapids, MI: Baker Book House, 1985), 351.

the word *law* in Romans 6:14, as well as Galatians 3:19 and 4:21, to mean *law as a covenant,* and we agree with him that it is an either/or proposition. You are either under law or you are under grace, but you cannot be under both at the same time in the sense in which Paul uses those words in these passages. Those two concepts, *under the law* and *under grace,* as used in these three passages, are antithetical. You cannot be under the law and under grace as covenants at the same time. The emphasis in the following quotation is mine. Owen says:

> First, the law *giveth no strength against sin* unto them that are under it, but grace doth. Sin will neither be cast nor kept out of its throne, but by a spiritual power and strength in the soul to oppose, conquer, and dethrone it. Where it is not conquered it will reign; and conquered it will not be without a mighty prevailing power: this the law will not, cannot give.
>
> The law is taken two ways: —
>
> 1. **For the whole revelation of the mind and will of God in the Old Testament,** In this sense [the law] had grace in it, and so did give both life, and light, and strength against sin, as the psalmist declares, Ps 19:7–9. In this sense it contained not only the law of precepts, but the promise also and the covenant, which was the means of conveying spiritual life and strength unto the church. In this sense [the law] is **not** here [Romans 6:14] spoken of, nor is it anywhere **opposed unto grace.**
>
> 2. [The law is taken] for the **covenant rule of perfect obedience: "Do this, and live."** In this sense men are said to be "under it," in opposition unto being "under grace." They are under its power, rule, conditions, and authority, as a covenant.
>
> In this sense the law was never ordained of God to convey grace or spiritual strength unto the souls of men;…

It is not God's ordinance for the dethroning of sin, nor for the destruction of its dominion.

There is, therefore, no help to be expected against the dominion of sin from the law.

Wherefore, those who are "under the law" are under the dominion of sin. ... "The law is holy ... just ... good," but it can do them no good, as unto their deliverance from the **power** of sin. God hath not appointed it unto that end. Sin will never be dethroned by it; it will not give place unto the law, neither in its **title** nor in its **power**.[88]

Owen, in this passage, says exactly what I believe about the law. The Old Testament Scriptures (the thirty-nine books written before Christ came), or *the law* in the first sense in Owen's definition, clearly revealed and declared the one gospel message of grace. The *law covenant* made with Israel at Sinai, however, had no grace at all in its covenantal terms. It was a killing covenant. God designed it to be a ministration of death (2 Cor. 3 and Rom. 7:1–11). The *law covenant* served a very gracious *purpose* in the history of redemption; it killed self-hope and prepared those under it for grace, but its *terms* were solely legal. The ceremonial feasts and holy days clearly preached the gospel of a coming Messiah, but even that proclamation came at the end of a sword. Scripture clearly presents the Mosaic covenant as a legal covenant of works.

Owen then goes on to his second major heading. "The law not only gives no strength against sin":

Secondly, The law *gives no liberty of any kind;* it gendereth unto bondage, and so cannot free us from any dominion,—not

---

[88] John Owen, *The Works of John Owen,* vol. 7 (Edinburgh: Banner of Truth Trust, 1965), 42, 43, 44. (bolding mine)

that of sin, for this must be by liberty. But this we have also by the gospel. There is a twofold liberty:—

1. Of state and condition; [referring to justification]

2. Of internal operation; [referring to sanctification] and we have both by the gospel.[89]

Owen then shows that we are delivered from the curse of the law and have internal liberty, which he calls "...the freedom of the mind from the powerful inward chains of sin, with an ability to act all of the powers and faculties of the soul in a gracious manner. Hereby is the power of sin in the soul destroyed. And this also is given us in the gospel."[90]

Owen goes on to show the inability of the law, used in his second definition as a covenant, to help a believer fight sin. Actually, the law not only gives no aid in the fight with sin; the law does the exact opposite. The law gives strength to sin (1 Cor. 15:56). If you ask the law to help you struggle against sin, the law will side with sin and condemn you for your guilt.

Thirdly, the law doth not supply us with effectual motives and encouragements to endeavor the ruin of the dominion of sin in a way of duty; which must be done, or in the end it will prevail. It works only by fear and dread... these things weaken, enervate, and discourage the soul in its conflict against sin...[91]

Fourthly, Christ is not in the law; he is not proposed in it, not communicated by it,—we are not made partakers of him

---

[89] Ibid., 549.

[90] Ibid., 550.

[91] Ibid., 550.

thereby. This is the work of grace, of the gospel. In it is Christ revealed; by it he is proposed and exhibited unto us...[92]

Can you say, with John Owen, *Christ is not in the law*? You can if you understand the twofold meaning of law as Owen has defined it.[93]

To follow Owen's argument, we must see that the first covenant—the old covenant given to Israel at Sinai—rested primarily on the tables of the covenant, or the Decalogue. The Ten Commandments were the basic covenant document or summary of the covenant terms. The Ten Commandments cannot be equated exactly with the old covenant, but they also cannot be separated from the old covenant. What happens to the old covenant happens to the Ten Commandments. If the old convent is done away, or cast out, then the Ten Commandments are also cast out.

The old covenant, as a legal covenant, had the primary purpose of conviction of sin and preparation for grace. We must separate a gracious *purpose*—the preparation of sinners for salvation—from grace itself, which, as Owen said, is found only in the gospel. One, sovereign, unchanging *purpose* of grace, which is biblical, and a theological covenant of grace, which is purely theological, are two different things. One is the product of biblical exegesis, and the other is the product of logic applied to systematic

---

[92] Ibid., 551.

[93] I am aware that I will be accused of misrepresenting Owen. I do not in any sense suggest that Owen would agree with my new covenant theology. All I am saying is that his definition of the meaning of the word "law" is exactly what I believe. How Owen himself could have reconciled these comments with his covenant theology is beyond me. His article on Romans 6:14 is one of the last things he wrote.

theology. John Owen is unerring in his twofold definition. When the Scripture refers to the law covenant at Sinai, it refers to a legal covenant with no grace in its terms. Conversely, the Old Testament Scriptures, as revelation, are inherently full of grace: it is an act of grace for God to reveal himself to his creatures, especially to those whom he has chosen unto salvation. The entire old covenant, as a part of that revelation, is gracious in that same sense, but not in its *covenantal terms* as given at Sinai.

In the same vein, there is not an ounce of covenantal law in the gospel of grace. There are clear, objective, moral standards, or laws, given to the new covenant people of God, but they do not come as law at the end of a sword. They do not come from Mount Sinai. They come from Mount Calvary. However, even though there is no law, as defined in Owen's second sense, in the gospel, true saving grace will always lead a child of God to seek to fulfill every command that God has revealed as his will for him today. The biblical gospel of grace will always produce a holy heart that pants after righteousness. The *law covenant* is powerless to either produce or sustain such an attitude; if the gospel cannot accomplish these goals, then it is just as weak as the law. Grace must reign in righteousness, or it is not grace.[94]

When we try to define the particular law to which Paul refers, we also raise the vexing theological problem of continuity and discontinuity. Clearly, Paul saw the Galatians' observation of "days, and months, and times, and years" (4:10) as evidence of their desertion of the truth of the new covenant and adoption of the old covenant. He saw this

---

[94] See our book, *Grace,* available from New Covenant Media.

observation as loyalty to the Mosaic law on the part of the Galatians, but at the same time, and by the same evidence, he saw very little of "Christ being formed" in them. In 4:11 and 20, Paul is so disturbed by this infatuation with the Mosaic law that he questions their salvation.

What does it mean to be under the law in a wrong way? First, we have to know what it means to be under the law in the right way. For that, we must know the purpose of the law. Paul's first question about the law, *"What, then, was the purpose of the law"* (3:19 NIV) is the place to start this discussion. Paul asks and answers the specific question of both the nature of the law and God's purpose in giving it. The heart of the problem in the theology of the Judaizers was their misuse of the law. They were using the holy, just, and good law for a purpose God never intended. It is tragic but true that good people can unknowingly misuse the holy law of God. Paul is quite clear about this fact: *"But we know that the law is good if one uses it lawfully"* (1 Tim. 1:8 NKJV). If no one ever misused the law, Paul would have never written what he did in verse 8. So what constitutes a misuse of the law? Any attempt to make the law to be the mother of holiness in either a sinner or a saint is to misuse it. The law was an executioner without an ounce of mercy. Bunyan showed this clearly in his picture of the man with club (Moses) who was beating poor Faithful nigh unto death. The law's designated job was to kill every hope a sinner had of saving himself and having done that, its ministry was finished. If we do not understand the function of the law, we are more likely to misuse it.

The question in 3:19 is quite clear. We could paraphrase the question this way: "What, in the light of what I have taught about the law, was God's purpose in giving it?" The word *then* implies that this is the thrust of Paul's question. Paul has argued that, on the surface, it appears that the covenant God made with Israel at Sinai contradicts the covenant he made with Abraham many years before. Paul admits this appearance of contradiction and shows that in spite of appearances, there is a clear consistency to God's one, sovereign, unchanging purpose of grace. On the one hand, Paul insists that the covenant at Sinai is law-based and the covenant with Abraham is grace-based, and they therefore are different in their *natures*. On the other hand, Paul also insists that the same God gave both covenants, and both covenants equally serve the one unchanging and ultimate purpose of God in redemption. God did not change horses in the middle of the stream of redemption at Mount Sinai. He saved sinners the same way before and after both Moses and Abraham, and continues to do the same today. Mount Sinai may be a legal covenant, but it still serves a vital and essential part in the scheme of grace.

Paul's answer to the question in 3:19 was radically different from the answer of his opponents. His answer would have both amazed and enraged the Judaizers. The apostle taught that the law was not given to curb sin and to produce holy living. The law does not have the power to do either of these things. The law was given to magnify sin by bringing the sin in a person's heart to the surface. We covered this before when we looked at 3:19. The law was like a mirror, which, when the sinner looks into it, reveals what he is really like.

Paul writes in the same vein when he addresses the church at Rome. Look again at Romans 7:1–11 and see Paul's theology of law worked out there. Paul consistently teaches that God designed the law to provoke sin and bring it to the surface. Paul is as emphatic in Romans as he is in Galatians that the law can neither justify a sinner nor sanctify a saint. It cannot deal with sin, period. Paul goes even farther and teaches that the law actually aggravates and hinders sanctification. Lloyd-Jones has stated this clearly. Let me quote a key section from his commentary on Romans 7.

> The Apostle sees at once that there was a likelihood of two main charges being brought against him. The first was the charge of antinomianism, the charge that he is more or less saying, 'Live as you like, sin as much as you like. All is well; grace will look after you and cover all your sin.' [95]

Lloyd-Jones then gives a short summary of Romans 6, showing how Paul refutes this unjustified charge of antinomianism. It should be noted that Lloyd-Jones has stated in another commentary dealing with Paul's statement in Romans 6:1 just how bold and different Paul's view of law was. After stating his view that "where sin abounded, grace did much more abound" (Rom. 5:20), Paul said, "You will probably accuse me of saying, 'Let's continue in sin so that grace may abound'" (Rom. 6:1). Lloyd-Jones makes this penetrating statement.

> First of all, let me make a comment, to me a very important and vital comment. The preaching of the gospel of salvation by grace alone always leads to the possibility of this charge being brought against it. There is no better test as to whether a man is really preaching the New Testament gospel of salvation than

---

[95] D. Marytn Lloyd-Jones, *Romans, An Exposition of Chapters 7:1-8:4, The Law: Its Functions and Limits* (Grand Rapids, MI: Zondervan Publishing House, 1973), 3.

this, that some people might misunderstand it and misinterpret it to mean that it really amounts to this, that because you are saved by grace alone it does not matter at all what you do; you can go on sinning as much as you like because it will redound all the more to the glory of grace. That is a very good test of the gospel preaching. If my preaching does not expose it to that misunderstanding, then it is not the gospel.[96]

If Lloyd-Jones is correct, and I believe he is, then many Reformed churches would fail the test of true gospel preaching. If our preaching of the gospel does not expose us to the same criticism that Paul endured, then we are not preaching the same gospel that Paul preached. You could attend some Reformed churches, especially some Reformed Baptist churches, for one hundred years and never come close to even thinking of charging them with antinomianism. They guard, protect, and qualify the gospel to the place they actually lose its glory and power. Some of them boast they have no false converts, but fail to add that they have no converts, period. They enthrone Moses in the conscience as the greatest lawgiver who ever lived and have our Lord ministering at the altar of Moses.

Some Jews who were professing Christ as the Messiah refused to leave the old covenant, or the religion of Judaism, *in its entirety*, and move into the new covenant, or Christian religion, completely. This also is a misuse of the law. These professing Christians wanted to trust Christ while hanging on to the law of Moses. From our perspective, such reluctance, while regrettable, is understandable. The old

---

[96] Marytn Lloyd-Jones, *Exposition of Romans 6. The New Man* (Grand Rapids, MI: Zondervan Publishing House, 1973), 8.

covenant had mediated God's will to them for centuries. Their national identity was tied to it. This same reluctance, when found a century-and-a-half later on the part of people who had never been Jewish is much harder to understand. Puritan theology evinces the same desire to have both Christ and the Mosaic law. On the one hand, the Puritans insisted, correctly, that the Old Testament must be understood in the light of the New Testament.[97] However, in fact, they built their system of theology on a theory of continuity that made it impossible for them to follow their own principle. A footnote on Galatians 4:10 in John Brown's commentary on Galatians illustrates this. Immediately after quoting Galatians 4:10, *Ye observe days, and months, and times, and years*, Brown writes, "Under the Christian dispensation, with the exception of the Lord's day, all days are alike."[98] After the words "Lord's day," in that sentence, Brown inserts the following footnote:

> That, under the Christian dispensation, the first day of the week is divinely appropriated for religious purposes, and that this is in reality the form in which the principle embodied in the Sabbath from the beginning is exhibited under that dispensation, are principles capable, I apprehend, of complete proof by a "conjugation of moral probabilities," which, on a fair mind, is fitted to produce an effect as powerful as

---

[97] "...[A] pure theology as will prove the suitable instrument of heavenly influence in transforming individuals, and churches, and nations, must be based on a well-understood Bible, and especially on a well-understood New Testament: for we run into no vicious circle when we say, we must learn to read the Old Testament in the light of the New, in order to our deriving illustration to the New Testament from the Old." From: Brown, *Galatians*, vi.

[98] Ibid., 208, 09.

demonstration. The dislike of the objects of the institution, it is to be feared, in many cases leads people to demand a kind and degree of evidence of which the subject does not admit; and I am afraid harm has been done by persons endeavoring, with the best intentions doubtless, to meet this unreasonable demand.[99]

That is an amazing statement, especially from a man like John Brown. I treasure every commentary John Brown wrote. He is one of my favorite writers. However, he was a consistent covenant theologian and realized that Paul appeared to be laying the Sabbath to rest under the new covenant. He felt compelled to defend his view of continuity. You can cut that quotation any way you like, and it will always mean the same thing. John Brown in effect is saying, "My theology dictates that the Sabbath must be a moral commandment and therefore still be in effect today. I do not have a shred of clear textual evidence in Scripture to prove this, but I believe it because of a 'conjugation of moral probabilities'." He then says that this conjugation of moral probabilities, should, on a fair mind, be enough evidence. We do not need an actual text of Scripture to establish the point. He accuses those of us who reject his view of the Sabbath of being "unreasonable" for demanding textual (biblical) evidence. We all understand that if John Brown had had textual evidence, he would have supplied it. By his own admission, there is no such evidence and we are being unfair to ask for it. Brown further accuses people who believe as I do of being motivated by a "dislike of the objects of the institution" [the Sabbath] when we reject the "conjugation of moral probabilities" as being equal to

---

[99] Ibid., 209.

biblical evidence. This is both an unfair and untrue accusation.

The second question that Paul asks as he unfolds his doctrine of law is in 4:21:*"Tell me, you that desire to be under the law, do you not hear the law?"* This question highlights not only where the Galatians were going wrong on their view of the law but also why their position was so dangerous.

So what does it mean to hear the law? To "hear" the law is to understand clearly the law's terms of perfect obedience and to realize you can never satisfy those terms and are therefore without hope of ever seeing, apart from sovereign electing grace, the face of God in peace.

It is tragic that neither the Judaizers in Paul's day nor many Christians today understand what it means to *hear the law*. The Scriptures are replete with statements that a person can "hear" without ever "hearing" (Matt. 13:10–17). This is true of the law as well as the gospel. If all you ever heard was, "Thou shalt not steal," you have not heard the law. All you heard was a commandment. You have not heard the law until you hear it say, "Thou shalt not steal and *if you do I will have you stoned to death."* Now you have *heard the law.* If all you heard was, "Remember the Sabbath day to keep it holy," all you heard was a commandment. If you heard, "Remember the Sabbath day and keep it holy, and *if you so much as pick up a few sticks you are a dead man,"* then you *heard the law.* It is the penalty aspect that gives law its status and authority. You could post a sign saying "50 mile-an-hour speed limit" every hundred yards on every highway in America, but without a fine for breaking that speed limit, police officers to arrest speeders, and judges to collect the fines, you do not have a law—you only have good advice.

In Galatians, Paul uses the term *the law* to refer to the old covenant in its entirety, including the Ten Commandments. He states that this law cannot provide help in the fight against sin—either in justification or in sanctification. The purpose of the old covenant was to expose sin and to drive a sinner to the only viable solution in the battle against sin— the Lord Jesus Christ. To view the old covenant in any other way is to misunderstand and misuse it. The ultimate goal of the old covenant was to do its killing work job and then pass out of existence. We will see this clearly in the next chapter when we will look at Paul's allegorical use of Sarah and Hagar. This section of Scripture contains some of the most astounding statements Paul ever made concerning the Christian and the law.

CHAPTER TWENTY

GALATIANS 4:21–31

In this chapter, I want to cover Paul's allegorical interpretation of Hagar's expulsion from Abraham's house. First, we will review the historical details as recorded in Genesis; then, we will look at Paul's interpretation and application of those facts. Finally, I will look at what that application means in the twenty-first century. Here are the historical facts of the allegory of Sarah and Hagar.

In Genesis 12, God promises Abraham that his seed will become a great nation. At this time, Abraham has no offspring. Twenty-five years pass, and Abraham remains childless.

In Genesis 15, Abraham observes that Eliezer of Damascus will inherit everything, because Abraham and Sarah are still without natural heirs. God affirms that Abraham, through Sarah, will have children, as many as the "the stars of sky." Abraham believes God and is justified.

In Genesis 16, Sarah has a bright idea about how to help God fulfill his promise to Abraham. She gives her servant to Abraham to serve as a surrogate mother. Abraham agrees and the plan seems to work. Hagar conceives. However, when Hagar discovers that she is pregnant, she taunts Sarah. Sarah becomes angry and treats Hagar so harshly that Hagar runs away. An angel meets her in the wilderness and sends her back. This is the story so far. We come now to the part of the account that Paul uses for his allegory.

And the LORD visited Sarah as he had said, and the LORD did unto Sarah as he had spoken. For Sarah conceived, and bare Abraham a son in his old age, at the set time of which God had spoken to him. And Abraham called the name of his son that was born unto him, whom Sarah bare to him, Isaac. And Abraham circumcised his son Isaac being eight days old, as God had commanded him. And Abraham was an hundred years old, when his son Isaac was born unto him. And Sarah said, God hath made me to laugh, so that all that hear will laugh with me. And she said, Who would have said unto Abraham, that Sarah should have given children suck? for I have born him a son in his old age. And the child grew, and was weaned: and Abraham made a great feast the same day that Isaac was weaned. And Sarah saw the son of Hagar the Egyptian, which she had born unto Abraham, mocking. Wherefore she said unto Abraham, Cast out this bondwoman and her son: for the son of this bondwoman shall not be heir with my son, even with Isaac. And the thing was very grievous in Abraham's sight because of his son. (Gen. 21:1–11 KJV)

Essential Facts! Miss these facts and you miss the meaning of Paul's allegorical use of the passage.

Historical Fact No. 1—Abraham has two sons by two different mothers.

1. Hagar gives birth to Ishmael.

2. Sarah gives birth to Isaac.

3. Textual evidence: *For it is written, that Abraham had TWO SONS, the one by a bondmaid* [Hagar], *the other by a freewoman* [Sarah]. (Gal. 4:22 KJV, emphasis added)

Note the words "Abraham had two sons." Ishmael is just as much a true son, or seed, of Abraham as is Isaac.

Historical Fact No. 2—There is a great difference in the nature of the two mothers.

1. Hagar is an Egyptian slave girl.

2. Sarah is an Israelite free woman.

3. Textual evidence: *For it is written, that Abraham had two sons, the one by a BONDMAID* [Hagar], *the other by a FREEWOMAN* [Sarah]. (Gal. 4:22 KJV, emphasis added)

Historical Fact No. 3 — There is a great difference in the manner of the birth of the two sons.

1. Ishmael is born "after the flesh," or by natural procreation and normal birth. They needed no power from God to produce Ishmael. Free will could do it all.

2. Isaac is born "by promise" and by a miraculous conception and birth. Isaac's birth needed the supernatural power of God.

3. Textual evidence: *But he who was of the bondwoman was born **after the flesh;** but he of the freewoman was **by promise.*** (Gal. 4:23 KJV, emphasis added)

Historical Fact No. 4 — There is a great difference in the natures of the two sons. One son, Ishmael, hated his brother Isaac.

1. Textual evidence: *At that time the son born in the ordinary way persecuted the son born by the power of the Spirit. It is the same now.* (Gal. 4:29 NIV)

2. Paul's point is not the two brothers per se, but what the two brothers represent. They both represent fruit: one symbolizes the fruit of legalism, begotten by the old covenant and the other the fruit of godliness, begotten by the new covenant.

Historical Fact No. 5—One mother and her son must be expelled from the house.

Textual evidence: *Nevertheless what saith the scripture?* ***Cast out the bondwoman and her son:*** *for the son of the bondwoman shall not be heir with the son of the freewoman.* (Gal. 4:30 KJV, emphasis added)

Again, Paul is talking (1) about casting out the law, or Hagar, and (2) all the fruit—Ishmael—that the law begets. Look carefully at Paul's theological points.

Paul's First Major Point—These two mothers, Sarah and Hagar, represent the two covenants around which most of the Scripture is centered.

Textual evidence: *Which things are an allegory: for these [the two mothers] are* ***the two covenants;*** (Gal. 4:24a KJV, emphasis added)

Paul's Second Major Point—Paul clearly identifies both of the two covenants represented by the two mothers in the allegory (Gal. 4:24b—26).

1. The one covenant, represented by Hagar, is the "old," or law covenant made with the nation of Israel at Sinai (Hagar is Mount Sinai in Arabia [v. 25]). It is impossible to make Paul's words refer to Adam and the Garden of Eden.

2. The other covenant, represented by Sarah, is the Abrahamic covenant fulfilled in the new covenant by the work of Christ that Paul has been discussing since 3:1.

3. Textual evidence: v. 24… *these are the two covenants; the* ***one from the Mount Sinai…*** 25 *For this* ***Agar*** **[Hagar]** *is Mount Sinai in Arabia, and answereth to*

Jerusalem which now is, and is in bondage with her children. 26 *But Jerusalem which is above is free, which is the mother of us all.* (Gal. 4:24a–26 KJV, emphasis added).

NOTE: We must remember that Paul lived before the writing of the *Westminster Confession*. He did not know anything about the two theological covenants around which that confession builds its theology of law and grace.

Paul's Third Major Point—Just as the nature of the mother determines the nature of her offspring, so the nature of the covenant each mother represents also determines the nature of both the worshipers and the worship begotten by that covenant.

1. Hagar, a bondmaid, can only produce a bondservant child who must be cast out with no inheritance.

2. Sarah, because she is a free woman, can produce free children who will inherit the promised blessing, justification, because they have all the rights and privileges of true sons.

The important question in this case is not "who is your **father?**" but, "who is your **mother?**" Both Ishmael and Isaac, the Jews and the Arabs, have equal claim to Abraham as their father. However, only one son is begotten (or "mothered") by grace and promise and not by law and works.

Paul's Theology of Law and Grace Illustrated. Just as mothers beget and bear children, so covenants beget and produce worshippers and worship.

1. The Sinai law covenant, represented by Hagar, can only gender, or give birth, to bondage. (Gal. 4:24).

2. The gracious covenant, represented by Sarah, mothers, or gives birth to, free children who live in the freedom of the new covenant (Gal. 4:26).

3. Textual evidence:... *two covenants; the one from the Mount Sinai, which* **GENDERETH** *to bondage, which is Agar* [Hagar]*... is in bondage with her children. But Jerusalem which is above is free, which is the* **MOTHER** *of us all.* (Gal. 4:24b–26 KJV, emphasis added)

Essential Points to Remember in the Allegory:

1. Hagar equals Sinai, or the law covenant given to Israel at Sinai (v. 24b, 25)—see also Exod. 24:1–8). Hagar is the covenant written on the tablets of the covenant (Exod. 34:27, 28; Deut. 9:9–11; and Heb. 8:6–13) given through Moses. This is the old or legal covenant. The law covenant is to be treated in the same manner that Hagar and Ishmael were treated! As Hagar and Ishmael were cast out, so must the law be cast out. If we miss this point, then we lose the entire allegorical interpretation and misunderstand Paul's view of law.

2. Sarah equals the new covenant, or the free grace of God (v. 26b). Sarah is the covenant of promise given to Abraham and is the gracious covenant fulfilled in Christ.

3. These points are neither figments of some exegete's imagination nor are they the good and necessary consequences deduced from a system of theology. The Holy Spirit of God himself, via the pen of the Apostle Paul said, "… these are the *two covenants;* the one from the *Mount Sinai,* which *gendereth to bondage,* which is Agar. For *this Agar is*

Mount Sinai in Arabia..." (Gal.4:24b, 25a KJV). I am constantly amazed that good and godly writers and teachers will choose an interpretation that flies in the face of clear texts of Scripture in order to protect a system of theology based only on good and necessary consequences deduced (by logic) from non-biblical presuppositions.

The Heart of Paul's Argument

Paul has set the scene. He has explained the identity of the characters. Now he provides the central point of the allegory. Paul uses the two mothers (Sarah and Hagar) and the fruit, or children (Isaac and Ishmael), gendered, or born, of each mother, to make the following comparisons:

1. The nature of the two covenants (the old law covenant given at Sinai and the new covenant of grace in Christ) represented by Hagar and Sarah are compared.

2. The nature of the mothers' offspring, or their children, is compared to the nature of the fruit produced by the two covenants. Just as the nature of the fruit, or the children, of each mother, is determined by the nature of the mother who begets that fruit, so *the fruit, or worship, that is produced by the two covenants, represented by the two mothers, is also determined by the nature of the covenant that begets the fruit or worship.* Just as Hagar, because of her nature as a bondmaid, can only produce a bondservant child, so the law covenant at Sinai, because it is a legal works covenant, can only produce work mongers in bondage to legalism.

3. Just as Sarah can produce free children because she is a free woman, so the gracious covenant promised to Abraham and fulfilled in Christ produces children born to be free, or in Paul's words, to be "not under the law, but under grace."

4. Verse 30 is the *heart of the allegory*. This is the point toward which Paul has been moving all along. This point is the foundation of Paul's theology of the relationship of law and grace and the Christian's relationship to the law. Some commentators barely mention this section of Scripture, and others skip right over it. Remember, Paul bases the command to "cast out the bondwoman" on the fact that she cannot produce legitimate children to Abraham. She can only produce children in bondage. Remember what Paul said about the two mothers being types of the two major covenants, the old covenant made with Israel at Sinai and the new covenant established by Christ. Both covenants, like the mothers who represents them, bear fruit or children (worshippers and worship). Just as the nature of the mother determines the nature of the fruit or children, so the nature of each covenant determines both the nature of those it begets (the worshippers) and the nature of their worship or fruit (v. 24–26). Paul's crucial point is the necessity for a Christian to "cast out the law" (Hagar).

Paul's Inspired Application of the Allegory

Paul sees the "Jerusalem which now is" as the fruit gendered by the old covenant, and the body of Christ as the fruit of the new covenant. Paul is saying in verse 30 that this casting out work is the solution to the problem in Galatia. *Both* the bondwoman (Hagar) and her son (Ishmael) must be cast out. **Remember, whatever happens to Hagar must happen to the law covenant that she represents.**

The bondwoman (Hagar, or the law covenant at Sinai) and her son (Ishmael, or the worship begotten by that covenant) must be CAST OUT! Paul is clear in his statements.

Nevertheless what saith the scripture? **Cast out the bondwoman** [Hagar—the law] *and her son* [Ishmael –the worship begotten by the law]: *for the son of the bondwoman shall not be heir with the son of the freewoman.* (Gal. 4:30 KJV, emphasis added)

The offspring of the law cannot inherit the true Abrahamic inheritance—the blessing of justification. Indeed, the offspring of the law cannot inherit *any* spiritual blessing.

We must maintain Paul's interpretation of the facts.

As you hear Paul admonishing believers to cast out the bondwoman (Hagar), remember that Paul has clearly identified the bondwoman as the law covenant at Sinai that genders bondage. Hagar equals the old covenant, including the Ten Commandments as the terms, or words, of the covenant made with Israel at Sinai (Exod. 34:27, 28).

Hagar's son, Ishmael, equals the fruit or worship begotten by that old covenant. Paul is emphatically saying, "Cast out the law (old covenant) and all of the legalism that it produces." We know the identity of the law to which Paul refers. He has clearly identified it as the old covenant recorded in Exodus 19 and 20 at Sinai.

Paul's bold statement raises some essential questions.

1. **From where** and **to where** do we cast out the law?

Answer: We do NOT cut it out of the Bible. The law is a part of the inspired Word of God in all ages, in all dispensations, and under all covenants. We must cast the law out of the conscience as an accuser or excuser. We must take the law out of Moses's hand, but never take it out of either Scripture or out of our minds. We place it into the category of "not my covenant, but still useful." (See Bunyan's classic, "The Christian and the Law.")

2. **How** do we cast out the law?

Answer: By allowing *nothing* between our conscience and God except the blood and righteousness of Christ.

3. **What** are the spiritual consequences if, instead of casting out the law, we continue to live under the law in a wrong manner, as the Galatians were doing?

Answer: We may fall from grace. This is not necessarily the same thing as losing one's salvation. We will lose the joy of assurance as well as losing the power to overcome sin. We cannot escape a legalistic coating in our spiritual lungs if we continue to breathe the smoke from Mount Sinai.

4. **How** could the holy law of God be in any way connected with Ishmael or be used to describe the Judaism of Paul's day that had crucified the very Lord of Glory?

This last question is the easiest to answer. Hagar is a good handmaid, but she was never meant to be Abraham's wife and raise seed with him. In the same way, the law, or old covenant, functioned as a wonderful handmaid of the gospel, but it was never meant to beget either worshippers or holiness in true worshippers. The moment the law is used as a means to *either* justify or sanctify, it will produce nothing but a legalist. Paul says the law is good when used in a lawful manner (1 Tim. 1:7–10). However, any attempt to empower the law with the ability to beget or sustain holiness is doomed to failure. This is precisely what the Galatians were attempting to do. It was also the great error of the Puritans. It is the error of many in Reformed circles today. In Galatians 4:21–5:1, Paul is emphatic that the law cannot be the mother of holiness.

Paul uses the allegory to show the difference between a child of grace and a legalistic Judaizer. He carefully compares (1) the differences between Isaac and Ishmael, as the fruit of two different mothers, and (2) the difference between the Jerusalem that now is and is in bondage, and the Jerusalem which is above and is free, as the fruit of the two covenants represented by Hagar and Sarah.

There are three basic differences between Ishmael and Isaac: (1) They are different in *birth*; (2) different in their *attitudes* toward each other; and (3) different in the *inheritance* they receive.

We have already examined the essential differences between the two sons. Now let us consider how we should apply Paul's point in this allegory.

Paul is pointing out the difference between those who live by works—who try to earn the blessing of God by striving to keep the law—and those who live by faith in the promises of God and the power of the Holy Spirit. The contrast is between those who believe in, and depend upon, themselves to make God's plan work, and those who rely solely on the power of God. We must ask ourselves which category describes our lives.

Note: These differences are just as true in sanctification as they are in justification. Fleshly zeal is just as fleshly when found in a believer as it is when found in a lost person. Old Adam can no more be sanctified by the law than he could be justified by the law.

Sarah would have testified, with tearful eye, that she was motivated by the glory of God and the good of Abraham, *but all her effort was of the flesh.* It was not of God, nor did it secure the blessing. Instead, her work greatly hindered the blessing. It also caused everyone concerned grief and pain, and events quickly revealed how fleshly the whole idea was.

The Great Lesson: *"That which is born of the flesh is flesh; and that which is born of the Spirit is spirit"* (John 3:6 KJV). God must reject all that the flesh produces. Only that which is produced by the Holy Spirit is acceptable worship or work. If we do not see this as the heart of this allegory, we are sure to balk at Paul's exhortation to cast out the bondwoman (the law) and her son (all the law produced.)

Whatever is produced by flesh literally stinks in God's nostrils, and no flesh stinks as badly as orthodox flesh.

"We are the only true 'Reformed' church within a hundred miles" —Ishmael! Flesh!

"God cannot really love born-again Anglicans as much as he loves Baptists" —come on now, be honest. Ishmael! Flesh!

"Surely God loves Calvinists more than Arminians!" —Ishmael! Flesh!

The most dangerous preacher in the church is the man who preaches law and duty without constantly standing you under the cross and reminding you of the power of the Holy Spirit.

The motivation and power that produce attitudes and actions are as important as the acts themselves. Are we controlled by flesh or by Spirit, by law or by grace, by fear or by love, by duty or by promise?

I remind you again of the key truth in Galatians 5:6 KJV. *"For in Jesus Christ neither circumcision availeth any thing, nor uncircumcision; but faith which worketh by love."* Notice the three essential ingredients: faith, works, and love.

1. Faith, not feelings, must motivate our hearts and lives.

It must be a faith that works and not just talks, or else it is a dead faith that will make our hell all the worse.

2. This working faith must be motivated by love and not by fear, or else it will be the works of the Judaizer and the legalist.

3. We need all three of these things, and we need them in the *right order*.

Sarah worked hard to secure the blessing for her husband, but the fruit of her labor was rejected because it was born of unbelief and not of faith. Ishmael stands for all the worship and worshippers begotten by the fear of the law. Isaac stands for the worship and worshippers begotten by the love of Christ and the work of the Holy Spirit. Worship or works produced by the flesh always produce strife, envy, and all the ugly attitudes that grow out of a partisan spirit. It always results in division, separation, and hatred. The fruit of the Spirit unites and brings peace.

An amazing truth about the flesh: God has never commanded you to do anything you are able to do!

I said it right. Let me say it again. *God has never commanded you to do anything you are able to do!*

The proof is John 15:5 KJV. *"I am the vine, ye are the branches: He that abideth in me, and I in him, the same bringeth forth much fruit: for **without me ye can do nothing.**"* I did not say, "It could not be done." I did say that flesh cannot do it. Notice that Jesus said "WITHOUT ME."

That is the awful truth of *total depravity.* If flesh produces it, then it stinks in God's sight.

Philippians 4:13 is the other side of the coin. *"I can do all things through Christ which strengtheneth me."* Do not ever preach John 15:5 without also preaching Philippians 4:13.

John 6:44, 45 sets forth both sides of this truth. We must never proclaim one side without the other.

(1) *"No man **can** come to me, **except** the Father which hath sent me draw him: and I will raise him up at the last day"* (John 6:44 KJV). That is universal and total depravity or inability. *"No man can ...except the Father...."*

(2) *"It is written in the prophets, And they shall be all **taught of God**. Every man therefore that **hath heard,** and hath **learned** of the Father, **cometh unto me"*** (John 6:45 KJV). That is effectual calling. There is a drawing of the Father that always produces a new birth and a conversion experience. On the one hand, you have *"no man can—unless,"* and the other hand you have *"every man will—when."*

The worst sin we commit against lost people is telling them to look to their own works and willpower to find the obedience of faith for salvation. The worst sin we commit against believers is telling them to look to the law for the help and strength they need to please God.

I realize that it is impossible for some theologians to look at what we have said with any objectivity. They are committed to a view of the so-called "unchanging moral law of God" and simply cannot allow Paul to mean what he says when he says, "Cast out the law" (Hagar, the bondwoman). I agree it is a radical statement that we would not even dare think, let alone state out loud, if Paul himself had not stated it so clearly.

John Bunyan, in a two-page article that he wrote just before he died, gave me more help in understanding law and grace than all other writers put together. Here are the concluding two points of his summary.

> Wherefore whenever thou who believest Jesus, dost hear the law in its thundering and lightning fits, as if it would burn up heaven and earth; then say thou I am freed from this law, these thunderings have nothing to do with my soul; nay even this law, while it thus thunders and roareth, it doth both allow and approve of my righteousness. I know that Hagar would sometimes be domineering and high, even in Sarah's house and against her; but this she is not to be suffered to do, nay though Sarah herself be barren; wherefore serve IT [the law] also as Sarah served her, and expel her out from thy house.[100]

This is classic Bunyan. His reference to Sarah and Hagar is from Galatians 4:30. Hagar represents the law, and just as Sarah expelled Hagar (the law) from her house, so Christians must expel the law from their consciences. Christians must do this in spite of the fact that they may, at the moment, have little or no fruits or evidences. They may be as barren as Sarah was, but they must still hold on to the promise of God alone, and not trust fruits and evidences. If anyone questions Bunyan's use of Sarah and Hagar, they may read his own clear explanation.

> My meaning is, **[Bunyan does not want you miss his point]** when this law with its thundering threatenings doth attempt to lay hold on thy conscience, shut it out with a promise of grace; cry, the inn is took up already, the Lord Jesus is here entertained, and there is no room for the law. **[Bunyan is emphatic that it is impossible for the law and the Lord Jesus to dwell in the same conscience at the same time. Moses and Christ**

---

[100] *Of the Law and a Christian, Works of Bunyan*, 2:388.

cannot be roommates in the same heart. It is in the area of law and conscience that covenant theology and Reformed Covenantal Baptists will not hear Bunyan. Their theology openly **opposes Bunyan at this point.**] Indeed if it will be content with being my informer, **[Teach my mind]** and so lovingly leave off to judge me **[Stay out of my conscience];** I will be content, it shall be in my sight, **[It will help me to see and understand the will of my Father]** I will also delight therein; but otherwise, I being now made upright without it, and that too with that righteousness, which this law speaks well of and approveth; I may not, will not, cannot, dare not make it my savior and judge **[That is referring to justification]**, nor suffer it to set up its government in my conscience **[That is referring to sanctification];** for by so doing I fall from grace, and Christ Jesus doth profit me nothing. Gal. 5:1–5.[101]

Bunyan's comments, like Paul's statements in Galatians 4:21–5:1 could not be clearer. If we misunderstand them, we do so willfully. The law covenant made at Sinai, with the Ten Commandments being the primary terms, must not be allowed into the Christian's conscience. I love Bunyan's exhortation about the inn being taken up by our Lord.

My meaning is, when this law with its thundering threatenings doth attempt to lay hold on thy conscience, shut it out with a promise of grace; cry, the inn is took up already, the Lord Jesus is here entertained, and there is no room for the law.

When Paul refers to the Jerusalem that now is, he means the Judaism that crucified Christ. It is the old covenant of law, without faith in the full sufficiency of Christ. Jerusalem above is the church, or body of Christ, whose children are begotten into freedom and liberty.

---

[101] Ibid.

Hagar, Horeb, Earthly Salem,
Works of flesh will not avail them.
Sarah, Zion, Heavenly Salem,
Christ their Lord will never fail them.

I would have loved to have heard Paul say, "Stand fast in the liberty of the gospel!" My dear reader, you will never engage in a more vital struggle than in protecting that liberty.

CHAPTER TWENTY-ONE

GALATIANS 4:19–31

In the preceding chapter, we examined Paul's allegorical interpretation of Hagar's expulsion from Abraham's household. In this chapter, I want to (1) show why Paul's concern for the Galatians resulted in his advocating the need to "cast out the law" (Hagar), and (2) look at three specific differences between Ishmael and Isaac. Paul sets his allegory in the section of the letter that addresses the Galatians' misunderstanding of what the law really says. This section follows Paul's explanation of slavery, the era of minority, and the era of adoption to adult sonship. He has pointed out that the Mosaic law, which seemed so attractive to the Galatians, belonged to the period of minority. The era of full sonship has come, and with it, a focus on Christ and his completed work: an impossible focus during the time of the Mosaic law.

Paul voices his great concern about the Galatians in verses 19 and 20 of chapter 4.

> *My little children, of whom I travail in birth again until Christ be formed in you, I desire to be present with you now, and to change my voice; for I stand in doubt of you.* (KJV)

His major concern was the obvious absence of Christ in their life. This is always the results when the emphasis on law becomes greater than the emphasis on grace. By saying, "I stand in doubt of you" (v. 20), Paul is literally questioning if the Galatians are truly saved. That shows the importance of our subject! The Galatians were forsaking both Paul and the gospel of grace that he preached and instead were following the Judaizers' false gospel of law-keeping. Paul is amazed not only that they were so carelessly and stupidly trading grace for law, but also that they were doing it so quickly. This rash acceptance of the Judaizers' message meant that the Galatians were not just a bit off theologically, but were adopting heresy of the deepest dye.

> *I am astonished that you are so quickly deserting the one who called you by the grace of Christ and are turning to a different gospel* —(Gal. 1:6 NIV)

Paul had hardly left Galatia before the church was ready to listen to the Judaizers.

Phillips paraphrases Galatians 3:1 as "You dear idiots. I think someone has cast a spell on you." Paul is perplexed. How can people who have believed that Jesus was indeed the promised Messiah turn to a system grounded in *waiting* for the Messiah? The Galatians were Gentiles who had been excluded from the Mosaic covenant. They had received the Spirit, as promised in the Old Testament Scriptures, because they believed what Paul had told them about the crucifixion of the Messiah, and not because they had been keeping the law. Paul's point is that since they had not needed to keep the law to benefit initially from what the Old Testament promised, neither would they need it subsequently.

Paul could well feel the same perplexity about some congregations in our day. In over fifty years of ministry, I have seen congregation after congregation forsake the glory of the free grace of God and follow a work-monger into bondage and despair. It is always done in the name of biblical holiness, but too often biblical holiness is confused with proving that I am more holy than you are. When this happens, strong corrective measures are needed. Paul's tone changes in Galatians 5:1–4, from perplexity to admonishment. This section contains strong words of rebuke that apply to anyone who forsakes Christ for Moses.

It is for freedom that Christ has set us free. Stand firm, then, and do not let yourselves be burdened again by a yoke of slavery. Behold, I Paul say unto you, that if ye be circumcised, Christ shall profit you nothing. For I testify again to every man that is circumcised, that he is a debtor to do the whole law. Christ is become of no effect unto you, whosoever of you are justified by the law; ye are fallen from grace. (my translation).

In verse 2, Paul says, *"Christ will profit you nothing."* Paul is addressing professing Christians. Paul aims verse 4, *"Christ is become of no effect"* and *"you are fallen from grace"* at people who profess to be children of God. Paul is talking to baptized church members like you and me.

The Judaizers did not, in any way, deny that a person must believe in Jesus as the Messiah in order to be saved. Their heresy was *adding law-keeping* to faith in Christ as the grounds of being a "true child of Abraham." "You must believe in Christ AND be circumcised AND keep the law." This position is both logically and theologically incoherent. Furthermore, it completely misses the truth of justification by faith alone in Christ alone. John Stott has written, **"To supplement Christ in any way is to supplant Christ altogether."**

Let me illustrate this point with a personal experience from thirty-odd years ago. I was the Bible teacher at a weekend retreat with thirty-one young people from four different Reformed Baptist churches. The first night, I gave them a sheet of paper with twenty-five questions, which they returned after writing the answers. Only four of the questions were of real interest to me. The rest were a smokescreen. One of the important questions was, "Do you believe it is possible to be sure you are going to heaven when you die?" All thirty-one answered yes. I then asked if they were individually sure they were going to heaven. Thirty of the thirty-one were sure. The next question was, "Do you believe that God is sure you are forgiven and coming to heaven?" All of the thirty who were sure they were going to heaven said no. None of them believed that God thought they were coming to heaven. As I read the papers after the meeting, I was amazed! How can a person believe that she or he is truly saved, but at the same time, also be convinced that God is not sure that she or he is saved? I found the answer when I came to the last significant question, "What must a person do to be sure she or he is going to heaven?" **Every answer, without exception, used the word** *and.* I was teaching in twentieth-century Galatia. I spent the rest of the weekend teaching about justification by faith.

Here are some sample answers the young people gave:

- You must trust Christ as Lord and Savior and keep the Ten Commandments.
- You must be born again and live a holy life.
- You must repent and believe in Christ and not sin.

All of the answers contained good things to do, but they missed the point by making those things the grounds of acceptance and assurance. The Galatian Judaizers were certainly urging good things. Law-keeping is surely a good thing, but it is not a means to become justified. I spoke to one of the pastors of the churches represented and he stated, very firmly, "I do not believe or preach that." I replied, just as firmly, "That is what your young people are hearing."

Paul tells his readers what he views as essential to one's salvation by first stating what is not essential.

> For in Jesus Christ neither circumcision availeth anything, nor uncircumcision; but faith which worketh by love. (Gal 5:6 KJV)

The text has four main points. First, neither keeping the law nor not keeping the law has any relevance to entering "into Christ." Second, faith alone, as opposed to works, is all that is essential to justification. Third, faith is more than just saying something; that is, Paul's understanding of faith disqualifies what we might term *dead faith*. It must be a living faith that "works." And fourth, true saving faith must be more than simply active and working, it must work, meaning that in order to be effective ("working"), faith must be motivated by love and not by the flesh. These last three things must all be present and in the order given. (1) There must be faith as opposed to works. (2) It must a faith that produces works as opposed to a dead faith. (3) The motivation of the working faith must be grace and love as opposed to law and works. I repeat, we must have all of these three things, and they must be in the *right order*.

Faith with no works is vain and futile and will cost you your soul. Faith with works produced by law and fear is just as vain and futile and will produce not the righteousness of God, but self-righteousness. An obedient faith that works by love is the evidence of the gospel of grace. Someone has said, "Faith without works is like a tree without fruit, and works without faith is like a tree without roots."

Paul was in doubt of the people he addresses because their lives did not manifest the faith he described in

Galatians 5:6. They exhibited great zeal in many works, but the wrong theology defined the work, and thus the works were evidence of the flesh and not of the Spirit. Paul, if he could have visited the Galatians, would have seen them earnestly striving to keep the law, but for the wrong reason. He *would not have seen* Christ and the fruit of the Spirit. He would have seen the image of Moses, but not "Christ formed in them."

By comparing 4:19 with 4:21, we see the real cause of Paul's perplexity and doubt. Paul correctly assumes that it is impossible for anyone who has tasted the truth and power of grace and really understood the true message of the law to want to place himself under its authority.

> *My little children, of whom I travail in birth again until Christ be formed in you (4:19). Tell me, ye that desire to be under the law, do ye not hear the law?* (4:21 KJV)

Paul was not satisfied with any result that fell short of lives truly transformed by the power of grace. He was not interested in zealots for the law who exhibited little or no evidence of true love to Christ, manifested in the fruit of the Spirit.

The Galatians lacked the fragrance of Christ and the fruit of the spirit. They were placing themselves under the law and thereby trading grace for law, faith for works. They were denying the gospel of sovereign grace for an unholy mixture of law and grace. There may have been plenty of fruit of the flesh, but no fruit of the spirit; lots of Moses and little of Christ; lots of law and duty, but no love and joyous assurance. We can test both our own lives and the results of a preacher's sermon by applying verse 19: Is the fragrance of Christ growing more and more evident? Paul laments the lack of evidence in the lives of the Galatian congregation. This short section of Paul's letter reveals a lot about both legalism and the Galatians.

First, these people had lost both their joy of salvation and their love of the man who had brought them the message of that salvation.

> *Even though my illness was a trial to you, you did not treat me with contempt or scorn. Instead, you welcomed me as if I were an angel of God, as if I were Christ Jesus himself. What has happened to all your joy? I can testify that, if you could have done so, you would have torn out your eyes and given them to me. Have I now become your enemy by telling you the truth?* (4:14–16 NIV)

This happened when they transferred their affection for Paul and the gospel of grace to the Judaizers and their gospel of works, which is no gospel at all (1:6, 7).

Second, by turning from grace to law they were biting and devouring each other (5:15). This biting and devouring took the form of judging and condemning each other. Whenever we, individually or as a church, become law or rule-centered, we soon begin to judge each other's holiness by outward conformity to our peculiar list of dos and don'ts. The fruit of the Spirit becomes secondary, if considered at all, in any setting of legalism. This leads to pride and boasting based on outward performance alone.

Third, the camp controlled by Judaizers is notable for its lack of joy, peace, and love. There is an emphasis on law, a preoccupation with self-examination, and little looking to Christ alone.

Fourth, we can summarize the Galatians as professing heirs of grace who were living like slaves of the law.

The immediate context, 4:21, shows that these people were adopting and following the law in such a way as to corrupt the gospel. Regardless of how we understand the relationship of law and grace, we can be positive that the Galatians were wrong in their understanding! Paul must have felt that these people were in grave danger, or he would never have been so vehement in condemning them. He uses harsh words:

> Behold, I Paul say unto you, that if ye be circumcised, Christ shall **profit you nothing**...Christ is become of **no effect unto you**...ye are **fallen from grace**. (Gal 5:2, 4 KJV, emphasis added)

The potential danger for professing Christians of being cut off from Christ and falling from grace should make us earnestly seek to know where the Galatians went wrong so we can avoid the same mistake. They were about to fall from grace by going under the law. What does Paul mean when he uses the phrase *under the law*? Here are some of the specific questions that we must ask and answer:

1. Precisely what law is Paul talking about? The word *law* has a variety of meanings.

2. What does it mean to be *under* that law in such a way that it is a denial of Christ and the gospel?

3. Why is being under law in this wrong way antithetical to the *under grace* gospel that Paul taught?

4. Why is this way of being *under the law* dangerous to a professing Christian's spiritual well-being?

5. How could Paul's own converts so quickly buy into such wrong theology and practice?

6. Why is a works mentality so appealing to sinners and saints alike?

7. Who are the present-day counterparts to the Galatian Judaizers, and how does a child of God recognize them and their message and so avoid the consequences of following them (enslavement to the law)?

Can anything be more important than correctly answering these questions? We answered the first three questions at length in Chapter Nineteen of this study. There, we established two working definitions of law: (1) The entire Old Testament Scripture—the thirty-nine books written before Christ came; and (2) the law covenant made with Israel at Sinai. We concluded that Paul's use of *under law* in Galatians is best understood when we use the second definition—the law as a covenant—and that as such, it is antithetical to *under grace* as a covenant. A person cannot be under both covenants at the same time. Their foundations, terms, and aims are different. The law covenant has no ability to overcome sin; it can only identify and condemn sin. We use the law wrongly when we try to make it do a job God never designed it to do—produce holiness in either a saint or a sinner. Before we go on to answer the last four questions listed above, let me make a few observations.

First, it is possible for sincere church leaders to advocate a wrong use of the law. If this were not the case, there would be no book of Galatians. The fact that the Holy Spirit put Paul's denunciation of the Galatians' folly into the canon of Scripture means that believers in all ages are in danger of being seduced by a corruption of the gospel that hides behind a zealous, but mistaken, use of God's law.

Second, in and of itself, no brand of theology, nor any great teacher, can keep believers free from bondage to the law. The Galatians were converts of the great Apostle himself and had been taught the truth of sovereign grace under his personal ministry. These people would have been among the most zealous and sincere in "truly Reformed" circles if those terms had been used in that day.

Third, the present law/grace controversy in our day evokes the identical charges and defenses used in that day. Books, conferences, sermons, etc., that address this issue make it seem as though we are living in Galatia presently. We see biting, devouring, and other symptoms of a critical spirit. Some sincere believers are being charged with being law-hating antinomians, simply because they reject covenant theology's view of the law and the Sabbath. Others are being called legalists, only because they sincerely believe the Sabbath is a moral law and not a ceremonial law. History is repeating itself in our generation. Look carefully at Paul's question: *"Do you really hear what the law says?"* He clearly implies that if you really hear the law's message, you will never want to go under it!

When you really hear the law, you will see how badly you need the gospel. When you hear the true gospel, you will see the law perfectly fulfilled and done away forever. You will see every claim the law justly makes fully supplied in the gospel. You will sing, *"Free from the law, oh, happy condition. Jesus has died and there is remission. Bruised by the fall and cursed by the law, grace has redeemed us once and for all."*

Stand at the empty tomb, and you will see the law forever perfectly satisfied. Hear me, now! You will also see the law dismissed and done away because its necessary work has been accomplished. As Newton wrote, you will hear "the law's loud thunder" at Calvary, but you will also hear that *thunder forever hushed at the empty tomb*. This is Paul's point in this passage.

Let me now answer the last four questions listed above:

1. Why is this wrong way of being under the law dangerous to a professing Christian's spiritual well-being?

2. How could Paul's own converts so quickly buy into such wrong theology and practice?

3. Why is a works mentality so appealing to sinners and saints alike?

4. Who are the present-day counterparts to the Galatian Judaizers, and how does a child of God recognize them and their message and so avoid the consequences of following them (into an enslavement to the law)?

Putting oneself under the law covenant is dangerous for a professing Christian because it hampers him from fulfilling the two greatest commandments that Christ identified: loving God with all of one's being and loving one's neighbor as oneself. A Christian who puts himself under the law dethrones Christ as the supreme authority in the conscience. This demeans Christ and his glory. Additionally, a conscience that is satisfied according to the law runs the danger of producing complacency, self-righteousness, and a critical spirit toward others who do not adhere to the same set of rules. A conscience that feels the just condemnation of the law runs the risk of producing spiritual despondency, the sinking conviction that "I can never do what God demands of me, so why try?"

The answers to questions two, three, and four go together. Paul's converts in Galatia may have embraced the Judaizers' brand of Christianity because Judaism was tolerated within the Roman Empire.[102] It had the stature of long-standing tradition. If the Judaizers presented their teaching as that which truly represented the traditions of Judaism, and Paul's teaching as an aberrant version of Judaism, the Galatians might well have been attracted by the respectability of the former. Paul's defense of his teaching by way of an appeal to Abraham provides some evidence for this reconstruction. A second factor to consider in the quickness of the Galatians' acceptance of the Judaizers' message lies in the appeal of a works mentality. The idea that I can do something for my spiritual status, and am not dependant upon something or someone outside me, is attractive because it puts me in control of my spiritual well-being. The appeal and the danger of legalism are the same and lie precisely in this aspect of ability. I **can** improve my spiritual estate; therefore, I do not need Christ. We are not usually as blunt as this; we often do not question why we are drawn to "works"; but the independence that lies at the heart of legalism is what attracts us. We can recognize present-day Judaizers and avoid them by analyzing their

---

[102] Roman officials regarded Judaism as one cultural 'club' among many others. In this way, Judaism did not threaten the state-sanctioned worship of the Roman pantheon of gods. Christianity, on the other hand, by distancing itself from traditional Judaism, posed a threat to the established order. One of the Roman criticisms of the Jewish-Christians was that they had broken with their ancestral traditions.

message through this lens of independence/dependence. Any teaching that replaces complete dependence upon Christ for every aspect of our standing before God (justification, sanctification, and glorification) is some form of Judaizing.

The second thing I want to cover is the difference between Isaac and Ishmael. In our last chapter, we saw that these two boys represented the fruit of the two major covenants in Scripture. Paul uses their differences to show the difference between a child born of the flesh and a child born of the free grace of God. We will look at three differences.

ONE: The two boys are different in their BIRTHS (Gal. 4:22, 23). Look first at Ishmael: *He was the product of the power of natural procreation.* Sarah and Abraham needed no special grace from God to produce Ishmael. They needed no special power from God. They accomplished the whole thing all by themselves. Ishmael was produced by free will and natural desire of the flesh. Sarah and Abraham conceived the idea; they liked their idea; and they had the will to carry out their idea, which they did. They produced an Ishmael all by their own power with no help needed from God.

I repeat what I said before: Sarah sincerely wanted Abraham to receive the promised blessing. She obviously loved him very much to suggest what she did, but the entire scheme was of the flesh. The legalist's hope of obeying the law to secure God's blessing is just as useless and just as fleshly as Sarah's scheme.

Ishmael stands for all of the works of the flesh, produced apart from the power of the Spirit. It includes the fleshly pride that, like the Judaizers, boasts about its holy zeal for the glory of God while mocking the love and grace of God that alone can produce true zeal. In reality, this zeal is pride under a thin veneer of pious Pharisaism.

Put another way, as Paul does, Ishmael stands for all of the fruit produced by a wrong use of the law, or the old covenant.

Let us now look at Isaac. *Isaac was born of more than just natural procreation.* He was a miracle child born to two people who were both physically unable to have children. Isaac was born as a result of Abraham and Sarah acting in faith in the power of God. Isaac was a child of promise and faith. This faith was not blind but had as its object a specific and clear promise from God. Isaac was born out of reliance on God's power to fulfill his oath and specific covenant promise.

Romans 4:20–22 is the best definition of faith that I know of in all of Scripture.

> He staggered not at the promise of God through unbelief; but was strong in faith, giving glory to God; And being fully persuaded that, what he had promised, he was able also to perform. And therefore it was imputed to him for righteousness. (KJV)

Abraham's body was as good as dead. Sarah was past the age of child bearing. Abraham and Sarah looked past all the impossibilities to the promise and power of God, and a miracle child was conceived in a womb long dead—beyond the natural ability to conceive a child.

Isaac represents the spirit-born child of sovereign grace (Gal 4:28), and the worship that is born of the Spirit by God's sovereign power, and is therefore acceptable to God.

Isaac is the religion, not of Moses, works, and the law; but the religion of Christ, grace, and faith. Do you see what

Paul is saying? He is saying that the basic difference between Ishmael and Isaac's births is the difference between *true and false worship and worshippers.* Isaac is a child of sovereign grace and sovereign power, and Ishmael is a child of free will and human power. Isaac is the worship that is begotten by the power of grace (and grace *has* a power) and the love of Christ, and Ishmael is the worship that is begotten by the law and the works of the flesh.

Isaac stands for all of those who wait upon God's promise and power, and Ishmael stands for all of those who depend on themselves to make God's plan work (vv. 25, 26).

TWO: The two boys are different in their NATURES. Remember, the nature of the mother determines the nature of the children she begets, and the nature of a covenant determines the nature of the fruit or worship that it begets. Hagar can only produce a legalist slave child, and a legalist always hates grace. Ishmael hated Isaac because he, Ishmael, knew Isaac was going to receive the inheritance. This is a replay of Cain's hatred for Abel. A legalist cannot stand really happy people. Legalists put forth every effort to try to keep the law in order to quiet their conscience. They fail, because nothing but the blood of Christ sprinkled on the conscience by the Holy Spirit can calm the conscience (Hebrews 9 & 10). The harder the legalist works, the more miserable they become. That is why a legalist resents a joyous child of God. The legalist looks at a happy Christian and says, "Look at that airhead. He is as happy as a lark, but he has no theological understanding. He probably never read a single Reformed book. What he needs is to spend some quality time studying the Ten Commandments."

If you question what I am saying, watch how a person with legalistic tendencies operates. The first person a legalist tries to instruct in the Lord "more fully" is the new convert who rejoices in the simple gospel. The legalist will not share great truths about sovereign grace simply because he cannot. The legalist has never experienced those great truths in his own soul. Instead, the legalist will share his doubts, fears, and struggles, and will earnestly warn the new convert about false assurance. A legalist will destroy a congregation if he is allowed free reign. Ishmaels and Isaacs cannot dwell in the same inn. Ishmaels will always hate and seek to destroy the freedom of Isaacs. One of them must be cast out.

THREE: The two boys are different in their INHERITANCES. One inherits the blessing and the other must be cast out, empty-handed. The law and works, no matter how sincere and diligently performed, will not inherit the blessing of justification and assurance. God's grace is given sovereignly to them "that worketh not," but to those "who believeth on him that justifies the ungodly" (Rom. 4:4, 5). The true child of Abraham not only has an inheritance; he has a gospel of free and sovereign grace to share with poor sinners. The poor legalist has only doubts and fears to share. Legalists confuse being pious with true piety. They claim to love the knowledge of the truth, but their knowledge is one that "puffs up" instead of one that leads to humility and assurance.

Ishmael must be cast out of your personal conscience, cast out of the local assembly, and cast out of your theology. Ishmael and Isaac, like Moses and Christ, cannot dwell in the same inn.

CHAPTER TWENTY-TWO

GALATIANS 5:1

We have reached Galatians 5:1, a pivotal verse in Paul's argument about the relationship of the law to the Christian. Here he transitions from illustration to explicit statement.

> *Stand fast, therefore, in the liberty wherewith Christ hath made us free, and be not entangled again with the yoke of bondage* (Gal. 5:1 KJV).

The word *therefore* indicates that this is an exhortation based on the theology implicit in his metaphor and analogy in 4:21–31. Paul had used an allegorical interpretation of Hagar and Ishmael's being cast out of Abraham's house to insist that Christians must cast out the law—just as Hagar was cast out. Most interpreters see 5:1 as the conclusion of chapter four. All agree that the yoke of bondage of which Paul speaks is some law whose rule and reign has ceased under the new covenant. It is clear that we are commanded to "cast out the bond woman and her son." It is just as clear that Hagar represents the law, and Hagar's son, Ishmael, represents all that the law produces—the fruit of worship produced by the law. That truth is clear in the text. However, not all agree on the identity of the law to which Paul refers and what it means to cast out that law. All do agree that this law is a "yoke of bondage" from which Christians are liberated. This law is contrary to the freedom of the gospel of sovereign grace. Paul is adamant on this point. The law of which Paul speaks is antithetical to the gospel, which Paul had preached and the Galatians had confessed they believed. Therefore, it is vital that we precisely identify the law Paul commands us to "cast out."

Freedom is a major theme in the gospel. During his time on earth, our Lord spoke clearly about the introduction of a freedom or liberty and the end of bondage. Our Lord preached that freedom was one of the certain results of believing the gospel message.

> *And ye shall know the truth, and the truth shall make you **free**.*
>
> *They answered him, We be Abraham's seed, and were never in **bondage** to any man: how sayest thou, Ye shall be made **free**?*
>
> *Jesus answered them, Verily, verily, I say unto you, Whosoever committeth sin is the servant of sin.*
>
> *And the servant abideth not in the house forever: but the Son abideth ever.*
>
> *If the Son therefore shall make you **free**, ye shall be **free indeed**.* (John 8:32–36 KJV)

The truth that sets people free is the gospel of sovereign grace. The bondage from which it frees us is the bondage to which Paul refers in Galatians 5:1 and Peter in Acts 15:10. The prophet Isaiah foretold the truth that the gospel would *"proclaim liberty to the captives, and the opening of the prison to those who are bound"* (Isa. 61:1b). When our Lord came and announced that the kingdom had come, he quoted this text and applied it to himself and his ministry (Luke 4:16–21). He was the great liberator. The mark of his kingdom rule is freedom. John 8:35 may well be a reference to the casting out of Ishmael and Isaac.

Galatians 5:1 functions as a transitional text. It links the truth stated and defended in chapters 1 through 4 with the practical application to the problem in the Galatian church. It sets forth the heart of Paul's theology of law and grace as well as his answer to the Galatians' defection from the truth of sovereign grace. This is Paul's usual method of teaching. He begins with theology and then applies the truth he has established to life.

Here is a paraphrase of the verse: The text contains two sentences: The first is a statement, *"Christ set us free to be free indeed,"* and the second is a command, *"Stand fast and protect the purchased liberty. Don't trade your liberty for bondage to the law."*

First, we must understand what Paul means by *freedom* and by *bondage*. This understanding will color our understanding of the entire book of Galatians. One system of theology reads Paul as teaching that our gospel freedom is freedom from the so-called ceremonial law. Others believe that Paul is talking about the entire Mosaic law viewed as the old covenant. I share the latter view.

The freedom to which Paul refers involves, among other things, freedom of conscience that enables us to *"come boldly to the throne of grace"* by the *"new and living way"* opened up by the blood of Christ (See Hebrews 4:14–16; 10:19–22; Eph. 2:13–19). This freedom is peculiar to new covenant believers. John Stott has caught the truth of the text. The emphasis in **bolding** is mine.

The best manuscripts divide verse 1 into two sentences, so that they are not a single command (as in the RSV) 'to stand...in the liberty wherewith Christ has made us free,' but first an assertion *(for freedom Christ has set us free)*, followed by a command based upon it *(stand fast therefore, and do not submit again to a yoke of slavery)*. John Stott has some excellent comments.

    a. The assertion

As the New English Bible puts it, 'Christ set us free, to be free men'. Our former state is portrayed as a slavery, Jesus Christ as a liberator, conversion as an act of emancipation and the Christian life as a life of freedom. This freedom, as the whole Epistle and this context make plain, is not primarily a freedom from **sin, but rather from the law.** What Christ has done in liberating us, according to Paul's emphasis here, is not so much to set **our *will* free from the bondage of sin as to set our *conscience* free from the guilt of sin.** The Christian freedom he describes is **freedom of conscience, freedom from the tyranny of the law,** the dreadful struggle to keep the law, with a view to winning the favor of God. It is the freedom of acceptance with God and of access to God through Christ.

b. The command

Since 'Christ has set us free' and that 'for freedom', we must 'stand fast' in it and not 'submit again to a yoke of slavery'. In other words, we are to enjoy the glorious **freedom of conscience** which Christ has brought us by His forgiveness. We must not lapse into the idea that we have to win our acceptance with God by our own obedience. The picture seems to be of an ox bowed down by a heavy yoke. Once it has been freed from this crushing yoke, it is able to stand erect again (*cf.* Lv. 26:13).

It is just so in the Christian life. At one time we were under the yoke of the law, burdened by its demands which we could not meet and by its fearful condemnation because of our disobedience. But Christ met the demands of the law for us. He died for our disobedience and thus bore our condemnation in our place. He has 'redeemed us from the curse of the law, having become a curse for us' (3:13). And now He has struck the yoke from our shoulder and set us free to stand upright. How then can we dream of putting ourselves under the law again and submitting to its cruel yoke?

This, then, is the theme of these verses. Christianity is freedom not bondage. Christ has set us free; so we must stand firm in our freedom.[103]

It is certainly true that Christ has set us free in respect to sin, in respect to food and clothing laws, and in respect to men by refusing to allow them to rule our conscience instead of Scripture. However, Stott is correct in stating that the freedom mentioned in Galatians 5:1 is not "a freedom from sin"—setting our will free from bondage to sin—but "setting our **conscience** free from the **guilt** of sin." Paul is exulting in the joy and assurance of a *complete* salvation. The idea of *deliverance* is surely one of the central themes in Scripture. In Romans 6:14–18, we are delivered from both the power of sin to control us as well the authority of the law to condemn us. In Hebrews 10:22 and Eph. 2:14, 15, we are delivered from an accusing conscience, and in Hebrews 2:14 we are delivered from the power of Satan and the fear of death.

The new covenant truth of a conscience set free from the law, resulting in an actual and a perceived peace with God, is the source of spiritual power that energizes new covenant believers. One aspect of gospel freedom is the result of understanding and believing grace—the "worketh not—but believeth" theology of Romans 4:5. Bunyan described this freedom allegorically by the release of the heavy pack on Pilgrim's back at the sight of the cross.

Now I saw in my dream, that the highway up which *Christian* was to go, was fenced on either side with a wall, and that wall was called *Salvation*. Isaiah 26:1. Up this way,

---

[103] Stott, *One Way*, 132, 33, emphasis mine.

therefore, did burdened *Christian* run, but not without great difficulty, because of the load on his back.

He ran thus till he came at a place somewhat ascending, and upon that place stood a *Cross,* and a little below, in the bottom, a sepulcher. So I saw in my dream, that just as *Christian* came up to the *Cross,* his Burden loosed from off his shoulders, and fell from off his back, and began to tumble, and so continued to do till it came to the mouth of the Sepulcher, where it fell in, and I saw it no more.

Then was *Christian* glad and lightsome, and said with a merry heart, "He hath given me Rest by his Sorrow, and Life by his Death." Then he stood still a while, to look and wonder; for it was very surprizing to him that the sight of the Cross should thus ease him of his Burden. He looked, therefore, and looked again, even till the springs that were in his head sent the waters down his cheeks. (Zech. 12:10). Now as he stood looking and weeping, behold, three Shining Ones came to him, and saluted him with, "Peace be to thee;" so the first said to him, "Thy sins be forgiven". (Mark 2:5); the second stripped him of his rags, and cloathed him with Change of Raiment, (Zech. 3:4); the third also set a Mark on his forehead, (Eph. 1:13), and gave him a Roll with a Seal upon it, which he bid him look on as he ran, and that he should give it in at the Celestial Gate: so they went their way. Then Christian gave three leaps for joy, and went on singing:

"Thus far did I come laden with my Sin,
Nor could aught ease the grief that I was in,
Till I came hither. What a place is this!
Must here be the beginning of my bliss?

Must here the Burden fall from off my back?
Must here the strings that bound it to me crack?

Blest Cross! Blest Sepulcher! blest rather be
The Man that there was put to shame for me!"[104]

We must speak not only of the negative perspective of the blessing of the gospel, that is, deliverance from various aspects of bondage, but we must also emphasize the positive experience of glorious gospel freedom—access into the Most Holy Place. It is true that the full experience of our freedom has just begun in this life and will not be complete until our Lord returns (Rom. 7:24–8:1), but the foretaste is so sweet we cannot help but long for that day of final deliverance from every vestige of the old creation. This is the religion of faith and hope. This is not a "do" religion but a "done" religion. Our blessed Lord has done for us what we could not do for ourselves. As the songwriter G. McSpadden said, "I owed a debt I could not pay; he paid a debt he did not owe."

Paul develops this theme of gospel freedom further by speaking of "walking in the freedom of the Spirit." We will cover that aspect when we come to Galatians 5:25. Here, in 5:1, his main concern is to point his readers to the "free" service to God, without fear or constraint, which is the birthright of every new covenant believer. We come to God as our father and friend, not as our judge. We experience valid, legitimate freedom to feel God's love and to confidently enter his presence because of the rent veil. William Hendriksen explains that gospel freedom is fuller than other kinds of freedom:

> Such true freedom is therefore always a freedom *plus*. When an accused man is declared not guilty, he is free. Likewise when a slave is emancipated, he is free. But the judge or

---

[104] John Bunyan, *The Pilgrim's Progress* (Uhrichsville, OH: Barbour and Co., Inc, 1985) 35, 36

emancipator does not adopt the acquitted individual as his son. But when the Son makes one free, he is free indeed (John 8:36). He then rejoices in the glorious liberty of sonship, with all this implies as to "access, right to inheritance, etc."[105]

We lose the assurance of the peace with God expressed in Romans 5:1 when we cease to view Christ alone as the only valid object of our faith. If we seek justification by standing any place except under the cross, we can expect nothing but bondage to result. We lose that bold access into the Most Holy Place when we try to ground that privilege in anything but the blood and righteousness of Christ. To gain access into God's presence at the throne of grace, we need to go through a "security check" to prove we are righteous and perfectly acceptable to a holy God. The only identification card that makes us acceptable and gets us past the security check is signed with the blood of Christ. Christ made all believers free to serve as sons by being made a curse for the believers who had been under the law, effectively removing the law that kept both Jews and Gentiles out of the Most Holy Place (Gal 3:13). Just as it was his blood that cleansed us and made us acceptable to the Father (Heb. 10:19), that atoning work continues to keep us acceptable despite our failures. In addition to losing peace with God when we forfeit the liberty of conscience Christ purchased for us, we also lose the power to overcome sin. Robert Haldane, in his excellent commentary on Romans, includes an apt quotation from William Romaine. Romaine provides a priceless, but little understood, piece of truth.

---

[105] William Hendriksen, *Galatians*, New Testament Commentary (Grand Rapids, MI: Baker Book House, 1968) p 192

The law has now no more right to condemn thee, a believer, than it has to condemn him. Justice is bound to deal with thee, as it has with thy risen and ascended Saviour. If thou dost not thus see thy complete mortification in him, sin will reign in thee. No sin can be crucified either in heart or life, unless it be first pardoned in conscience; because there will be want of faith to receive the strength of Jesus, by whom alone it can be crucified. **If it be not mortified in its guilt it cannot be subdued in its power.**

Many Reformed teachers, especially among Reformed Baptists, when addressing the subject of sanctification, not only ignore the truth pointed out by Romaine, they seek to reinforce the exact opposite. They seek to produce a quiet conscience by teaching obedience to the law. In their theology, the Mosaic Law is the greatest aid to sanctification. A quiet conscience follows obedience to the law. Romaine, following Paul, insists the exact opposite is true. There can be neither a true motive nor an energizing power to "be holy as he is holy" until the conscience is set free by totally accepting the satisfaction to the law Christ rendered in our place—as our substitute. Hear again what Romaine says about sin: **If it [sin] be not mortified in its guilt it cannot be subdued in its power.**

There are at least three serious mistakes that interpreters of Galatians 5:1 make concerning the bondage from which a Christian is set free. Let me list all three, with brief objections, and then examine them one at a time.

1. A Christian is free from any and all law. This interpretation leads to antinomianism. Paul will deal with this perversion in Galatians 5:13, 14. We will cover this when we reach those verses. We must follow Paul and avoid

an antinomian reading of texts that speak of our freedom from the law.

2. The law from which a new covenant believer is set free is the so-called ceremonial law. The death of Christ gives us the liberty to eat bacon with our eggs and frees us from the entire ceremonial system given to the Jews. This interpretation misses the greater import of what Christ's death accomplished.

3. The Christian is free to do anything not specifically forbidden in Scripture. When we engage in debatable practices, we are free from condemnation by other Christians. This interpretation leaves out qualifiers that Paul adds in other places when he addresses this issue.

Paul answers the first wrong approach in 5:13, 14. We will examine it more carefully when we reach that point in our analysis, but for now note that Paul realizes that some people will misunderstand his theology of law and grace and will use their liberty in Christ as a license to sin.

The second misunderstanding concerns the nature and cause of the bondage from which we have been set free. We have already noted that the primary freedom is freedom of conscience before God. If you have any questions or doubts as to what Paul means, I suggest that you re-read John Stott's quotation. The presupposition that lies behind this misunderstanding is the insistence that the law from which we are freed cannot be what some theologies term the moral law. The problem is that the text means exactly that!

The interpreters who divide the law of Moses into three different codes—moral, ceremonial, and civil—are quick to insist that whatever law Paul is referring to in Galatians 5:1, he cannot include the so-called moral law or Ten

Commandments. In their system of theology, the moral law is eternal, unchangeable, and transcends all ages, dispensations, and covenants. Obviously, an eternal, transcendent law admits no exemptions. It is clear that the law to which Paul refers was a "bondage too heavy to bear" (Acts 15:10), and believers have been not only delivered from it, but they will "fall from grace" (Gal. 5:4) if they go under its authority. To describe the Ten Commandments this way (as bondage) would be considered gross heresy in the theology of Covenant Theology.

Is there warrant for believing that the law to which Paul refers *does* include the Ten Commandments considered as covenant terms? Let us look more closely at Galatians 5:1.

> *It is for freedom that Christ has set us free. Stand firm, then, and do not let yourselves be burdened again by a yoke of slavery.* (NIV)

As I mentioned earlier, all agree that the "yoke of slavery" is some law in some sense. The context of the letter from the middle of chapter two and on into chapter five makes that clear. Paul is continuing his argument that the Christian is not (and should not be) "under the law." Covenant theology insists, correctly that Paul's yoke of bondage in Galatians 5:1 and Peter's in Acts 15:10 is the same yoke. They also insist, but incorrectly, in my view, that the reference in both places is to the "ceremonial" law. Their reason for that view is obvious. In Covenant Theology, neither Peter nor Paul can mean, or include, the so-called moral law in their concept of expendable law, since all people of all ages, present-day Christians included, are under that law as a rule of life. The law to which Peter and Paul refer is the "Mosaic administration," but with the moral law, or Ten Commandments, excised out of it. This view cannot be reconciled with the rest of Scripture. This is a vital point. Let us look at the meaning of the word _law_ in both texts.

First: The setting of Acts 15 is the meeting of the Jerusalem council to discuss the relationship of the Gentile converts to the law of Moses or old covenant. Judaizers had come to Antioch and were insisting that the Gentiles there must be "circumcised according to the custom of Moses" in order to be saved. Paul and Barnabas disagreed sharply, precipitating the council meeting in Jerusalem. In Jerusalem, professing believing Pharisees supported the Judaizers, stating that the Gentiles had to be circumcised and were required to obey the law of Moses. Peter, arguing against this view, referred to the law of Moses as a yoke. Peter uses the term _yoke_ figuratively here to refer to that which is the antithesis of saving grace. If we adopt Covenant Theology's definition of law here, we have Peter in effect arguing that the Judaizers' position is that observing the ceremonial law justifies a person. It is as if he were saying, "We believe that grace saves a person. You believe that salvation comes by obeying the ceremonial law."

> And certain men which came down [to Antioch] _from Judaea taught the brethren, and said, Except ye be circumcised after the manner of Moses, ye_ **cannot be saved.** _...There rose up_ [in Jerusalem] _certain of the sect of the Pharisees which believed, saying, That it_ **was needful** _to circumcise them_ [the Gentiles], _and to command them to_ **keep the law of Moses.** _...And ...Peter...said...Why tempt ye God, to put_ **a yoke** _upon the neck of the disciples, which neither our fathers nor we were able to bear?_ (Acts 15:1, 5, 7, 10 KJV)

The phrase _keep the law of Moses_ cannot be restricted here to mean "keep the ceremonial law." It refers to the entire law of Moses or the old covenant. The freedom Peter speaks of is liberty of conscience grounded in justification by faith alone. The Ten Commandments, or so-called moral law, do not equal the law of Moses, but the law of Moses certainly **includes** the Ten Commandments. The "tables of the covenant" upon which were written the "words of the covenant," or Ten Commandments (Deut. 9:9–11; Ex. 34:27, 28), are the core summary document of the old covenant. The Ten Commandments are, without question, a vital part of Peter's "yoke of bondage."

Second: The yoke the Judaizers were seeking to impose on the Gentiles was, according to Peter, a yoke "which neither our fathers nor we were able to bear" (Acts 15:10). The "ceremonial law" is not a yoke too heavy to bear. The present Seven-Day Adventist and the "back to nature" crowd, as well as the Jewish nation, willingly observe the ceremonial law without any complaint. Freedom from the yoke of the law is described in Ephesians 2 and Hebrews 9 and 10: in those places, the result of gospel freedom is a conscience devoid of offense toward God. Freedom from the yoke of the law allows for freedom of conscience in full assurance of salvation and enables us to enter boldly, but not brazenly, into the Most Holy Place without fear (Heb. 4:14–16). If Paul, in Galatians, and Peter, in Acts 15, are using the idea of the yoke of the law to talk about the ceremonial law, then our consciences were justifiably guilt-ridden by our failure to observe the ceremonial law, and Jesus shed his blood to purchase for us the liberty of eating bacon with our eggs. In addition, the Jerusalem council would have been all about eating ham and shrimp, planting a garden, wearing certain kinds of clothing, and circumcising. That may appear to protect the "holy law," but it does so at the expense of minimizing the cross.

Peter's argument in Acts 15 focuses on justification and salvation and not on diet and clothing. The topic under debate was what was essential for a Gentile to be saved and to have assurance of that salvation. Peter, in Acts 15:10, was talking about the yoke of the law on the conscience from which there was no release until Christ shed his blood and redeemed sinners from the holy and just claims of the law.

Third: The Jerusalem council imposed some ceremonial laws upon Gentiles—no meat offered to idols and no eating blood (verse 29), some of which Paul later rescinded under certain circumstances. Additionally, Peter's recommendation of what the Gentiles ought to do included moral laws (abstain from sexual immorality). Covenant Theology's tripartite division of the Mosaic law creates more problems than it solves. No apostle or writer of Scripture ever divided up the Mosaic law into three **codes.** We may recognize that a specific law addresses a ceremony, or a civic function, or something that fits neither category, but we have no warrant to divide the law into specific different **codes.** Scripture, in both Testaments, treats the law of Moses as a single, cohesive unit synonymous with the old covenant that is done away in Christ.

Four: Neither the general nor the immediate context of Galatians 5:1 has anything to do with the ceremonial law. Paul, in verses 2 and 3, is dealing with the effects of allowing your conscience to come under the "whole law" as a covenant of life and death. He addresses the same subject here as he has in the rest of the letter, namely, a religion of law versus a religion of grace. Circumcision in itself is no burden at all. However, as a religious rite carrying the theological meaning the Judaizers gave it, namely, that it is a rite essential to salvation, it then becomes a denial of the gospel. When circumcision is an act that commits you to keep the whole law in order to be saved, then it indeed becomes a "yoke too heavy to bear." It becomes what Paul calls "trying to be justified by law" (v. 4). It seems that John Stott is correct in defining freedom from the yoke too heavy to bear as "freedom of conscience, freedom from the tyranny of the law, the dreadful struggle to keep the law, with a view to winning the favor of God. It is the freedom of acceptance with God and of access to God through Christ."

We have often noted that legalism and antinomianism are equally deadly enemies of the gospel. In Galatians 4 and 5:1, Paul deals with legalism as it grows out of the misuse of the law. In Galatians 5:13-26, Paul will deal with the second enemy of the gospel, antinomianism. We have already noted the stern words of warning in 5:2–12. I wish we could tattoo verse 6 on the conscience of every preacher and in every pulpit.

> For in Christ Jesus neither circumcision nor uncircumcision has any value. The only thing that counts is faith expressing itself through love (NIV).

Paul feels deeply about the wickedness of adding circumcision to the gospel. His choice of words to express his disgust and dismay may make a few people blush, but it shows the strength of his passion about the purity of the gospel message.

> As for those agitators, I wish they would go the whole way and emasculate themselves! (v. 12 NIV)

Elder D. J. Ward said, "In preaching, the main thing is to keep the main thing the main thing." The main thing in preaching is "faith," but not faith in some kind of a god of your own imagination. It is faith in Christ, God's Son, crucified, buried, raised from the dead, ascended to heaven, and seated at the right hand of God. One of the tests of all preaching and of your religion is what place the words *do* and *done* play. When it comes to your relationship with God, it should be one-hundred percent **done.** Preachers of false doctrine will tell us what we must do and will neglect to tell us what Christ has done for us that we could not do for ourselves.

We now come to the third mistake made concerning the bondage from which a Christian is set free (Gal. 5:1). Some teachers interpret freedom from the yoke of slavery here to refer to Christian liberty—being free from the opinions of people (usually other Christians) in debatable areas. While it is true that Paul's teaching here implies that Christians are free from the opinion of anyone who would impose law-keeping for salvation, that is not how we generally understand the topic of Christian liberty. Usually when the subject arises, it is in the context of sanctification—behavior that is appropriate for someone who is already a Christian: "Is it permissible for a Christian to smoke or to drink wine?" The list could extend indefinitely. This kind of question misses the main point of biblical liberty. It is true that one aspect of liberty involves not placing our consciences under the control of fellow believers when it involves debatable subjects. When the Reformed Baptist movement was just beginning, our young seminary students went to Westminster and later to Reformed Seminary in Jackson,

Mississippi, because there were no Baptist schools that taught the doctrines of grace. Some of the professors at these schools smoked and drank wine. Nearly all of the Baptist students had been raised in Arminian churches that placed smoking and wine on a taboo list. These Baptist students not only adopted a "free in Christ" philosophy about smoking and drinking wine on campus; some of them flaunted their new-found freedom when they went home.

Many Reformed Baptist pastors also started drinking wine. I refrained from both tobacco and wine, not because I believed partaking of either was a sin, but because I had many Arminian friends who believed you became a Calvinist on Monday, started smoking on Tuesday, and got drunk on Wednesday. I did not want them rejecting Calvinism because of associations with smoking and drinking wine. Fellow pastors often chided me when I politely refused a glass of wine. "What is the matter, John, don't you believe you are free to drink wine?" I always replied, "I am well aware that I have freedom to either smoke or drink wine. However, I am also free to abstain from either one for my brother's conscience sake." I was not sure that some of those pastors were free to do the same.

We must understand that we are not free to smoke or to drink wine, or to engage in any other debatable practice, until we can say both yes and no. If we must have it, we are its slave. We are not free to do something until we are just as free to refrain from doing it. Freedom means that Christ alone is our master. To be free in Christ means that we are not enslaved to anything but Christ. We do not *have* to have anything but him. We must not confuse liberty with rights. Christian liberty is not having the right to do as we please, regardless of how our actions affect others. The only *right* we have is the right to go hell, humbly, because we deserve it! We renounced all our rights when we bowed to the lordship of Christ. We take our orders from him. Unless we can put that wine glass on the table and ask, "Lord, what would you have me to do, drink it or leave it?" we are not free! If we cannot refrain from reaching for a cigarette or a pipe, then we cannot claim Christian liberty in the matter of smoking. If we simply must have that nightcap or cigarette before bed, we are slaves and not free people at all. If we can receive either as a gift of God and partake with a conscience void of offense, then we are free to go right ahead. When people ask me whether a specific debatable behavior is legitimate, I say, "I approve of anything of which our Lord approves."

If the main point of Christian liberty is not about legitimate debatable behaviors, then what is it about? What is true Christian liberty? Look at verses 13 and 14. Notice how Paul protects liberty against both legalism and antinomianism.

> You, my brothers, were called to be free. But do not use your freedom to indulge the sinful nature; rather, serve one another in love. The entire law is summed up in a single command: "Love your neighbor as yourself." (NIV)

In verse 13, Paul tells his readers that they were called. This word *calling* is important. Let me again quote John Stott.

> 'Called to freedom'! This is what it means to be a Christian, and it is tragic that the average man does not know it. The popular image of Christianity today is not freedom at all, but a cruel and cramping bondage. But Christianity is not bondage; it is a call of grace to freedom. Nor is this the exceptional

privilege of a few believers, but rather the common inheritance of all Christians without distinction. This is why Paul adds 'brethren'. Every single brother and sister has been called by God to freedom.

What are the implications of Christian freedom? Does it include freedom from every kind of restraint and restriction? Is Christian liberty another word for anarchy? Paul himself was being criticized for teaching this, and it was an easy jibe for his detractors to make. So, having asserted that we have been called to liberty, he immediately sets himself to define the freedom to which we have been called, to clear it of misconceptions and to protect it from irresponsible abuse. In brief, it is freedom from the awful bondage of having to merit the favour of God; it is not freedom from all controls.[106]

First, Paul shows what Christian liberty is not. *It is not freedom to indulge the flesh!* If it were not possible for a Christian to abuse this liberty, Paul would never have warned against it. An unbridled license is not liberty at all but another form of bondage. It is merely changing one bad master for another one. When self rules an individual, then self is king and we are its slaves. Our present society boasts loud and long about its freedom. Comedians often ridicule Christians and boast of having won the battle against the Bible and its commandments. But the chains that bind their lives rattle and tell another story. So-called free love and free lifestyles become frightfully expensive in terms of destroyed personal relationships and disastrous consequences. Those who indulge the flesh become slaves of their appetites to which they must give free reign because they cannot control them. John Stott explains how liberty differs from license.

---

[106] Stott, *One Way*, 140

Christian freedom is very different. Far from having liberty to indulge the flesh, Christians are said to have 'crucified the flesh with its passions and desires' (verse 24). That is to say, we have totally repudiated the claim of our lower nature to rule over us. In vivid imagery which Paul borrows from Jesus, he says we have 'crucified' it, nailed it to the cross. Now we seek to walk in the Spirit and are promised, if we do, that we shall 'not gratify the desires of the flesh' (verse 16). Instead the Holy Spirit will cause His fruit to ripen in our lives, culminating in self-control (verse 23).[107]

Then Paul tells his readers what Christian freedom looks like: *"through love be servants one of another."* Many people in the world (both the first-century Greco-Roman world and the twenty-first-century American world) operate on the principle, "you scratch my back, and I will scratch yours." We serve another person only if we get something out of it. Our first question is, "What's in it for me?" Or, "What have you done for me lately?" The Christian has drunk the water of life that quenches the thirst of the soul and eaten the bread of life that satisfies the hunger of the soul. Christians are no longer motivated by self and are free to love the unlovely and to give ourselves to others without needing anything in return. Instead of saying, "How can I benefit from a relationship with you?" we can say, "How can I help bear your burdens?" (Gal. 6:2).

We are not only free to serve others, but free to do it in love and feel it as a privilege. Christian liberty does not use people as if they were things. Christian liberty enables us to respect others as persons in their own right—as made in the image of God. No matter how debauched by sin an

---

[107] Ibid., 141.

individual may be, that person is worthy, as a creature of God, of my love and to hear the gospel. The Christian is free from the ego massaging that controls the world. Christian liberty is service, not selfishness. True love does not seek to possess a person for myself, to meet my needs. Biblical love enables a child of God to serve others for their own sake and to help meet their needs. We either serve or use everyone with whom we have some kind of a relationship, and using people instead of serving them winds up with us biting and devouring one another (verse 15).

Paul feels so strongly about the importance of love that he posits it as the fulfillment of all law.

> *The entire law is summed up in a single command: "Love your neighbor as yourself." (v. 14 NIV)*

We are forever free from the law as a means of finding acceptance with God. We are not free to make our own laws and live as we please. We are willing bond-slaves of Christ and his law. The more we obey our Lord's law, the more we will be people who truly love and serve others.

CHAPTER TWENTY-THREE

GALATIANS 5:1–12

In the our last chapter, we considered what it meant to be set free from what Paul, in 5:1, calls the "yoke of bondage." The essence of Christianity is that it is a religion of freedom and not of bondage. However, we must guard and defend that liberty against those who, by either abuse or distortion, would rob us of its power.

In this chapter, we will examine the first twelve verses of chapter five.

1 It is for freedom that Christ has set us free. Stand firm, then, and do not let yourselves be burdened again by a yoke of slavery.

2 Mark my words! I, Paul, tell you that if you let yourselves be circumcised, Christ will be of no value to you at all. 3 Again I declare to every man who lets himself be circumcised that he is obligated to obey the whole law. 4 You who are trying to be justified by law have been alienated from Christ; you have fallen away from grace. 5 But by faith we eagerly await through the Spirit the righteousness for which we hope. 6 For in Christ Jesus neither circumcision nor uncircumcision has any value. The only thing that counts is faith expressing itself through love.

7 You were running a good race. Who cut in on you and kept you from obeying the truth? 8 That kind of persuasion does not come from the one who calls you. 9 "A little yeast works through the whole batch of dough." 10 I am confident in the Lord that you will take no other view. The one who is throwing you into confusion will pay the penalty, whoever he may be. 11 Brothers, if I am still preaching circumcision, why am I still being persecuted? In that case the offense of the cross has been abolished. 12 As for those agitators, I wish they would go the whole way and emasculate themselves! (NIV)

John Stott, in his commentary, uses the title "False and True Religion" in the chapter addressing these verses. In the first six verses, Paul deals with gullible believers who are in danger of practicing false religion, and in verses 7 through 12, he describes the false religion that some teachers in the Galatian church were promoting, and the danger of listening to their corrupted gospel. In both cases, Paul uses strong language to condemn the message, the messengers, and the foolish listeners.

In verse 2, Paul unpacks the theme of bondage he has introduced in verse 1. He warns Gentile converts against allowing themselves to be circumcised. As you read these words, remember that the Judaizers were insisting that Gentile converts be circumcised in order to be saved (Acts 15:1–5). In what way does Paul see circumcision as contributing to bondage? John Stott provides an answer.

> The false teachers in the Galatian churches, as we have already seen, were saying that Christian converts had to be circumcised. You might think this a very trivial matter. After all, circumcision is only a very minor surgical operation on the body. Why did Paul make so much fuss and bother about it? Because of its doctrinal implications. As the false teachers were pressing it, circumcision was neither a physical operation, nor a ceremonial rite, but a theological symbol. It stood for a particular type of religion, namely salvation by good works in obedience to the law. The slogan of the false teachers was: 'Unless you are circumcised and keep the law, you cannot be saved' (*cf.* Acts 15:1, 5). They were thus declaring that faith in Christ was insufficient for salvation. Circumcision and law-

obedience must be added to it. This was tantamount to saying that Moses must be allowed to finish what Christ had begun.[108]

Notice how Paul describes what the Galatians were saying implicitly about themselves by their rejection of the gospel of sovereign grace that he had taught them and their acceptance, in its place, of the gospel of works the Judaizers preached. The moment they "receive circumcision" (verses 2, 3) they will be duty bound to *keep the whole law* (verse 3), since this is exactly that to which their circumcision would commit them. Circumcision, in the scheme of the Judaizers, meant trying to be justified by keeping the law (verse 3). By submitting to circumcision, the Galatians were binding their consciences with the very "yoke of bondage" from which the gospel had freed them.

How does Paul respond to their folly? He warns them that the moment they submit to circumcision, *Christ will be of no advantage to* [them] (verse 2), and [they will be] *severed from Christ,* and [they will] *have fallen away from grace* (verse 4). The nature of the gospel makes it an either/or situation. It is all grace or all law. It is all Christ or all self-effort. It is all circumcision or all faith. To add law-keeping or circumcision to the gospel is to corrupt and destroy the gospel.

Although the implication of the warning in verse 2 seems self-evident, Paul explicitly states it in verse 3.

> Mark my words! I, Paul, tell you that if you let yourselves be circumcised, Christ will be of no value to you at all. Again I declare to every man who lets himself be circumcised that he is obligated to obey the whole law.

---

[108] Stott, *One Way*, 133.

Circumcision commits those who receive it to earn their justification before God by perfectly obeying the law. The Galatian men, by allowing themselves to be circumcised, were committing themselves to keep the whole law. This meant they could receive no benefit at all from the cross work of Christ. Their circumcision rendered all that Christ did useless and insufficient. *You who are trying to be justified by law have been alienated from Christ; you have fallen away from grace* (v.4). John Stott explains that grace and works are mutually exclusive with regard to justification.

> It is impossible to receive Christ, thereby acknowledging that you cannot save yourself, and then receive circumcision, thereby claiming that you can. You have got to choose between a religion of law and a religion of grace, between Christ and circumcision. You cannot add circumcision (or anything else, for that matter) to Christ as necessary to salvation, because Christ is sufficient for salvation in Himself. If you add anything to Christ, you lose Christ. Salvation is in Christ alone by grace alone through faith alone.[109]

In verses 5 and 6, Paul changes the pronoun from *you* to *we*. He has been warning the Galatians (*you*) of losing hold of Christ and grace. He now shifts his focus to include himself and all believers. He describes how true believers seek righteousness—by faith—implicitly contrasting that with what he has just described—the method of justification employed by a false believer. Paul first says that believers, by faith, wait in hope for the fulfillment of the promise of the second coming. We live in expectation, inspired by the Holy Spirit, for the day when faith gives way to sight and we experience full redemption and perfect righteousness

---

[109] Ibid., 133-4.

(verse 5). Two things are significant in these verses. In verse 5, we *wait* (in hope) through the Spirit, by faith; we do not *work,* through the flesh, by sight, for righteousness. In verse 6, we see that faith alone will bring us to Christ and bring Christ to us. Christ, and Christ alone, is all that really matters.

> 5 But by faith we eagerly await through the Spirit the righteousness for which we hope.
>
> 6 For in Christ Jesus neither circumcision nor uncircumcision has any value. The only thing that counts is faith expressing itself through love.

In verse 6, Paul states his point in two ways. First, he approaches it from a negative standpoint—he explains what does not have value. Paul is clear that neither circumcision nor uncircumcision, nor anything else, has any spiritual value in itself. Circumcision does not make, or help to make, anyone a child of God. A male believer is "no more a Christian" if he is circumcised and "no less a Christian" if he is uncircumcised. If circumcision mattered for salvation, women would be excluded completely. All that matters is whether a person, male or female, is in Christ.

The final sentence of verse 6 contains Paul's positive approach. Here he explains what does have value. Consider three vital points: *The only thing that counts is* [1] *faith* [2] *expressing* [KJV—working] *itself through* [3] *love.* These three go together and all are essential to true religion. First is faith: not a dead faith, but a faith that works and expresses life. It is not merely a working faith, but one that is motivated by love in its work. In Christ, what matters is faith (v. 6). John Stott explains what this necessary faith looks like.

Again Paul denies the false teaching. When a person is in Christ, nothing more is necessary. Neither circumcision nor uncircumcision can improve our standing before God. All that is necessary in order to be accepted with God is to be in Christ, and we are in Christ by faith.

A word of caution is needed here. Does this emphasis on faith in Christ mean that we can live and act as we please? Is the Christian life so completely a life of faith that good works and obedience to the law simply do not matter? No. Paul is very careful to avoid giving any such impression. Notice the phrases which I have so far omitted. Verse 5: 'For *through the Spirit*, by faith, we wait for the hope of righteousness.' That is to say, the Christian life is not only a life of faith; it is a life in the Spirit, and the Holy Spirit who indwells us produces good works of love, as the apostle goes on later to explain (verses 22, 23). Verse 6: 'faith *working through love.*' It is not that works of love are added to faith as a second and subsidiary ground of our acceptance with God, but that faith which saves is a faith which works, a faith which issues in love.[110]

True believers keep living by faith; we keep waiting in hope, looking for the second coming of our blessed Lord. We do all of this by the power of the Holy Spirit, given us as our heavenly comforter. Paul expresses this same assurance to the Corinthians.

I always thank God for you because of his grace given you in Christ Jesus. For in him you have been enriched in every way—in all your speaking and in all your knowledge— because our testimony about Christ was confirmed in you. Therefore you do not lack any spiritual gift as you eagerly wait for our Lord Jesus Christ to be revealed. He will keep you strong to the end, so that you will be blameless on the day of our Lord Jesus Christ. God, who has called

---

[110] Ibid.,134.

you into fellowship with his Son Jesus Christ our Lord, is faithful. (1 Cor.1:4–9 NIV)

Paul's hope for the sure and final perseverance of all the saints is always in the faithfulness of God to fulfill his promise and sovereign purpose. Paul always "thanks God" for every evidence of grace, whether initially, at conversion, or in enabling grace to *"keep you strong to the end"* when you shall finally be *"blameless on the day of our Lord Jesus Christ."*

In verse 7 of chapter 5 of his letter to the Galatians, Paul turns his attention to the false teachers who were leading his readers astray. He first reminds them of their past zeal for the truth and their love for him when he had brought the gospel to them. It is obvious they were now embracing a radically different gospel than the one Paul had taught them.

> *You were running a good race. Who cut in on you and kept you from obeying the truth?*

John Stott unpacks Paul's race metaphor. He writes:

> Paul loved to liken the Christian life to a race in the arena. Notice that to 'run well' in the Christian race is not just to believe the truth (as if Christianity were nothing but orthodoxy), nor just to behave well (as if it were just moral uprightness), but to 'obey the truth' applying belief to behaviour. Only he who obeys the truth is an integrated Christian. What he believes and how he behaves are all of a piece. His creed is expressed in his conduct; his conduct is derived from his creed.[111]

The Galatians had started the Christian race with what looked like successful running. But somewhere during the course of their race, someone had cut between them and the

---

[111] Ibid., 135.

goal. These intruders were hindering the Galatians from running in the right direction, and in some cases, actually stopping them from running at all. In verses 8–10, Paul goes into detail about the false teaching. First, he traces this hindrance to its true origin: it was not of God (v. 8). He then warns of its corrupting effect: it was corrupting their entire Christian life (v. 9). And last, he expresses his believe that the truth will win out (v. 10).

Verse 8 is both clear and logical. _That kind of persuasion does not come from the one who calls you._ Any influence that draws a believer away from total confidence in Christ cannot be of God. God had called the Galatians in sovereign grace (1:6); he had NOT called them by works. It seems self-evident to Paul that the message of the One who had called them was radically inconsistent with the message of those who were now calling them. The two messages lead in two mutually exclusive directions.

In verse 9, Paul warns of the natural effect of heresy. It not only hinders the Christian's life; it also unsettles him and makes steadfast faith impossible. Paul adopts a well-known proverb to demonstrate not only the certainty of the corrupting influence of heresy, but also the fact that tolerating "just a little bit" is not possible. _"A little yeast works through the whole batch of dough."_ We remember a similar proverb from Ben Franklin's old nursery rhyme:

For want of a nail the shoe was lost.
For want of a shoe the horse was lost.

For want of a horse the rider was lost.
For want of a rider the battle was lost.

For want of a battle the kingdom was lost.
And all for the want of a horseshoe nail.

If we can adapt that sentiment for our purposes, we can say that a lack of faith in one area leads to a lack of faith overall. A lack of faith leads to a loss of Christ.

In verse 10, Paul expresses his confidence that truth will win out. He has no confidence in either his ability to argue or the inherent integrity of the Galatians, but he does have great confidence in God's grace. The Galatians will return to the truth, and God will judge the false teachers. *"I am confident in the Lord that you will take no other view. The one who is throwing you into confusion will pay the penalty, whoever he may be."*

Verse 11 implies that the false teachers were claiming that Paul, on other occasions, taught circumcision as a means of currying favor with the Jews and avoiding criticism. They likely assured the Galatians that their message was no different from the one that Paul himself preached or practiced. They may have had in mind that Paul had Timothy circumcised before the two of them set out on an evangelistic journey (as recorded by Luke in Acts 16:1–3).

> *He* [Paul] *came to Derbe and then to Lystra, where a disciple named Timothy lived, whose mother was a Jewess and a believer, but whose father was a Greek. The brothers at Lystra and Iconium spoke well of him. Paul wanted to take him along on the journey, so he circumcised him because of the Jews who lived in that area, for they all knew that his father was a Greek.* (NIV)

In this circumstance, Paul was not trying to avoid persecution; he was going on a missionary journey and did not want the Jews he might encounter to use Timothy's lack of circumcision as an excuse not to listen to Paul preach. Timothy was already a believer (a disciple) when Paul met him. Timothy was indeed circumcised at Paul's request, but not in order to become a child of God or to add to the justification he already had. His circumcision falls into the category of Christian liberty. He acquiesced to avoid his presence being a hindrance to the gospel. Paul's question in verse 11 is another clear and logical refutation of what the Judaizers were claiming about him. _"Brothers, if I am still preaching circumcision,_ [as these false teachers claim,] _why am I still being persecuted?_ [If I were actually teaching circumcision, no one would be upset with me.] _In that case the offense of the cross has been abolished_ [but I am still hated and persecuted]."

Paul has now clearly set himself and the false teachers in stark contrast. They were preaching circumcision and works, and he was teaching Christ and grace. Preaching circumcision and works panders to a sinner's flesh and has him looking inside himself to find the will and power to please God and earn grace. To preach Christ crucified is to strip sinners of any hope in themselves and urge them to cast themselves on the mercy of God alone. One message is inoffensive to pride and therefore popular; the other is offensive and not popular at all. The treatment Paul received was proof that his message about the cross of Christ was not popular or acceptable to the carnal mind.

Verse 12 seems uncouth and harsh to modern ears. Paul is literally saying, I wish the knife would slip and they would castrate themselves. _As for those agitators, I wish they would go the whole way and emasculate themselves!_ Paul may have had in mind the eunuch priests of the Great Goddess of Syria, proverbial in their day for the disgust they raised in those who encountered them. These eunuchs dressed in garish colors, wore startling face makeup, and cavorted about the countryside hawking their goddess to passersby. At times, as atonement for sins against their goddess, these eunuchs would savagely bite or cut themselves.[112] If this is the comparison Paul has in mind, his sentiment is shocking indeed. The Judaizers, in his mind, are as offensive to him as the frenzied, wild priests of a pagan goddess are to the rest of the Roman world. Some will say, "Shame on Paul for being so intolerant." No, I think it should be, "Shame on us for being so wrongly tolerant. Shame on us for not loving Christ and his truth enough to have our spiritual sensibilities shocked by open and clear error." Stott concludes his chapter on these verses by putting *tolerance* into perspective for us.

> Ours is an age of tolerance. Men love to have the best of both worlds and hate to be forced to choose. It is commonly said that it does not matter what people believe so long as they are sincere, and that it is unwise to clarify issues too plainly or to focus them too sharply.
>
> But the religion of the New Testament is vastly different from this mental outlook. Christianity will not allow us to sit on the fence or live in a haze; it urges us to be definite and decisive, and in particular to choose between Christ and circumcision. 'Circumcision' stands for a religion of *human* achievement, of what man can do by his own good works; 'Christ' stands for a religion of *divine* achievement, of what God has done through the finished work of Christ. 'Circumcision' means law, works and bondage; 'Christ' means grace, faith and freedom. Every man must choose. The one impossibility is what the Galatians were attempting, namely to

---

[112] For an early second-century account that demonstrates the aversion of one Roman to these eunuch priests, see Apuleius' *The Golden Ass*, chapter 12, "With the Eunuch Priests."

add circumcision to Christ and have both. No, 'circumcision' and 'Christ' are mutually exclusive.

Further, this choice has to be made by both the people and the ministers of the church, by those who practise and those who propagate religion. It is either Christ or circumcision that the people 'receive' (verse 2), and either Christ or circumcision that ministers 'preach' (verse 11). In principle, there is no third alternative.

And behind our choice lurks our motive. It is when we are bent on flattering ourselves and others that we choose circumcision. Before the cross we have to humble ourselves.[113]

The "preaching of the cross" is the clear declaration that the Lord Jesus Christ is the promised Messiah, delivered up to death on the cross for our sins. He who knew no sin was made sin for us (2 Cor. 5:21). That act of obedience to his Father fulfilled all the Old Testament types, shadows, and promises. The cross broke down the middle wall of partition between Jews and Gentiles, and left all, without exception, guilty before God, with no hope but the gospel of sovereign grace.

It is not possible to declare clearly the true gospel without experiencing persecution. As we saw in 4:29, the Ishmaels will always persecute the Isaacs. It happened to Jeremiah, to Daniel, to Amos, and to a host of others. It has happened to godly believers in every age. Preaching the cross is especially offensive to a generation like ours that boasts of its ability to tolerate any and every form of sin under the guise of being open-minded. On the one hand, the worst cultural sin possible today is to be positively sure that you

---

[113] Stott, *One Way*, 137-38.

know and believe absolute truth. On the other hand, we cannot deny the presence of legalists in our midst who have rulebooks an inch thick, filled with small print. While the first group would deny there is any absolute truth, the "work mongers" would deny anyone the right to think and believe something a bit different from their particular understanding.

Many believers cannot understand why the worst persecution a Christian receives is usually not from pagans but from professing Christians. It is not the "lawless" who become most upset; they usually could not care less about what a Christian thinks. It is the people whose religion consists of rules and laws for everything who choke on the concept of full and free justification by grace and faith alone. Preaching the cross is preaching blood atonement for hell-deserving sinners. It is a message that slams the door to heaven as tight as a drum to all who would come to God with their own righteousness. This same preaching of the cross opens that door wide to let the worst of sinners come in. Horatius Bonar expressed it well in his hymn.

> Not what my hands have done
> Can save my guilty soul;
> Not what my toiling flesh hath borne
> Can make my spirit whole.
>
> Not what I feel or do
> Can give me peace with God;
> Not all my prayers and sighs and tears
> Can bear my awful load.
>
> Thy work alone, O Christ,
> Can ease this weight of sin;
> Thy blood alone, O Lamb of God,
> Can give me peace within.

Thy love to me, O God,
Not mine, O Lord, to thee,
Can rid me of this dark unrest,
And set my spirit free.

Thy grace alone, O God,
To me can pardon speak;
Thy pow'r alone, O Son of God,
Can this sore bondage break.

No other work, save thine,
No other blood will do;
No strength, save that which is divine,
Can bear me safely through.

I bless the Christ of God;
I rest on love divine;
And with unfalt'ring lip and heart,
I call this Savior mine.

His cross dispels each doubt;
I bury in His tomb
Each thought of unbelief and fear,
Each ling'ring shade of gloom.

I praise the God of grace,
I trust his truth and might;
He calls me his, I call him mine,
My God, my joy, my light.

'Tis he who saveth me,
And freely pardon gives;
I love because he loveth me,
I live because he lives.

CHAPTER TWENTY-FOUR

GALATIANS 5:1, 13–15

We often have noted that both legalism and antinomianism pose constant threats to the true gospel of sovereign grace. In Galatians 5:1, Paul warns against the first, and in 5:13–15, he cautions against the latter.

> *It is for freedom that Christ has set us free. Stand firm, then, and do not let yourselves be burdened again by a yoke of slavery...You, my brothers, were called to be free. But do not use your freedom to indulge the sinful nature; rather, serve one another in love. The entire law is summed up in a single command: "Love your neighbor as yourself." If you keep on biting and devouring each other, watch out or you will be destroyed by each other. (Gal. 5:1, 13–15 NIV)*

In a previous chapter, we demonstrated that the "yoke of slavery" to which Paul refers in Galatians 5:1 is the law, as a covenant, pressed on the conscience. New covenant theology sees the salient connection between freedom and law, as Paul expresses it in Galatians 5:1, as the effect of that freedom on the conscience. This is one tenet that distinguishes new covenant theology from covenant theology. Covenant theology divides the law into three categories—moral, civil, and ceremonial—and views the law from which the Galatians are free as the ceremonial category. This interpretation preserves covenant theology's commitment to the perpetuity of the Decalogue, but misses Paul's point in the allegory of Sarah and Hagar, which immediately precedes his exhortation in 5:1. Thus, covenant theology fails to consider the text on its own terms. Paul has compared Sarah and Hagar to *two covenants*, not to *two categories* of *one covenant*.

A second interpretation of "freedom from the yoke of slavery" reads Paul as reminding his readers that Christ has freed them from their former bondage to sin. In this view, Paul is referring not to the conscience, but to the will, which previously had been bound by sin, but now is bound to Christ. This is indeed the point that Paul makes in his letter to the Romans (Rom. 6:1–23), but it is not his point in Galatians. John Stott nicely captures the essence of Paul's argument in Galatians about freedom from the law. The **bolding** in the following quotation is mine; italics are in the original.

> This freedom, as the whole Epistle and this context make plain, is not primarily a freedom from sin, but rather from the law. What Christ has done in liberating us, according to Paul's emphasis here, is not so much to set our *will* free from the bondage of sin as to set our *conscience* free from the guilt of sin. The Christian freedom he describes is **freedom of conscience,** freedom from the tyranny of the law, the dreadful struggle to keep the law, with a view to winning the favour of God. It is the freedom of acceptance with God and of access to God through Christ.[114]

The key words in this quotation are *freedom, conscience, acceptance,* and *access.* As Stott describes the tyranny of the law, he includes the essential qualifier, "the dreadful struggle to keep the law with a view to winning favor with God," and so must we. We must not sever the last phrase from the first. Paul never understands being free from the law to mean being free to discard God's will, clearly

---

[114] Stott, *One Way*, 132 emphasis mine.

revealed in Christ, and to be ruled instead by our wicked hearts.

Throughout the letter to the Galatians, Paul wages his war against the Judaizers on two fronts: sanctification and justification. He appeals to sanctification—acting in accordance with the truth of the gospel—as he criticizes the manner in which believers who have adopted the Judaizing position respond to each other (Gal. 2:11–14). He grounds appropriate in-group behavior in the fact of justification, reminding his readers that justification is by faith and not by observing the law (Gal. 2:15, 16). In 5:1, Paul applies the truth of justification that he has been laboring to establish: sinners are put right with God by faith in the merit of Christ's atoning work and not by their own works. Assurance of salvation, or acceptance with God, is what gives the sinner both the sincere desire, as well as the joyous boldness, to enter into the Most Holy Place. Access into God's presence is tied to the conscience's being set free from the law. The assurance that we are eternally secure in Christ and can never be condemned (Rom. 8:1) because God has buried our sins in the deepest sea and will remember them against us no more, is the freedom of the conscience that comes only from the knowledge of full and free justification. In Christ, we have the very justification we so desperately need. No one can revoke our access into God's holy presence.

This knowledge and experience of free access comes to believers only through the new covenant. It did not, and could not, be known or experienced by believers under the old covenant. As long as the veil of the tabernacle was in place, no one except the high priest could enter the Most

Holy Place, where God's presence was manifest. Even he could not enter without blood, and then, only on the Day of Atonement. Access to God was severely restricted. The day the veil was rent from top to bottom was the day that established free access into the Most Holy Place. The only conscience that is free, however, is one that grounds its freedom in the act that caused the rending of the veil—the sacrifice of Christ that satisfied the just demands of God. A free conscience sees a sign that says, "Come, and welcome," that has replaced the sign that said, "No admittance upon pain of death."

Paul brackets his argument about freedom from the law by appealing to both justification (5:4) and sanctification (5:13–15). The conscience that is free from the demands of the law as a means to earn favor with God is free to love others as God loves them—unconditionally in Christ. In the case of the Galatians, circumcision had become a condition for peer acceptance. Those who saw it as necessary for salvation could not accept those who professed faith in Christ but lacked circumcision. Loving and accepting fellow believers is an inherent part of sanctification. Biting and devouring (v. 15) is contrary to sanctification. The practical aspects of sanctification Paul mentions in verse 15—the knowledge and experience of freely loving and accepting each other, regardless of circumcision or the lack thereof— also come only through the new covenant. Under the old covenant, fellowship between Jews and Gentiles was restricted. The old covenant erected a barrier—a dividing wall of hostility—between Jews and Gentiles. That wall remained in place as long as the covenant that established it remained in place. When Christ abolished the law with its commandments and regulations, he broke down that barrier and ended that hostility (Eph. 2:14, 15). The new covenant brings freedom for both Jews and Gentiles to love and serve one another in Christ. The only conscience, however, that is free to love others this way is one that grounds its freedom in the act that caused the demolished wall—the sacrifice of Christ that satisfied the just demands of God and gave both Jews and Gentiles access into the Father's presence (Eph. 2:18).

By recognizing sanctification as part of Paul's argument (especially as it is manifested in horizontal behavior), we are downplaying neither theology nor the vertical aspect of sanctification. Paul's finely-tuned theological arguments are not academic and unrelated to real life. Paul's theology provides the rationale behind both the desire and the blood-bought privilege of the worst of sinners to come boldly to the throne of grace to find help in time of need (Heb. 4:14–16). That rationale is the fact of a new and living way of access to God (Heb. 10:19, 20), opened up by the atoning work of Christ. To argue, as Paul does, for the doctrine of freedom from the law is to argue for the freedom of the gospel itself. It is to fight for a full and free justification that frees the conscience and allows the redeemed sinner to take advantage of that new access. What can be more desirable for a child of God than the knowledge that there is a welcome mat at heaven's gate with his name on it? What can be more practical and essential than the privilege of visiting the throne of grace to find grace to help in times of need? God's grace is available for help in both the vertical and horizontal aspects of sanctification. John Stott explains the apostle's exhortation:

Since 'Christ has set us free' and that 'for freedom', we must 'stand fast' in it and not 'submit again to a yoke of slavery'. In other words, we are to enjoy the glorious freedom of conscience which Christ has brought us by His forgiveness. We must not lapse into the idea that we have to win our acceptance with God by our own obedience. The picture seems to be of an ox bowed down by a heavy yoke. Once it has been freed from this crushing yoke, it is able to stand erect again (*cf.* Lv. 26:13).

It is just so in the Christian life. At one time we were under the yoke of the law, burdened by its demands which we could not meet and by its fearful condemnation because of our disobedience. But Christ met the demands of the law for us. He died for our disobedience and thus bore our condemnation in our place. He has 'redeemed us from the curse of the law, having become a curse for us' (3:13). And now He has struck the yoke from our shoulder and set us free to stand upright. How then can we dream of putting ourselves under the law again and submitting to its cruel yoke?[115]

I wish every sovereign grace preacher understood what Stott means by, "set our **conscience** free from the guilt of sin," "freedom of **conscience**," "freedom from the tyranny of the law," and "the glorious liberty of **conscience** which Christ has brought us by His forgiveness." If more preachers understood, believed, and preached these phrases, joy, assurance, and the power of the Holy Spirit would replace gloom, despair, and the lack of assurance so prevalent in many Reformed circles. The freedom of conscience from the law is the great new covenant blessing, predicted in the Old Testament and fulfilled in the New Testament with the advent of the Holy Spirit at Pentecost. The church needs a

---

[115] Ibid., 132-33.

clear and exhaustive study on the role of the law in the conscience in new covenant sanctification.

Previously, I have mentioned that John Bunyan's teaching on law and grace opened my understanding of the relationship between the two and their effect on the conscience. In his work, "The Law and the Christian," Bunyan insists that the Christian must dismiss the law out of his conscience the same way that Sarah dismissed Hagar from Abraham's house. He then clarifies exactly what he means by that analogy.

> My meaning is, when this law with its thundering threatenings doth attempt to lay hold on thy **conscience,** shut it out with a promise of grace; cry, the inn is took up already, the Lord Jesus is here entertained, and there is no room for the law.[116]

The word *conscience* here is the key word. We must remember that conscience is not a lawgiver. It does not teach us what is right and wrong. It functions as a judge to apply the law that has been given to it. Conscience is not an infallibly safe guide, because it can be trained to obey wrong standards. Some people can commit the most horrible deeds and feel they are doing what is right. John 16:1–3 is a clear example of this.

> *"All this I have told you so that you will not go astray. They will put you out of the synagogue; in fact, a time is coming when anyone who kills you will think he is offering a service to God. They will do such things because they have not known the Father or me."* (NIV)

Jesus is saying that people can, with clear consciences, kill someone who disagrees with them about religion. The

---

[116] *Of the Law and a Christian, Works of Bunyan,* 2:388. Emphasis added.

Apostle Paul, by his own admission, is a classic example of this truth.

> *Paul looked straight at the Sanhedrin and said, "My brothers, I have fulfilled my duty to God in all good conscience to this day."* (Acts 23:1 NIV)

What did Paul mean by "his duty to God?" Prior to his conversion, he sincerely believed it was his duty to God to beat Christians, to put them in jail, and in some cases, even to put them to death. Paul's conscience as a Jew who did not follow Christ not only allowed him to give vent to his hatred, but also demanded that it was his duty to do so. Hear his testimony: "I believed it was my duty to persecute and kill Christ-followers (because they were aberrant Jews), and I did my duty with zeal and a clear conscience."

We see this also in twenty-first century religious terrorism. When a militant Islamic terrorist beheads a "pagan" American or Canadian, his conscience does not in the least protest. In fact, his conscience cheers and applauds his action! How can that be? His conscience, instructed by his religion, is trained to wrong standards, from the perspective of Christianity. The terrorist thinks he is doing a service to God, but his action is wicked when viewed from a conscience instructed by Jesus's teaching. When we apply Jesus's words to the Muslim terrorist, we understand him as doing what he does because he is one of those who "*do such things because they have not known the Father or me.*" It is impossible for a person to know God the Father, or Jesus Christ his Son, and commit wicked acts in the name of God.

A person born and raised in a terrorist household will not feel any qualms of conscience when he kills in the name of religion. Yet if that person is a devout Muslim, he would feel terrible guilt upon eating ham or bacon, or consuming alcohol. A person born in a Christian home will feel no pangs of conscience at all when eating pork, but if that person is a devout Christian, he could not kill in Christ's name without offending his conscience. The Muslim's conscience will 'condemn' the person who eats pork, but the Christian's conscience will 'approve' someone who eats pork. The Muslim terrorist's conscience will approve of killing in the name of Allah; the Christian's conscience will condemn that action. The difference does not lay in a good or a bad conscience, but in the standards given to conscience.

Conscience accuses saying, "You are a hypocrite" when you do what you believe to be wrong or fail to do what you believe to be right. Likewise, conscience applauds, "You are a good person" when you do what you believe to be right and refrain from doing what you believe to be wrong. The Muslim terrorist's conscience says, "You are a good Muslim" when he beheads a pagan, but will scream at him for sinning when he eats pork.

Conscience does not, and cannot, tell you what is, or is not, the right thing to do. That is the role of parents, society, education, and for the Christian, the Bible. All human beings have a conscience, but the law that a specific conscience uses to accuse or excuse certain actions or intentions will vary greatly according to the individual's environment and background. Obviously, the higher the standard that trains the conscience, the more conscience will 'accuse.' When the law of God trains the conscience, it is impossible for that conscience ever to approve completely, since that law demands sinless perfection.

Paul, in Romans 2:14, 15, addresses this very point.

Indeed, when Gentiles, who do not have the law, do by nature things required by the law, they are a law for themselves, even though they do not have the law, since they show that the requirements of the law are written on their hearts, their consciences also bearing witness, and their thoughts now accusing, now even defending them. (NIV)

Too often preachers and teachers misuse this text because they misunderstand it. Rarely do they even quote it correctly. I have heard many preachers say, "Romans 2:14, 15 states that the law is written on the hearts of all people." They then use this text to try to prove that the Ten Commandments are written on the hearts of all people, Jewish and Gentile. Paul does not say, in this text, that the law itself is written on the heart, but that the **work** of the law is written on the hearts of all men and women. Later, in Romans 4:15, Paul tells his readers explicitly what that work of the law is. "The law worketh **wrath**" by defining transgression. This proves that all people have some law and a conscience that condemns them when they fail to obey that law. When the law comes as clear and unmistakable revelation from God, the conscience informed by that law will condemn offenses against that specific law.

At Sinai, God put Israel's conscience under a codified law and made that law the terms of a covenant. The primary purpose of that law was to work wrath, or to convict people that they were guilty sinners in need of grace. Nothing could satisfy a conscience that was under the law, since it was impossible for sinners to meet the covenant demands of sinless perfection. When even unavoidable, involuntary bodily experiences such as an infectious skin disease, a swelling, or a rash counted as transgressions that rendered one unclean and required a sacrifice to purify the afflicted person (Lev. 14:1–32), the people would have realized that they were helpless to refrain from transgressing. One of the greatest mistakes of covenant theology is their insistence that the law aids in sanctification. Paul's allegorical interpretation of the casting out of Hagar and Ishmael proves that God never meant the law to be the mother of holiness. Hagar was a handmaid, just as the law is a handmaid to the gospel, but she was never meant to be the mother of the children of the promise any more than the law was meant to produce the children of the promise or the fruit of the Spirit.

The law of God had a definite function in the history of redemption. It still has a function, but it is not the same function as it had in Israel's experience. The law that worked wrath in Israel's conscience has been fully silenced and does not work, in any sense, either wrath or blessing in the Christian. The law of God can neither curse nor bless a Christian. It cannot *curse* a Christian because Christ has endured every curse the law threatened, and it cannot bless a Christian because even with a new heart, the child of God cannot earn the blessing that is the reward for perfect obedience. However, just as Christ endured every curse the law threatened, he also earned every blessing the law promised. If you read the law and feel guilt and despair, you do not understand justification, and if you read the law and feel good about your progress in sanctification, you are a deceived, self-righteous hypocrite.

Bunyan saw this twofold work of the law in justification and sanctification. He was both clear and emphatic that law and grace could not room together in the heart or conscience of a child of God under the new covenant. Moses was a faithful servant in the old house, but he has no place or service in the new house our Lord built (Heb. 3:1–6).

After writing that *we must not allow the law to lay hold of our conscience, but must instead shut it out with a promise of grace, and cry that the inn is full, there is no room for the law, because Jesus occupies the inn completely,* Bunyan goes on to write words that should be written with gold ink.

> Indeed if it [the law] will be content with being my informer, and so lovingly leave off to judge me; I will be content, it shall be in my sight, I will also delight therein; but otherwise, I being now made upright without it, and that too with that righteousness, which this law speaks well of and approveth; I may not, will not, cannot, dare not make it my saviour and judge, nor suffer it to set up its government in my conscience; for by so doing I fall from grace, and Christ Jesus doth profit me nothing. (Gal. 5:1–5)[117]

First, Bunyan sees that with the coming of the new covenant, the function of law to work wrath or to accuse and/or excuse has ceased. The law is now helpful as a teacher, or as Bunyan says, "it shall be in my sight." However, he insists the law dare not "set up its government in my conscience." The law, along with the rest of Scripture, helps us to understand our Father's will for our conduct, but we dare not allow it to rule our conscience. Our Lord Jesus Christ alone is our lawgiver; actually, he himself is the law for the child of God.

Bunyan is clear as crystal that the law can no more sanctify us than it can justify us. The old tinker felt deeply

---

[117] Ibid.

about this point. His language is quite passionate. **"I may not, will not, cannot, dare not,"** is deliberately emphatic—and what is it that he "may not, will not, cannot, dare not" do? Again, Bunyan is clear. He sees that there are two things involved in a right understanding and use of the law of God in the Christian's life. First, I must not treat the law as a savior or a judge. Bunyan is here talking about justification. The law cannot be my savior; it cannot bring me salvation. It cannot be my judge; it cannot tell me whether I am saved or lost. In this respect, I am beyond the reach of the law. It has no authority over me. Second, I dare not allow the law to "set up its government in my conscience." Bunyan is now talking about sanctification. He is saying, "The law can neither justify me nor can it sanctify me." I must not allow the law to dwell in my conscience as a welcome guest. The inn—a metaphor for our heart and conscience—is "took up already, the Lord Jesus is here entertained, and there is no room for the law."

The goal of many Reformed preachers is to plant Moses in the believer's conscience in order to help him fight and conquer sin. They believe that God gave the law to curb sin. Yet that is precisely what the law *cannot* do. It cannot help a believer to fight sin. In fact, the law hinders sanctification. In the fight against sin, the law takes the wrong side. Paul tells his Corinthian readers that the law gives strength to sin.

The sting of death is sin, and the power of sin is the law. (1 Cor. 15:56 NIV)

In Romans 7, Paul writes that sin was dead without the law (v. 8). The coming of the commandment, instead of giving life, killed (vv. 9, 10). Sin used the commandment to declare Paul guilty and thus to condemn him to death.

In Romans 5:20, we find Paul's classic summary of God's purpose for the law. He states that the purpose of God in giving the law was to make the "offense **abound.**" This is the opposite of what covenant theology teaches about the purpose of the law.

> *Moreover the law entered, that the offense might abound. But where sin abounded, grace did much more abound.* (KJV)

If Paul had taught what covenant theology thinks he taught—that God gave the law to curb sin—then Paul's question in Romans 6:1 would not make sense. Here he responds to an imaginary, but obvious, objection to his teaching about the purpose of the law. Paul's question in Romans 6:1 seems, on the surface, the logical conclusion to his "where sin abounds, grace abounds even more" theology.

> *What shall we say then? Shall we continue in sin, that grace may abound?* (KJV)

Paul realizes that his teaching on this subject lays him open to the charge that he is promoting sin. The obvious course, it would seem, is for the law to remain so that it can continue to increase sin. Then, grace can increase to meet the need, and God will be glorified. Paul answers this objection, not by explaining that what he really meant was that the law aids in sanctification, but by declaring that the law does not have that effect on a person who is dead; i.e. not under it, and that it therefore is impossible for sin to reign over a Christian. The Christian is both "dead to sin" (v. 2) and "not under the law, but under grace" (v. 14).

We must protect the glorious truth of our freedom from misunderstanding and abuse. The question is how to do so. Can we believe that we are totally free from the law and eternally secure in Christ and cannot lose our salvation, and at the same time avoid a careless, casual attitude toward both sin and righteousness? In other words, in escaping from legalism and the "bondage to the law," which destroys the freedom of the gospel, how do we stay out of an antinomian lifestyle that also destroys the gospel of grace? Biblical grace must reign in righteousness, or it is not true grace. Paul answers this question for us in both Romans 6–8 and Galatians 5:13–26. He calls the fruit of true liberty "walking in the Spirit" and the abuse of liberty "walking in the flesh."

In Galatians 5:1, Paul exhorted his readers to stand fast in their liberty and to not become tangled in the bondage of the law. In 5:13, Paul shows that Christians can destroy their liberty in ways other than by succumbing to legalism. Please note that legalism, as we are using it here, does not describe the attitude of a Christian who earnestly seeks to please God, but uses the law as a means to that end. A sincere desire to please God is not legalism. Nor does it cause legalism. Legalism results from the actual misuse of the law. Nor does legalism in any sense diminish the goodness of the law. There is nothing wrong with God's holy law. Woe to the person who disparages the holy law that God wrote on stone with his finger. We must, however, use the law properly, as the author of the letter to Timothy explains.

> The goal of this command is love, which comes from a pure heart and a good conscience and a sincere faith. Some have wandered away from these and turned to meaningless talk. They want to be teachers of the law, but they do not know what they are talking about or what they so confidently affirm.
>
> We know that the law is good if one uses it properly. We also know that law is made not for the righteous but for lawbreakers and

rebels, the ungodly and sinful, the unholy and irreligious; for those who kill their fathers or mothers, for murderers, for adulterers and perverts, for slave traders and liars and perjurers—and for whatever else is contrary to the sound doctrine that conforms to the glorious gospel of the blessed God, which he entrusted to me. (1 Tim. 1:5–11 NIV)

Note that these words imply that there is a right and wrong use of the law for the Christian. The author does not explicitly explain what constitutes the proper or improper use of the law, but he spells out in detail **whom** the law is for. It is not for the righteous. Righteousness comes by faith, not by performing works of the law. Therefore, it is wrong to make the law our "savior or judge," as Bunyan affirmed. However, it is not wrong for us to allow the law to "instruct our minds," as long as we filter that instruction through the new covenant. The final authoritative yardstick that validates any truth or law for the child of God is the gospel. Sound doctrine is doctrine that conforms to the glorious gospel of the blessed God. Every truth that we accept as sound doctrine and part of our rule of life must conform to that gospel.

In Galatians 5:13, Paul begins to unpack the nature of true gospel freedom. He describes true liberty in terms of (1) manifesting itself in service to my brothers and sisters in genuine love, (2) subduing the flesh by the grace of God and the power of the Holy Spirit, and (3) joyfully seeking to obey the law of love. In the next chapter, we will follow Paul's argument about living in the liberty of conscience to the glory of God's grace.

CHAPTER TWENTY-FIVE

GALATIANS 5:13–15

The topics of freedom and individual rights have historically dominated and continue to dominate American political conversation. Americans talk about these ideas as much today as they ever have. These concepts loomed large for our founding fathers and figured prominently in the platforms of subsequent political leaders. In 1941, President Franklin Roosevelt talked about four freedoms that he perceived as universal ideals: freedom of speech everywhere, freedom of worship everywhere, freedom from want everywhere, and freedom from fear everywhere. The American psyche holds the idea of God-given rights as an inherent part of our framework of social justice. Americans believe that the freedoms alluded to by President Roosevelt are theirs by virtue of their identity as Americans; by extension, those freedoms belong to all people, regardless of nationality, by virtue of their humanity. The greatest of all freedoms, however, is one that is not a natural birthright; it is an earned freedom—the freedom purchased by Christ for his people. The Apostle Paul had experienced this liberating power of gospel freedom; it had delivered him from prejudice, hate, conceit, and spiritual bondage. Paul had experienced all these things as a result of living under the Mosaic law. It is no wonder, then, that he loved and extolled the freedom from the law that Jesus purchased for us.

Two great fears plague every child of Adam, and only the gospel can free us from either. First, we fear the unchangeable past. We cannot go back in time and undo the wrongs we have done. When presented with unmistakable evidence and called to give an account of our lives, we will have nothing to say. The record is fixed, and it stands against us. We deserve condemnation, and we know that we deserve it; therefore, we fear the righteous judgment of our past. The truth of justification by faith in the blood of Christ sets us free from that fear forever. We can sing, "He has hushed the law's loud thunder/ He has brought us nigh to God." The atoning work of Christ blots out our past forever.

Our second great fear is of the unpredictable future. Again, only the gospel can free us from this fear. We do not know what will happen to us tomorrow or next year. Will our situation tomorrow be the same as it is today? Better? Worse? What will it be in five years? Ten? Twenty? When we hear the one who died for us say, "I will never leave you or forsake you," we can sing, "I know not what the future holds/ but I know who holds the future." Paul knew what it was to be free from both of these fears, but his point in Galatians seems to focus mostly on the first—fear of God's disapproval and just condemnation.

In the last chapter, we looked at Galatians 5:1 where Paul exhorted his readers to "stand fast in the liberty" that Christ had purchased for them. We determined that the context of the letter defined the liberty of which he spoke as liberty of conscience, or freedom from the condemnation of the law and a boldness to enter the Most Holy Place. In this way, Paul's understanding of freedom encompasses both justification and sanctification. We also recognized that Paul's argument addresses both the vertical aspect of sanctification (I am free to come to God to find grace and help in time of need) and its horizontal aspect (I am free to love my fellow believers in Christ regardless of their other identities, specifically, their ethnic identity). We saw that a system of legalism destroys that freedom in all its facets. We now look at a different danger that can destroy gospel liberty, namely, antinomianism. Paul warns against this danger in Galatians 5:13–15.

> *You, my brothers, were called to be free. But do not use your freedom to indulge the sinful nature, rather, serve one another in love. The entire law is summed up in a single command: "Love your neighbor as yourself." If you keep on biting and devouring each other, watch out or you will be destroyed by each other.* (NIV)

What are the implications of the Pauline doctrine of Christian freedom? Does it include freedom from every form of restraint and restriction? Is Christian liberty another word for anarchy? It is essential that we realize what a real possibility there is of misusing our liberty in Christ. If the misuse of liberty that Paul describes in these verses were not a potential danger, Paul would never have given such a clear warning. Likewise, Paul would never have written Romans 6:1–15 if his doctrine of grace did not, on the surface, imply the potential for the misuse of grace. Before we were believers in Christ, we were habituated to either legalism or antinomianism. Old habits die hard, even for those who acknowledge and rejoice in the freedom Christ has granted them. It is a testimony to the awesome power of remaining sin in the best of believers that the seeds of both legalism and antinomianism are ever present in all people, even true Christians. Paul recognizes that it is possible for those who are children of the promise to use their legitimate freedom for illegitimate ends, so he immediately cautions against potential abuse.

The specific kind of illegitimate use envisioned by Paul provides a clue to his concept of the legitimate use of freedom. Paul's readers are not to use freedom as a means to the end of indulging the flesh; rather, they are to use freedom to serve one another in love. The category of indulging the flesh is broad—staggeringly so—but Paul narrows it for his readers by placing it in contrast to the correct goal of freedom: serving one another in love. Self-centeredness is one specific outcome of an antinomian mindset, and one that Paul has already addressed earlier in the letter. He reminds his readers that he had chided Peter for shunning Gentile believers in order to enhance his reputation with the Jerusalem brothers who visited Antioch and were of the circumcision party (Gal.2:11–13). Before we go on to consider this specific aspect of indulging the flesh, let us consider its broader implications. Paul lists some ways that we can deny or distort our freedom in Christ.

First, we can use the doctrine of freedom, or security, to indulge the flesh instead of conquering it. The carnal mind has little trouble jumping from the truth that a child of God can never lose their salvation to thinking that it does not matter to God whether his children obey him or not. We cannot separate the truth that we are "free from the law" from the truth that we are "bondslaves of Christ." We are made free from the power of sin and the tyranny of the law so we can love and obey our new Master. We are not made free from the law in order to be a law unto ourselves. We are set free to serve our Lord in love. We now belong to him. Let me illustrate.

A professing Christian dreamt he was driving in the backwoods and came across an old country store. He stopped and went in to look around. There he saw the most beautiful pearl he had ever seen. The man said, "I would give anything to own that treasure. I would give all I have." The storeowner replied, "Are you sure you know what you are offering?" The man answered, "Yes, I am." The owner said, "Fine. It is a deal." The man emptied his pockets and wallet and came up with a little over two-hundred dollars. He said, "That is all I have." The storeowner put the money in the cash register and started to wrap the pearl. The man then asked, "Could you lend me five dollars for gas for my car?" The storeowner replied, "Oh, you have a car. I will take the title and the keys." The man protested, "But I need my car to get to my job." "Oh," said the storeowner, "You have a job. Here is my address for your employer to send me your wages." The man pleaded, "But I need those wages to pay the mortgage on my house." "Oh, you have a house. I will take the keys and the deed." The man cried, "But I need the house for my family to live in." The storeowner said, "I see I am getting a family in this deal."

The poor man was stunned. The storeowner smiled, returned the car keys, and said, "I am loaning you my car, but you must remember it is mine. I have some elderly friends who sometimes need a ride to church. I will expect you to use my car to help them." He gave him back the deed and house keys and said, "You may use my house. I have friends all over the world and sometimes they visit here and need a place to stay. I'm sure you will not mind letting them use a few rooms in my house. I also have enterprises all over the world and need bright young people to work for me. I may need one or more of my new children that I will entrust to your care to go to Africa or India to work for me."

The man woke up and realized the message of the dream.

If you are a Christian, this is the kind of deal to which you willingly agreed when you bowed in repentance and faith to Jesus Christ as your Lord. You gave Jesus, your savior and lord, all that you had (and will have) and all that you are—including your so-called rights. When Paul wrote to the Corinthians, "You are not your own, you are bought with a price," he meant that all they had belonged to Christ. This principle has not changed. You may no longer view either your possessions or talents as belonging to you, to do with as you please, but you must see yourself as a steward, and consider everything you have as on loan from God.

If our freedom from the tyranny of the law consisted of freedom to indulge the flesh, we would merely be trading one kind of bondage for another. Self is concerned only with my personal happiness and sees God and others as a means to that end; the new man in Christ is concerned with holiness and serving the Lord and is happy to use his freedom as a means to that end. Self is a cruel master that can never be satisfied. Serving self is sin, no matter what name we give it. John Stott explains that much of what we call freedom is really slavery to self.

> So Jesus said to the Jews: 'every one who commits sin is a slave to sin' (Jn. 8:34), and Paul described us in our pre-conversion state as 'slaves to various passions and pleasures' (Tit. 3:3).
>
> There are many slaves in our society today. They proclaim their freedom with a loud voice. They speak of free love and a free life; but in reality they are slaves to their own appetites to which they give free rein, simply because they cannot control them.

Christian freedom is very different. Far from having liberty to indulge the flesh, Christians are said to 'have crucified the flesh with its passions and desires' (verse 24). That is to say, we have totally repudiated the claim of our lower nature to rule over us. In vivid imagery which Paul borrows from Jesus, he says that we have 'crucified' it, nailed it to the cross.[118]

Let us return now to consider more closely the specific way Paul thinks of misusing freedom in verse 13—to use people for our selfish ends instead of loving and serving them. *But do not use your freedom to indulge the sinful nature* [flesh]; *rather,* **serve one another in love** (Gal. 5:13c).

The world functions like a giant massage parlor. It runs on the principle, "you scratch my back, and I will scratch yours." It goes without saying that you must scratch my back first. The term currently in vogue to describe this attitude is "meet my needs." I am not denying we have legitimate needs that are inherent in the very fact of our humanity. But modern psychology has hijacked the biblical truth that people have basic God-given needs and has turned that truth into the science of manipulation. We think that it is natural and right that we get what we want at any cost, and manipulation is the most efficient means to that end. Motivational courses and sales seminars are forums to learn how to get other people to do what we want them to do. By labeling such courses as "motivation seminars," we blur the subtle but real difference between *motivation* and *manipulation.* Motivation has positive connotations; manipulation does not.

It is my duty as a pastor to try to motivate people. It is a grievous sin when I try to manipulate them. One of the main

---

[118] Stott, *One Way*, 141.

differences between those two actions is not so much *what* I am urging the person to do as *why* I am urging them to do it. I motivate people when I seek to help them reach their goals and their full potential. My concern is for their well-being, growth, success, and personal satisfaction. I manipulate a person when I urge him to do things, which on the surface, seem right and good, but in reality are things that help *me* reach *my* goals. Self-serving pastors and politicians are masters of manipulation. They have made a science out of using "concern for the people" to enhance their own power. It seems to me that Washington is using our current financial crisis as an opportunity to gain more power under the guise of alleviating the immediate pressing need of society for a stable economy.

For many people, "What have you done for me today?" has become a personal slogan. We will see in a future chapter that this attitude destroys the freedom of the gospel. It allows us to treat people as objects, as means to an end, instead of as individuals in their own right. Christian liberty is service, not selfishness. It is freedom to approach God without fear, not freedom to exploit my neighbor without love.

Every true need a person has, whether physical, emotional, or psychological, is God-given, and can be traced to the early chapters of Genesis. This includes the need for food, drink, love, sex, security, companionship, accomplishment, acceptance, and other such needs. God not only created a perfect humanity; he also put that perfect humanity in a perfect environment where they could satisfy every need in a way that glorified God their creator and made themselves supremely happy and satisfied. Sin destroyed all of that. Adam and Eve were banished from the perfect environment; the nature that had previously been their friend was now their enemy. The ground that had freely supplied all their basic survival needs now brought forth thorns and thistles. For the first time, a human being knew what it was to sweat and to fight to survive. The companionship that had existed between male and female became a competition for the right to rule. Two people who had been made for each other and who had freely and joyously met each other's needs now became primarily interested in using each other to meet their own needs.

Although humanity lost their perfect environment, they did not lose their basic needs. They retained every one of their God-given needs, but polarization between people made it impossible to fulfill all of those needs. Some of those needs required the heartfelt cooperation of others. The problem was that the others also had needs crying out to be met, and everyone now had a sinful and selfish nature that said, "Me first! You meet my need and then I will meet yours." This meant, of course, "you meet my needs fully so that I am completely satisfied." No sinner, however, can ever be totally satisfied, nor can he totally satisfy another sinner. That is the story of how Eden became a massage parlor that catered to giant selfish egos.

Paul narrows his focus on the misuse of freedom even more in verse 15, where he specifies what form the fleshly indulgence that is the opposite of love takes:

> If you keep on biting and devouring each other, watch out or you will be destroyed by each other. (NIV)

At first glance, this verse seems to come from nowhere. It just jumps out at you. Paul has not mentioned anything in either the immediate or broader context about the Galatians fighting with each other. But he has mentioned eating, way back in chapter 2, verses 11 through 14. With exquisite irony, Paul links Peter's unloving, self-serving refusal to eat with the Gentiles (a legalistic approach that allows him to be antinomian in indulging the flesh) to the Galatians' willingness to devour each other by observing identity markers such as circumcision (Gal.5:6). If the Galatians persist in recognizing and heeding in-group status markers, not only will they be subverting the fellowship meal in the same manner as Peter did; they will be destroying the basis of the fellowship meal. They will have metaphorically eaten each other, instead of having symbolically eaten Christ. Eating Christ sustains the covenant community; eating each other destroys it.

Here, and in 5:24–26, Paul lays out an important truth about personal relationships. In every relationship you have, no matter how close or casual, the thing that determines how you treat the other person is your attitude toward yourself. Your attitude toward yourself is determined by your attitude toward God. You love and serve the other person, or you use the other person to meet some need you have. How you view yourself determines whether you "love and serve" or "try to use." That is not psychology; that is Paul's theology! This is what it means to "walk by the Spirit and not gratify the desires of the flesh" in our relationships (Gal. 5:16). We will see this more clearly in the next chapter.

Although Paul uses the phrase *biting and devouring* to refer to the legitimization of status markers in the specific context of the fellowship meal, we can see that the attitude of biting and devouring is present whenever we reduce religion to keeping rules. In such a situation, it is easy to measure who is really holy—who has the highest status— they are the ones who keep the rules most faithfully. Sadly, the rules, in most cases, will have nothing to do with the fruit of the Spirit. The admonition to "owe no man anything, but to love one another, for he that loveth another hath fulfilled the law" does not figure in this holiness scheme. It is impossible for such an atmosphere to not breed pride and spiritual conceit, because in such a setting, "I am holy," translates into "I am more holy than you are," which means, "I keep more of the rules on our list than you do."

Paul presents the legitimate use of freedom in verse 14:

> *The entire law is summed up in a single command: "Love your neighbor as yourself."* (NIV)

The person who lives under the freedom of the gospel does not make laws; he gladly submits to the law of the new master. Christians are not a law unto themselves, either collectively or individually, but are under law to Christ (1 Cor. 9:21). If you want to think about observing a list of rules, start with Galatians 5:14. Here is the chief commandment on the list. If you keep this one law, you will have kept the entire law and will have no need for further rules. Why do churches and professing Christians bite and devour one another for breaking their respective list of rules, yet completely ignore the specific rule that fulfills all of the law? Paul holds that observing this law specifically describes the real heirs of God. John also is quite clear on this point. He tells us over and over that we know we are God's children if we keep his commandments. He then tells us that loving—especially loving my brother and my sister—is Christ's commandment (See 1 John 2:3, 4, 9–11; 3:4,

14; 5:2–4). I wish all the "law" preachers who use 1 John to make Christians doubt their salvation for not keeping the law would also preach that the chief commandment in the law is to show genuine love.

Did you ever read in Scripture, "We know we are children of God because we do not smoke? Or because we never miss prayer meeting or Sunday school?" How many rules, written and unwritten, do you and your church have that are purely traditional, and have nothing to do with Scripture itself? How many fights, some that have led people to leave churches, have been caused by a list of rules that were about ten percent Scripture and ninety percent tradition and prejudice?

Years ago, I listened to a southern preacher preaching on the radio on worldliness. He was doing a fair job on the text, "love not the world." He then asked, "And exactly what is worldliness? Any honest person will know without doubt that God is talking about playing baseball." He then launched a tirade against playing baseball. I thought then, and still do, that such a gross misunderstanding of the truth would be amusing if it did not have such tragic results. Stott summarizes verse 14 well, as he explains that Christian freedom is not freedom to disregard the law.

> *For the whole law is fulfilled in one word, 'You shall love your neighbour as yourself.'* We must notice carefully what the apostle writes. He does not say, as some of the 'new moralists' are saying, that if we love one another we can safely *break* the law in the interest of love, but that if we love one another we shall *fulfil* the law, because the whole law is summed up in this one command, 'You shall love your neighbour as yourself.'[119]

---

[119] Ibid., 142. Emphasis in the original.

Stott then concludes his analysis of Galatians 5:13–15 by applying the truth of Paul's doctrine of Christian freedom to our contemporary setting.

> This paragraph [Gal. 5:13–15] speaks relevantly to the contemporary situation in the world and in the church, especially regarding the fashionable 'new morality' and modern rejection of authority. It is concerned with the relationship of between liberty, licence, law and love.
>
> It tells us at the outset that we are 'called to freedom', the freedom which is peace with God, the cleansing of our guilty conscience through faith in Christ crucified, the un-utterable joy of forgiveness, acceptance, access and sonship, the experience of mercy without merit.
>
> It goes on to describe how this liberty from systems of merit expresses itself in our duty to ourselves, our neighbour, and our God. It is freedom not to indulge the flesh, but to control the flesh; freedom not to exploit our neighbour, but to serve our neighbour; freedom not to disregard the law, but to fulfil the law. Everyone who has been truly set free by Jesus Christ expresses his liberty in these three ways, first in self-control, next in loving service of his neighbour, and thirdly in obedience to the law of his God.
>
> This is the freedom with which 'Christ has set us free' (verse 1) and to which we 'were called' (verse 13). We are to stand firm in it, neither relapsing into slavery on the one hand, nor falling into licence on the other.[120]

In the next chapter, we will ask how to live in the power of the threefold freedom Paul has just described. The answer is, "walk in the Spirit and you will not fulfill the desires of the flesh." We will begin with 5:16 and discuss what it means to "walk in the Spirit."

---

[120] Ibid., 143-44.

CHAPTER TWENTY-SIX

GALATIANS 5:16–23

In the last chapter, we saw that the Galatians, true to form, were ready to misuse their liberty in Christ. Paul cautioned them against using freedom as an opportunity to serve themselves rather than as an opportunity to serve each other. Freedom from the law meant that they could ignore the identity markers that had formerly separated Jews and Gentiles; it did not mean that they were free to ignore Christ's command to love each other. John Brown has keen insight concerning liberty and its misuse.

> There is a strange disposition in mankind to misapprehend the meaning and tendency of religious truth however plainly stated, and to turn it to purposes which it was never intended to answer, and which, when rightly understood, it obviously appears that it was never intended to answer. The Apostle Paul was well aware of this tendency, and accordingly he often connects with a statement of a Christian doctrine a caution against its abuse.[121]

We started our study of Galatians by showing that Paul addresses three major issues in his letter: (1) the issue of authority, (2) the issue of salvation, and (3) the issue of victory over sin. His goal in the letter was to reveal to his readers the impotence of the Mosaic law to aid them in gaining victory over sin and self and in living a God-honoring and satisfying life. Paul pointed out that he, as an

---

[121] Brown, *Galatians*, 283

apostle sent by Jesus Christ and God the Father, had the authority to tell his readers what they ought to believe and how they ought to live. He told them that they ought to believe the gospel he had brought to them, because salvation comes only by grace through faith. Any other message of salvation is a false gospel. He used Abraham to support this claim. They needed to live in a manner that reflected faith in Christ rather than faith in the law. We now come to the section in the letter where Paul deals specifically with victory over the flesh. As Paul addresses the issue of victory over personal sin, he implicitly raises and answers three questions: How do we attain true victory over sin and self? How can we control our selfish and sinful desires? How can we be happy, loving, sharing, godly people? His answers apply in practical ways such as establishing and maintaining lasting and meaningful relationships, building happy homes and marriages, and avoiding fighting, demanding our own way, and being egocentric.

I remind you here of what we said at the beginning of this study. Are not the issues that Paul addresses still with us today? He raises real questions that define our contemporary problems, as well as those of his first-century audience. Are not these three basic problems the subjects of many books, conferences, seminars, retreats, and experience-oriented meetings? I list them again. First: The question of *authority*—who has the right to tell me what I can and cannot do. Second: The question of *salvation*—peace of mind about my relationship with God. How I can be sure I am justified before God and sure of heaven? Third: the question of *victorious living*. These things are the stuff of which real life is made.

Why is Galatians such a good book to use to answer these momentous questions? The answer: Paul, writing as an inspired apostle, demonstrates the necessary relationship between the three questions, specifically in the aspect of cause and effect. You cannot begin with question number three, that of victory over self and sin. This is the reason that so many attempts to solve these problems actually make the problems worse. They start at the wrong end. Nor is this approach confined to those outside of Christ—many Christians are unable to answer these problems correctly. They start with trying to discover how to live victoriously without first being certain why they are not already living victoriously. Too often, we start with personal happiness. People talk about "finding themselves," "being fulfilled and really happy," and "having their needs met." Starting at this point, however, only intensifies the problem of selfishness and delays our finding the only real answer to victory over self and the flesh. Starting with our personal happiness—with ourselves—only feeds the selfishness that created the despair and frustration in the first place. That is a lesson we should have learned from studying Ecclesiastes as well as Galatians.

Humanity's foremost problem is not our interpersonal relationships (human to human), but our relationship to our creator and judge (human to divine). The first chapter of Romans clearly shows that we become "ungodly," that is, we first have a wrong attitude to God, and then become "unrighteous" in our attitude to our fellow creatures. Our treatment of our fellow creatures grows directly out of our knowledge of, and attitude toward, the true and living God—our creator. Our knowledge of, and attitude toward, the true and living God is in direct proportion to our knowledge of, and attitude toward, the Word of God, the Bible! Nothing we do, think, decree, or imagine can ever change that reality.

We start at the wrong end when we only want to talk or think about how to feel good about ourselves. The wrong end ignores truth, doctrine and, theology. How often do victorious-living seminars focus on theology? More often than not, self-help advice minimizes the importance of _what_ we _believe._ All that matters is that we are _sincere_ in what we believe, regardless of the _content_ of our faith. Behavior, not belief, is the target of change. To accomplish this goal, someone will study us and treat us as _animals_; that is, they will attempt to change our behavior by using methods akin to training animals in a Skinner box. This methodology follows logically from a commitment to evolution. Granted, many people acknowledge that a human being is the highest form of animal, but nonetheless, a human being is still _only_ an animal, produced by some unknown _natural_ cause, and not by a creative act of a Creator God. Behavioral change fails to consider human beings as _spiritual beings_ made in the image of God.

We certainly agree that people must be sincere in what they believe, but it is just as important that they be _correct_ in what they believe. We shall go even further and say that when the content of belief is wrong, sincerity becomes dangerous. A zealot with a machine gun is a dangerous monster—but he is surely sincere! A professor in college or superintendent in a high school who rejects the authority of God's Word is potentially more dangerous to a society than are bombs and missiles. Bombs can send you to the grave, but the rejection of God's Word will send you to hell.

Approaching life and its problems by starting at the wrong end ignores the reality of sin and of a sinful nature. It ignores the basic need of fallen humanity—to know God and to be at peace with him. It refuses to accept the full and clear revelation of God in his Word, and thus rejects the only clear explanation and answer to humanity's deepest needs and problems. This refusal and rejection is nothing less than a human being pretending that he is God.

We simply must see the relationship between the problems of authority, salvation, and victory. Until we do so, we can never expect to receive lasting help with the last problem. Lasting happiness and joy will not come until we achieve victory over self and sin. Real and lasting peace of mind concerning our relationship with God cannot come to us until we *know* that God himself is satisfied with our personal salvation. This glorious reality of assurance of acceptance with God will be our personal possession the moment we understand and believe the doctrine of *justification by faith*, but we will never grasp this soul liberating truth until we understand, believe, and personally apply the gospel of God's saving promise revealed in God's word to our hearts and lives. Justification before God is by *faith*, and faith that is to be genuine must have *truth* (the promises of God) as its foundation.

The book of Galatians is clearly God's answer to the vital questions of *authority, salvation, and victory over personal sin.* The apostle Paul does answer the question of victory and happiness, but he does so by answering the other two questions first. He begins to address the issue of victory over personal sin and selfishness in 5:16–26. As you read these verses, notice Paul's emphasis on the Holy Spirit and the nature of holiness produced in believers by the Spirit.

> *This I say then, Walk in the Spirit, and ye shall not fulfill the lust of the flesh. For the flesh lusteth against the Spirit, and the Spirit against the flesh: and these are contrary the one to the other: so that ye cannot do the things that ye would. But if ye be led of the Spirit, ye are not under the law. Now the works of the flesh are manifest, which are these; adultery, fornication, uncleanness, lasciviousness, idolatry, witchcraft, hatred, variance, emulations, wrath, strife, seditions, heresies, envyings, murders, drunkenness, revellings, and such like: of the which I tell you before, as I have also told you in time past, that they which do such things shall not inherit the kingdom of God. But the fruit of the Spirit is love, joy, peace, longsuffering, gentleness, goodness, faith, meekness, temperance: against such there is no law. And they that are Christ's have crucified the flesh with the affections and lusts. If we live in the Spirit, let us also walk in the Spirit. Let us not be desirous of vain glory, provoking one another, envying one another.* (KJV)

The only way to conquer the flesh is by walking in the spirit. Paul uses several phrases that need careful explaining. He talks about "living by the Spirit," "walking in the Spirit," and "being led by the Spirit." Look at his uses of the word *spirit* in chapters 4 and 5. Sometimes he is referring to the Holy Spirit and other times to the new spiritual frame of mind given to believers in regeneration (as opposed to the mind of the flesh).

4:6 God sent the Spirit of his Son into our hearts.

4:29 Born according to the Spirit.

5:5 Wait through the Spirit

5:16 Walk [live] in the Spirit.

5:17 Flesh lusteth against the Spirit (and vice versa).

5:18 Led by the Spirit.

5:22 Fruit of the Spirit.

5:25 Live in the Spirit.

5:25 Walk in the Spirit.

(1) To "live in the Spirit" is the same as saying we have been born of the Spirit and have spiritual life. It is the same as saying that we are Christians. Every Christian lives in the Spirit in that he has been born of the Spirit and has spiritual life.

(2) "To walk in the Spirit" is to live out, in day-to-day conduct, the new life given to us at conversion. We will look at both of these phrases carefully when we come to verses 24 and 25.

(3) "To be led by the Spirit" is a little more difficult. It has something to do with living under the new covenant because Paul contrasts "being led by the Spirit" with "being under the law" (verse 18: *"But if you are led by the Spirit, you are not under the law."*) John Brown's comments on this passage are excellent.

> The introductory formula, "This I say," [v. 16] is obviously intended to mark the apostle's sense of the importance of the sentiment he is about to utter. "To walk" is a common figurative expression for conduct. "To walk in the law of the Lord" is to regulate our conduct according to its precepts. To "walk in the Spirit," is to act like spiritual persons—to follow out to their fair practical consequences those views and affections to which, through the faith of the gospel, by the agency of the Holy Spirit, they were formed—to live habitually under the influence of the faith of Christ, and those dispositions which it naturally inspires. 'Deliver yourselves up

to the native force of those new views and affections, and ye will not fulfil the lusts of the flesh.'

"The flesh," as we have just remarked, is the mode of thinking and feeling which is natural to man in the present state of human nature, and "the lust of the flesh" are the desires which naturally rise out of this mode of thinking and feeling. From experience and observation, as well as from Scripture, we know that this mode of thinking and feeling is depraved—wholly depraved. Every man may truly adopt the apostle's language, "In me, that is, in my flesh, dwells no good thing," [Rom. 7:18]. The desires of the flesh then are foolish and criminal desires; and to "fulfil" these desires is to endeavor to gratify them, to adopt the course of conduct to which they naturally lead.

The apostle's statement, then, is this, 'The best way of opposing the criminal biases of our depraved nature, is to yield ourselves up to the practical influence of that new and better mode of thinking and feeling into which we are brought by the faith of the gospel. This will put a more effectual check on the desires of the flesh than the most rigid observance of Mosaic ceremonies. Nothing mortifies pride, malignity, and impure desire, these lusts of the flesh, like walking in the Spirit.' Clear views of Christian truth, accompanied by corresponding affections, followed out to their obvious practical results, will do more to deliver a man from the power of vicious habits than the most minute, laborious series of external services or ritual observances.[122]

Brown assumes that we want to oppose and indeed are engaged in opposing "the criminal biases of our depraved nature." It is important to realize that when we were converted, we went to war against sin. Both Galatians 5 and

---

[122] Brown, *Galatians*, 292, 93.

Romans 7 describe a spiritual war that began the day the life of God was planted in us. The combatants in this war are the flesh—our carnal nature, and the spirit—our new spiritual nature. Or you can say that it is battle between the Devil and the Holy Spirit. In this war with sin and the flesh, the Christian loses many battles, but does not, yea, cannot, lose the war. Likewise, no matter how fierce the battle, the true child of God will not give up the fight and quit the battlefield, nor will he sit down at a conference table and negotiate peace terms. The flesh is the avowed enemy of the spirit. The Christian life is one of unrelenting warfare.

In this war with the flesh, the law of God takes the side of sin and gives the child of God no help. This is a greatly misunderstood truth. Paul makes two statements in this context that are vital to understanding our war with sin. The first one is verse 18, *"But if ye be led of the Spirit, ye are **not under the law**,"* and the second one is verses 22 and 23, *"But the fruit of the Spirit is love, joy, peace, longsuffering, gentleness, goodness, faith, meekness, temperance: **against such there is no law**."*

According to verse 18, it is impossible to be led by the Spirit and to be under the law at the same time. This is an either/or situation. If you are motivated by the Holy Spirit, then you will automatically manifest the fruit of the Spirit. Just as the sap in a tree rises when the sun shines, so the fruit of the Spirit always appears when we are motivated by the love of Christ. Likewise, when the flesh is motivating us, the works of the flesh are in evidence. Works of the flesh and the fruit of the Spirit are the evidences of being under the law or being led by the Spirit. We must be delivered from the law before we can produce the fruit of the Spirit.

Paul says the same thing in Romans 6:14; *"For sin shall not have dominion over you: for ye are not under the law, but under grace."* That is not a promise that you claim by faith; this is a reality experienced by every child of God. It is impossible for sin to have dominion over a Christian! No matter how badly he fared in a battle with temptation, nor how wounded in that battle, the child of God will not quit the field, but will surely rise again and fight, and win, another day.

How can we be so sure that sin cannot possibly have dominion over the Christian? Paul answers in the next verse. The verse says: because the Christian is *"not under the law but under grace."* It is sin that gives the law its power or dominion over us. It is the law that justly condemns us in our sin. But the law cannot condemn sin if the sin has already been punished—and our sin debt has been fully paid by Christ. The child of God is forever free from the law's authority. It cannot touch him. It is the law that gives sin its strength (1 Cor. 15:56), and it is sin that gives law its power or dominion. You must see the law totally satisfied in order to be free from both the authority of the law and power of sin. Our Lord's complete atoning work both fulfilled and satisfied the law and also freed us from its power and tyranny. We can now cry out in victory with Bunyan, "…when this law with its thundering threatenings doth attempt to lay hold on thy conscience, shut it out with a promise of grace; cry, the inn is took up already, the Lord Jesus is here entertained, and here is no room for the law."[123] We can sing with John Newton, "He has hushed the law's loud thunder, He has quenched Mount Sinai's flame; He has

---

[123] *Of the Law and a Christian, Works of Bunyan*, 2:388.

washed us with his blood, He has brought us nigh to God" (John Newton, 1774).

The "lust of the flesh" in 5:16, 17 is, unfortunately, usually associated with sexual lust. This is wrong. Actually the specific things the flesh desires are not necessarily evil in themselves. The Greek word means *strong desire*. What Paul is saying is this, "the flesh sometimes feels a strong desire for something and is tempted to satisfy that desire in a way which is against the clearly revealed will of God." Of course, there are times when the person's lust is after something that is sinful in itself, but that is not necessarily the case. The Holy Spirit does not sin when he 'lusteth after righteousness' (verse 17).

There is no middle ground or basis for compromise in our war with sin. The principle of sin and selfishness is an indelible part of our old nature that will not be totally eradicated until we land in heaven. The Spirit and the flesh are totally contrary to each other. It is impossible for this antagonism to not have a direct bearing on our personal conduct. The flesh keeps us from doing the things we would like to do. In Romans 7, Paul says the same thing, "The good that I would, I do not." The apostle is not saying he is one bundle of frustration and defeat and never obeys God in anything. The "good" in Romans 7:19 is the same as the "things he would, but cannot" in Galatians 5:17—sinless perfection. Paul lusts after perfection, but cannot attain it because of remaining sin. He is resigned to do battle with the flesh until faith gives way to sight and he is delivered from this body of death. He fights with the assurance he will ultimately gain the total victory.

But what about today? Is our only hope for the future when our Lord returns? Paul, in Galatians 5, is talking about the time before the return of Christ. There is a present victory over the flesh. It is not a total victory, nor is it a constant victory, but there is a true victory over sin and self. Anyone whose life is being described in Galatians 5:22, 23 surely cannot be classified as spiritually defeated. Paul's entire exhortation in this section emphasizes walking in the Spirit and not fulfilling the desires of the flesh.

In verses 19 through 23, Paul compares the works of the flesh and the fruit of the Spirit. After listing the works of the flesh, he adds "and the like" to show his lists are not exhaustive. The works list can be divided into four categories—sexual activity, religion, society, and drink.

In the category of sexual activity, Paul lists *immorality, impurity, and licentiousness* (verse 19).

In the category of religion, he lists *idolatry and sorcery.* It should be noted that idolatry is just as much a work of the flesh as is immorality.

In the category of society, the apostle lists eight examples of interpersonal relationship breakdowns. Again, these things are just as much works of the flesh under the curse of God as are sexual impurity and drunkenness. The New English Bible translates 'hostilities, strife, jealousy, outbursts of anger, selfish rivalries, dissensions, factions, envying, murder, (verses 20, 21).

In the category of drink, he lists drunkenness and carousing (or drinking bouts and orgies, verse 21).

Paul warns in verse 21 that they who do these things will not enter the kingdom, but he does not mean that doing any one of these things even once will cause a person to be cast out of the kingdom. It is possible for a person to commit a grievous sin in a given instance after he is converted. David is a clear example of this. However, it is not possible for a Christian to have a lifestyle *dominated* by any of these works of the flesh. The Greek verb tense denotes a habitual practice and not a single instance of succumbing to temptation.

In verses 22 and 23, Paul lists nine Christian graces. John Stott's comments are excellent.

> Here we have a cluster of nine Christian graces which seem to portray a Christian's attitude to God, to other people, and to himself.
>
> Love, joy, peace. This is a triad of general Christian virtues. Yet they seem to primarily concern our attitude towards God, for a Christian's first love is his love for God, his chief joy is in God, and his deepest peace is with God.
>
> Next, patience, kindness, goodness. These are social virtues, manward rather than Godward in their direction. 'Patience' is longsuffering toward those who aggravate or persecute. 'Kindness' is a question of disposition, and 'goodness' of words and deeds.
>
> The third triad is faithfulness, gentleness, self-control. 'Faithfulness' (AV 'faith') appears to describe the reliability of a Christian man. 'Gentleness' is that humble meekness which Christ exhibited (Mt. 11:29; 2 Cor. 10:1). And both are aspects of the 'self-mastery,' or 'self-control,' which concludes the list.[124]

The 'works' of the flesh (verse 19) are plural, and the 'fruit' of the Spirit is singular. Not all unbelievers manifest all of the works of the flesh, but all Christians manifest the

---

[124] Stott, *One Way*, 148

fruit of the Spirit. Not all Christians manifest the fruit of the Spirit to the same degree, but they do have the seeds of the fruit in their hearts. The contrast between 'works' and 'fruit' is deliberate. The flesh literally works hard to produce its efforts, but the Holy Spirit produces his fruit without our efforts. The works of the flesh are the product of our work, and the fruit of the Spirit is the product of the Spirit working in us, "both to will and to do."

After listing specific examples of fruit, Paul adds, "Against such there is no law." We have already seen that when the Spirit leads us, we are not under the law. Paul now adds that there is no need for a law when we are led by the Spirit. Can you imagine making a law saying you are not allowed to show too much love? How about a law restricting kindness? Martin Luther said, "Love God with all of your heart and do as you please." Theoretically, Luther was correct. Paul, in 1 Corinthians 13, describes how a person who loved God with all of his heart would live. When Paul says, "Love is kind," he does not add "because that is what the law demands." Love is kind just because it is the nature of love to be kind. If you made a law that forbad being kind, love would break that law and still show kindness.

Having said all that, we must add that it is impossible for redeemed and regenerated sinners to love God *perfectly*. We need objective definitions of right and wrong, because without them, we would abuse love by turning it into lust for our own ends. The problem is not the weakness of love, but the depravity of the sinner, even the reborn sinner. And having said that, we must add that the answer is not to bring the law into the Christian's life as a means to combat that depravity. One thing Paul is emphatic about in both Romans and Galatians is the inability of the law to conquer sin, whether it be in the lost person or the saved person. The law is like a big club that can be used to control a lion. However, you would be advised not to turn your back on the lion. Preachers can use the law to cower a congregation into subjection, but how effective is the law when the preacher is absent? No, no, my friends, the threat of the law cannot tame the wildness in a heart. Walking in the Spirit is the only answer. We will see this spelled out in 5:24–26.

CHAPTER TWENTY-SEVEN

GALATIANS 5:24–26

We now come to a section of application that has profound implications. Paul continues his discussion of what it means to walk in the Spirit as opposed to walking in the flesh. We will learn a vital truth in these three verses.

> And they that are Christ's have crucified the flesh with the affections and lusts. If we live in the Spirit, let us also walk in the Spirit. Let us not be desirous of vain glory, provoking one another, envying one another. (Gal. 5:24–26 KJV)

Verse 24 is a fact experienced by every child of God. Crucifying the flesh, in the sense Paul uses that phrase in verse 24, is essential to conversion. Every true Christian has "crucified the flesh." That does not mean the Christian no longer sins.

Verse 25 is a positive exhortation based on the fact stated in verse 24. Paul is saying, "Let's prove we really have eternal life, which is living in the Spirit, by the way we live. Let's 'walk in the Spirit' in our day-to-day life and demonstrate the fruits of the Spirit." All Christians, without exception, "live in the Spirit." They "live in the Spirit," or have spiritual life, because they have been born of the Spirit. Paul is not describing some "super" Christians who live in the Spirit as opposed to second-class Christians who know nothing of life in the Spirit. The whole paragraph is addressed to "those that are Christ's," or *all Christians*. All Christians have spiritual life. All Christians "live in the spirit." Those two things are the same. However, all

Christians do not 'walk in the Spirit' with the some consistency. Living in the Spirit and walking in the Spirit are two different things.

Verse 26 is a negative exhortation. We are here told what not to do. We must not be "desirous of vainglory." Vainglory is another word for conceit. Let us not become conceited. Conceited people think too highly of themselves. It is impossible for a conceited person to have a God-honoring relationship with another person. If you think you are better than the other person, you will find a way to challenge them and demonstrate your superiority. If you feel the other person is superior to you, then you will envy them and stay out of their way. The moment you become conceited one of two things will automatically follow. You will either "provoke," meaning challenge, or else you will "envy." Either provoking or envying must inevitably follow a conceited attitude.

The great lesson in verse 26 is this: Your attitude toward yourself totally controls your attitude toward other people. That is not "good psychology;" that is biblical Pauline theology. 1) Your attitude toward yourself determines your attitude toward others, and 2) your attitude toward God determines your attitude toward yourself. If you are conceited or self-righteous, you are not thinking straight about yourself. You are not viewing yourself as God views you in his Word. When you are not honestly facing the truth about yourself as it is revealed in Scripture, then you will automatically act in one of two ways, both of which are wrong. You will either provoke or envy other people depending on how strong or weak you perceive them to be. If you feel stronger than the other person, you will a find a way to challenge them and prove how superior you are. If you feel they are stronger than you, then you will avoid any situation where a challenge shows up your weakness. You will envy these people and try to find ways to see them criticized. You will try to "bring them down a notch." We will work this out in a moment.

The first thing we must do is compare Galatians 5:24 with Romans 6:6. There are both similarities and differences in the two texts. It is vital that we understand these two texts and their relationship to each other.

First, both texts speak of the flesh being crucified.

Second, both texts use the aorist tense for the word *crucify*. This tense is used to denote a 'once and for all action.' An action that is described with an aorist tense never gets bigger or smaller and never happens to the same person again. It never changes; it is done once and for all. It is the difference between something going "boom," once and for all; and going "boooooom," starting and growing; and "boom-boom-boom," happening again and again. Romans 5:1 is an illustration: "Therefore having been justified by faith..." You are just as justified the moment you trust Christ as you will be the day you die. You are just as justified the day you are converted as the Apostle Paul was at the height of his Christian life. Likewise, the act of crucifying the flesh in both Galatians 5:24 and Romans 6:6 is a once and for all act. Those who belong to Christ Jesus have—once and for all-aorist tense—crucified the flesh.

Third, Romans 6:6 is in a *passive* voice and Galatians 5:24 is in an *active* voice. It is vital to see this distinction. The passive voice is used when you want to emphasize that the person involved is being acted upon and not doing any acting. If I say, "Bill threw the ball to me and I was hit by the ball," I am using the active voice to describe what Bill did (threw the ball) and using the passive voice when describing what the ball did to me (it hit me). I did nothing; I was passive. I was acted upon. If I would say, "Bill threw the ball and I caught it," I would use the active voice to describe Bill's action of throwing the ball and also use the active voice to describe what I did in catching it.

Romans 6:6 declares that our old life, or old man, was crucified with Christ at the cross. 'Was crucified' is aorist passive. We did not act at the cross. Christ did it all, and He did it once and for all. It is a finished work, and it was 100% his work. We were passive and did nothing. We were put to death when Christ died for us; we were buried with him, rose from the dead with him, ascended to heaven in him and at this moment we are "seated together in heavenly places in Christ Jesus." We did not have one single thing to do with any of that work. We were passive, and Christ did all the acting in our place. Galatians 5:24 is not in a passive voice. *It is not describing the same thing as Romans 6:6.* It is not describing something that was *done to us*, as described in Romans 6:6; it is describing something *we did.* We consciously and deliberately 'crucified the flesh.' When I say *we*, I mean every Christian. The text says, "They who belong to Christ," and that means each and every Christian "has crucified the flesh." It was the Christian's action. True, we did it 'by grace' and the power of the Holy Spirit, but it was still our action and it was a once for all time action just as much as 'having been crucified with Christ' was a once for all action. If you have never crucified the flesh, in the sense that Paul teaches in verse 24, you are not a Christian.

Obviously, we better be sure what it means to 'crucify the flesh.'

Verse 24 is another way of saying, "We repented of our sin and admitted to the truth of total depravity." The word *repentance* means a change of mind that leads to a change of direction. It is a change of mind about God and his character. We see that he is more than just love and mercy; he is also holy and righteous. It is a change of mind about ourselves. We are not good and nice people who deserve heaven; we are guilty sinners who deserve God's wrath. We change our mind about grace being the only ground for hope of ever being saved. We forever jettison good works as a way to earn God's favor. It is the Holy Spirit who gives us both the insight and desire to obey the truth, but it is our act that changes us. The Holy Spirit does not repent 'for us' nor does Christ believe the gospel in our place.

When we repented, we went from big #1 in our eyes to zero. We went from "hot stuff" to a dung heap. Instead of boasting about how good we were, we acknowledged we were totally depraved. Romans 7:18, "I know that in my flesh dwelleth no good thing," was a personal biography that we willingly signed and acknowledged as our own. We admitted that we deserved judgment and offered no excuse or justification for our sin and guilt. We openly confessed that everything about us deserved the fire, and nothing was worth salvaging. That is how we began our Christian life and that is how we continue in our Christian life. We once for all agreed with God and his Word about what we were in God's sight apart from grace. We repented and confessed that we deserved to die. We continue to remind ourselves every day of what we did at conversion. In an act of confession and commitment, we mentally put to death our old life. All boasting and self-righteousness were gone. We were stripped naked spiritually and came to God "with nothing in our hands" except our sin and his promise.

Our Lord taught us that we must deny ourselves and take up our cross daily and follow him. Taking up the cross is a vivid image of speech that Christ intended to show self-denial. It is a picture, metaphorically, of taking our flesh, our sinful self, and nailing it to a cross because we are convinced there is no good thing about the flesh. It is a picture of our turning our back on the old nature and all of its lusts. John Stott suggests that a Christian's rejection of his old nature is to be *pitiless,* it will be *painful,* and it must be *decisive.*

It is not possible to crucify the flesh until you are convinced that you owe the flesh nothing but death. Romans 8:12 tells us we are not debtors to the flesh. We owe it nothing but death. We must not coddle the flesh or try to protect some pet sins that may seem harmless. We must see the totality of the flesh to be an enemy that must be crucified. The work of crucifixion must be without pity.

Our rejection of our old nature will indeed be painful. There are things and relationships that are very dear to the flesh. They bring us much creature comfort and enjoyment. They also often draw us away from God and godliness. It is a great mistake to deny the reality of sin's appeal. Much sin is pleasant and enjoyable. The hymn writer was correct when he said, "For thee all the *pleasures* of sin I resign." Modern hymnbooks have changed that to, "For thee all the *follies* of sin I resign." It is certainly true that sin is utter folly, but it is also true that sin is very pleasant to the flesh.

John Stott has some excellent thoughts on the need to be decisive in our crucifying the flesh.

Now 'those who belong to Christ Jesus', Paul says, 'have crucified the flesh with its passions and desires'. The Greek verb is in the aorist tense, indicating that this is something we did decisively at the moment of conversion. When we came to Jesus Christ, we repented. We 'crucified' everything we knew to be wrong. We took our old self-centred nature, with all it sinful passions and desires, and nailed it to the cross. And this repentance of ours was decisive, as decisive as a crucifixion. So, Paul says, if we crucified the flesh, we must leave it there to die. We must renew every day this attitude toward sin of ruthless and uncompromising rejection. In the language of Jesus, as Luke records it, every Christian must 'take up his cross *daily*' (Lk. 9:23).

So widely is this biblical teaching neglected, that it needs to be further enforced. The first great secret of holiness lies in the degree and decisiveness of our repentance. If besetting sins persistently plague us, it is either because we have never truly repented, or because, having repented, we have not maintained our repentance. It is as if, having nailed our old nature to the cross, we keep wistfully returning to the scene of its execution. We begin to fondle it, to caress it, to long for its release, even to try to take it down again from the cross. We need to learn to leave it there. When some jealous, or proud, or malicious, or impure thought invades our mind we must kick it out at once. It is fatal to begin to examine it and consider whether we are going to give in to it or not. We have declared war on it; we are not going to resume negotiations. We have settled the issue for good; we are not going to re-open it. We have crucified the flesh; we are never going to draw the nails.[125]

---

[125] Stott, *One Way*, 151, 152

There is an old saying that no matter what time of day you cut off a copperhead snake's head, the snake will not fully die until the sun goes down. I do not know if that is true or not. I do know that sin in us will not fully die until the day we land in heaven. We need the same advice about sin that the old-timers gave about copperhead snakes. Even though the snake's head is cut off, if it wiggles, hit it again!

Verse 24 is stating that we admitted we were totally depraved sinners. We openly confessed there was no good thing in us. In other words, we repented. We agreed with God that we deserved to perish because we were guilty, depraved, hopeless and helpless sinners with no excuse or self-justification. We quit trying to blame our condition on bad parenting, a cruel and non-understanding environment, a temperament inherited from parents that said, 'that is just the way I am.' All of those hiding places were exposed and renounced. We agreed that the flesh, in its totality, deserved death (Rom. 8:12). We did not make any 'provisions' for the flesh (Rom. 13:14) by trying to hang on to some really favorite sins.

Verse 25 is a positive exhortation that logically follows the fact established in verse 24. Paul here exhorts us to prove we have the life of God in us by living that life out in our relationships. Let us prove by the way we live that we are born of God and have his life in us.

If we live in the Spirit, let us also walk in the Spirit. (Gal. 5:25 KJV)

Remember that all Christians live in the Spirit but all Christians do not walk in the Spirit with the same speed or consistency. Exactly what is Paul exhorting Christians to do in this verse? What does it mean to "walk in the Spirit"?

Walking in the Spirit is nothing less than walking in obedience to the revealed will of God in Scripture. It is manifesting the fruit of the Spirit in our relationships instead of the works of the flesh. If a child of God walks in the flesh and manifests the works of the flesh in his life, he is in essence denying what he confessed in verse 24. You can't say, "I am a depraved sinner who deserves his flesh to be crucified" and at the same time be living to please the flesh. That is a contradiction. The moment you start claiming 'rights' and feel justified in using other people for your own ends to meet your needs, you have denied your confession of depravity. How can a person walk in the kind of lifestyle he totally renounced at conversion and, at the same time, claim to love God? Only by forgetting what he confessed to in verse 24 or by proving that he never believed what he confessed in the first place. It is impossible for verse 25 to be true in your experience without verse 24 also being true. One experience is built on the other. You cannot walk in the Spirit and deny total depravity at the same time.

The negative exhortation in verse 26 is, "let us not be conceited." We are told in Scripture to honestly evaluate ourselves. We are to know our strengths and weaknesses. As Clint Eastwood says in one of his Dirty Harry movies, "A man's got to know his limitations." However, we must be honest in our evaluating.

> For by the grace given me I say to every one of you: Do not think of yourself more highly than you ought, but rather think of yourself with sober judgment, in accordance with the measure of faith God has given you. (Rom. 12:3 NIV)

Notice we are to specifically avoid thinking "too highly" of ourselves. Thinking too little of ourselves is far less common but it is just as wrong as thinking too highly of ourselves. For a child of God, it is just as wrong to have an inferiority complex as it is to have a superiority complex. Both of these attitudes grow out of wrong thoughts about yourself and a refusal to evaluate yourself in the light of God's truth. In both cases you are disobeying the Word of God and not accepting what it says about you. There are two vital doctrines you must understand and believe at the same time.

First of all, you must remember the doctrine of total depravity. If you are truly totally depraved, then that means you are better than no one. You cannot look down your nose at any other person nor can you despise anyone for supposedly being worse than you. "Total" depravity admits of no degrees.

Secondly, you must believe and remember the doctrine of unconditional sovereign election. That means no one is better than you. You are one of God's special people. You are the apple of his eye. You were a dead dog, but you are now a child of God. The world may tar and feather you and then light a fire under you, but you are still one of God's elect! No one can cause you eternal hurt. If you can get these two things written in your soul, you are "free" and untouchable in your real life which is hidden in Christ.

We need to look more carefully at the exhortation in Galatians 5:26. What happens when you become conceited? Your actions will deny and contradict what you said and did in verse 24. You start thinking and acting like you really aren't so bad after all. You start believing that there are still some good things about you that deserve recognition. You start feeling you deserve far better treatment than you have gotten. When this happens you have forgotten that you confessed you deserved nothing but damnation. What has really happened? Your wrong thinking is leading to wrong feelings about yourself, and the wrong feelings are starting to produce wrong actions. The "old self" patterns of thinking and actions that you renounced in your repentance return and start controlling and destroying your relationships.

This kind of thinking grows out of having wrong expectations, and wrong expectations grow out of not understanding Scripture. When conceit starts to rule your thinking, then thoughts like "it's not fair" begin to occupy your mind. If we were thinking biblically, we would know that we had no right to think it ever would be fair. It was not fair that they stoned Steven to death; it was not fair that his brothers hated Joseph and sold him to the Egyptians as a slave. We live in a world of sin. We live in a world that hates grace and anyone who exemplifies grace. Where did anyone ever get the idea they had a right to expect fairness? Surely not from the Bible.

Feelings that lead to moods and ultimately to wrong actions do not float in through the window and grab hold of your thoughts and emotions. They come from inside of us. They grow out of the things we believe, out of the way we understand and respond to what we believe to be reality. We start defining reality on our own terms instead of what God says. Your feelings, especially about yourself, are based upon your conviction that the thoughts you believe about yourself are true even if the Devil may have planted those thoughts in your mind. Who told you that you were "hot stuff" and deserved more recognition? Likewise, who told you that you were a useless failure who could not make it? Who convinced you that you had the right to think for another person and control them into serving you to help you reach your goals? In each of these instances it was not the Holy Spirit controlling your mind. It was your old conceited sinful self. Your wrong thoughts about yourself were giving you bad information.

It is no accident that the Bible says a lot about thinking correctly. Look at two representative texts.

For as he thinks in his heart so is he (Prov. 23:7a NKJV)

So Jesus said, "Are you also still without understanding? Do you not yet understand that whatever enters the mouth goes into the stomach and is eliminated? But those things which proceed out of the mouth come from the heart, and they defile a man. For out of the heart proceed evil thoughts, murders, adulteries, fornications, thefts, false witness, blasphemies. These are the things which defile a man, but to eat with unwashed hands does not defile a man." (Matt. 15:16–20 NKJV)

Everything hinges on the thought life. He who controls the mind controls the whole man. How you think determines how you feel, and how you feel determines how you act. This is especially true of your attitude toward, and your treatment of, the people with whom you have any kind of a relationship. If you are conceited enough to think you are #1, it will not be long before you start trying to prove you are #1. Being recognized and treated as #1 is part of the enjoyment of occupying that position.

We keep emphasizing how important it is that we think correctly (biblically) about ourselves and avoid becoming conceited because one or two wrong attitudes must follow. You will challenge those weaker than you to some kind of a contest that enables you to put the other person down and demonstrate your superiority. Since you are superior, you feel justified in using the weak person for your own ends. In your own eyes, you believe using other people is part of the turf that belongs to the strong. One thing is sure, you cannot "love and serve" another person (Gal. 5:13) in any relationship when you feel superior to them. It is vital that we see how inevitable it is that either challenging or envying must follow a conceited attitude.

You have three choices in every relationship.

1. You serve me on my terms because I am better than you. Both of us will grow to despise each other. I will have no respect for you because you are gutless, and you will hate me for using you and taking advantage you.

2 You can reverse the above, and I serve you on your terms. The same painful relationship will follow. In every relationship based on either of these two situations, one person is insignificant and unnecessary. A deacon at a wedding said, "I think that will be a good marriage. Mary loves Jim, and Jim loves Jim."

3. We serve each other on Christ's terms. This is walking in the Spirit. In such a relationship, two people will grow in their love to Christ and to each other.

Who defines the roles and responsibilities in a marriage? Who tells a man how he is to treat his wife and what he has a right to expect from her? Playboy magazine? His father or grandfather–"That's the way we have always done it in this family." The majority in society or the politically correct crowd? A man's own feelings and expectations? Or does the Word of God alone teach him his duty to his wife?

Who tells a woman how to treat her husband? The feminist movement? Her mother and grandmother? The majority or politically correct people? Her own ideas and expectations? Or is the Scripture alone her rule book for her duty to her husband?

Can you imagine a man who spent an hour reading and looking at Playboy magazine and absorbing its philosophy coming home at 5 o'clock from work to a wife who spent half of her afternoon watching soap operas and the other half reading a feminist magazine? The false and selfish expectations imbibed by both would explode in short order.

One of the greatest hindrances to "walking in the Spirit" is confusing duty and feelings. Your feelings have nothing to do with doing your duty. You perform your duty simply because it is your duty. If you do it only because it is duty, you receive no reward. If you do not do your duty, you will always be wrong. That sounds like being between a rock and a hard place. What you do is this: Do your duty even when you don't feel like it and pray to God to enliven your heart to enjoy it! God has made loving your mate a duty whether you feel like it or not. The next time someone tells you they are leaving a mate and children in order to "find themselves," smile, lay your hand on their shoulder and say, "My dear friend, I hope you are successful. I pray you will really find yourself, and when you do you will discover what a conceited self-centered nerd you really are." Try the "I did not feel like going to work" argument on your boss and see if you still have a job.

I suggest every husband and wife read carefully Ephesians 5:22–33. After thinking about it, go back and read verse 21.

You have only two choices. You can walk in the flesh and seek to satisfy needs by using other people, or you can walk in the Spirit and crucify the flesh. It is flesh or Spirit, law or grace, works or faith. Or put another way, you use or serve others. We can walk in the Spirit and keep remembering that we once and for all crucified the flesh and consciously put to death the deeds of the flesh. We can understand that "No, I do not owe my flesh any gratification at all. It is my sworn enemy, and its every promise is really a ticket to trouble." We must keep reaffirming our repentance in order to maintain the right attitude and actions. When the flesh tempts us to satisfy a lust, get out the canceled check signed in our Lord's blood and say, "Flesh, I owe you nothing." Reaffirm again your biography as recorded in Romans 7:18. Also remind yourself of your sovereign election and "the blessed hope" set before us.

I repeat what I said earlier. It is impossible to believe in total depravity and sovereign election and have either a superior or inferior attitude. A religion that uses rules to control people can easily engender a false loyalty and will soon lead to legalism. The same is true in any relationship. Where rules reign, judging soon follows, and a superior condemning attitude is not far behind. Such an atmosphere will always use guilt for breaking the rules as a means of control. Pastors and parents are experts at manipulation by guilt. *God never uses guilt to motivate us. He uses the love of Christ.*

Those who use guilt to motivate have all kinds of ways to lay false guilt on you. It is called "putting you on a guilt trip." False guilt is more difficult to deal with than true guilt. True guilt can be confessed and be forgiven. Even God cannot forgive false guilt. The only person who can remove false guilt is the one who laid the guilt on you. If your Mama put the guilt on you, then Mama is the only one who can take it off. If the pastor put you on a false guilt trip, then he alone can remove the false guilt. The price you pay for him to remove such guilt is for you to give him your conscience and blindly obey without question his every whim. He will call it your God-given "duly authorized" responsibility. Paul calls it stupidity.

Whenever a relationship demands that you must "earn" the other person's love and approval, then Galatians 5:16 and 5:26 are in motion. We love and forgive "for Christ's sake" even as Christ loved and forgave us. A husband cannot love and serve his wife if he really believes he deserves a better wife. If a wife honestly feels she is superior to her husband, she may outwardly submit to him, but it will not last. The lid will blow off. A pastor cannot love and serve a congregation if he believes his gifts deserve a much bigger hearing. Likewise a congregation cannot love and serve a pastor when they believe their present pastor is "below their status in the community." This is what walking in the flesh versus walking in the Spirit is all about.

One last thing, how should a Christian who is caught red-handed in sin respond when reminded of what they did by an unsaved person? Let's say a Christian woman is married to a non-Christian man. She is goaded into a fight with her husband. She gets angry and says some awfully mean things to him. He smiles and says, "So that is the way Christians act when they get upset." That is not the time to try to justify yourself by saying, "Well, at least I sincerely try to get along and you could not care less." No, don't say that. You sinned and you know it, your husband knows it, and God knows it. Sin must be confessed. In such a situation the wife should say (even if the husband deliberately provoked the fight), "Honey, you are right. I sinned and I am sorry. I was not a good example of a Christian." When he wakes up (he will faint), say, "I asked God to forgive me and I want you to forgive me also." Give him a little kiss and say, "I wish you were a Christian and could help me in my Christian life to be a better wife. I really do love you." That is walking in the Spirit. That is manifesting the fruit of the Spirit.

In the next chapter we will look at more ways the new life in the Spirit is worked out in everyday life.

CHAPTER TWENTY-EIGHT

GALATIANS 6:1–5

Brethren, if a man is overtaken in any trespass, you who are spiritual restore such a one in a spirit of gentleness, considering yourself lest you also be tempted. Bear one another's burdens, and so fulfill the law of Christ. For if anyone thinks himself to be something, when he is nothing, he deceives himself. But let each one examine his own work, and then he will have rejoicing in himself alone, and not in another. For each one shall bear his own load. (Gal. 6:1–5 NKJV)

At first glance, these verses seem to have minimal connection with the preceding verses, which have been detailing the fruit of the Spirit and encouraging the Galatians to walk by the Spirit. If, however, we read carefully, we will see a vital connection. Paul, in 5:26, has described walking in the Spirit negatively, that is, not becoming conceited, not provoking each other, and not envying each other. As we think about that connection, let us note five obvious problems that appear in the passage. We will not have space to answer them all, but we will deal with some of the more pressing ones.

First, how can a person think of himself as spiritual without already being conceited—having the wrong attitude? Are not people who identify themselves as spiritual and therefore capable of restoring someone overtaken in sin already fallen into the sin of pride themselves? Would not their judgment of themselves as spiritual prove they were proud—conceited?

Second, the first section deals with restoring a fellow believer overtaken by sin, but most of the caution and warning is given to the one attempting the restoring.

Third, what does Paul mean by "the law of Christ"? This is the only place he uses that phrase in any of his epistles.

Fourth, why would Paul bring up law-keeping here when elsewhere in his letter he continually emphasizes that the Christian is not under the law? In chapter 5, he contrasted law and Spirit. There is no law against the fruit of the Spirit (vv. 22, 23). Now he seems to equate walking in the Spirit with fulfilling the law of Christ. Is there a law that is for (commands) the fruit of the Spirit?

Fifth, Paul instructs his readers in verse 2 to "bear one another's burdens," and then in verse 5, he writes that everyone is to "bear his own load." On the surface, the two instructions seem contradictory. Which instruction of the two (if either) fills the requirement of walking by the Spirit?

Let us look at the first problem. It seems to me that if individuals carefully evaluated themselves to see if they were spiritual enough to have a restoring ministry with the person overtaken, only self-righteous, conceited people would ever attempt such a ministry. The author of Proverbs writes, *"The righteous are bold as a lion"* (Prov. 28:1). Unfortunately, the self-righteous are just as bold.

What makes a person truly spiritual, and how does such a person know that he is spiritual enough for the ministry of restoring a fallen fellow believer? In chapter 5, Paul describes a spiritual person (one who walks by the Spirit [vv. 16, 25]; one who is led by the Spirit [v. 18]) as someone whose life exhibits the fruits of the Spirit. He is a person who shows, among other things, genuine love and compassion. When such a person sees a brother hurting, it does not occur to him to ask, "Am I spiritual enough to help?" These people automatically reach out to help. They make an effort to help because their hearts want to help. They cannot keep from reaching out to help, because they sincerely desire to do all they can for the person overtaken.

On the other hand, a person who looks at the overtaken person and thinks, "he really asked for the trouble he is in," or, "it is not my concern and I will not get involved," or "let him learn the hard way," is not spiritual enough to help the overtaken person. Such a person has disobeyed our Lord's commandment against judging. The non-spiritual person has judged the fallen brother as not worthy of help. This conceited person is acting in the undesirable ways described in our last chapter. The attitude toward self as better than the person overtaken makes it impossible for the self-righteous, conceited person to love the fallen and try to help. If ever we needed to remember our own depravity, it is when we see someone overtaken by sin. This is why Paul, as per number two above, gives sharp warnings to those seeking to help. If ever we needed to guard our hearts against thinking too highly of ourselves, it is when we are confronted by someone overtaken by sin. Even those who are spiritual and who try to help the fallen face the danger of falling themselves into a self-righteous, judgmental attitude.

When Paul cautions helpers against being tempted (6:1), he does so on two fronts: watch yourselves so that you do not fall into the same sin as that committed by the fallen one, and watch yourselves so that you are not tempted to be proud, judgmental, and self-righteous. Any person who consciously feels spiritual enough to qualify for this ministry probably is not spiritual enough. Paul himself writes as much in verse 3, *"For if anyone thinks himself to be something, when he is nothing, he deceives himself."* The author of the letter to the Hebrews, when reminding his readers about the qualifications of the high priest, also points to a humble, compassionate, self-awareness of personal sin:

> For every high priest taken from among men is ordained for men in things pertaining to God, that he may offer both gifts and sacrifices for sins: Who can have compassion on the ignorant, and on them that are out of the way; for that he himself also is compassed with infirmity. And by reason hereof he ought, as for the people, so also for himself, to offer for sins. (Heb. 5:1–3 KJV)

This Hebrews author seems to distinguish between those who through ignorance go astray (*the ignorant*) and those who deliberately and knowingly sin (*them that are out of the way*). We often do the same in our own experience. It is far easier to love and pity a person who has fallen through ignorance than it is to love and pity someone whose problem resulted from deliberate rejection of loving warnings and exhortations. However, true compassion for those in either group (the ignorant or the out-of-the-way) cannot co-exist with pride and self-righteousness in the heart. It is essential that every Christian, and especially every leader, remember their own total depravity. No one should approach the ministry of restoration without feeling, "There, except for the grace of God, go I."

I was recently asked to speak at a sovereign grace conference on the subject of how to be gracious in preaching the doctrines of grace. I was looking forward to preaching, but health reasons forced me to cancel. Had I been able to preach, I would have mentioned Hebrews 5:1–3. One problem with preaching grace is being certain that you first feel its power in your own soul. 'Hard' Calvinists scare me. They can win theological arguments, but they often leave destroyed lives behind them. Some of these leaders are ready and willing to use church discipline for any reason, but too often they lack compassion. They use church discipline as a tool of intimidation and control. Hyper-Calvinists are not happy people. The only things they have to share are law, wrath, and condemnation. When they seek to restore a fallen brother, all they can use is a club. If only they felt the power of grace in their own hearts, they would know how to weep when they talk about **both** repentance and assurance of forgiveness. Since, however, they have never experienced heartfelt assurance themselves, they cannot share it with others. They cannot share love and joy, since they themselves are loveless and joyless.

I once shared my personal testimony at a large CBMC meeting in Toronto. During the message, I used an illustration about God's sovereignty and then said, "You can tell from that illustration that I am one of those people known as Calvinists." That night at 11:00 PM my phone rang and a young man asked, "Are you the man who spoke at the St. George Hotel this evening?" I said, "Yes." He then asked to see me at my earliest convenience. When we got together he said, "I am not a Christian. I am from the Netherlands. I can quote the *Canons of Dort* and the *Heidelberg Catechism* forwards and backwards. I have heard the greatest Reformed preachers in the world." I asked him, "Why did you want to talk to me? I doubt I can tell you anything you have not already heard many times." He said, "You are the first Calvinistic preacher I ever heard that preached with a smile on his face!" Why do so many Reformed preachers have such difficulty smiling?

When Paul refers in Galatians 6:1 to those caught in any transgression, he does not mean people whose whole lifestyle contradicts the gospel they claim to believe. Being overcome by temptation and living in habitual sin are two different things. Paul's immediate exhortation in the following verse to "bear one another's burdens" implies that the fall into sin was in some way associated with a personal burden that led to the transgressor's being overtaken. The individual who fell was simply unable to handle a trial or test of his faith. Committing a sin was the easy way out. In such a situation, restoration would involve not only helping the individual out of that sin, but also helping to bear the burden that the Devil used to tempt the individual into sin in the first place.

The word *restore* is used when speaking of re-setting a broken bone in place or restoring a function to a part of the body that has been damaged. When one part is not functioning as it was made to function, the entire body suffers. Paul uses the term metaphorically to refer to the relationship between a single believer and the entire body of Christ. When an individual follower of Christ is overtaken in temptation, the entire body of Christ suffers. The new covenant doctrine of the priesthood of believers is involved in the ministry of the restoration of a fallen brother.

We have looked at the first two problems listed above: self-evaluation and restoration of a fallen brother. Now let us consider the third issue. The phrase, *the law of Christ*, is not easy to identify positively. Paul is the only author of Scripture to use this precise phrase (νομον του Χριστου), and he only uses it here in Galatians 6:2. He implies it in his first letter to the Corinthians (1 Cor. 9:19–21 NIV), where he writes about being under the law of Christ (εννομος Χριστου):

> Though I am free and belong to no man, I make myself a slave to everyone, to win as many as possible. To the Jews I became like a Jew, to win the Jews. To those under the law I became like one under the law (though I myself am not under the law), so as to win those under the law. To those not having the law I became like one not having the law (though I am not free from God's law but am **under Christ's law**), so as to win those not having the law.

What does Paul mean by the phrase *the law of Christ*? In the letter to the church at Corinth, Paul equates the law of God with the law of Christ and then contrasts the law of Christ with the law of Moses. The law of Christ may have some similarities with the law of Moses, but the law of Christ is radically different in other ways. In this way, the phrase distinguishes between the basis of the old and new covenants. The apostle John records John the Baptist's clear annunciation of the most radical difference:

> John testifies concerning him. He cries out, saying, "This was he of whom I said, 'He who comes after me has surpassed me because he was before me.'" From the fullness of his grace we have all received one blessing after another. **For the law was given through Moses; grace and truth came through Jesus Christ.** (John 1:15–17 NIV)

John was not saying that before Christ came, there was no grace or truth at all in God's dealings with his people. The Hebrew Scriptures, the Scriptures to which John had access, stated otherwise. *"Noah found **grace** in the eyes of God"* (Gen. 6:8), and the psalmist wrote, *"mercy and **truth** are met together"* (Psa. 85:10). John would have been aware of these passages, and he would not have contradicted them. Nor is he saying there are no commandments in the new covenant. John is speaking here the same way Paul will speak when he writes in 2 Corinthians 3 that the new covenant is superior to the old. Paul acknowledges that the old covenant was glorious, but when its glory is compared to the glory of the new covenant, the old is so inferior it is as if it had no glory at all (2 Cor. 3:7–11).

When John writes in 1:16, *"From the fullness of his grace we have received one blessing after another,"* he is pointing out that God's people never received the blessings promised by the law of Moses. All that they received from Moses was death and just condemnation, because they had failed to keep the terms of the covenant. God's new covenant people, however, enjoy every spiritual blessing through the fullness of the grace of Christ.

The law of Christ and the law of Moses are radically different in nature. Peter argued against putting Gentile converts under the law of Moses because it was a yoke too heavy to bear (Acts 15:5, 10). During his earthly ministry, our Lord insisted the law-yoke that he put on the neck of his disciples was easy and the burden they were called to bear was light. Instead of struggling in despair under Christ's law, we find that law provides comfort and rest for our entire being (Matt. 11:28–30). The law and the gospel are two different things. The law of Moses was the old covenant. The old covenant was summarized and written on the tables of the covenant, or Ten Commandments.

Then the LORD said to Moses, "Write down these words, for in accordance with these words I have made a covenant with you and with Israel." Moses was there with the LORD forty days and forty nights without eating bread or drinking water. And he wrote on the tablets the words of the covenant—the Ten Commandments. (Ex. 34:27–28 NIV)

The tables of the covenant upon which were written the "words of the covenant" (Deut. 9:9–11) were then placed into the ark of the covenant. The box was called the ark of the *covenant* because it housed the covenant document, the Ten Commandments.

There was not an ounce of grace *in* the ark of the covenant. It contained a law that said, "do and live, disobey and die." That box was holy because it contained the covenant terms of Israel's relationship with God: it was so holy that even to touch it meant death. The lid of the ark, however, was called the mercy seat, and when it was sprinkled with blood on the Day of Atonement, it spelled nothing but grace. The tables of the covenant in the box said, "stay away, do not touch," but the blood on the lid said, "come and welcome." The words on the tables of the covenant in the box were the summary of the terms of the old covenant, and the blood on the mercy seat foreshadowed the terms or foundation of the new covenant. This was what John meant when he said,

> For the law was given through Moses; grace and truth came through Jesus Christ. (John 1:17 NIV)

We will better understand the meaning of the phrase, *law of Christ*, if we understand exactly how that law is fulfilled and how it is disobeyed. We may have trouble identifying the specific content of the law of Christ, but we cannot miss the fact that we fulfill it when we bear one another's burdens. Paul specifically commands us to *"bear one another's burdens,"* and declares that in so doing we *"fulfill the law of Christ"* (verse 2). From this text, we can legitimately conclude that the law of Christ includes a commandment to "bear one another's burden." In his commentary, John Brown explains that bearing one another's burdens is to love mutually:

> The apostle enforces his injunction to bear one another's burdens by a powerful motive: by doing so, Christians "fulfil the law of Christ." "The law of Christ" seems here plainly to be the law of mutual love, so often and so explicitly enjoined, and so powerfully and affectionately enforced,–John xiii. 34, 35; xv. 12. There does not seem to be anything emphatic in the word "fulfil." It just signifies to obey. When Christians bear one another's burdens, they obey the law of Christ; and when they do not, they violate that law. When they act in the manner in which we have described, they show that they really love one another; and when they act in an opposite way, they show that they do not love one another. It is a very powerful motive with a Christian mind to reflect, 'If I do this, I do what is well pleasing to my Saviour— what he has required of me as a proof of my love and obedience—and if I do not this, I displease him, I trample on his authority, I dishonour his name.'

> There seems to be a tacit contrast between the law of Moses and the law of Christ. It is as if the apostle had said, 'This bearing one another's burdens is a far better thing than those external observances which your new teachers are so anxious to impose on you. To be sure, it is not like them, a keeping of the law of Moses, but infinitely better, it is a fulfilling of the law of Christ—the law of love.'[126]

The law of Christ is not a new covenant list of laws that replaces or contradicts the old covenant list. The law of Christ neither explicitly nor implicitly permits theft or

---

[126] Brown, *Galatians*, 325, 26.

adultery. The law of Christ moves and motivates by love, and not by threat based on objective law, no matter how holy, just, and good that objective law may be. Paul points out his contrast by his command to restore the fallen member of God's people with gentleness. This was not the way of keeping God's people pure under the law of Moses. The law of Moses required sacrifice or expulsion. Love reaches out to a fallen believer and law, rightly so because of its nature, starts gathering stones (Heb. 10:28).

On several occasions, we have quoted Luther's statement, "love God with all your heart and do as you please." Many current Reformed people vehemently insist that love without law is blind. When we understand correctly the true law of Christ and the true nature of love, we will see that Luther was correct and the Reformed folks are wrong. Let me explain. *Love, by its very nature, does not need any law.* No one who loved his neighbor would steal from him, molest his wife, or kill him. Anyone who hated his neighbor may possibly do any or all of those things. Adam did not have a law that told him not to steal or not to murder. His loving nature controlled his life. Adam was just as incapable of committing any sin, except one— eating the fruit from the tree of the knowledge of good and evil— as we will be in heaven. I infer from the sermons of some preachers that the Ten Commandments will be posted on every street corner in heaven. Adam had no law simply because he did not need a law. The law was never made for a righteous man (1 Tim. 1:8–11).

The problem is that you and I, and all other sinners, have a sinful nature instead of a pure nature, as Adam had. We cannot possibly love God with all of our hearts. We desperately need objective definitions of God's will for how we should live. In no sense is our inability the fault of a weakness in love. The fault lies in our inability to truly love and not in the nature and power of love. Paul, in 1 Corinthians 13, defines love as being kind. Is true love always kind? Yes. Can true love be anything other than kind? No. If you made a law that forbids kindness, would true love disobey that law and show kindness? Yes. That is precisely Paul's point in Galatians 5:22–23 as he describes the fruit of the Spirit and concludes that there are no (nor can there be) laws against these things. There are (and must be) laws against the desires of the flesh, but the nature of the desires of the Spirit precludes them from laws against them. Why is love always kind? Why **must** love be kind? Does the law and its just threats have anything at all to do with why love is kind? None at all! Love is kind just because it is the nature of love to be kind! True love does not need law in any sense. However, sinners need law to keep them from abusing love and turning it into lust. If we could desire, feel, and practice love as Paul describes it in 1 Corinthians 13, we could indeed "do as we please." Since that is impossible because of indwelling sin, we need clear objective standards that describe love for us. We can know that love is the right thing to do, but we do not always know *what* is the loving thing to do. The Holy Spirit informs us through the Scripture, transforming us thereby so that we become more like Jesus, who always loved God with all his being and his neighbor as himself. We need to explore the relationship between law and love more fully.

The fifth problem we identified with this passage was the seeming contradiction between bearing one another's burdens and bearing one's own load (vv. 2 and 5). We can resolve the apparent contradiction by recognizing that in his exhortation to *bear one another's burdens* in verse 2, Paul refers to a different kind of burden than he does in verse 6: *each man shall bear his own burden.* Our English translations do not clearly make the distinction that would have been obvious to Paul's audience. Paul uses two different Greek words that distinguish between kinds of loads. The word in verse 2 means a heavy, weighty load (with the emphasis always on the weight), and the word in verse 6 means responsibility—something that is borne (without reference to its weight): it could mean the cargo of a ship or something as light as a knapsack. All of us have sometimes been forced to carry a heavy load of responsibility, a mental anguish, a bitter defeat, a sickness, or some other weighty burden. That is what verse 2 is talking about. We can help to lighten many of these burdens for each other. We should not be ashamed to ask a fellow believer for help to bear this kind of a burden when possible. It is no sign of spiritual weakness to ask for needed help, nor is it presumptuous of us to offer help when we can. I know there are some Christians that insist it is sufficient that we "roll our burden on the Lord," but we cannot ignore Paul's words by appealing to piety.

The word in verse 5 is another matter. There are some things that only the individual can carry. Each of us has personal responsibilities. We all bear the cross alone. No one can crucify our own fleshly desires for us. We do that alone (by loving Christ through the power of the Holy Spirit). Additionally, we all have some burdens that no human ear has ever heard about, simply because it is impossible that a human being could either understand or help. Paul assures us that God's grace will enable us to carry those things by ourselves. They will never be too heavy (1 Cor. 10:13).

I want to mention one more issue that arises from reading Galatians 6:1–5. We need to compare the "restoring of a man taken in a trespass" (Gal. 6:1) and dealing with a brother who has "trespassed against thee" (Matt. 18:15–17). Jesus, in Matthew 18, was teaching about greatness in the kingdom of heaven and referred to the required attitude toward a trespass that was personal, i.e. a sin against you. This breach of relationship, if not repaired privately, could lead to church discipline. Paul, in Galatians 6:1, was teaching about walking by the Spirit, and referred to the required attitude toward a trespass that was not necessarily personal, i.e., a sin not against you. This sin, if left without correction, could well lead to church discipline, but that was not the focus of his paragraph. One of the surprising things about both passages is that neither mentions *elders or any other church officials!* Matthew 18 mentions church discipline in terms of the entire church (*tell it to the church*). In both passages, it is "one another" that are involved.

Let me conclude with a quote from John Stott, who points to the Christ-like nature of burden bearing.

> …to love one another as Christ loved us may lead us not to some heroic, spectacular deed of self-sacrifice, but to the much more mundane and unspectacular ministry of burden-bearing.

To be a burden-bearer is a great ministry. It is something that every Christian should and can do. It is a natural consequence of walking by the Spirit. It fulfils the law of Christ. 'Therefore', wrote Martin Luther, 'Christians must have strong shoulders and mighty bones'—sturdy enough, that is, to carry heavy burdens.[127]

For Paul, one of the benefits of the freedom to which Christ calls his followers is living by the Spirit. This living results in a lifestyle characterized by the fruit of the Spirit, which manifests itself in attitudes that make for positive interpersonal relationships. One aspect of a positive interpersonal relationship is a humble, gentle willingness to help our fellow believers live Christ-like lives, while at the same time, taking responsibility for our own attitudes. Paul sees this kind of interaction between believers as the purpose of our calling to be free: we need to be free from whatever enslaves us so that we can serve one another in love.

---

[127] Stott, *One Way*, 158-59.

CHAPTER TWENTY-NINE

GALATIANS 6:6–10

Throughout his letter to the Galatians, Paul forcefully asserted his authority as an apostle of Christ. He systematically and clearly laid out the doctrine of justification by faith alone. He both refuted and condemned the Judaizers who, by seeking to place the Galatian Christians under the Mosaic law, denied the gospel of sovereign grace. At the close of chapter 5, Paul wrote that living by the Spirit ought to produce walking by the Spirit. In the opening verses of chapter 6, he described some specifics of walking in the Spirit: gently restoring those who stray, bearing one another's burdens, and shouldering individual responsibilities (vv. 1–5). As Paul nears the end of his letter, he continues to exhort his readers to walk by the Spirit, providing practical details about bearing each other's burdens.

> *Anyone who receives instruction in the word must share all good things with his instructor. Do not be deceived: God cannot be mocked. A man reaps what he sows. The one who sows to please his sinful nature, from that nature will reap destruction; the one who sows to please the Spirit, from the Spirit will reap eternal life. Let us not become weary in doing good, for at the proper time we will reap a harvest if we do not give up. Therefore, as we have opportunity, let us do good to all people, especially to those who belong to the family of believers.* (Gal. 6:6–10 NIV)

The relationship Paul describes between teachers and learners is one practical way in which Christians bear each other's burdens. Learning about Christ is necessary in order to imitate him. Therefore, ignorance about Christ is a burden that those who teach about Christ alleviate. But teaching about Christ creates other burdens: specifically, time management. Those who spend time in study cannot use that time to earn money to provide for their own needs. Therefore, those who are taught lift that burden when they share what they can earn with those who teach them. Each group (the learners and the teachers) has particular needs that the other group is particularly suited to meet.

This relationship between those who learn and those who teach can be difficult to discuss. On the one hand, the Christian ministry is a calling and not a vocation. It is hard to imagine the clergy forming a union and having their union representatives negotiate, among other things, a salary. What would we think of an individual who was called to serve as a missionary comparing health programs or retirement benefits of various foreign mission boards as a means to determine where the Lord wanted him to serve? On the other hand, who could fault a pastoral candidate for deciding against serving a church that believed, "God will keep the pastor humble and we will keep him poor"?

The potential exists for both groups to shirk their responsibility to bear each other's burdens. The teacher could abuse it by being lazy and not studying, which would result in shallow sermons that would not lift the burden of needing to know more about Christ from those entrusted to his care. Conversely, he could spend all his time in his study and thus remain unaware of the particulars of his congregation's ignorance of Christ. In such a case, he would not know the needs of his congregation and would not be able to minister to those needs. The members of the congregation would remain burdened. A pastor has no direct supervisors to whom he is accountable for his time and work. John Stott, in his commentary on Galatians, addresses this problem:

> Is there any safeguard against this possible abuse? I think we may find one in I Timothy 5:17: 'Elders who do well as leaders should be reckoned worthy of a double stipend, in particular those who labour at preaching and teaching. For Scripture says, "A threshing ox shall not be muzzled"; and besides, "the workman earns his pay"' (NEB). It is not particularly flattering, perhaps, to find the preacher likened to a threshing ox! But he is also called a 'workman' or labouring man. The Greek word is strong and indicates that he 'toils' at the Word with all his might and main, seeking to understand and apply it. Perhaps preaching is at a low ebb in the church today because we shirk the hard work involved. But if the minister throws himself into his ministry with the energy of a labouring man, and sows good seed in the minds and hearts of the congregation, then he may expect to 'reap' a material livelihood.[128]

A true gospel-ministry is not at all an easy task. Those who fulfill its responsibility earn whatever they receive just as surely as if they had labored manually. Paul likens a pastor's work of caring for a flock to the work of both a shepherd and a mother. A person who seriously cares for the souls of others experiences deep spiritual struggles, emotional pain, and distress. This is hard work.

Paul, in more than one letter, makes it clear that those who proclaim the gospel should get their living by the

---

[128] Stott, *One Way*, 168.

gospel (1 Cor. 9:14). Paul deliberately gave up this right and earned his living by making tents, but in none of his writings does he suggest that this should be the practice of every preacher. Paul faced a cultural situation that made it expedient for him to forgo his right to financial support. In the first-century Greco-Roman world, Sophists earned a living by teaching men how to argue either side of a question. Effective persuasive public-speaking (rhetoric) was a highly-prized skill in this culture, and the Sophists provided training in this art. The problem (from a Christian viewpoint) lay, however, in their beliefs about truth. The Sophists were skeptics who believed that there was no way to prove whether truth existed or not. Even if it did exist, there was no way to know if it corresponded to a person's perception of it. Therefore, the question of the truth of a matter was irrelevant: the ability to argue well was what was desirable. Paul, by refusing to accept payment for his teaching, distanced himself from the Sophists. If he had accepted what was his due (financial support from those who learned from him), he might have undermined the truth claims in his teaching by seeming to be no different than the Sophists—in it for the money.

Teachers are not the only group that has the potential to fail in this particular burden-bearing relationship. No learners have the right to neglect their responsibility to bear the financial burdens that those who teach must of necessity bear. Paul writes that *the Lord* has commanded this (1 Cor. 9:14). Learners could abuse their responsibility less overtly, however, by trying to control what a teacher says. Such a congregation might feel that since it pays the teacher, it has the right to tell him what to teach: "Whoever pays the piper must be allowed to call the tune." It is sinful for a congregation to use financial pressure to control a teacher's message, and it is also sinful for him to yield to such tactics. However, if a minister has a wife and children to support, he faces the particular temptation to tickle the ears of his congregation. A congregation has no right to put such a temptation in the path of a pastor. He has a responsibility to provide for his family's financial needs. These competing relationship demands pose a dilemma for a tender conscience. If he meets his congregation's true needs against their wishes, he fails in his familial duties. If he concedes to his congregation's unbiblical demands, he provides for his family at the expense of his biblical responsibility to his congregation. In the long run, a congregation will suffer as much from a minister yielding to such a temptation, as will the minister himself.

In most of the churches with whom I am familiar, the congregations faithfully fulfill their responsibility to bear the financial burdens of their teachers. Those who are eager to learn more about Christ respond well to those who teach the truth about Christ. If there is any problem at all in these churches, it is that the congregation loves its pastor too much! Often, in my personal experience, I felt I was paid more than I was worth.

Once, when I was a candidate for the pastorate of a church, the congregation raised the subject of my salary before we had come to any decision about whether or not they were going to call me and whether or not I would accept. I suggested that we should settle those matters first. I said I did not think salary amount should be a factor in my decision. If they offered me a very generous salary, I might be influenced to accept, even if I had reservations. If they offered me too little, I might be influenced not to accept when other things seemed to indicate I should come. I told them I trusted them to do what was right. I found out later (after I accepted the call) that they changed their budget and added hospital insurance to my salary.

In verse 7, Paul illustrates the nature of teacher/learner burden-bearing by applying an agriculture metaphor: a person reaps what he sows. This principle, established by God in Genesis 8:22, applies equally to learners and teachers. *As long as the earth endures, seedtime and harvest, cold and heat, summer and winter, day and night will never cease.* Both groups have to make a choice. They may sow to the flesh (acting selfishly by refusing to bear each other's burdens) or they may sow to the Spirit. The first sowing results in a harvest of fleshly corruption; the second in a harvest of Spiritual life. Paul uses the same metaphor in one of his letters to the Corinthians as he points to the reciprocal nature of the teacher/learner relationship:

> *If we have sown spiritual seed among you, is it too much if we reap a material harvest from you? If others have this right of support from you, shouldn't we have it all the more?* (1 Cor. 9:11, 12a NIV)

In 1 Corinthians 3, Paul likens those who learn to a garden and those who teach to those who tend the garden. Some teachers plant, others water. If we can extend that metaphor a bit, we can say that teachers also pull weeds. A successful harvest depends on the kind of seeds sown, the right amount of water applied during the growing season, and careful weeding.[129]

---

[129] In the same letter, Paul also likens the learners to a temple and the teachers to the builders of that temple. Some teachers use gold, silver

Let us unpack this metaphor to see how it applies to the responsibilities of teachers.

(1) Someone must sow if there is to be a harvest.

(2) What is sown determines what is harvested.

(3) God has promised that a harvest is certain if there is a sowing.

Notice that the *nature* of the harvest is determined by the kind of seed that is sown. We cannot harvest wheat where we planted corn. Tomato plants will never yield potatoes. The same principle applies in behavior and morals. Teachers who do not "plant Christ" cannot expect to see Christ-like qualities in their congregations.

Not only does the seed determine the *nature* of the harvest, it also determines the *quality* of the harvest. Inferior seed will produce an inferior crop just as superior seed will yield a superior harvest. The best of ground cannot compensate for a poor quality of seed. Teachers can plant an inferior Christ by failing to present a full Scriptural account of Christ. Teachers who choose to present only certain qualities of Christ while neglecting to teach about other qualities will produce congregations who fail to embody all the Christian virtues.

Lastly, the *quantity* of the harvest is also determined at the planting time. If we sow sparingly, we will have a sparse harvest. There is no plentiful harvest without a generous

---

and precious stones; others use wood, hay and stubble. In the day when God judges each teacher's labor, the verdict will depend on the kind of building material used. The great lesson for teachers in Galatians 6 and 1 Corinthians 3 is to be faithful to the truth as found in God's book.

sowing. Teachers sow generously by modeling Christ to their congregations as well as by formally teaching about him.[130]

John Stott integrates these three points about the harvest thusly,

> ...if a farmer wants a bumper harvest of a particular corn, then he must not only sow the right seed, but good seed and that plentifully. Only if he does this can he expect a good crop.[131]

Paul prefaces his remarks about reaping and sowing with a clear warning, *"Do not be deceived: God cannot be mocked."* You can no more fool God than you can fool the ground in your garden. You may foolishly believe that your tomato plants will yield potatoes, but you will be sorely disappointed every time. This principle applies beyond the burden-bearing relationship between teachers and learners: it extends to every kind of sowing and reaping. You may sow the world, believing that the world and the things of it will yield satisfaction and meaning, but your expectations will prove futile at the time of harvest or judgment. You may believe that if you give your heart, efforts, and resources to the world and its goals, you will receive a harvest of satisfaction, but you will be mocked when harvest time comes. You cannot deny God's principle of sowing and reaping in any area. To think or act as if you are exempt

---

[130] Paul also applied this particular aspect (generous sowing) to financial giving in 2 Corinthians 9:6, 7a,"Remember this: Whoever sows sparingly will also reap sparingly, and whoever sows generously will also reap generously. Each man should give what he has decided in his heart to give..."

[131] Stott, *One Way*, 165-66.

from God's fixed law is to blind yourself to reality. John Stott explains why Paul links this principle to the command "do not be deceived:"

The possibility of being deceived is mentioned several times in the New Testament. Jesus said the devil was a liar and the father of lies, and He cautioned His disciples against being led astray. [John 8:44; Mark 13:5, 6, 22]. John warns us in his Second Epistle that 'many deceivers have gone out into the world'. [2 John 7. *Cf.* 1 John 2:18–27; 4:1–6]. Paul begs us in his Letter to the Ephesians: 'Let no one deceive you with empty words.' [Eph. 5:6. *Cf.* 1 Cor. 6:9; 2 Thess. 2:3]. Already in Galatians he has asked 'who has bewitched' his readers (3:1) and spoken of the person who 'deceives himself' (6:3).

Many people are deceived concerning this inexorable law of seed-time and harvest. They sow their seeds thoughtlessly, nonchalantly, and blind themselves to the fact that the seeds they sow will inevitably produce a corresponding harvest. Or they sow seed of one kind and expect to reap a harvest of another. They imagine that somehow they can get away with it. But this is impossible. So Paul adds: *God is not mocked.* The Greek verb here *(muktērizō)* is striking. It is derived from the word for a nose and means literally to 'turn up the nose at' somebody and so to 'sneer at' or 'treat with contempt'. From this it can signify to 'fool' (NEB) or to 'outwit' (Arndt-Gingrich). What the apostle is saying is that men may fool themselves, but they cannot fool God. They may think that they can escape this law of seed-time and harvest, but they cannot. They may go on sowing their seeds and closing their eyes to the consequences, but one day God Himself will bring in the harvest.[132]

---

[132] Ibid., 166-67.

A joyous life with a sense of true meaning and worthwhile fulfillment does not happen by chance. It is the product of right thinking and right acting. Biblical joy and security are no more the fruit of chance than are tomatoes and potatoes the fruit of carrot seeds. A life filled with meaning, purpose, and spiritual satisfaction does not "just happen" any more than a garden filled with tasty vegetables "just happens." In both cases, someone made a deliberate choice of seeds to sow that would guarantee the desired harvest.

In verse 8, Paul continues to encourage mutual burden-bearing by providing a specific example of the sowing/reaping principle:

> *The one who sows to please his sinful nature, from that nature will reap destruction; the one who sows to please the Spirit, from the Spirit will reap eternal life.* (NIV)

Earlier in the letter, Paul explained that the freedom to which the Galatian Christians had been called was not the freedom to indulge in selfishness. Freedom from the Mosaic law was not to result in self-promotion, segregation, or superiority, but in love. Love is the goal of the Christian community: living by the Spirit is the means to that end. Paul, in verse 8, reminds his readers of this truth by repeating the key contrast he established in 5:16: *desires of the flesh versus desires of the Spirit*. Within the immediate context of 6:6, Paul's warning is to learners who will sow to the flesh if they fail to share material goods with those who teach them. The result of such a selfish action is corruption—they will remain ignorant of Christ and will not become more like him. Paul contrasts this condition with eternal life, which, according to Jesus himself, is to know him and thus to know

God (John 17:3—"*And this is eternal life, that they know you, the only true God, and Jesus Christ whom you have sent.*" [ESV]). The universal nature of the sowing/reaping principle, however, allows a much broader application of sowing to the flesh and sowing to the Spirit. Paul's warning/encouragement extends beyond the burden-bearing relationship of learners and teachers into all of life. John Stott explains that Paul uses the sowing/reaping principle to move from the particular to the general:

> ... [Paul] reverts to the theme of the flesh and the Spirit which he has treated at some length in Galatians 5:16–25. There in Galatians 5 the Christian's life is likened to a battleground, and the flesh and the Spirit are two combatants at war with each other upon it. But here in Galatians 6 the Christian's life is likened to a country estate, and the flesh and the Spirit are two fields in which we may sow seed. Further, the harvest we reap depends on *where* and on *what* we sow.
>
> This is a vitally important and a much neglected principle of holiness. We are not the helpless victims of our nature, temperament and environment. On the contrary, what we become largely depends on how we behave; our character is shaped by our conduct. According to Galatians 5 the Christian's duty is to 'walk by the Spirit', according to Galatians 6 to 'sow to the Spirit'. Thus the Holy Spirit is likened both to the path along which we walk (Gal. 5) and to the field in which we sow (Gal. 6). How can we expect to reap the *fruit* of the Spirit if we do not sow in the *field* of the Spirit? The old adage is true: 'Sow a thought, reap an act; sow an act, reap a habit; sow a habit, reap a character; sow a character, reap a destiny.' This is good, biblical teaching.[133]

---

[133] Ibid., 169-70. Italics in the original.

Paul has specifically mentioned the burden-bearing relationship between teachers and learners. He identified one way in which those groups sow to the Spirit (sharing of material goods). We have considered ways in which both groups might sow to the flesh within that relationship. What are other ways, outside the learner/teacher relationship, that Christians might sow to the flesh or to the spirit? Paul warns that sowing to the flesh leads to corruption. Anything that in any way encourages us to coddle or pander to our flesh or sinful nature is sowing in the wrong field and will lead to a harvest of destruction. We are to crucify the flesh; we are not to pity it or pamper it. We are to sow to the Spirit by following the Word of the Spirit or the Scriptures. The moral seeds we thusly sow (either fleshly or spiritual) are thoughts and values: the harvest is deeds of the same nature. John Stott provides some specific ways we might sow to the flesh:

> Every time we allow our mind to harbour a grudge, nurse a grievance, entertain an impure fantasy, or wallow in self-pity, we are sowing to the flesh.[134]

We sow to the flesh by keeping company with people whose lives are marked by self-centeredness. This might include people who profess to follow Christ as well as those who have no interest in the gospel. Self-centered people, by their very nature, will have values that do not conform to the gospel. Whether consciously or unconsciously, these people's lives will constantly urge us to adopt values and perform actions contrary to the gospel. By making self-centered people our companions and role-models, we ask to be tempted into areas of thinking and acting where we do

---

[134] Ibid., 170.

not belong and which are difficult to resist. It should not surprise us then, when we become selfish, considering ourselves better than others, and making our wants and needs paramount.

Sowing to the Spirit involves setting the mind on what the Spirit desires (Rom. 8:5) and being led by the Spirit (Gal. 5:16, 22–23). It includes walking by the Spirit, which manifests itself in humility, encouragement to holiness, and esteeming each other (Gal. 5:25–26). Just as sowing to the flesh involves thoughts and deeds, so sowing to the Spirit involves the life of the mind. Sowing to the Spirit means that we make deliberate choices about the kinds of books we read (especially THE Book), the places of entertainment we frequent, and the kind of company we choose, including our faithful fellowship with Christians at worship and prayer services. A life that imitates Christ is an intentional *harvest*. It is not an accident. The question is this; "How much do we want to look like Christ? How much do we want our lives to be a harvest of holiness?"

Life is not static. We constantly grow one way or the other. We grow better or worse. Life is like a field. Every field produces a harvest of some sort. Even unplanted and uncultivated fields produce a harvest. In those fields, weeds predominate. If we do not sow to the Spirit, the weed called the flesh will take over. The flesh will always "lust against the Spirit" (Gal. 5:17). We do not have to teach and train the flesh to love sin and self. A harvest of shame follows "doing nothing," simply because doing nothing is really actively doing something–it is sowing to the flesh! John Stott points out that growing toward holiness (becoming more like Christ) has both a negative and a positive aspect:

Therefore, if we want to reap a harvest of holiness, our duty is twofold. First we must avoid sowing to the flesh, and secondly we must keep sowing to the Spirit. We must ruthlessly eliminate the first and concentrate our time and energies on the second. It is another way of saying (as in Gal. 5) that we must 'crucify the flesh' and 'walk by the Spirit'. There is no other way of growing in holiness.[135]

In verses 9 and 10, Paul equates sowing to Spirit with doing good:

Let us not become weary in doing good, for at the proper time we will reap a harvest if we do not give up. Therefore, as we have opportunity, let us do good to all people, especially to those who belong to the family of believers. (NIV)

By employing a metaphor with universal applicability (the sowing/reaping metaphor), Paul moves his readers from an "in-house" responsibility (bear one another's burdens) to a responsibility that has universal applicability (it encompasses all people): do good to all (sow spiritual seed among everyone). Christians have no excuse to act selfishly toward those who are outside the faith. I know some Christians who will not in any way help nonbelievers. They are the first to help a Christian who has suffered a tragedy. They will provide food, clothing, and shelter for a brother or sister whose house has burned, but they feel no compulsion to help an unbeliever in a similar situation. This attitude is contrary to Paul's teaching. We do not sow half our field with loving seed and half with selfish seed. Our life, whether we are in the company of fellow believers or in the company of those who do not believe, is to be marked in its entirety by love. The double-duty we have to do good

---

[135] Ibid., 171.

among believers does not negate the responsibility we have to love all of God's image-bearers.

Paul does not specifically define "doing good" here, nor does he describe the harvest that follows. We can surmise from his placing it in the context of sowing and reaping that the harvest is the fruit of the Spirit, which he has described in some detail in 5:22 and 23: love, joy, peace, patience, kindness, goodness, faithfulness, gentleness, and self-control. We know from the principle just stated that if we wish to harvest this fruit, we must sow its seed. So it would seem that doing good, according to Paul in this passage, is to spread love, joy, peace, patience, kindness, goodness, faithfulness, gentleness, and self-control. This is the harvest we will reap, whether as a confirmed way of life for ourselves (a settled disposition to do good) or as an attitude those around us show toward us. Either way, the results are not likely to be immediate; hence Paul's encouragement not to give up. We cannot let the remaining self-centeredness that we see in our own lives discourage us to the point that we stop trying to be other-centered. We cannot let the self-centeredness that we see in others prevent us from acting selflessly toward them.

It is all too easy today to justify not doing good in our broader community (the community comprising believers and non-believers). It sometimes seems as if we not only are *not* seeing a harvest of love, joy, peace and the like from those outside the faith, but we are also seeing those very qualities under attack when demonstrated by Christians. In fact, Christians often stand accused of exhibiting the opposite qualities. Our love is called hate. Our joy is called dourness. Our self-control is called repression. Our peace is called smugness. There may indeed be some who claim to follow Christ who deserve such censure, but it is difficult to persevere in genuine love, joy, peace, and the like when we all stand accused of being hypocrites. Nor is this the only reason we may feel discouraged. The nation our forefathers shed their blood to give us—a nation with freedom of religion enshrined as one of its basic rights—is also under attack. Do not misunderstand me: I am not at all interested in the church endorsing a political party or candidate. I am interested in encouraging believers to let their convictions be known. I think that doing good certainly includes doing all we can to stop the downhill slide of our culture. It may be, however, that our cultural malaise is God's judgment. If he has turned our country over to judgment (and the evidence for that seems to be mounting every day), then all our efforts to stop that slide will fail. We cannot outwit God's sovereign purposes. However, we cannot see what God's sovereign purpose has ordained; therefore, we do good and keep on doing good in spite of the outcome.

John Stott sums up the ways in which Paul applies the principle of sowing and reaping in this section of Galatians:

> We have considered the three spheres of the Christian life to which Paul applies his inexorable principle that 'whatever a man sows, that he will also reap'. In the first, the seed is *God's Word*, sown by teachers in the minds and hearts of the congregation. In the second, the seed is *our own thoughts and deeds*, sown in the field of the flesh or the Spirit. In the third, the seed is *good works*, sown in the lives of other people in the community.
>
> And in each case, although the seed and the soil are different, seed-time is followed by harvest. The teacher who sows God's Word will reap his living; it is God's purpose that

he should. The sinner who sows to the flesh will reap corruption. The believer who sows to the Spirit will reap eternal life, an ever-deepening communion with God. The Christian philanthropist who sows good works in the community will reap a good crop in the lives of those he serves and a reward for himself in eternity.

In none of these spheres can God be mocked. In each the same principle invariably operates. And since we cannot fool God, we are fools if we try to fool ourselves! We must neither ignore nor resist this law, but accept it and co-operate with it. We must have the good sense to allow it to govern our lives. 'Whatever a man sows, that he will also reap.' We must expect to reap what we sow. Therefore, if we want to reap a good harvest, we must sow, and keep sowing, good seed. Then, in due time, we shall reap.[136]

Whether or not we see the harvest in our own individual lives, in the life of the church, or in the life of the larger community, our duty is to keep on doing good. In due season, we will reap. Paul does not tell us when "due season" is; he simply tells us that it exists and it will reveal the good harvest. In the light of this certainty, we continue to do good. We continue to sow spiritual seed. We continue to love and to imitate Christ.

---

[136] Ibid., 172-73.

CHAPTER THIRTY

GALATIANS 6:11–18

Paul has now reached the end of his letter. He reminds his audience of the main point of the letter: the purity of the gospel and his determination to protect that purity. We could label 6:11–18, "The Essence of the Gospel of Sovereign Grace." Let us read the entire section and then study it.

> *Ye see how large a letter I have written unto you with mine own hand. As many as desire to make a fair shew in the flesh, they constrain you to be circumcised; only lest they should suffer persecution for the cross of Christ. For neither they themselves who are circumcised keep the law; but desire to have you circumcised, that they may glory in your flesh. But God forbid that I should glory, save in the cross of our Lord Jesus Christ, by whom the world is crucified unto me, and I unto the world. For in Christ Jesus neither circumcision availeth anything, nor uncircumcision, but a new creature. And as many as walk according to this rule, peace be on them, and mercy, and upon the Israel of God. From henceforth let no man trouble me: for I bear in my body the marks of the Lord Jesus. Brethren, the grace of our Lord Jesus Christ be with your spirit. Amen.* (KJV)

Paul directs the Galatians' attention to the fact that in this section, he is no longer dictating the letter through a secretary, but has picked up the pen himself. We know from his second letter to the Thessalonian church that Paul included a mark in his letters to distinguish them from letters that *seemed* to be from him (2 Thess. 2:2; 3:17). It would seem from these passages that other people were writing letters in Paul's name and that he did not want the church to be misled. To prevent confusion, Paul always added something to every epistle in his own handwriting. Sometimes he merely signed his name, other times he wrote a blessing, and here he wrote an entire paragraph. Perhaps he used the size of the words ("see with what large letters I am writing to you") to draw the reader's attention to this distinguishing mark of authenticity or to signify both the mark and the importance of his upcoming words.

Why might Paul's next words be so important? In verses 12–14, he contrasts the motives of his opponents with his own motives. This is consistent with his strategy throughout the letter to contrast the true gospel that he preached with the false gospel the Judaizers preached. In verse 15, he once more clarifies and exalts the heart of the gospel: what is important is a new creation.

This portion of the passage (Gal. 6:12–15) raises and answers two questions concerning the nature of true Christian faith.

1. Is the nature of the gospel outward or is it inward?

2. Is the essence of faith human or is it divine?

If the nature of the gospel were external, then we would find Paul promoting circumcision and the works of the Mosaic law. What we find, however, is the opposite. In this letter, Paul stresses the point that faith in Christ does not manifest itself as a religion of external ceremonies administered by "holy men." The gospel that Paul preaches deals with the heart and is inward and spiritual. It deals with the individual's personal and immediate dealings with God. As we explore these verses, it is good to remind ourselves that the problem Paul addresses in this letter is not restricted to the first century. The enemy that Paul fought so fiercely still exists today.

John Stott, in his commentary on Galatians, points out that the Judaizers, typical of all legalists, were concerned primarily with something outward, in this case, circumcision.

> In verses 12 and 13, they [the Judaizers] are described not only as 'those who receive circumcision' themselves, but as those who 'would compel you to be circumcised' or (NEB) 'are trying to force circumcision upon you'. It is with justice that they are sometimes called 'the circumcision party'.[137]

As Stott notes, the Judaizers were rightly labeled the circumcision party, because their religion was primarily interested in circumcision and law-keeping. In effect, they denied that the gospel taught that salvation was by grace through faith alone. According to Luke, the gist of their teaching was, 'unless you are circumcised and keep the law of Moses, you cannot be saved' (Acts 15:1). Peter rejected that teaching by directing attention to God's work of cleansing the heart (Acts 15:9). Heart cleansing is internal. Paul picks up the external/internal contrast as he refutes the Judaizers' claim.

It is important to note in verses 12 and 13 that Paul exposes the motivation behind the Judaizers' teaching. Why were they so insistent that Gentiles be circumcised, and even more importantly, why did they want to put the Gentile believers under the law? Look closely at these two verses.

> *As many as desire to make a fair shew in the flesh, they constrain you to be circumcised; only lest they should suffer persecution for the*

---

[137] Stott, *One Way*, 176.

cross of Christ. For neither they themselves who are circumcised keep the law; but desire to have you circumcised, that they may glory in your flesh. (KJV)

Under the old covenant, Jewish people could have no personal fellowship with Gentiles. This prohibition placed the first-century Judaizers in a dilemma. On the one hand, they professed to believe that Jesus was the Messiah. They were part of the "knowing ones" for whom Nicodemus spoke: *"We know thou art a teacher come from God: for no man can do these miracles that thou doest, except God be with him"* (John 3:2b KJV). Our Lord had all of the necessary credentials to prove he was the Messiah and on the strength of that evidence, the Judaizers had "believed." On the strength of that confession, they had joined the group of believers, a group that eventually included Gentiles. On the other hand, they did not actually submit to Jesus Christ as Lord, and they certainly were not willing to forsake the old covenant and move into the new covenant. This reluctance manifested itself in their insistence on circumcision for the Gentile believers. Earlier in this epistle (Gal. 2:4), Paul had called the Judaizers "false brethren." They were *brethren* in the sense that they had made a profession of faith, but they were *false* brethren whose behavior invalidated their profession. Their commitment to Judaism included their desire to be accepted by those of their Jewish brethren who did not view Jesus as Messiah. They wanted to add Jesus to their Judaism without forsaking Moses and the old covenant.

Paul believed that the Judaizers' motivation was clear. They wanted to have the approval of the Jewish community, but that was impossible as long they had any fellowship with the uncircumcised Gentiles. If they could persuade, or force, the Gentiles to be circumcised and to keep the law of Moses, they could then boast that they had actually made Jews out of the Gentile converts. The Judaizers hoped they could glory in the flesh—circumcision—of the Gentiles and thereby have both the approval of their unbelieving Jewish brethren and the acceptance of the Gentile believers. This solution, however, suffered from several flaws. One problem was that the Judaizers themselves did not keep the law (v. 13). How ridiculous to impose law-keeping as essential to salvation when you yourself did not keep the law! Their position was ludicrous.

Another problem was that the real persecution came from the *preaching of the cross* (v. 12). The preaching of the cross is hated today, but it was especially odious to the Jews in Paul's day. Preaching the cross meant that all people, without exception, were equally guilty sinners before God. Only the blood of Christ shed on the cross could bring forgiveness. Paul preached, *"There is no distinction: for all have sinned and fall short of the glory of God,"* and that *all* included every Jew (Rom. 3:22b–23 ESV). To imply or suggest in any way that a Gentile was even remotely close to being equal to a Jew would have seemed heretical. It would have eliminated the distinction the old covenant enforced. In order to join the group of believers, the Judaizers had to confess that "no distinction" applied also to the gift of justification by grace through the redemption that is in Christ Jesus (cf. Rom. 3:24 ESV), but they could never profess it to their non-believing Jewish brethren without incurring their wrath. Circumcising the Gentiles—in effect, making them Jewish and giving them an elevated status—seemed like an answer.

Preaching the cross also meant declaring the sacrificial death of the Messiah. That sacrifice superseded and ended all the other sacrifices of the old covenant: the Jewish paschal lambs, the Day of Atonement, and all the priestly rituals of that religion. Everything that made Judaism God's old covenant religion was forever finished because it was fulfilled. It was all fulfilled and thus done away with. It is not difficult to see why an unbelieving Jew would hate the very mention of the cross. His religion—his entire way of life—consisted of rituals and ceremonies. The function of religious rituals and ceremonies was to ensure that one approached the deity properly. Thus, there was a visible temple, a visible altar, and visible sacrifices and offerings. There was a visible high priest with colorful clothing. There was the history and glory of a visibly manifesting and intervening God. With the end of the old covenant, all of that is gone. In the new covenant, all is now spiritual. Sight has given way to faith and the visible to the invisible. The outward has given way to the inward and spiritual. It no longer matters which mountain you worship on, because there are no longer any holy mountains or any other holy places, including what was once the Most Holy Place in the tabernacle.

When the veil in the temple was rent from top to bottom (Matt. 27:51), the Most Holy Place (a place that only one man on one day of the year was allowed to enter) was no longer holy. I say this reverently: the Most Holy Place became an ordinary, mundane place that could have been rented out for a pigpen. The ark of the covenant (an object so holy that no human hands were permitted to touch it) was no longer holy and could have been melted down and sold on the gold market. We can understand to some degree the Jews' plight upon the inauguration of the new covenant.

We can see the significance of the new covenant as it relates to worship when we read John 4:19–24.

> *The woman saith unto him, Sir, I perceive that thou art a prophet. Our fathers worshipped in this mountain; and ye say, that in Jerusalem is the place where men ought to worship. Jesus saith unto her, Woman, believe me, the hour cometh, when ye shall neither in this mountain, nor yet at Jerusalem, worship the Father. Ye worship ye know not what: we know what we worship: for salvation is of the Jews. But the hour cometh, and now is, when the true worshippers shall worship the Father in spirit and in truth: for the Father seeketh such to worship him. God is a Spirit: and they that worship him must worship him in spirit and in truth. (KJV)*

Paul, in Galatians 6:12–16, repeats the essence of what Jesus said to the woman at the well, recorded in John 4. The nature of the gospel is inward, not outward.

The answer to the second question raised in this passage, *Is the essence of faith human or is it divine?* is that it is divine. What is meant by this question is whether Paul's message primarily focuses on "… what we do for God or [on] what He has done for us?"[138] In verse 12, Paul describes the motive of the Judaizers as making "a good show in the flesh" and in verse 13 as desiring to "glory in the flesh." If they have their way, they will be able to say, "Look what we have done! We have brought the Gentiles into the kingdom. We have done something (circumcision) that joins them to the people of God; we have given them something (the law

---

[138] Ibid., 178.

of Moses) that allows them to remain as part of the people of God; and we have done all this for God." Paul contrasts the Judaizers' human-centered religion with his God-centered gospel. Human hands and human agencies can produce everything involved in a human-centered religion, but only God can produce a true spiritual and eternal change in sinners. The Judaizers may glory in the flesh but Paul is emphatic—he will glory in nothing but the cross (v. 14). Verse 14 is one of Paul's great Christ-centered "glory shouts."

> But God forbid that I should glory, save in the cross of our Lord Jesus Christ, by whom the world is crucified unto me, and I unto the world. (KJV)

Paul's theology allows for a single object of glorying, or boasting: the cross of Christ. In 1 Corinthians 1:18, Paul writes, *"the preaching of the cross is to them that are perishing foolishness,"* and in the same chapter, verse 31, he adds, *"that, according as it is written, he that glorieth, let him glory in the Lord."* He is quoting from Jeremiah 9:24, which states, *"But let him that glorieth glory in this, that he understandeth and knoweth me, that I am the Lord who exercises loving-kindness, justice, and righteousness ..."* We glory in something when we are proud of it. We boast about something when it makes us feel special and exceptional. But before God, sinners do not have anything of their own about which to boast. Winning seven gold medals at the Olympics certainly gives a person the right to be proud of his accomplishment before fellow humans, but God is not really impressed. Gold medals are not made of the stuff that never rusts or corrodes. The only source of gospel glorying is when we glory in the fact of God's loving-kindness in electing us to know and understand his revelation of himself. You may glory in your baptism, or in your church, or in your pastor, or in your theology, but I will glory in the fact that "Jesus loves me, this I know, for the Bible tells me so."

Note that Paul glories in the very thing, the cross, that those who are perishing call foolish. Why is the preaching of the cross foolishness to unbelievers? Many unbelievers do not ridicule the preaching of the love of God. In fact, these people object to preaching that omits the love of God. Not everyone becomes upset when we preach the miracles in the Bible. What is it about preaching the cross that so upsets people? Preaching the cross is preaching that we are so guilty before God that nothing less than a bloody sacrifice could effect forgiveness of sins. It is preaching that God's holy and just character must be propitiated, and nothing less than the vicarious atoning work of Christ on the cross could accomplish that job. People hate the cross because it condemns them in their sin.

In verse 14, Paul shows that there are two sides to the crucifixion. He is crucified to the world, and the world is crucified to him. When we glory in the cross, we demonstrate the irreconcilable natures of the world where self reigns and the preaching of the reign of God's sovereign grace. As John Stott notes, it is impossible to boast in the Lord and boast in ourselves at the same time. By choosing to boast in Christ, we have drawn a line in the sand.

As a result, we and the world have parted company. Each has been 'crucified' to the other. 'The world' is the society of unbelievers. Previously we were desperately anxious to be in favour with the world. But now that we have seen ourselves as sinners and Christ crucified as our sin-bearer, we do not care what the world thinks or says of us or does to us. 'The world has been crucified to me, and I to the world.'[139]

Being crucified to the world means more than just being crucified to its immorality. We have declared as criminal the entire world and life-system and philosophy that suggest that we can live a meaningful and satisfying life apart from Christ. We must not seek or yield to its smiles of approval any more than we yield to its allurement of sensual sins. I have known some great people who would not succumb to the fiercest temptation, nor abandon the faith under the most severe trials; yet they yielded to the world's smile of approval.

In verse 15, Paul sets forth the great truth concerning the nature of faith in Christ.

> *For in Christ Jesus neither circumcision availeth any thing, nor uncircumcision, but a new creature.*

We can substitute anything a person does in the place of *circumcision* and the meaning of the verse remains. When it comes to our relationship to God, all that avails is the cross. Our ancestors, even if they were the holiest people who ever lived, avail us nothing. Baptism, as a child or an adult, by sprinkling or immersion, counts for nothing. No individual action or accomplishment can put grace into our hearts. Nothing that a human being can do, or can have done to him by another human being, can earn an ounce of grace with God. In order to inherit the kingdom of God, we must be born of the Spirit. It is not circumcision made with hands but the circumcision of the heart by the Holy Spirit that counts with God. Paul wants the Galatians to realize the real

---

[139] Ibid., 180.

issues involved. John Brown, in his commentary on Galatians, explains:

> [It is] [a]s if the apostle had said, 'Your false teachers glory or boast in their influence over you, proved by your submitting to the initiatory rite of Judaism in consequence of their urgency; but I have a more solid ground for my boasting. I glory not in the blind submission of men to my authority; I glory in the cross of my Savior.'[140]

One of the key words in Paul's assertion is *avails* or *counts*. The idea of contrast between covenants is clear. Paul is teaching that under the new covenant, it does not matter if you are or are not circumcised. Under the old covenant, circumcision was not only important; it was vital. It had great significance and counted for much. Moses almost lost his life for not having his son circumcised (Ex. 4:24–26). It did not, in and of itself, secure salvation, but those who had the mark qualified for important privileges. Those who were uncircumcised were without these privileges and consequent blessings (see Eph. 2). John Brown details this contrast between covenants:

> A Gentile, on being circumcised, was admitted to the participation in all the external privileges of the chosen nation; and, on the other hand, a Jew, a descendant from Abraham, Isaac, and Jacob, if he did not submit to circumcision, was cast off from the people of the Lord, and had no more interest than an uncircumcised Gentile in the blessing of the natural covenant. But under Christ it is otherwise: circumcision is nothing; it has no force in introducing a man into the enjoyment of its privileges: uncircumcision has no force in excluding him from them. Submitting to the initiatory rite of

---

[140] Brown, *Galatians*, 363.

Judaism has nothing to do with Christianity. He that has submitted to it is not on that account the nearer the enjoyment of the blessings Christianity promises: he that has not submitted to it is not on that account the farther from the enjoyment of these blessings. The circumcised and the uncircumcised stand, in reference to them, on the same level.[141]

Under the new covenant, all that avails (counts for) anything before God is that which is wrought by the Holy Spirit. The contrast between that which humans do and that which the Holy Spirit does cannot be starker. Every blessing and privilege of the new covenant is contingent on our "being in Christ." That, and that alone, is what is vital. Only the Holy Spirit can baptize us "into Christ." This sovereign work of God (placing us into Christ) will always produce a new creation. Throughout his letters, Paul uses the phrase *new creation* two different ways. He sometimes refers to the new age, or dispensation, brought into being by the advent of the Holy Spirit. Second Corinthians 5:17 is an illustration of this use. In that passage, Paul is not talking about a dramatic change in a person's mindset and lifestyle. He is talking about the age of grace that replaces the old Adamic age. In Christ, a new creation came into being—the old creation had passed away. Paul uses *new creation* to refer to the advent of the kingdom. In Galatians 6:15, however, Paul seems to be talking about the radical change in a believer's mindset and lifestyle. The person himself is the new creation. Both aspects are equally true of every believer living under the new covenant. We may separate them for the purpose of study, but we must never separate them in experience. Christians live on this side of the cross and

---

[141] Ibid., 378.

resurrection. They have been born into a new kingdom characterized by grace instead of the old kingdom based on law. They have also been born of God and given the Holy Spirit as a personal teacher. John Stott summarizes verses 12–15.

> So, then, Paul has contrasted false and true religion. On the one hand was circumcision, standing for the outward and the human, a formal external religion and our own efforts to save ourselves. On the other is the cross of Christ and the new creation, the finished work of Christ on the cross to redeem us and the inward work of the Spirit in our hearts to regenerate and sanctify us. These are fundamental parts of the gospel. No-one has understood the gospel who has not grasped that Christianity is first inward and spiritual, and secondly a divine work of grace.[142]

Having established the necessity and the sufficiency of the new creation, Paul pronounces a blessing on all who walk by this rule (the necessity and the sufficiency of the new creation) and refers to them either *in addition to* the Israel of God or to them *as* the Israel of God.

> *And as many as walk according to this rule, peace be upon them, and mercy, and upon the Israel of God.* (Gal. 6:16 KJV)
> *Peace and mercy to all who follow this rule, even to the Israel of God.* (Gal. 6:16 NIV)

The Greek text allows for either translation. Thus, commentators disagree over the meaning of *the Israel of God.* The two most widely held interpretations are (1) the Israel of God is all Jewish Christians, or (2), the Israel of God is the new covenant church. John MacArthur's Study Bible takes the first view, which is dispensational:

---

[142] Stott, *One Way*, 180.

Israel of God. All Jewish believers in Christ, i.e., those who are both physical and spiritual descendants of Abraham (see notes on 3:7, 18; Rom. 2:28, 29; 9:6, 7).[143]

The *NIV Study Bible* takes the second view, which is non-dispensational:

Israel of God. In contrast to "Israel according to flesh" (a literal rendering of the Greek for "people of Israel" in 1 Co 10:18), the NT church, made up of believing Jews and Gentiles, is the new seed of Abraham and the heir according to the promise (3:29; *cf.* Ro 9:6; Php 3:3)—though some limit the phrase here to Christian Jews (translating the conjunction [*kai*] as "and" instead of "even").[144]

Most, but not all, non-dispensational Calvinistic commentators assume the phrase is referring to the church. John Stott is typical.

a. The church is the Israel of God

'All who walk by this rule' and 'the Israel of God' are not two groups, but one. The connecting particle *kai* should be translated 'even', not 'and', or be omitted (as in RSV). The Christian church enjoys a direct continuity with God's people in the Old Testament. Those who are in Christ today are 'the true circumcision' (Phil. 3:3), 'Abraham's offspring' (Gal. 3:29) and the 'Israel of God'.

b. The church has a rule to direct it

God's people, God's 'Israel', are said to 'walk by this rule'. The Greek word for 'rule' is *kanon*,[145] which means a measuring

---

[143] MacArthur Study Bible, 1800.

[144] NIV Study Bible, 1788.

[145] This is the word we use when we speak of the "canon of conduct for the Christian" or of the "canon of Scripture." The whole of Scripture, all sixty-six books, as understood through the lens of the new covenant, is the Christian's "canon" of conduct.

rod or rule, 'the carpenter's or surveyor's line by which a direction is taken'. (Lightfoot, p. 224). So the church has a 'rule' by which to direct itself. This is the 'canon' of Scripture, the doctrine of the apostles, and especially in the context of Galatians 6 the cross of Christ and the new creation. Such is the rule by which the church must walk and continuously judge and reform itself.

c. The church enjoys peace and mercy only when it walks by this rule

'Peace and mercy be upon all who walk by this rule, upon the Israel of God.' How can the church be sure of God's mercy and blessing? How can the church experience peace and unity among its own members? The only answer to both questions is 'when it walks by this rule.' Conversely, it is sinful neglect of 'this rule', the apostolic faith of the Bible, which is the main reason why the contemporary church seems to be enjoying so little of the mercy of God and so little internal peace and harmony. 'Peace upon Israel' (for this phrase cf. Nu. 6:24–26; Pss. 125:5; 128:6) is impossible when the church departs from its God-given rule.[146]

Paul closes the epistle with verses 17 and 18, where he insists that he has no need to prove his love of God and his readiness to follow without question the rule that God has revealed in his Son, our Lord Jesus Christ.

From henceforth let no man trouble me: for I bear in my body the marks of the Lord Jesus. Brethren, the grace of our Lord Jesus Christ be with your spirit. Amen. (KJV)

In essence, he wrote, "Don't hassle me. I don't need your approval, and I have no intention of discussing with you the authority of God's perfect rule."

---

[146] Stott, *One Way*, 180-81.

The Greek word for *marks* is *stigmata*. In the secular Greek, the word described the branding of a slave. It is possible that Paul is emphasizing that he is a slave of Jesus Christ. He received his branding in the many persecutions and beatings he endured. In 2 Corinthians 11:23–25, Paul writes that he 'received countless beatings'—five times the thirty-nine lashes of the Jews, three times beaten with rods, and once stoned. The scars from these persecutions were "the marks of Jesus."[147] Paul may be contrasting his scars with the mark of circumcision that the Judaizers insisted was necessary, implying that his marks are more legitimate. The Judaizers, by insisting on the mark of circumcision, did all they could to appease the unbelieving Jews and avoid persecution. Paul bore the marks that proved he faithfully proclaimed the truth, knowing that hateful persecution would result.

Paul also may be directing his readers' attention back to his comment in verse 11, making a parallel between the mark of authentication in the letter and the mark of authentication (his scars) in his body. Just as Paul's distinguishing writing mark proves the authenticity of the letter, so his physical scars prove the authenticity of his ministry. No one is to trouble him for further proof. Thus, he opens and closes his letter with an appeal to his authority to write as he does—as a spokesman for the risen Christ. This authority gives his words a weight that the Judaizers cannot match.

Paul bookends the letter with grace and peace as well as with an appeal to his authority. Paul started by praying that

---

[147] Ibid., 182.

the Galatians would experience both grace and peace (1:3). In verse 18, he asks that the grace of the Lord Jesus Christ would be with them. There is no greater blessing we can ever pray for our fellow believers than to ask God to increase their awareness and enjoyment of his amazing grace, bestowed on us through Jesus Christ.

We have finished our comments on this mighty epistle. I trust Paul's letter to the Galatians has become more meaningful to you. I hope you have enjoyed reading this book as much as I have enjoyed writing it. I pray the same prayer for you that Paul prayed for his first-century readers:

Brethren, the grace of our Lord Jesus Christ be with your spirit. Amen. (Gal 6:18 NKJV)

9213630R0

Made in the USA
Charleston, SC
21 August 2011